Earth Polyphony

Environment and Society

Series Editor
Douglas Vakoch

As scholars examine the environmental challenges facing humanity, they increasingly recognize that solutions require a focus on the human causes and consequences of these threats, and not merely a focus on the scientific and technical issues. To meet this need, the Environment and Society series explores a broad range of topics in environmental studies from the perspectives of the social sciences and humanities. Books in this series help the reader understand contemporary environmental concerns, while offering concrete steps to address these problems.

Books in this series include both monographs and edited volumes that are grounded in the realities of ecological issues identified by the natural sciences. Our authors and contributors come from disciplines including but not limited to anthropology, architecture, area studies, communication studies, economics, ethics, gender studies, geography, history, law, pedagogy, philosophy, political science, psychology, religious studies, sociology, and theology. To foster a constructive dialogue between these researchers and environmental scientists, the Environment and Society series publishes work that is relevant to those engaged in environmental studies, while also being of interest to scholars from the author's primary discipline.

Recent Titles in the Series

Earth Polyphony: Law, Ecocriticism, and Eco-Activism in Postcolonial India, by Suhasini Vincent
Staying Together: Natureculture in a Changing World, Edited by Kaushani Mondal
Learning in the Anthropocene: Reimagining Education in the Twenty-First Century, by Carl A. Maida
The Social Life of Unsustainable Mass Consumption, by Magnus Boström
Everyday Life Ecologies: Sustainability, Crisis, Resistance, by Alice Dal Gobbo
Environmental Legacies of the Copernican Universe, by Jean-Marie Kauth
Anticipatory Environmental (Hi)Stories from Antiquity to the Anthropocene, edited by Christopher Schliephake and Evi Zemanek
Mapping the Environmental Humanities: The Emerging Role of GIS in Ecocriticism, edited by Mark Terry and Michael G. Hewson
The Bangladesh Environmental Humanities Reader: Environmental Justice, Developmental Victimhood, and Resistance, by Samina Luthfa, Mohammad Tanzimuddin Khan, and Munasir Kamal
Loren Eiseley's Writing across the Nature and Culture Divide, by Qianqian Cheng
The Saving Grace of America's Green Jeremiad, by John Gatta
Art and Nuclear Power: The Role of Culture in the Environmental Debate, by Anna Volkmar
Contesting Extinctions: Decolonial and Regenerative Futures, edited by Luis I. Prádanos, Ilaria Tabusso Marcyan, Suzanne McCullagh, and Catherine Wagner
Embodied Memories, Embedded Healing: New Ecological Perspectives from East Asia, edited by Xinmin Liu and Peter I-min Huang

Earth Polyphony

Law, Ecocriticism, and Eco-activism in Postcolonial India

Suhasini Vincent

LEXINGTON BOOKS
Lanham • Boulder • New York • London

Published by Lexington Books
An imprint of The Rowman & Littlefield Publishing Group, Inc.
4501 Forbes Boulevard, Suite 200, Lanham, Maryland 20706
www.rowman.com

86-90 Paul Street, London EC2A 4NE

British Library Cataloguing in Publication Information Available

Library of Congress Cataloging-in-Publication Data

Names: Vincent, Suhasini, author.
Title: Earth polyphony : law, ecocriticism, and eco-activism in postcolonial India / Suhasini Vincent.
Description: Lanham, Maryland : Lexington Books, [2024] | Series: Environment and society | Includes bibliographical references and index. | Summary: "Earth Polyphony revels in a polyphony of voices that favor dialogic discourse to save our planet Earth in the era of the Anthropocene" —Provided by publisher.
Identifiers: LCCN 2023054609 (print) | LCCN 2023054610 (ebook) | ISBN 9781666951561 (cloth) | ISBN 9781666951578 (epub)
Subjects: LCSH: Climatic changes—Law and legislation—India—History. | Ecocriticism—India. | Human ecology—India. | Nature—Effect of human beings on—India.
Classification: LCC KNS1509.5 .V56 2024 (print) | LCC KNS1509.5 (ebook) | DDC 363.700954—dc23/eng/20231214
LC record available at https://lccn.loc.gov/2023054609
LC ebook record available at https://lccn.loc.gov/2023054610

Earth Polyphony

ENVIRONMENT AND SOCIETY

Series Editor
Douglas Vakoch

As scholars examine the environmental challenges facing humanity, they increasingly recognize that solutions require a focus on the human causes and consequences of these threats, and not merely a focus on the scientific and technical issues. To meet this need, the Environment and Society series explores a broad range of topics in environmental studies from the perspectives of the social sciences and humanities. Books in this series help the reader understand contemporary environmental concerns, while offering concrete steps to address these problems.

Books in this series include both monographs and edited volumes that are grounded in the realities of ecological issues identified by the natural sciences. Our authors and contributors come from disciplines including but not limited to anthropology, architecture, area studies, communication studies, economics, ethics, gender studies, geography, history, law, pedagogy, philosophy, political science, psychology, religious studies, sociology, and theology. To foster a constructive dialogue between these researchers and environmental scientists, the Environment and Society series publishes work that is relevant to those engaged in environmental studies, while also being of interest to scholars from the author's primary discipline.

Recent Titles in the Series

Earth Polyphony: Law, Ecocriticism, and Eco-Activism in Postcolonial India, by Suhasini Vincent
Staying Together: Natureculture in a Changing World, Edited by Kaushani Mondal
Learning in the Anthropocene: Reimagining Education in the Twenty-First Century, by Carl A. Maida
The Social Life of Unsustainable Mass Consumption, by Magnus Boström
Everyday Life Ecologies: Sustainability, Crisis, Resistance, by Alice Dal Gobbo
Environmental Legacies of the Copernican Universe, by Jean-Marie Kauth
Anticipatory Environmental (Hi)Stories from Antiquity to the Anthropocene, edited by Christopher Schliephake and Evi Zemanek
Mapping the Environmental Humanities: The Emerging Role of GIS in Ecocriticism, edited by Mark Terry and Michael G. Hewson
The Bangladesh Environmental Humanities Reader: Environmental Justice, Developmental Victimhood, and Resistance, by Samina Luthfa, Mohammad Tanzimuddin Khan, and Munasir Kamal
Loren Eiseley's Writing across the Nature and Culture Divide, by Qianqian Cheng
The Saving Grace of America's Green Jeremiad, by John Gatta
Art and Nuclear Power: The Role of Culture in the Environmental Debate, by Anna Volkmar
Contesting Extinctions: Decolonial and Regenerative Futures, edited by Luis I. Prádanos, Ilaria Tabusso Marcyan, Suzanne McCullagh, and Catherine Wagner
Embodied Memories, Embedded Healing: New Ecological Perspectives from East Asia, edited by Xinmin Liu and Peter I-min Huang

Earth Polyphony

Law, Ecocriticism, and Eco-activism in Postcolonial India

Suhasini Vincent

LEXINGTON BOOKS
Lanham • Boulder • New York • London

Published by Lexington Books
An imprint of The Rowman & Littlefield Publishing Group, Inc.
4501 Forbes Boulevard, Suite 200, Lanham, Maryland 20706
www.rowman.com

86-90 Paul Street, London EC2A 4NE

British Library Cataloguing in Publication Information Available

Library of Congress Cataloging-in-Publication Data

Names: Vincent, Suhasini, author.
Title: Earth polyphony : law, ecocriticism, and eco-activism in postcolonial India / Suhasini Vincent.
Description: Lanham, Maryland : Lexington Books, [2024] | Series: Environment and society | Includes bibliographical references and index. | Summary: "Earth Polyphony revels in a polyphony of voices that favor dialogic discourse to save our planet Earth in the era of the Anthropocene" —Provided by publisher.
Identifiers: LCCN 2023054609 (print) | LCCN 2023054610 (ebook) | ISBN 9781666951561 (cloth) | ISBN 9781666951578 (epub)
Subjects: LCSH: Climatic changes—Law and legislation—India—History. | Ecocriticism—India. | Human ecology—India. | Nature—Effect of human beings on—India.
Classification: LCC KNS1509.5 .V56 2024 (print) | LCC KNS1509.5 (ebook) | DDC 363.700954—dc23/eng/20231214
LC record available at https://lccn.loc.gov/2023054609
LC ebook record available at https://lccn.loc.gov/2023054610

Dedication
For my son

*R*emember those Chinese elephants of Yunan
*O*n their last legs after an epic 400-kilometer errant journey
*S*pent and exhausted after the long trek
*H*abitat lost, flopped down on the hard-forest earth
*A*nd quite unlike stand-sleep elephants
*N*uzzled together on their flanks to finally drift into sleep!

—Suhasini

Contents

Acknowledgments

I was able to do my research for *Earth Polyphony* in India in 2023 thanks to the research grant of the SAES (Société des Anglicistes de l'Enseignement Supérieur). I am honored that the SAES singled out my proposal for the second time during my research track. I received the first grant in 2004 when I was a doctoral student. This second grant was for the preparation of my HDR (Habilitation à diriger des recherches) that entails the writing of a monography. My research director, Professor Kerry-Jane Wallart, was supportive and encouraged me to write and not lose the thread of thought. I spent many hours at the Bibliothèque Universitaire Robert de Sorbon in Reims and am thankful to the librarian Mrs Justine Deschamps who found me almost all the books referenced in this book over a period of twenty years. My research trips to give ecocritical papers at conferences were funded by my University—Paris Panthéon Assas and my research unit VALE (Voix anglophones, littérature et esthétique) of Sorbonne University.

I would like to thank the different photographers and artists who willingly agreed to let me use their splendid photos in *Earth Polyphony*.

Graphic artist Stephanie Léonard of Thylacine designed the cover image captioned the "Earthshot." Polyphonic synchronicity in art is evident in her use of mixed techniques of aquarelles, penciling and computer graphics. Her "Earthshot" is one that engages the reader-viewer to return home to Earth—*Nostos Erda*.

Sudeep Sen, poet and photographer, was extremely kind and generous while sharing his photos of the skies, lakes, trees, and rocks. His creative artifice mingles various genres of poetry, music, and photography. The Earth was his muse inspiring art and literature through its varied hues, tints, shades, and voices. He granted me permission to configure his poetry as diptych and triptych frames.

Vincent Rahir photographed his sculpture of "Rudy, the fiercely hot Penguin" for *Earth Polyphony*. I touched Rudy when he was exhibited in front of the Reims railway station in 2021. He was a bright-blue-colored

Emperor Penguin before being bleached white by the sun. Rudy was consequently displayed in the courtyard of the Champagne House Champagne Jacquart before being gifted by Rahir to the town hall of Dormans, where he now stands, white and majestic, in his creator's hometown.

Shanthi Palaynkottai, my childhood friend, who now lives in Santa Clara photographed Stan, the dinosaur during one of her early morning walks. Stan guards the entrance of Googleplex in Mountain View, California.

I would like to thank Suniti Namjoshi for letting me use her fables in *The Blue Donkey Fables* and *Dangerous Pursuits* for ecocritical analysis. Sudeep Sen also gave me permission to use whole sections of his poems as diptych and triptych frames from *Red* and *Anthropocene: Climate Change, Contagion, Consolation*.

My family encouraged me to write *Earth Polyphony*. My father, M.A. Vincent, though no longer with us, was a constant gardener who inspired the writing of the chapter "Seeds of the Future." His voice still lives in his children. My mother, Ramola Vincent's voice is heard in her favorite biblical parable "The Parable of the Sower" that also figures in the "Seeds of the Future," reminding me that we reap what we sow. She read my manuscript and expressed varying emotions of surprise, joy, and happiness each time she discovered something new. My brother Sujit Vincent inspired the writing of the chapter "Animals in the Forum." Engineer at work, but an ardent animal welfare activist at heart, he houses an animal welfare shelter called Paws at Shollinganallur in Chennai, rescuing deserted and ill-treated animals from the jaws of death. Head in the clouds but feet firmly planted on *Terra Firma*, my son Roshan Vincent whose favorite genre is fantasy, can still make me believe that the mighty Ents of old can carry us safely to a better world.

Abbreviations

ACEA	Azienda Comunale Elettricità e Acque (Electricity and Water Municipal Utility of Rome)
AFA	Asia for Animals Coalition
AFADA	Association of Officials and Lawyers for Animal Rights
ASHA	Alliance for Sustainable and Holistic Agriculture
ASO	Assistant Settlement Officer
ASPCA	American Society for the Prevention of Cruelty to Animals
AWG	Anthropocene Working Group
BHI	Black Hills Institute of Geological Research
BOD	Biological Oxygen Demand
BT or Bt	Bacillus thuringiensis
CAG	Comptroller and Auditor General of India
CEJU	Court of Justice of the European Union
CEO	Chief Executive Officer
CETP	Common Effluent Treatment Plant
CIA	Central Intelligence Agency
CJI	Chief Justice of India
CMWSSB	Chennai Metro Water Supply and Sewerage Board
CNN	Cable News Network
COD	Chemical Oxygen Demand
COP	Conference of the Parties
CRZ	Coastal Regulation Zone
DAPL	Dakota Access Pipeline
DDT	Dichlorodiphenyltrichloroethane

DNA	Deoxyribonucleic Acid
DSS	Director of Survey and Settlement
DYFI	Democratic Youth Federation of India
EC	Environmental Clause/Clearance
ECHR	European Convention on Human Rights
ECPHR	European Convention for the Protection of Human Rights
EIA	Environmental Impact Assessment
EIS	Environmental Impact Statement
EPA	Environmental Protection Act
EROL	Environmental Rule of Law
FCA	Forest Conversation Act
FNH	Fondation pour la Nature et l'Homme
FRA	Forest Rights Act
GBM	The Green Belt Movement
GCZMA	Gujarat Costal Zone Management Authority
GEO	Geostationary Orbit
GERD	Grand Ethiopian Renaissance Dam
GHG	Greenhouse Gas
GIDC	Gujarat Industrial Development Corporation
Gt	Gigatons
HCW	*Habeas Corpus* writ
HLC	High Level Committee
ICS	International Commission of Stratigraphy
IEA	International Energy Agency
IMD	Indian Meteorological Department
IPCC	Intergovernmental Panel on Climate Change
ISRWD	Inter-State River Water Disputes Act
IT	Information Technology
IUCN	International Union for Conservation of Nature
IUGS	International Unit of Geological Scientists
IWT	Indus Waters Treaty
LEO	Lower Earth Orbit
MEO	Medium Earth Orbit
MIC	Methyl Isocyanate

MMDR	Mines and Minerals Regulation and Development Act
MoEF	Ministry of Environment and Forests
MoUs	Memorandums of Understanding
NAS	Nucleic Acid Sequence
NASA	National Aeronautics and Space Administration
NATO	North Atlantic Treaty Organization
NBA	Narmada Bachao Andolan or Save the Narmada Movement
NGO	Non-governmental Organization
NGT	National Green Tribunal
NhRP	Nonhuman Rights Project
NRW	North Rhine Westphaliaand
OTFD	Other Traditional Forest Dwellers
PCA	Permanent Court of Arbitration
PCA	Prevention of Cruelty to Animals
PETA	People for the Ethical Treatment of Animals
PIL	Public Interest Litigation
PKK	the Kurdistan Workers' Party
POPs	persistent organic pollutants
RAF	Royal Air Force
RSPCA	Royal Society for the Prevention of Cruelty to Animals
RTI	Right to Information
SCRC	Special Collections Research Center
SEZ	Special Economic Zone (SEZ) projects
SIR	Special Investment Regions
SNCF	Société Nationale des Chemins de Fer français
SPA	La Société Protectrice des Animaux
TDS	Total Dissolved Solids
TRIPS	Treade-Related Aspects of Intellectual Property Rights
TTZ	Taj Trapezium Zone
UCC	Union Carbide Corporation
UCIL	Union Carbide India Limited
UKSC	United Kingdom Supreme Court
UNCCC	United Nations Climate Change Conference
UNEP	United Nations Environment Program

UNFCCC	United Nations Framework Convention on Climate Change
UNICEF	United Nations International Children's Emergency Fund
UNOSSA	United Nations Office for Outer Space Affairs
UPA	United Progressive Alliance
VCS	Verified Carbon Standard
WASH	Water, Sanitation, and Hygiene Sector
WHO	World Health Organization
WPS	Water, Peace, and Security Partnership
WRI	World Resources Institute
WRP	Water Reclamation Plant
WTO	World Trade Organization
WWF	World Wildlife Fund

Chapter 1

Earth Rise: A Voice for Our Blue Planet

On November 7, 2022, *Time* magazine entitled its cover page as "The Planet We Made."[1] The image of an orange-and-red Earth with a green heart at its centre, was accompanied by a message from the picture's creator, Olafur Eliasson, requesting the viewer to stare at the green heart for twelve seconds before turning the page and continuing to stare.[2] The Icelandic-Danish artist applied the technique of an optical illusion of an afterimage to enhance and reimagine the viewer's experience of the ordinary. The red-orange colours of a planet on fire get transformed into blue and green in the viewer's imagination of a healthy Gaia. Eliasson depicts a globe that is dangerously tilted on its axis with a blue heart at its centre. The visual anchor of the blue heart expands with the reader's stare and sends waves of cognitive recognition to the perceptual apparatus of the eyes and the brain, reminding the viewer of the true colours of Gaia even after the flip of the page. The *Time* magazine cover page coincided with the COP 27 talks held in the Egyptian coastal city of Sharm el-Sheikh in November 2022, where ninety-two heads of state and delegates of 190 countries decided on "the urgent need for deep, rapid and sustained reductions in global greenhouse gas emissions"[3] to limit global warming to 1.5°C in keeping with the Paris Agreement (2015).[4] Earth figured, too, on the cover of *Time* magazine on January 2, 1989, as a Person of the Year, bearing the image of a plastic globe fettered with twine by the artist-duo Christo.[5] The dark crepuscular sun in the background sent the message of an imperilled Earth accompanied with the caption "Planet of the Year: Endangered Earth."[6] The idea of our Earth, our unique life-sustaining planet, our Blue Marble, stems from the photo captured by the astronauts of Apollo 17 on December 7, 1972, when the crew viewed the silver and blue Earth with its marble hues from outer space. Eliasson's accompanying ode to the "The Planet We Made" in 2022 makes a plea to the reader to view our Earth from within and not just from outer space.

Your planet seen from within
Moves you to shape your own earth . . .[7]

In *The Vanishing Face of Gaia*, James Lovelock though skeptical of today's space-age race to other planets by rocket billionaires, expresses the whim of being on a shuttle in space to be able to "share that transcendental feeling of astronauts that our home is not the house or the street or the nation where we live, but the Earth itself."[8] Lovelock's Gaia theory warns us that our planet is facing unprecedented stress, and that inaction to climate change crisis could result in impoverished ecology and climate catastrophe.[9]

GRASPING THE CLIMATE SCIENCE

The Earth Rise photo serves as an iconic symbol for environmental protection. Our solar-powered Blue Planet is tilted at an axis of 23.5° from the plane of its orbit around the sun. Earth's tilted axis results in the Sun's rays being radiated differently on the two hemispheres of the planet. Our planet's yearlong loop around the sun causes seasons, produces darkness and winter in the Northern Hemisphere in the second half of the year; and brings in summer to the Southern Hemisphere, where it stimulates plant and animal life forms. This annual, alternated cycle drives moments on Earth, sparks migration, triggers rainstorms, and sustains life on our planet. The tilt of the Earth's axis varies between 22.1° and 24.5° every forty thousand years. Due to these tilt changes, the seasons are likely to change gradually. More axis tilt may provoke severe seasons of warmer summers and colder winters; whereas less axis tilt may result in less severe seasons of cooler summers and milder winters. A lesser axis tilt would be ideal for Gaia as it enables snow and ice to last from year-to-year in high latitudes, thus permitting the existence of massive ice sheets. Snow has the propensity to reflect the sun's energy into space, causing additional cooling for our Blue Planet. Our planet is habitable as it revolves at the right distance from the Sun with its magnetic field protecting it from harmful solar radiation. Its insulating atmosphere is kept warm by its magnetic field and its greenhouse gases like carbon dioxide (CO_2), water vapor (H_2O), methane (CH_4), and nitrous oxide (N_20), bouncing heat around and ensuring that heat does not escape the Earth's atmosphere. Water and carbon are the two essential ingredients for life on our planet and it is on our hands to use them efficiently.

Enveloping the Blue Planet is a giant bubble of magnetism called the magnetosphere that protects it from the Sun's powerful rays. Its magnetic field deflects most of the solar particles emanating from the Sun, and thus protects the Earth with its protective layers that shield it from the Sun's ultraviolet radiation. It is this magnetic bubble that makes the Earth a habitable planet. Greenhouse gases occur naturally and are part of the Earth's structure. They make the Earth an amenable place to live in with the natural greenhouse effect, which keeps the planet at a friendly 15°C (59°F) on an average. But increased burning of fossil fuels by humans has resulted in an accumulation of CO_2 in the air, thus resulting in extra heat getting trapped near the Earth's surface, resulting in Gaia on fever. In a report prepared by the Intergovernmental Panel on Climate Change (IPCC), the United Nations body for assessing the science related to climate change, forecasts the impact of an average global warming of 1.5°C on a tested 105,000 species.[10] It predicts that the Earth will lose more than half of its habitat including 6 percent of insects, 8 percent of plants, and 4 percent of vertebrates. With a 2°C level of global warming, the percentage of species that will lose over half of their habitats is expected to be double. Associated risks regarding forest fires and other extreme weather conditions will be less at 1.5°C than at 2°C. According to the Global Climate Report of January 2023, the global surface temperature was 1.75°F (0.97°C), well above the twentieth-century average of 12.1°C (53.8°F).[11] In 2023, the Northern Hemisphere winter temperature was the fifth warmest on record and marks the thirty-eighth consecutive winter with global temperatures ostensibly above the twentieth-century average in the Northern Hemisphere; the Southern Hemisphere summer temperature ranked tenth warmest on record (tied with 2003 and 2006) and marks the forty-seventh consecutive warmer-than-average summer in the Southern Hemisphere.[12] At the COP 27, delegates reiterated that the impacts of climate change will be much lower at the temperature increase of 1.5°C compared with 2°C; they resolved to pursue further efforts to limit the temperature increase to 1.5°C; and they insisted on the need to understand and grasp the climate science.[13] The science of climatology though fascinating, fills me with pangs of Mermosity, the "anticipated state of being worried about the possible passing of the familiar" and its adverse effect to my sense of place.[14]

ECOCRITICISM, THE STORIED FORMS OF KNOWLEDGE

Both the material and the non-material worlds are endowed with meanings and are storied forms of knowledge. Sean Cubitt in *Anecdotal Evidence: Ecocritique from Hollywood to the Mass Image*, states that there is no boundary between human beings and the environment as the two exist in a complex interweaving of conditions and situations that create stories and this contingency pave the way for "unexpected results of criss-crossing influences and causal chains—that makes events real, and grounds ecocritical politics."[15] The ecocritical principle exists on the principle that all kinds of matter connect with everything else.

> Living starts from the ecological principle that everything mediates everything else. Media mediate of course, including media such as money and transport systems, but non-human mediation is even more fundamental. Plants mediate sunlight, oceans mediate atmospheric carbon, earthquakes mediate heat from the Earth's interior, and our bodies mediate all of these. From water's point of view, human life is just a phase that water goes through.[16]

In other words, there are numerous entwined stories of astronomy, geology, history, ecology, and life embodied in every form of matter both human and non-human. Material Ecocriticism is based on the premise that matter and meaning coalesce in these narrative potentialities of the physical world, or "narrative agency."[17] In the context of climate change, postcolonial ecocritical writing is involved in the enterprise of unsettling the centre-periphery model of world systems theory and making a turn to studying how climate change events influence cultural and literary life across national, regional, imperial, and even planetary boundaries. Ecocriticism is "an earth-centred approach to literary studies . . . and an application of ecology and ecological concepts to the study of literature."[18] It may also refer to study of environmental texts that contain a scrutiny of ecological implications and human-nature relationships, as well as texts that seem, at first glance, unmindful of the nonhuman world.[19] Though there is no definitive map of environmental criticism, trend lines may be traced as "waves in the ecocritical palimpsest."[20] While the first wave of ecocriticism in the 1980s focussed on nature and wilderness fiction and spoke for nature as one that stemmed from earlier romantic representations of nature, the second wave in the 1990s was characterized by a preoccupation with environmental justice issues and green cultural studies and questioned the breaking down of the assumed distinctions between human and non-human entities.[21] Arne Naess, the proponent of the Deep Ecology Movement proposed an entirely new worldview and philosophical perspective whereby he opposed shallow approaches that took a merely instrumental approach to nature, arguing for the preservation of natural resources only for the sake of humans. Instead, he advocated a deep approach of Deep Ecology that recognises nature's intrinsic importance and denotes a "shift from a human-centred to a nature-centred system of values."[22] In its present third wave trend, ecocriticism's analysis of climate change is done either through the lens of a cultural phenomenon by considering Derrida's deconstruction theory or Foucault's analyses of power and discourse or Latour's actor-network theory, or feminist perspectives of gender consciousness examining the interplay of women and nature, thus adopting an Earth-centred approach to literary studies.[23] Contemporary environmental problems have prompted theorists of the third wave to make a profound historical shift where the geologic is entangled with human history, and where the term Anthropocene serves as "a measure not of geological time but of the extent of human impact on the planet."[24] The idea of climate change being contingent and slippery has been imagined as one that challenges our known ontological and epistemological assumptions of knowledge, thus being aptly classified among hyperobjects that "occupy a high-dimensional phase space that makes them impossible to see as a whole on a three-dimensional human-scale-basis."[25] As all "discursive practices are related to the material world,"[26] there is consequently ample space for "an interpretive horizon for the complex interrelations between discourse and matter."[27] Material Ecocriticism as a form of engagement with nature and stories draws inspiration from the stories of matter and their narrative performance, thus partaking in the "dynamic process of material expressions seen in bodies, things, and phenomena."[28]

In his ecocritical work of nonfiction, *The Great Derangement: Climate Change and the Unthinkable*, Amitav Ghosh contends that in the present era of unpredictable climate phenomena like flash floods, killer tornadoes, wild storms, landslides, long spells of drought, and unprecedented heat, "we are confronted suddenly with a new task: that of finding other ways in which to imagine the unthinkable beings and events of this era."[29] His description of the climate change *status quo* fills the reader with Meteoranxiety, "the anxiety that is felt in the face of the threat of the frequency and severity of extreme weather events,"[30] which stem from climate change. By configuring these natural phenomena in the time and the space of his novels, Ghosh creates texts that conjure up worlds that become real precisely because of their finitude and distinctiveness. Ghosh delves into the challenges facing humanity in the era of the Anthropocene. He contends that humans as geological agents not only change the most basic physical processes of the Earth, but also that the "Anthropocene presents a challenge not only to the arts and the humanities, but also to our commonsense understandings and beyond that to contemporary culture in general."[31] Ghosh's literary enterprise aims at being a full-fledged form of engaged cultural critique and he wonders if contemporary writers are blind to potentially life-changing hazards and threats of climate change.

> But why? Are the currents of global warming too wild to be navigated in the accustomed barques of narration? But the truth, as it is now widely acknowledged, is that we have entered a time when the wild has become a norm: if certain literary forms are unable to negotiate these torrents, then they will have failed—and their failure will have to be counted as an aspect of the broader imaginative and cultural failure that lies at the heart of the climate crisis.[32]

Ghosh's contention that writers lack imaginative stirring to engage in different genres is not true. This book endeavors to highlight other experimental writing forms—like the science-fiction of Vandana Shiva, the animal fables of Suniti Namjoshi, the haiku poetry of Sudeep Sen's, the oral folklore of Mahasweta Devi, the anecdotes of Indra Sinha, and the parables of Amitav Ghosh—that revel in polyphonic voices engaging to protect the planet. Unlike Ghosh who posits that "the climate crisis is also a crisis of culture, and that of the imagination,"[33] I assert that material and non-material forces, human and non-human entities provide agency to the environmental debate of climate change and that there is no dearth nor lack of imagination. This study on the diverse narratives and polyphony of voices, shall endeavor to show through an Earth-centered approach how these forces contribute to material practices in material worlds. In adopting such an approach, it is imperative to consider each voice with its own thematic, ideological, social, and historical perspective of the world to analyze how an Earth-centered ecocritical approach takes the reality of climate crisis into account.

POLYPHONY IN LAW, ECOCRITICISM, AND ACTIVISM

Our present time is one rife with activism for political, economic, and social change. The Occupy Wall Street Movement in 2011 stirred thousands of individuals to set up an encampment at Zuccotti Park and occupy the business hub of New York, to challenge the power held by a few (1 percent), and to highlight the widespread economic and material inequality experienced by 99 percent of Americans. It triggered Mumbai's Occupy Dalal Street Movement (2011), when left-leaning activists decided to occupy the premises of the Bombay Stock Exchange to express strong discontent against greedy capitalism and corporate greed. Occupy Wall Street thus stirred other similar movements like the Occupy Gezi Park Movement in 2013, when protesters contested plans to redevelop Istanbul's Gezi Park into a complex with a new mosque and a shopping centre and fought to preserve their green spaces. These protests sometimes peaceful as in the uniting of hands in Seattle at the World Trade Organization (WTO) conference in 1999 to voice support for workers' rights, sustainable economies, and environmental and social issues; have also been violent with vociferous demands for a reduction in oil prices launched by the French Gilets Jaunes (Yellow Vests) in May 2018. This book, *Earth Polyphony*, is a study of the 'Material Turn,' and the 'Narrative Turn,' a cross-disciplinary study of how law meets literature, mingles, and allows for an exploration of the storied forms of knowledge in Indian ecocritical fiction and eco-activism. These narratives in law, ecocriticism, and eco-activism combine and influence each other and have sparked judicial activism in the courtroom. While many literary works deal with law as a subject or the scene of a trial to set the drama or as a kind of critique; judicial opinions in law have both literary and judicial merit as they demand both a substantive understanding of the principles of law and an endeavour to review, interpret and advance judicial activism. In the present-day global political context of low carbon economies, ecocritical works of Indian authors like Amitav Ghosh, Arundhati Roy, Suniti Namjoshi, Vandana Singh, Mahasweta Devi, Sudeep Sen, Indra Sinha, and Vandana Shiva have highlighted the need to protect the environment and avert ecological calamity and environmental crises. We shall see how these eco-narratives have been absorbed, reimagined, reframed, reconfigured, and retold by judges in their written opinions, thus making environmental law a kind of expressive, literary enterprise.

It is essential to remember that we do not attempt to apply a theory of ecocriticism to an Indian text, but we analyze it in its entirety, its existence in the context of the theme of climate change in a global paradigm. The written text is not the only form of illuminating environmental issues as it derives its driving force from other narrative voices with which it coexists in the polyphonic space. Similarly, activists do not read nonfiction or the newspapers to become environmental activists. Nor do law makers track the latest news of environmental activism to catch a case for application. These voices are all influenced by the media, the news they read, the sites they surf on the worldwide web, the art on display in museums, the films they watch, the TV news broadcasts they see, and the songs they hear. Students and youth develop an ecocritical perspective, not just from reading legislative Acts of Parliament, but they gain an insight or an eco-perspective in different ways, by reading or listening to the news, surfing the web, interacting on social media, playing eco-video games, observing climate change memes, watching animated cartoons and documentaries of eco-media.

The word *crisis*, which stems from the Greek word *krinein*, refers to the turning point of a disease. The idea of our planet on fever has stirred ecocritical imagination of writers who have embarked on a "study of the relationship between literature and the physical world."[34] Narratives of climate change by lawyers, judges, writers of ecocritical fiction, and environmental activists play a vital role in making the law count in postcolonial India. There is thus a polyphony of voices to be heard, through different forms of rhetoric in the arena, each portraying its individual stance while favoring the existence of multiple perspectives. *Earth Polyphony* seeks to show how voices coexist as in the Bakhtinian description of Georgian polyphonic music, where there is no domination by one side, but a multiple coexistence of perspectives with contradictions and differences, that permit interaction.[35] In an age of new models of narrativity, like Material Ecocriticism or narratives of matter, more emphasis is being placed on the ethical dimension of the bonds between language and matter. Furthermore, the environmental philosophy of Deep Ecology has awakened awareness of the need to protect the scarce natural resources, flora, and fauna of our planet Earth. As India steps into an era of 'Rights of Nature' Laws, justices influenced by ecocritical writing, decisions made in foreign forums, and global eco-activism have rendered court rulings that aim to give ecosystems, animals, and water spaces legal rights like those held by humans, trusts, and corporations. This book will refer to these court decisions that have resulted in creating a legal order where human-like status is conferred on voiceless nature.

Court judgments as a genre compel attention, enforce justice, incite interest and when rendered in court they become jurisprudential precedence whose *ratio decidendi* and *obiter dicta* get cited in other cases across countries. The *status quo* is one where there is a growing awareness and reception from different stakeholders, acknowledging that the protection of the environment is the responsibility of everyone, namely, citizens, decision-makers, justices, activists, states, regions, and international partners. My reading is to enquire into how opinions of justices are instrumental in shaping legislation, play an important role in establishing a progressive and informed judiciary that is engaged in an active exercising of the Environmental Rule of Law (EROL). Opinions of justices in different tribunals of justice around the world are scrutinized by jurists and are often subject to discussion and debate by the press for being revolutionary when they depart from the legal norm. The rhetoric in each judicial opinion varies depending on the doctrines of activism or restraint of the forum country and reflect the views of concurring and dissenting judges. *Earth Polyphony* will show how justices in the developing world while rendering decisions are increasingly aware of being under the scrutiny of the public eye and are aware of the need to include issues of equity, fairness, rights, and standing while considering issues related to environmental governance and ecological conservation.[36] While speaking of two entirely different disciplines, law, and ecocritical literature, I am aware that I may be addressing different forums of readership, who would appreciate an unpacking of these terms. The glossary of terms in law, ecocriticism, climate science, and Indian words have been explained and translated accordingly in the last section of this book.

NOSTALGIA, THE LONE KINGFISHER, SOLASTALGIA

My wish to pen *Earth Polyphony* stems from a yearning to write about my home in India and describe the homesickness and the environmental distress that is awakened when I see a changed and destroyed home space. Academia brought me to France in 1999 to pursue my studies and resulted in my laying new roots on French soil. I was born in the Indian capital city of New Delhi, but grew up in Chennai in South India, formerly known as Madras. Chennai is the Gateway to South India as it is situated on the Coromandel coast on the Bay of Bengal and has the second largest beach in the world with a wide sandy foreshore. The Senate Hall of the University of Madras that once housed the French department where I studied, though dilapidated now, still stands on the banks of the Buckingham canal, a remnant of the majestic Indo-Saracenic style, an edifice built in 1879 by the architect Robert Chisholm. The Madras University campus in Chepauk overlooks the Marina Beach and is situated in the erstwhile palace of Muhammad Ali Walajah, the Nawab of Arcot and the Senate Hall was built in the Nawab's artillery park in 1920. As a student of Ewart School and Ethiraj College in Chennai in the 1980s and 1990s, I lived in India at a time when the world was in flux, ever-changing in the decade of private enterprise that saw the rise of conservatism, and other political upheavals. News gleaned from the newspapers was of Olympic boycotts (1980 and 1984), the famine in Ethiopia (1984), the Bhopal gas tragedy (1984), the shredding of the Iron Cut (1989), the fall of the Berlin Wall (1989), Tiananmen Square student protests (1989), Mandal Commission protests against reservation in government jobs based on caste in India (1990), the assassination of Indian prime ministers Indira Gandhi (1984) and Rajiv Gandhi (1991), and the end of the Cold War (1992). News gathered from the newspapers was debated on with peers and family and not collected on the worldwide web. Doordarshan, India's sole national television network in the 1980s, moaned its gloomy tune only at 6:00 p.m. on TV sets at home. My father, an agricultural consultant who had worked for the Indian subsidiaries of the American Cyanamid Company and the Swiss Ciba-Geigy, was an avid, green-thumb gardener who could make any seed sprout. We rarely shopped at vegetable markets but consumed home-grown fruits and vegetables of the season on a cyclical rotation: fruits of banana, grape, papaya, guava, palm, and coconut trees were collected seasonally; aromatic herbs like mint, coriander, curry leaves were plucked daily; and vegetables ranging from okra, brinjals, tomatoes, spinaches, and gourds of different kind yielded in plenty. My mother pickled vegetables and stocked bottles of jam and juices that lasted for months. The supermarket shelves in today's metropolises are logistically and mechanically stocked and restocked with bottles, packets and boxes of mass-prepared food that are a far cry from the homemade cuisine my mother prepared in her little kitchen without the aid of modern robots and gadgets. The garden where my brother and I played with our many pets, had button and wood roses, sunflowers, jasmines, and lilies that nodded their heads and released their gentle perfume in the air still leaving lingering memories. Female papaya trees thrived thanks to the existence of a single male papaya tree. Female papaya trees gave fruit, while the male papaya tree offered white-yellow, bell-shaped flowers that attracted rare birds of different feathers who feasted on the stalks and permitted cross-pollination. Birds like wrens, weaver birds, sparrows, finches, ravens, parrots, tailor birds, and mynahs chirped happily in the free space of the garden. One lone kingfisher visited the male papaya tree each season. He was my silent companion near the large basin of fish in the garden where I spread out my books to study. While penning these words, I am filled with nostalgia of my childhood in India. I realize that it is ages since I have caught sight of a kingfisher amidst the high-rise buildings in Reims and Paris. My migration to France has brought me to a world, where I cross highways, railroads, metro lines, tramways, and parking lots to get to my university in Paris on record time. I traverse a city that looks like it has been built for cars and not humans. I stray occasionally into the Jardin du Luxembourg in the Latin Quarter, near my university, Paris Panthéon Assas, to escape the city's noises and admire the garden commissioned by Marie de Medicis in 1612. The regent queen of Italian descent yearned for the verdure spaces of the Boboli gardens in Florence and bought the small palace premises of the Jardin du Luxembourg to escape the constrained palatial enclaves of the Louvre. The Jardin du Luxembourg had once been her green space where she escaped all scrutiny and attention. I indulge in nostalgic thought.

When I visited Chennai in 2022, I realized that the once silvery beaches like the Eliot's beach on the foreshore estate in Chennai, are now polluted with trash, plastic bottles, broken glass shards of bottles, cigarette stubs and other used-plastic trappings of our present-day modern existence. It was impossible to take a barefoot walk on the sandy beach. Huge, air-conditioned shopping malls, temples of consumerism, and IT parks bustling with cyber activity, had sprung up in different parts of the city to welcome throngs of shoppers. The city's roads had been spruced up with median blocks painted fresh in black and white like the chess checkerboard to welcome international players from two hundred countries to the 44th Chess Olympiad. While taking a walk in Perungudi, a residential-commercial area near the sea in Chennai, I was filled with distress stirred by adverse environmental change. Here was a view safely veiled from the eyes of foreign delegates to the Chess Olympiad. This 191-acre-wide area in Perungudi is the lieu of a huge dumping ground of toxic waste that is unloaded daily causing the production of greenhouse gases like methane (CH_4) to escape into the atmosphere.[37] The decomposing waste generates leachate, a contaminated liquid that seeps into the ground water. The uncontrollable stench that permeates the air has affected the lives of residents who use Chennai's IT corridor at Perungudi, while the stagnant water in the dumping site is the breeding ground for mosquitoes and disease-spreading flies. In April 2022, a major fire in the dump resulted in further air pollution when the smoke spread across a five-kilometer radius.[38] The Perungudi dump is also being subject to a process of bioremediation and biomining projects that aim to excavate, treat, segregate, and utilize waste that has been accumulated at the dump site, leading to further pollution and stench.[39] One may wonder if it is truly biomining or yet another attempt at ecological marketing and eco-governance!

My encounter of the distress faced by environmental change while in the home space and the feeling of absolute helplessness at being able to do nothing in the face of ecological breakdown, was one akin to what Glenn Albrecht calls Solastalgia,[40] the etymological alchemy of nostalgia, solace, and desolation. *Earth Polyphony* attempts to show how solastalgic Earth Emotions in the Anthropocene prompt and spark the awakening for the quest to find Biophilia or the love for life, a requisite to enter the next era of the Symbiocene. An era that will require the symbiotic interconnectedness between different types of beings on this planet. Each chapter of this book envisages how human endeavor be it for the protection of animals, forests and rivers or the conservation of natural resources like water or carbon, encompasses ways and means of collaborating and working with other life forms. We shall see how the Symbiocene Youth of Generation Z and Generation Alpha are contemplating inter-generational action to pull down existing structures and are thus engaged in planting the seeds for a future of Sumbiocracy, a form of government where humans govern for the symbiotic, mutually beneficial relationships. The future is one where everyone will participate in the rule for the Earth, by the Earth, so that all might live together. My voice for the Blue Planet is not one characteristic of monologic discourse, but one that aims to let various voices have their say in the polyphonic space of *Earth Polyphony*.

NOTES

1. Justin Worland, "The Selfish Case for Climate Justice," *Time*, November 7, 2022.

2. D. W. Pine, "Behind Time's Optical Illusion Climate Change Cover," *Time*, October 27, 2022, https://time.com/6224632/olafur-eliasson-time-magazine-cover/. Olafur Eliasson (1967–) is an Icelandic-Danish artist whose sculptures and large-scale installation art contain elemental materials such as light, water, and air temperature to highlight the viewer's experience of the ordinary.

3. "COP27 Ends with Announcement of Historic Loss and Damage Fund," UNEP, accessed June 24, 2023, https://www.unep.org/news-and-stories/story/cop27-ends-announcement-historic-loss-and-damage-fund.

4. The Paris Agreement aimed to substantially reduce global greenhouse gas emissions to limit the global temperature increase in this century to 2° Celsius while pursuing efforts to limit the increase even further to 1.5 degrees. The Paris Agreement. Accessed June 24, 2023. https://www.un.org/en/climatechange/paris-agreement.

5. Christo Vladimirov Javalcheff (1935–2020) and his wife, Jeanne-Claude (1935–2009), wrapped world-famous buildings, transformed landscapes, and portrayed ephemeral nature in their works of art. Mentioned again in the chapter "Seeds of the Future."

6. "Time Magazine Cover: Endangered Earth, Planet of the Year," *Time*, January 2, 1989, https://content.time.com/time/covers/0,16641,19890102,00.html.

7. Olafur Eliasson, "Read Olafur Eliasson's Poem to Accompany His New *Time* Cover," *Time*, October 27, 2022, https://time.com/6224840/olafur-eliasson-time-climate-poem/.

8. James Lovelock, in *The Vanishing Face of Gaia* (London: Penguin, 2009), 2.

9. James Lovelock, *Gaia: A New Look at Life on Earth* (Oxford: Oxford University Press, 1979).

10. Chapter 3—Global Warming of 1.5° Celsius–IPCC, accessed July 5, 2023, https://www.ipcc.ch/sr15/chapter/chapter-3/.

11. "January 2023 Global Climate Report," January 2023 Global Climate Report | National Centers for Environmental Information (NCEI), accessed July 5, 2023, https://www.ncei.noaa.gov/access/monitoring/monthly-report/global/202301.

12. Idem.

13. Decision -/CP.27 Sharm el-Sheikh implementation plan–UNFCCC, accessed July 5, 2023, https://unfccc.int/sites/default/files/resource/cop27_auv_2_cover%20decision.pdf.

14. Glenn A. Albrecht, *Earth Emotions: New Words for a New World* (Ithaca: Cornell University, 2019), 200. More Earth Emotions are referred to in the chapter "Solastalgic Earth Emotions."

15. Sean Cubitt, *Anecdotal Evidence: Ecocritique from Hollywood to the Mass Image* (New York: Oxford University Press, 2020), 1.

16. Sean Cubitt, *Anecdotal Evidence: Ecocritique from Hollywood to the Mass Image*, 1.

17. Serpil Oppermann, "Material Ecocriticism and the Creativity of Storied Matter," *Frame* 26, no. 2 (November 2013): 55–69.

18. *Ecocriticism* is a term coined by William Rueckert. Cheryll Glotfelty, *The Ecocriticism Reader: Landmarks in Literary Ecology*, edited by Cheryll Glotfelty (Athens, Georgia: University of Georgia Press, 1996), xx.

19. Scott Slovic, "Ecocriticism: Containing Multitudes, Practising Doctrine," in *The Green Studies Reader: From Romanticism to Ecocriticism*, ed. Laurence Coupe (London: Routledge, 2000), 160–62.

20. Lawrence Buell, "The Emergence of Environmental Criticism," in *The Future of Environmental Criticism* (Malden: Blackwell, 2005), 17.

21. Greg Garrard, *Ecocriticism* (London: Routledge, 2004).

22. Garrard, *Ecocriticism*, 24.

23. Cheryll Glotfelty, "Introduction: Literary Studies in an Age of Environmental Crisis," essay, in *The Ecocriticism Reader: Landmarks in Literary Ecology*, edited by Harold Fromm (Athens: University of Georgia Press, 1996), xix.

24. Dipesh Chakrabarty, "Anthropocene Time," *History and Theory* 57, no. 1 (2018): 7. https://doi.org/10.1111/hith.12044.

25. Timothy Morton, *Hyperobjects: Philosophy and Ecology after the End of the World* (Minneapolis: University of Minnesota Press, 2013).

26. Karen Barad, Meeting the Universe Halfway: Quantum Physics and the Entanglement of Matter and Meaning (Durham: Duke University Press, 2007), 34.

27. Serenella Iovino and Serpil Oppermann, *Material Ecocriticism* (Bloomington: Indiana University Press, 2014), 2.

28. Iovino and Oppermann, 7.

29. Amitav Ghosh, *The Great Derangement: Climate Change and the Unthinkable* (London: University of Chicago Press, 2016), 33.

30. Albrecht, *Earth Emotions*, 77.

31. Ghosh, *The Great Derangement*, 9.

32. Idem, 8.

33. Idem, 9.

34. Cheryll Glotfelty, *The Ecocriticism Reader: Landmarks in Literary Ecology*, xviii.

35. Mikhail Mikhailovich Bakhtin, *Problems of Dostoevsky's Poetics* (Minneapolis: University of Minnesota Press, 1984), 27–28.

36. Ryan Holifield, Michael Porter, and Gordon Walker, *Spaces of Environmental Justice* (Chichester, West Sussex: Wiley-Blackwell, 2010).

37. Ananth Kumar, "How Perungudi Dump Yard Has Made Life Difficult for Residents in Chennai's IT Corridor," *Citizen Matters*, Chennai, June 8, 2023, https://chennai.citizenmatters.in/perungudi-dumpyard-mashland-pallikaranai-fire-pollution-biomining-75904.

38. "Major Fire in Perungudi Dumpyard," *Hindu*, April 27, 2022, https://www.thehindu.com/news/cities/chennai/major-fire-in-perungudi-dumpyard/article65361006.ece.

39. "Thoraipakkam Residents Raise a Stink Over Biomining at Perungudi Dump Yard," *Hindu*, November 30, 2022, https://www.thehindu.com/news/cities/chennai/thoraipakkam-residents-raise-a-stink-over-biomining-at-perungudi-dump-yard/article66206156.ece.

40. Albrecht A. Glenn, "Solastalgia: A New Concept in Human Health and Identity," *PAN (Philosophy, Activism, Nature)* 3 (2005): 44–59.

Chapter 2

Anthropocene—The Clock Ticks

The Doomsday Clock ticks . . . Its long arm wavers each year to signal the distance to a "time of unprecedented danger."[1] In 2023, it stands at ninety seconds to midnight! Its voice, a ticking metaphor of our times, warns the planet of how long to midnight humanity has before its self-destruction. The clock of the Anthropocene, a techno-scientific sword of Damocles, was conceived in 1947 by a group of atomic scientists. It symbolizes the perils facing humanity in the present time from nuclear weapons to the melting Arctic snow. The cautionary warning from physicists Leo Szilard and Albert Einstein to US president Harry S. Truman in 1946, on the irreversible dangers of nuclear bombs, fell on deaf ears, leading to the end of World War II with the dropping of nuclear bombs on Hiroshima and Nagasaki.[2] Scientists from the Manhattan Project decided to inform the public about science and its implications for humanity. So, the secret government service that had worked on producing the first atomic bomb formed the Bulletin of the Atomic Scientists of Chicago. Martyl Langsdorf, an artist and a member Bulletin scientist designed and illustrated a minimalist, but eye-catching clock of the Anthropocene with its large minute hand set at seven minutes to midnight. She chose this time configuration as it suited her eye and seemed aesthetically right.[3] Ever since, the Bulletin Scientists, comprised of scientists and Nobel laureates, have used the Doomsday Clock to depict the climate change threats facing humanity by resetting the minute hand's distance to midnight.

Hands that once figured only nuclear threats now encompass a larger array of catastrophic climate change phenomena. The furthest minute-hand span of the clock to midnight was a relatively safe record of seventeen minutes in 1991 after the collapse of the Soviet Union and the signing of the Strategic Arms Reduction Treaty signed by US president George H. W. Bush and Soviet general secretary Mikhail Gorbachev on July 31, 1991. So, the reduction of nuclear arsenal gave the clock more time space to midnight. In 1953, the hands crept to display approaching climate change doom with the minute needle angled at two minutes to midnight. It was the year when the

United States and the Soviet Union had engaged in similar missions of testing their nuclear bombs. Scientists from the Bulletin of the Atomic Scientists of Chicago include climate scientists and experts in nuclear technology, including thirteen Nobel laureates. They meet to discuss world events, voice their views, and reconfigure the hands of the Doomsday Clock each year. In 2016, the clock hand was moved to three minutes before midnight consequent to the Iran Nuclear Agreement (2015) and the Paris Climate Accord (2015). After the recent pandemics that rocked the planet, Russia–United States–China tensions, Russia's invasion of Ukraine, and revived fears of nuclear war, the clock's hands are now at the closest gap of ninety seconds to midnight.

The references to the clock are many in popular culture. Like the canary in the gold mine, which chirps a signal to the miners to exit the crumbling mines, the Doomsday Clock, when it meets with the small-hour hand, will chime, as in the pop star Prince's lyrics: "It's party over, oops out of time."[4] The clock settled into pop culture, with the rock group The Smashing Pumpkins launching the song "Doomsday Clock" as the opening track on their album *Zeitgeist*[5] to hammer the mood of the time. The British heavy metal band Iron Maiden in 1984 rocked the world with the lyrics: "Two minutes to midnight, the hands that threaten doom."[6] The idea of standing at the threshold of doom's doorstep was also expressed by the rock band R.E.M in their tune "It's the End of the World As We Know It."[7] Batman, in the movie *Justice League* (2017), reminds humanity that "the Doomsday Clock has no snooze button,"[8] and that time cannot be stopped in the era of the Anthropocene. At the COP 26 climate talks in Glasgow in 2021, former prime minister Boris Johnson referred to the Doomsday Clock: "It's one minute to midnight on that Doomsday Clock, and we need to act now."[9]

HYPEROBJECTS IN TIME AND SPACE

The International Union of Geological Sciences (IUGS),[10] the professional organization in charge of defining Earth's time scale, says that we are officially in the Holocene, an entirely recent epoch, which began 11,700 years ago, after the last major ice age. But in the last decade, a new label for our present era—Anthropocene—has slowly been accepted by scientists and environmentalists to describe our time. Our time is one in which humankind has contributed to the mass extinctions of plant and animal species. The Holocene, a relatively stable time for the Earth, has slowly degenerated into the Anthropocene, when humans have reduced 30 percent of fish stock to critical levels; have cut down over fifteen billion trees every year; have replaced wild forests with tame monoculture; and have transformed the planet into one run by humankind for humankind.[11] Human beings have overrun the world, have polluted the oceans, and have altered the atmosphere, among other lasting climate change phenomena. In 2011, the magazine *The Economist* had the words, "Welcome to the Anthropocene" on its cover page[12] to highlight how humans have changed the way the world works, signaling that it was now imperative that we change the way we think about it. In 2014, Professor Lise Autogena, from the University of Toulouse, organized a four-month exhibition and symposium performance called the *Anthropocene Monument* at Les Abattoirs Museum in Toulouse, to showcase human entry into the monumental time of the Earth. The exhibition considered the possible forms of a monument to the Anthropocene in art.[13] In 2015, *Nature*, a science magazine, ran a similar cover story entitled "The Human Epoch: Defining the Anthropocene," in which it attempted to stamp a name on the new geological age and find a possible marker to locate it in apocalyptic time discourse.[14]

The word *Anthropocene*, from the Greek derivation of *anthro* for "man" and *cene* for "new" was coined by Nobel prize laureate for chemistry, Paul Crutzen, and limnologist Eugene Stormer in 2000 to name the geological era of our time. From its name, *Anthropocene*, we know that this age is anthropogenic, during which atmospheric, biospheric, geologic, and hydrologic systems have been altered by human existence. The age is symbolic of a time when the emphasis is on humanity being the vital force shaping the Earth and thus prompting the logic of viewing "humanity taken as a whole and as a single unit."[15] This geological time, or chronostratigraphic unit, is one subject to profound alterations that stem from human influence on the planet.[16] Scientists and geologists have fixed the beginning of the Anthropocene from 1950. Our planet Earth has been through ice ages that are glacial periods with large ice sheets. The last ice age occurred 120,000 to 11,500 years ago. Since then, our planet Earth has existed in an interglacial age, the Holocene, and now the Anthropocene. Today, the International Commission of Stratigraphy (ICS) studies geological time. Its component body, the Anthropocene Working Group (AWG),[17] has the task of analyzing the case and determining if the term *Anthropocene* should be formally adopted to designate our present epoch. In 2019, the panel of thirty-four members of the AWG voted in favour of designating this new geological epoch as the Anthropocene. Even though the majority opinion within the AWG deems the Anthropocene to be stratigraphically existent and recommends formalization, this geological name is yet to be validated. Many new neologisms have been as proposed alternatives to the Anthropocene, namely Capitalocene, Plantationcene, Homogenocene, Myxocene, Thanatocene, Planthroposcene, Symbiocene, and Bandwaggonocene.[18] These new lexicons for articulating the impact of climate change show how the idea of the Anthropocene is no longer fettered to the earth sciences but is one that is poised on an entry into wider public discourse. Anthropocene discourse is evident in the social sciences and humanities, literature, and art, with these disciplines accepting the new, unsettling conventional distinctions between man and nature, the redistribution of agency between humans and non-humans, and radical new ideas on the place of the humans in Earth systems and deep time.

We human beings live time as 'human time,' in which we sense the passage of time as the present, the past, and the future, based on our understanding of physical space and countable time. We link tangible events in time and space by dividing events into measurable units, including the imperceivable, such as milliseconds or time spans that transcend our lifespan, like eras or millennia.[19] It is, however, difficult for us to imagine and fathom the passage of geological time or deep time. Human history spans just a fragment or a few milli-microseconds of the deeply incomprehensible immensity of deep time,[20] or planetary time. The abstract complexity of deep time is difficult to grasp as geological time space is unfathomable and unmeasurable. Tim Flannery elicits the idea of Dr. Who's time travel adventures through time's epochal gateways, as well as the passage through the relative dimensions of time and space, thus maneuvering the closure of one geological period and the beginning of a new one.[21] Deep time can be understood through the metaphor of the Doomsday Clock, with humanity poised one millimeter off the cosmic mile or its tryst with doom. Scholars have explored this claim of an existence of anthropogenic influence,[22] have attempted to archive both lost, frozen, and living narratives of people, flora, and fauna of the polar ice,[23] and have documented palaeoecological records.[24] In his work of nonfiction, *The Great Derangement: Climate Change and the Unthinkable*, Amitav Ghosh writes that we have entered a time when "the wild has become the norm."[25] Similarly, Timothy Morton writes that in wild time, the uncanny becomes the norm.[26] He contends that humanity in the era of global warming is "now in the uncanny valley."[27] Time may be wild, uncanny, but it remains unyielding, inescapable, and relentless, as Jeannette Winterson says in *The Stone Gods*: "You can change everything about yourself—your name, your home, your skin color, your gender, even your parents, your private history—but you can't change the time you were born in, or what it is you have to live through.[28] Hence, we are products of our time, and we have to accept time as it unfolds itself during our existence on the planet.

A certain "disenchantment of the world"[29] is evident in numerous apocalyptic motifs of our times: the biblical Great Flood, the Apocalypse, the Armageddon, the destruction of the world in the biblical book of Revelation, and references in film and other modes of popular culture. Our times are beset with "new fears,"[30] with artificial intelligence taking over human operations, nanotechnology, environmental catastrophes caused by GMOs, Malthusian predilections, nuclear holocausts, viral mutations, and pandemics. In his seminal essay, "Anthropocene Time," Dipesh Chakrabarty observes that humanist scholars will have to revise many of their fundamental assumptions about humans being the sole geological agents of climate change as the present epoch tends to be "Capitalocene," with capitalism or the global economic system being also to blame for climate change and the depletion of resources.[31] He explains that to understand the Anthropocene, we must see it as a "socio-ecological phenomenon" that originated from two centuries of capitalist development or a period of vast economic and social change during which the Holocene ended and the Anthropocene began.[32] In today's world, terms like *climate change*, *economy*, *capitalism*, and *neoliberalism* are what Timothy Morton labels as "hyperobjects," or massively distributed objects in time and space.[33] Present in a kind of non-locality, none of their manifestations can be pinned down as an independent system existing on its own, with the general being affected by the particular. They exist in a state described by Morton as a space of "interobjectivity" with lines drawn around them to establish a demarcation excluding non-humans.[34] As systems, these hyperobjects exist as a mesh comprising a plurality of different objects[35] and in a state of "viscosity," where hyperobjects, like the economy or capitalism, stick like oil to everything they enter in contact with, making it feel like they have been omnipresent all along.[36] Global warming is a hyperobject with its capacity to penetrate our planet Earth, neighboring stars, and the whole universe across galactical time and space. Morton draws a picture of hyperobjects enveloping us, and tapering off, like a long street stretched into an unimaginable distance. He reasons that hyperobjects are malleable as "Time bends and flattens them, the same way that an electromagnetic wave front shortens at its leading edge. Because we can't see to the edge of them, hyperobjects are necessarily uncanny."[37] The cosmic celestial sphere that affects our planetary existence is the focus of attention of space-age billionaires of today, aiming to conquer this uncanny, terrestrial, and planetary intergalactic space. Like the term *Anthropocene* referring to the end of the geological age in which human activity has a dominant influence on the climate and ecology of the Earth, the term *Anthropocosmos*, coined by C.A. Doxiadis Constantinos and John G. Papaioannou, refers to the age in which human activity has influenced the ecology of the entire universe.[38] Since the beginning of the Space Age era in 1957, when the Soviet Union launched Earth's first artificial satellite, *Sputnik 1*, expenditure by governments to be part of the International Space Station has escalated, with participating countries investing about one hundred billion euros.[39] As humans colonize orbital space, films and science fiction have contemplated the possible colonization of the stars and sending probes to alien planets. The space thus falls also under the category of a hyperobject that has the dual purpose of serving as a home to human space stations as well as the lieu of interstellar displacement of debris and junk.

Simonetta Di Pippo, the director of outer space affairs for the United Nations Office (UNOOSA), is a strong advocate of exploration and peaceful uses of outer space for a better future for humanity but has however acknowledged the dual threat of climate sustainability and space debris.[40] The published UNOSSA index has referenced 8,261 individual satellites orbiting the Earth, an increase of 11.84 percent compared to April 2021; 58 percent of these satellites orbiting the Earth remain active, while others are inactive.[41] The UNOOSA lists 12,293 objects launched into space from planet Earth through air-based, sea-based, and submarine launching sites. Their benefits[42] are no doubt many with satellites being an indispensable support for global efforts to climate change, existing in Low Earth Orbit (LEO), Geostationary Orbit (GEO), and Medium Earth Orbit (MEO).[43] But with countries vying with each other to be part of the Space Age,[44] and creating space events and spatial partnerships, there is also orbital debris as these space programs are organized in clusters or collaborative units in orbital space, often resulting in overcrowding or clustering of spacecraft. These space orbits also contain debris, and waste from old spatial missions. Space Surveillance Networks have tracked and catalogs 32,490 of a total mass of 10,500 tons from breakups, explosions, and collisions.[45] Di Pippo warns us that it is impossible to monitor and track the proliferation of space debris or space junk that may at any moment be on a collision course to Earth. She says it is time to listen to scientific narratives before it is too late. The project of removing debris of obsolete satellites and expended rockets from space orbit means injecting more millions into space research and missions. Astrophysicists have already contemplated the use of lasers, space nets, solar sails, drones, gecko-mimicking adhesive structures, and space garbage nets with robotic tools to catch the ever-elusive debris. How do the gains from space technology outweigh the costs of launching these satellites into outer space? It is evident that solving the debris problem would require new technologies. It stirs the need for new space regulations and international treaties.

DANGEROUS PURSUITS OF OUR TIME

In *Dangerous Pursuits*,[46] Suniti Namjoshi relates the fable of the lonely giant who swiftly tilled the land with his fingers, diverted a river to water his fields, reaped a rich harvest, and multiplied his monetary gains until he possessed the whole world. This tale is typical of the rocket-age billionaires of today, aiming to conquer terrestrial and planetary intergalactic space. The fable's watchwords signal that it is *money* that makes the world go round, as "Money breeds itself."[47] This adage could well apply to the galactic exploration of deep space in the missions of Elon Musk, Jeff Bezos, and Richard Branson.

They are aspiring billionaire-space entrepreneurs of our time involved in dangerous pursuits of conquering and exploiting planets surrounding the Earth. Elon Musk, in the Netflix documentary *Return to Space*, enunciates his ambitious, Space Age dream of humans becoming a multi-planet species: "Earth is the cradle of humanity, but you cannot stay in the cradle forever. It is time to go forth and be out there among the stars, expand the scope and scale of human consciousness."[48] SpaceX launches now boast of reusable orbital launch rockets capable of precision landings and advanced emergency-abort systems. Jeff Bezos, who heads Blue Origin LLC, the privately funded aerospace manufacturing and sub-orbital spaceflight services company, has even suggested offloading destruction to other planets, while preserving what remains of the Earth as a kind of pleasure garden and pastoral space. "We have a choice," Bezos persuades the audience. "We can have a life of stasis, because earth is finite. . . . Or . . . if we continue to grow . . . all the polluting industry will be done in space where we have infinite resources."[49] In 2021, Richard Branson and his crew of three astronauts flew above 80 kilometers (or about 262,000 feet), which is the altitude that the NASA recognizes as the boundary of space. His company, Virgin Galactic, besides taking an Italian crew of research astronauts to space, is now poised to send commercial flights into space and organize recurring commercial space line operations with the aim of "providing an unrivaled experience for private astronauts and researchers."[50] One may well wonder if there will soon be an Industrial Revolution in space, with new star men bringing space down to Earth and moving Earth to space!

In the Netflix film *Don't Look Up*,[51] while observing supernovas, Jennifer Lawrence, playing the role of a PhD student, discovers a 10-kilometer-large asteroid descending from the Oort cloud, the outermost part of the solar system. The comet named after her as Dibiasky is on its killer course toward Earth, and according to NASA's computers in the film, is all set to hit the Pacific Ocean sixty-two miles due west of the coast of Chile. Dr. Mindy, an astrophysicist played by Leonardo Di Caprio, warns the world through global media that the comet's impact would create a catastrophic tidal wave, generate mule-size tsunamis that would fan out across the globe, and have the impact of a billion Hiroshima bombs. Climate scientists in the film presage the event of a magnitude 10- or 11-earthquake intensity. But, as they articulate the science, the president of the United States does not understand the magnitude of the situation and asks them to "sit tight and assess."[52] Sitting tight and assessing is exactly what policymakers do in the film. A planet killer comet with a 100 percent certainty of impact stirs debate in the film on whether defense drones will be capable of changing the orbit of the comet. While executive and legislative decision-makers sit tight and assess, they finally attribute to the climate disaster the same credibility given to such events in video games.

As the meteoroid prepares to strike Earth, scientists in the movie contemplate how to split the comet and use its rare resources to remove poverty and social injustice on the Earth. Science fiction controls these narratives and highlights how presidents execute their role as the executive head of the planet. These climate change narratives in films have the potential to awaken and/or sway public opinion about the planet being fragile and endangered.

CLIMATE CHANGE WARRIORS IN THE ZERO HOUR

In the wake of the Anthropocene, grassroots movements around the world have manifested dissent and demonstrated activism in public spaces to have their voices heard. In 2018, after the United States pulled out of the Paris Agreement signed in 2015 in COP21, sixteen-year-old activist Jamie Margolin inspired young Generation Z activists to voice protest.[53] Her group, Zero Hour, chose the logo of the Doomsday Clock with the continents figuring in the clock's background face. The post-millennial group of activists—comprised of teens from Brazil, England, Germany, Kenya, India, and the Democratic Republic of the Congo—have joined forces to create awareness of the need to mitigate climate change. As heads of state assembled for the Global Climate Action Summit in San Francisco between September 12 and 14, 2018, Margolin picked up the loudspeakers to be the spokesperson of those affected by bad climate change decisions: "We're here to say that not everything is for sale, and that the leaders need to listen to indigenous people, people of color, low-income communities and immigrants, who have been paying the worst price for the climate crisis and have been victims of these systems."[54] In October 2015, indigenous people of the small, low-lying Pacific islands, calling themselves "Pacific Climate Warriors,"[55] traveled halfway around the world to spread out mats on the grounds of Saint Peter's Square in Vatican City. During their three-day vigil, these Pacific Climate Warriors prayed together for world climate leaders. Fervent voices expressed through prayers was followed by a traditional quiet session, during which they cried silent tears of anguish and concern for nature in the epoch of the Anthropocene. Their woven mats from another continent were symbolic of the journey to a place of prayer where they could create a space to talk about the trauma of climate change in their little Pacific islands. Their traditional coir mats were interwoven with stories and prayers uttered during their fabrication. The crashing of the ocean waves can be heard in the stories of these fisherfolk.[56] Lawrence Buell writes, "A place is seen, heard, smelled, imagined, loved, hated, feared and revered,"[57] and expresses the view that ecocritical insistence can be a "commitment deeper than professionalism."[58] The travel narrative of the islanders highlights their voyages of having traversed the high seas to voice their concern in another place, far from home. The Pacific Climate Warriors insist, "That's not the only story about us, we are also warriors standing up for our home and our people."[59] Their message—to fight and not wither in global warming—has incited young people in fifteen countries to form a network that engages in protecting their island homes.

Other grassroots, indigenous tribal movements have merged inside the global movement for climate justice. In 2016, native American tribes flocked together to protest and prevent the installation of the Dakota oil pipeline. Tribal leaders voiced protest to protect lands and artifacts they considered to be sacred. Donald Trump vowed to support the pipeline's developer, Energy Transfer Partners, saying it had the capacity to create thousands of construction jobs and millions in tax revenue.[60] Despite tireless opposition from tribes and environmental groups, the Biden administration continues to support the construction of the pipeline. On May 3, 2021, the Army Corps of Engineers announced its intention to keep the pipeline operational while preparing a court-ordered Environmental Impact Statement (EIS). The draft of EIS is expected in 2023.[61] The pipeline's opponents pointed out the fact that the pipeline ran within a half mile of the Standing Rock Sioux Reservation and that it endangered the drinking water facilities for local Native Americans. Tribal groups, joining hands together around the pipeline to align their activist movements, resulted in a merging of voices to create a stronger collective voice to express dissent. In this idea of polyphonic activism, each activist movement has a different activist propaganda, distinct in its tactical, strategic, and campaigning objectives, but their voices unite to address the incoherent legislative decisions of our time. As in a polyphonic rendering where there "are different voices singing variously on a single theme,"[62] this polyphonic activism is characterized by "multivoicedness, exposing the diversity of life and the great complexity of human experience."[63]

On March 3, 2023, the indigenous Sami tribes dispersed in Norway, Sweden, and Finland, who were dressed in traditional Sami garments, assembled outside the Norwegian royal palace. They voiced silent dissent to their sovereign, King Harald V. They squatted on the ground on reindeer skins in below-freezing temperatures to stop further installation of wind turbines at Europe's largest onshore wind farm in the Fosen district, situated 450 kilometers north of Oslo. The peaceful protest resulted in talks with the Norwegian prime minister, Jonas Gahr Støre. He made a public apology for having endangered the reindeer herders' way of life.[64]

In October 2022, the Kharia tribe in Odisha in India alerted the world of the illegal land acquisition of the Dalmia group. A 65-kilometer trek was organized with thousands of *Adivasis*, the indigenous tribes of India, taking part in the protest march to meet the Sudargarh collector. They chanted, "The forest is our mother, and we cannot be tricked into separating from it."[65] They slept outside the district collector's office and drew public attention to the seventy-seven-acre land project through which the government had permitted Dalmia Bharat Cement Limited to mine for limestone in forests, which were their habitat. In 2018, river activists who lived on the banks of the Yamuna River in India, marched with banners to protect the Taj Mahal from pollution. They called attention to the dry riverbed and alerted the public on how the monument was subject to sandblasts in hot weather. They contended that the "Taj Corridor Project." which was supposed to upgrade tourist facilities near the Taj Mahal, was a political scam with scarcely any improvement in the air they inhaled.[66]

These activist movements of the Zero Hour irrespective of their race, color, and creed, all have a part to play in this symphony or agreement or concord of voices. They support different causes and highlight their engagement in different ways. They draw attention to each other and inspire new causes to be heard along with their symphonic rendering of different notes.

ECOCRITICAL SCIENCE FICTION NOVUMS

Novelists and filmmakers use the futuristic time frame to portray the time of the Anthropocene. Science fiction that specializes in constructions of other-worlds, or what Suvin has called "novums" or a new thing,[67] that are extraterrestrial and futuristic is the favored genre for depicting climate change. Science fiction is the ideal mode for depicting tsunamis, rising sea levels, wildfires, energy scarcity, intense heat, melting polar ice caps, genetically modified diseases, pandemics, thus setting the otherworldly 'novum' of an apocalyptic end. The settings have components that are not present in the "author's and implied reader's norm of reality,"[68] so there is potential for exploration. The genre of science fiction thus enables "the presence and interaction of estrangement and cognition." where the reader discovers an imaginative framework alternative to the author's empirical environment."[69] One of the core preoccupations faced by ecocritical writers is the adoption of a sleight-of-hand that portrays more than a human voice while avoiding the techniques of traditional literary anthropomorphisms. Science fiction enables this acceptance of a "challenge of speaking for an ecosystem that may operate on scales of time and space that often elude normal human perception or judgment."[70]

Questioning the story of our time through the empirical environment of science fiction can highlight what it means to be 'human' and 'non-human' as well as partake in ecocriticism's project of rethinking the relationship between humans and our world. Vandana Singh,[71] in her collection of short stories entitled *The Woman Who Thought She Was a Planet*,[72] uses the genre of fantastic science fiction to imagine horrific scenarios in which man, nature, and the environment are no longer in harmony. In "Three Tales from Sky River: Myths for a Starfaring Age," Singh figures myths and folklore, elements of magic, to question the 'Anthropocene,' the story of our time. The three tales take readers on adventures in an age when humans on faraway galaxies look longingly at the planet Earth and crave to rewind the clock back to a life on *terra firma*. Alien, apocalyptic stories show the dark side of climate change, but they heighten awareness by exploring hypothetical questions: What if the Sky People returned to planet Earth? What if life really did exist on planet Omasa in the star system Proxima? What if humans had listened to nature and heard the warning of global warming? What if stones and trees did marry? Voices from faraway galaxies that experience the same climate change dilemmas as humans are evident in the polyphony in the three tales despite the improbability of occurrence. Singh builds pluralistic worlds in the three science-fiction tales, where fantasy permits entry into an alternative universe and contains a "novum" with a story that revolves around it.[73] In the three tales, alternative reality is mediated by fantastic events to highlight the pluralistic voicing of realities and experiences. In science fiction, ecological change in extraterrestrial terms is often allied to the theme of terraforming, as it draws attention to the climate change issues of our times and energizes environmental activism. In *Grimus*, Rushdie's science-fiction novum features a debate between the eagles Gribbs, Elfrida, and Irna at the Conference of Birds on whether stories should be well tied together or not. Elfrida sums up the novum of *Grimus* as one that portrays life as "slightly frayed at the edges, full of loose ends and lives juxtaposed by accident rather than some grand design. Most of life has no meaning so it must surely be a distortion of life to tell tales in which every single element is meaningful."[74] Like Rushdie's *Grimus*, which has often been subject to debate on whether it falls under the genre of science fiction or magic realism, Singh's postmodern sleight-of-hand also resorts to a hybrid blend of the two. While Rushdie's *Grimus* with its assorted intertexts features the twelfth-century Sufi narrative poem called "The Conference of the Birds," Singh's flock of Tipi-Birds are ones that congregate to warn and alert on the impending doom of climate change. The tale is set in an alternate time space where humans have begun to terraform the imaginary planet Jehana, meaning "destiny" in Hindi. *Jehana*'s tale of destiny is configured in a fictional-galactical star system called Kamboja, which is the name of an ancient tribe of Transoxiana and the Paropamisus in Iron Age India. Like the Iron Age on planet Earth, when humans smelted iron for weaponry, the galactical time span in this science-fiction tale is set at a primitive state of time when the *Saras*, or 'stork' people, were engaged in the process of terraforming, of building dams and reconfiguring their space settlements.

Planet Jehana, like planet Earth, has rivers, mountains, plains, and valleys. In this faraway galaxy, magical realist time moves in circles of three hundred years. Planetary existence revolves in a time circle; history repeats itself going back to the start. The beginning of a new era is the end, and the end of one epoch is the beginning. Warning of a new cycle of time is conveyed in the universal tone of magical-realist gossip by Tipi-Birds. These imaginary birds float; they do not fly. Their time is spent gossiping and ingesting river fish and algae during the day near the river settlements of Jehana. And at nightfall, their wings swell up with gas that lifts them to the blue skies. These fabled birds in Singh's fantastic extraterrestrial universe can enunciate only a single word: "Listen."[75] In the tale entitled "'Listen!' said the Tipi-Bird," Singh merges genres, inventing creation myths of a star-faring age when the creator of the universe, or the Great Shaper, descends every three hundred years to destroy civilization. As the god of the planet Jehana, the Great Shaper confesses to the Tipi-Bird, "I am tired of them changing and reshaping my river valleys, building dams, and blowing up hillsides, and I don't want them to get too arrogant. Therefore, I have made a plan to destroy their civilization every three hundred years."[76] The tale is related in the scientific, fantasy mode mingling elements of magical realism that lend to an allegorical interpretation. The plot deals with the quest motif of the protagonist, the Tipi-Bird, on planet Jehana, the fantastic locale. In this human settlement in outer space, spatial dimensions are in a state of fluidity and constant flux. The omniscient narrator warns the reader by predicting how terrible floods and earthquakes would destroy the Saras people in never-ending cycles. He forewarns that a destroyer in the form of the star akin to the Sun on Earth, named Eenah the Wanderer, would stray closer to planet Jehana, wiping out its valleys with floods and annihilating those who attempted to walk through its marshes.

By portraying hyper-reality in lieu of reality, Singh shows how humanity can survive if they would only 'listen.' The Great Shaper shares his intent of destroying the Saras peoples with a Tipi-Bird but swears her to silence. Unable to keep her secret, the Tipi-Bird whispers the tale of oncoming doom to an old woman, called Rema, who was fast asleep, by beginning her tale with the word "Listen."[77] On discovering that the garrulous bird had revealed his plans, the Great Shaker curses the Tipi-Bird, "you broke your word. . . . I now curse you and all your kind. You will lose your ability to talk, except for one word. I leave you the word 'listen.'"[78] When the star Eenah began to shine fiercely, the Tipi-Bird pays yet another visit to old Rema and makes a plea to listen. With this word of caution, the Tipi-Bird awakens Rema's memory of a nightmare where the floods and earthquakes forced the Saras people to seek shelter in the high mountains of Jehana. By endowing her Tipi-Bird with the ability to speak, albeit monosyllabically, Singh builds a pluralistic world of voices mediated by fantasy, which permits access into an unconventional universe. In the tale, she uses the myth of the Tipi-Bird to make the improbable possible. The tale ends with the few who had listened and heeded the warning of the old woman, returning from the mountains to the plateaus to continue with their lives for the next three hundred years. Nature voices her concern through the ripples and bubbles of the riverbanks. The Earth quakes and announces the arrival of Eenah, thus voicing further disapproval of the terraforming. Even secrets are voiced through one-word sentences of warning by the Tipi-Bird. Birds chatter, and women gossip and dream in this polyphonic tale.

In the second tale, "Haiho's knife," Singh's etiological myth imagines the origin of the serrated knife and how it came into use. The 'novum' is built in an imaginary world plausibly different from the author's current world.[79] In another galaxy faraway, on a star system bearing the princely name of Alamir on planet Kutch, dwelt former earthlings called the Sonhali people. They roamed the galaxies in silver-sky boats, exploring its unfathomable spaces. Having quenched the quest for the unknown, the sky people, in their silver boats, long once again to return to the rich pastures and bathe bare-bodied in the inviting, warm seas of the islands on planet Earth. The only living creatures they had taken with them to outer space were the peaceful, dormant micro-organisms that cover the surface of human skin. Their splash into the warm waters of the Earth resulted in freeing the tentacle-like beings that resided deep in their hair and glands. As they step out 'golden' out of the waters onto the beach sand, the Sonhali people, typical of their name,[80] rejoiced to see their golden bodies shine in the light of the new Sun. After a carnivalesque revelry of drinking and feasting for a couple of generations, the sky people are woken up from their dream-like existence when mysterious Amaila emerges from the sea with her head covered with finger-thick tentacles that writhed and moved. Naming them the Medusa for the creature that had once inhabited the bodies of the Sonhali sky people, she unwittingly transmits the Medusa to Haiho's lovesick son. Haiho creates the first serrated knife, a notched or toothed blade edge, to scrape out the Medusa and burn the contagious protagonist. The distinct authorial voice states the idea that serrated knives were needed for survival—one soft side for daily use and the other sharp and deadly face serving to combat the deadly viruses of climate change. The tale ends with the note that "ever since then, every hunter on every island in the archipelago has made sure that his knife has one serrated edge and one edge that is smooth, sharpened and deadly."[81] Self-complacency is evident in the collective voice of the Sonhali people: "We are beautiful."[82] Haiho bellows caution, while those who catch Amaila's Medusa moan in agony. In her article entitled "A Speculative Manifesto," Singh writes on the use of the genre of fantasy and science fiction as "stories about what cannot ever be, or what cannot be as yet."[83] In her relating of stories on sky-faring planets, where the impossible is the norm, she shows how alternative reality, mediated by fabulation and fantasy, can serve as a powerful tool to address the issue of climate change. Voices in the fictional space are ones engaged in transmitting their ideological stance from a different Space Age. The reader engages in the deciphering of meaning through a 'dialogic process,'[84] whereby one hears another's voice filled with its own experience, permeated with the interpretations and ideological stance of others. This plurality experience, with its ideas from diverse sources, underwrites the fact that ideas are never closed-off, but they transform and regenerate themselves through a constant interaction of other voices that have their own stances to maintain. Devoid of one-sided or dogmatic opinions, the tale abounds with different points of view, with Singh enabling these voices to collide and get together in the 'great dialogue' of the tale, leaving that dialogue open without a finalizing period at the end.[85]

Another galactical-age tale relating "The Marriage of Tree and Stone" is set on the imaginary planetary continent of Zakrug on planet Omasa in the star system Proxima. Here, Singh imagines the existence of nature on Alpha Centauri, a star system, which is our solar system's closest neighbor. This system has been under surveillance of the astronomical eye, as its three-star planetary surface seems habitable to the human gaze. Its stars, Alpha Centauri A and Alpha Centauri B, form an inner binary, whereas Proxima Centauri is its peripheral star, which is situated the nearest to our planet Earth. This science-fiction tale is set in Time's childhood, when trees could walk purposefully with long strides like the Ents in Tolkien's *The Lord of the Rings*.[86] The authorial voice paints the picture of a planet with trees that were capable of displacement. They even walked to dip their roots into the waters of the river to drink. Stones that could move and talk, fell in love with walking trees, and they even married. Their offspring were green, pliant, soft-skinned, and rootless. These hybrid children were nourished by the fruits from the trees, and they dwelt in the water channels created by the stones. It was a time when the "world sounded with the creaky, whispery voices of the trees, and the low, grating language of the stones."[87] However, strife on planet Omasa began when children rebelled against their parents, scoffed when a tree father walked, or a stone mother rolled, thus resulting in parent stones and trees standing still and voiceless forever. Apart from Angud, a lame boy who hid from his bigger tree and stone brothers due to the fear of being ridiculed, the rest of the hybrid-offspring grew proud and vain. Angud's voice is heard only when he blows his whistle to soothe the trees and the stones. But his whistle is rudely snatched away by his stronger siblings in this tale. He lives to witness the trees cover the stones with roots and mud. As his infant children grow, he teaches them to love the trees and stones by relating the yarns of old times, when nature lived in harmony.

Angud's offspring, the Angudka, learned to live and protect the forests. On his death, Angud is buried with his whistle. The ungrateful children in the tale cut down trees to build houses, lose the green tint of their tree ancestors, and in time forget their origins and their language. But the trees and stones still remember their old sorrow. When the ungrateful come to chop them down, they hear a whistle that blows amidst the trees. The trees and stones awoken by the whistle shake the Earth with their shudders. Stones split and trees uproot as the Earth erupts in agony. Voices of nature erupt in a polyphony of sorrow and distress. The ground shudders and rumbles, the trees wail, the stones crack. The ungrateful children take to their heels and run in fear. The whistle still blows, reminding us of the union between trees and stones and keeps that memory alive through a science-fiction tale.

> The ground thunders in the old tongue of tree and stone, and they say to the ungrateful children: You are our offspring. We made you, they say, but the ungrateful ones don't understand. They turn in fear and run? They do not remember their mother tongue.[88]

Angud laments as his whistle emits a quavering note. The tale is one devoid of human speech, but the voices are many. Tales that matter are silenced in today's world, as language often eludes recognition. The science-fiction lens enables the reader to make a significant correlation between broader environmental issues and specific human behavior patterns that lead to natural disasters. The mode of science fiction enables an alternative description of reality and engenders the possibility of looking at reality from other dimensions. Singh's tales portray the real and the hyper-real by setting the tales in outer space.

Portraying the theme of climate change through the frame of science fiction also enables the hearing of voices where the discourse is dialogic favoring the existence of a plurality of independent and unmerged voices. In these fantastic science-fiction tales, voices stand beside that of the author. They do not lose their identity and are not submerged within it. As polyphony entails an active participation of dialogue, the polyphonic author "means to question and to listen, to try out new orientations, to combine some and expose others."[89] In the three tale sequences, different voices surface to voice their stance. The Tipi-bird says just one word: "Listen"; the Great Shaper voices concern over the destruction of the landscape and spells out the dire need to stop human activity; the old woman's voice warns of and predicts the coming future. Similarly, in "The Tale of Haiho's Knife,," the Sonhali in their vain contemplation of themselves speak: "We are beautiful";[90] Amaila's voice reassures, "Do not be afraid,"[91] despite the climate change dangers just ahead. In the tale of "The Marriage of Tree and Stone," the only two joyful human words spoken are onomatopoeic: "My whistle."[92] The rich and complex texture of these internal and external dialogues exemplify the dialogic interactions that are typical of a polyphonic literary work. The reader hears many explicit and implicit voices in these science-fiction tales with the characters. The characters are engaged in the polyphony taking on different roles and voices in different contexts of time, space, and culture, the voices we hear in the polyphony thus multiply. In *The Value of Ecocriticism*, Timothy Clark observes that "ecocriticism has become a diverse and vast field, a mix of literary, cultural, political, scientific, and activist strands. . . . Its mantra is that the environmental crisis demands a reconsideration of society's basic values, constitution, and purposes, and that art and literature can be vital in that work."[93] Singh's choice of the genre of science fiction revels in its aesthetic capacity to accommodate environmental issues at a global scale irrespective of which continent one lives on our planet Earth.

THE PRECAUTIONARY PRINCIPLE

Common Law, with its principle of precedence or *stare decisis*, permits an expression of multiple voices. Judges render decisions by referring to the *ratio decidendi* of a previous case and hand down a similar decision in a future case, thus providing the legal basis for future cases. In the polyphonic model of judicial discourse, the judicial opinions from foreign forums of justice often influence tribunals in other corners of the globe to render groundbreaking decisions. Decision-making is part of a continuing dialogue where judges embrace dialogue and complexity, recognizing the independent validity of multiple perspectives in future judgments. Such opinions are in keeping with the principle of the Rule of Law that excludes arbitrary law-making but strives to encourage dialogue and the consequent elaboration of meaning. Principle 10 of the Rio Declaration (1992) states that courts must serve as a forum for voices to be heard.[94] The forms of rhetoric in the courtroom arena are many, with multiple perspectives from lawyers, judges, defendants, claimants, and court watchers. Grievances may be voiced by minority groups or by those who may hold minority dissenting opinions. The environment apocalyptic narrative of different forums leaves avenues open for human intervention to still avoid the catastrophe of climate change. Judges in courts around the world in the current trend of Anthropocene judgments deliberate and render decisions by "deploying reason in the global, collective life."[95]

In *Massachusetts et al. v. Environmental Protection Agency* (2007),[96] the state of Massachusetts, twelve other states in the United States and environmental organizations petitioned the EPA, questioning the efficacy of the independent executive agency in regulating the emissions of carbon dioxide from new motor vehicles as they contributed to global warming. Massachusetts voiced the opinion that the EPA was required to regulate greenhouse gasses as per the Clean Air Act (1970)—which states that Congress must regulate pollutants and anticipate action to protect public health and welfare. The EPA opposed the petition, claiming that the Clean Air Act did not require the EPA to regulate greenhouse gas emissions. The EPA defended its stance by stating it had the discretion to defer a decision until it was sure of the causes, extent, and significance of climate change regarding the matter on greenhouse emissions. Massachusetts decided to appeal the denial of the petition at the Court of Appeals for the D.C. Circuit, where a divided panel ruled in favor of the EPA. By a 5–4 vote, the USSC reversed the D.C. Circuit and ruled in favor of Massachusetts, thus becoming the first Supreme Court in the world to address the issue of standing in claims related to environmental justice. Justice John Paul Stevens opined that the State of Massachusetts had standing to sue the EPA over potential environmental climate change disasters like greenhouse emissions or the submerging of its coastline, and that the state had presented clear evidence of actual and imminent harm. The Court ruled that the EPA, as the country's executive agency for climate change, had the duty to protect the country and was unjustified in delaying action on the grounds of prudential decision-making.

In *Friends of the Earth, Incorporated v. LaidLaw Environmental Services* (2000),[97] the United States Supreme Court, while ruling on mootness in a case of voluntary cessation of activity, established that the burden was on the defendant to show that the conduct cannot reasonably be expected to occur in the future. The Court observed that, in this case, the defendant had not demonstrated why or how the polluting actions will not reoccur in the future. In the same vein of thinking, it is possible to assume that if a defendant can make a case moot simply by ceasing the dangerous activity, the defendant could stop and restart the same act an infinite number of times without facing a judicial decision on the activity. Justice Ruth Bader Ginsburg in her opinion wrote that a defendant's voluntary cessation of allegedly unlawful conduct ordinarily did not suffice to moot a case, and that Friends of the Earth had standing and enough cause to bring the suit on behalf of its members before the forum.

In *Friends of the Earth v. The Governor in Council and Others* (2008),[98] the petitioner, a not-for-profit organization, filed a suit in the Canadian federal court alleging that the Canadian government had breached its duties to its citizens under the Kyoto Protocol Implementation Act (2007) by missing deadlines and failing to publish regulations. The court's ruling, that there was no justiciable issue, was reaffirmed in 2009 by the Federal Court of Appeal. The Supreme Court of Canada's panel of three justices declined to accept the leave application without stating the reasons for its decision as is usually the case when it is not considered as a case of public importance.

The collective strong voice of the petitioner, a Dutch environmental group and nine hundred Dutch citizens, resonated in *Urgenda Foundation v. The Netherlands* (2019).[99] In the first instance, in 2015, the District Court of Hague declared that Urgenda could not rely on either the European Convention on Human Rights (ECHR) or the Dutch constitution and determined that the State had breached its duty of care under the Dutch civil code, which requires parties to take precautionary measures to mitigate a hazardous situation.[100] On appeal, in 2016, the Urgenda Foundation alleged that the Dutch government had to take more action to prevent global climate change.[101] In 2019, the Netherlands Supreme Court found that the government's existing pledge to reduce emissions by 17 percent was insufficient and increased the objective to be reached as 25 percent of reductions. The court cited various principles, namely, Article 21 of the Dutch Constitution regarding the right to the fundamental right of a clean environment; referred to EU emissions reduction targets; mentioned principles under the European Convention on Human Rights; applied the 'no harm' principle of international law; discussed the doctrine of hazardous negligence, the principle of fairness, the Precautionary Principle, and the Sustainability Principle embodied in the UN Framework Convention on Climate Change to conclude that the state has a duty to take climate change mitigation measures to limit greenhouse gas emissions.[102]

Similarly, in *ClientEarth, R (on the application of ClientEarth) v. The Secretary of State for the Environment, Food and Rural Affairs* (2013),[103] the petitioner, an environmental charity that uses the law to create a powerful voice to protect the planet, had filed an action in the High Court of Justice Queen's Bench Division Planning Court, challenging the UK government's decision to approve plans for Europe's largest natural gas plant in 2013. The proceedings concerned the failure of the United Kingdom since 2010 to obtain compliance in certain zones with the limits for nitrogen dioxide levels set by European Union law, under Directive 2008/50/EC.[104] In 2013, the Supreme Court of the United Kingdom referred certain questions to the Court of Justice of the European Union (CJEU) concerning the interpretation of articles 13, 22, and 23 of the Directive. The CJEU addressed these issues in a judgment dated November 14, 2014, C-404/13.[105] Consequently in 2015, in *R (on the application of ClientEarth) v. Secretary of State for the Environment, Food and Rural Affairs*,[106] the UKSC unanimously ordered that the government must put forward new air quality plans to the European Commission no later than December 31, 2015.[107]

In the case *Virender Gaur and Ors. v. State of Haryana and Ors.* (1994),[108] the Supreme Court of India held that the right of people to a healthy environment was protected by Article 21 of the Indian Constitution.[109] It ruled that the constitutional rights to life and dignity included a right to a hygienic environment. It noted that the state and citizens were under the obligation to maintain a hygienic environment for present and future generations. It maintained that the right to human dignity granted environmental protection to ensure good hygiene and ecological balance. The Court referred to Principle 1 of the Stockholm Declaration (1972),[110] whereby it deemed that environmental protection was a matter that was essential to maintaining well-being and the enjoyment of basic human rights. India was a signatory to the declaration and inserted Articles 48A and 51A (g), conferring on the State and its citizens the obligation to conserve, perceive, protect, and improve the environment.

THE EPISTOLARY JUDGMENT

India became an independent country free from British rule on August 15, 1947. The task of drafting the Constitution was entrusted to the Constitution Drafting Committee led by Bhimrao Ramji Ambedkar. The Constitution came into force on January 26, 1950. The Indian Constitution is the longest constitution in the world, containing 395 articles and eight schedules. It is a hybrid constitution influenced by other constitutions in the world, and it now contains additional 105 amendments and twelve schedules pertaining to specific government policy.[111] The Indian Judiciary's three-tier system, consisting of the Supreme Court, the High Courts, and the Subordinate Courts, territorial, subject matter and pecuniary jurisdiction is detailed in Articles 124–147 of the Indian Constitution. Indian Supreme Court decisions take precedent and are binding on lower courts as is typical in Common Law jurisdictions. Article 124(1) establishes the existence of a chief justice of India (CJI) and thirty-three judges who are appointed by the president of India. In the Indian Supreme Court cases mentioned in the following chapters, most cases were heard in an Indian Supreme Court Division Bench of two or three judges. However, Article 145(3) provides for the formation of exceptional constitutional benches of five to seven judges to decide important questions of fact or legal and/or constitutional interpretation. On 27 August 2022, Uday Umesh Lalit took the oath as India's forty-ninth chief justice of India, and he has decided to have at least one constitutional bench functioning throughout the year.[112]

In the context of climate change litigation, judgments from foreign jurisdictions figure as convincing arguments in Indian court opinions showing how this domain of justice is one influenced by comparative jurisprudence, as well as national and international legal frameworks of climate change law. It is this use of comparative jurisprudence that has produced justices who dare to step out of the precincts of judicial restraint and issue judgments that can be considered as activist and interfering with legislative and executive structures. The Precautionary Principle was applied in *M.C. Mehta v. Union of India & Ors* (1996),[113] also known as the Taj Trapezium case, when the petitioner filed a writ of mandamus in 1986 to preserve the Taj Mahal, one of the wonders of the ancient world, from industrial pollution. The 10,400 square kilometer area around the Taj Mahal is labeled as the Taj Trapezium Zone (TTZ) and encompasses five districts in the Agra region. The TTZ has around forty protected monuments, including three World Heritage Sites—namely the Agra Fort, the Taj Mahal, and the Fatehpur Sikri. The continuing mandamus writ procedure or structural interdict or structural injunction enables the court to keep a matter open so it can monitor a government agency's progress against orders and issue fresh orders where needed. The Taj Mahal was declared a UNESCO World Heritage Site in 1983. Mahesh Chander Mehta, popularly known as M.C. Mehta, is a public interest attorney known as India's green lawyer or green avenger. He is the pioneer of public interest litigation (PIL) in India. In this landmark case involving an oleum gas leakage in Delhi (1985), like the events of the Bhopal Gas Tragedy (1984), the Indian Supreme Court used the principle of Absolute Liability. Unlike the rule of Strict Liability, which was applied in the UK case, *Ryland v. Fletcher* (1868),[114] where the industry owner in the event of a hazardous act on his property could invoke the Defense of an 'Act of God,'[115] in *M.C. Mehta v. Union of India & Ors* (1996), the Indian Supreme Court replaced the principle of Strict Liability with Absolute Liability, holding the company Shriram Food and Fertilizers Ltd. completely responsible for the gas leakage, irrespective of its defense and claimed loss.

Justice Kuldip Singh rendered a poetic judgment on the beauty of the Taj Mahal by quoting Frederick Sleigh Robert's memoir, entitled *Forty-one years in India: From Subaltern to Commander-in-Chief* (1901).

> Neither words nor pencil could give to the most imaginative reader the slightest idea of all the satisfying beauty and purity of this glorious conception. To those who have not seen it, I would say, 'Go to India; the Taj alone is well worth the journey'. . . . It is too pure, too holy to be the work of human hands. Angels must have brought it from heaven and a glass case should be thrown over it to preserve it from each breath of air.[116]

In this case presented in table 2.1, instead of having his judicial writing dismissed as a "runaway judgment,"[117] the Supreme Court of India accorded the petitioner the right to form a committee of experts. This is evidence of how the narrative of the judiciary permits the mingling of the activist voice. The Agarwal Committee, set up by the petitioners, inspected the caustic chlorine

Table 2.1: *M.C.* Mehta v. Union of *India & Ors* (1996)

[Writ Petition (12739) of 1985]
IN THE SUPREME COURT OF INDIA
Judgments rendered on December 17, and December 20, 1996

Constitutional Bench: P.N. Bhagwati (CJ), R. Misra, G. L. Jamnalal Oza, M.M. Dutt, K. Singh

Rule: Examining the scope and ambit of the jurisdiction of the Supreme Court under Article 32(i), whereby an aggrieved person can move the Supreme Court for a legal remedy in case of an alleged infringement of his fundamental right.

Facts of the case: Pursuant to the oleum gas leak from an industrial unit of Shriram Foods & Fertilizers Industries, M. C Mehta filed the first Civil Writ Petition 12739 of 1985 under Article 32 of the Constitution of India to direct the closure of various industrial units owned by the company. M.C. Mehta's writ of mandamus alleged that, despite the strides in legal jurisprudence, government authorities had not taken effective steps to prevent atmospheric pollution. He claimed that the Taj Mahal was facing serious threat of acid rain and there was inherent danger of the white marble turning yellow due to pollution caused from the Mathura Refinery, iron foundries, glass, and chemical industries in the Taj Trapezium Zone. After two incidents of oleum gas leakage, the Delhi administration issued an order under Section 133(1) of the Code of Criminal Procedure, directing Shriram Industries to stop its activity. The Supreme Court appointed a team of experts, called the Varadharajan Committee, to inspect and report on the matter. It gave the petitioner the liberty to appoint his own team of experts to inspect the site for possible sources of hazards. It directed the Secretary of Delhi State Legal Aid and Advice Board to conduct a medical checkup of the victims and decide on the right mode of compensation.

Issues of public interest: Whether the Supreme Court had the authority under Article 32 to decide if Shriram Industries could restart its caustic chlorine plant. What the necessary conditions were to be met.

Issues of constitutionality: Whether applications for compensations to victims can be claimed under Article 32 of the Constitution of India. What the amount of compensation in a hazardous accident caused by an industry should be. Whether decisions of foreign courts as in Ryland v. Fletcher (1868) are binding on the Supreme Court of India. Whether a new legal principle can be applied when the existing legal principles are not applicable.

Reasoning of the court: The court applied the 'Precautionary Principle' and extended the principle of strict liability to one of absolute liability for those engaged in hazardous activities, thus providing the grounds for precautionary action when dealing with toxic materials.

Conclusion: In the first judgment on December 17, 1985, a three-bench Division Panel, examined the scope of public interest litigation in environmental laws. The Court granted temporary permission to Shriram Industries to reopen its plant and set ten conditions to be strictly followed, along with fines. The Court also mentioned that failure to maintain the conditions would result in the cancellation of the permission granted by the Court. In the second judgement on December 20, 1985, a five-bench Constitutional Panel dealt with constitutional questions. The Court decided to establish a new principle of liability. It did not find the applicability of the rule of strict liability as determined in Rylands v. Fletcher (1868), where the defendant is liable for damage caused to the plaintiff even if it was unintentional on the part of the defendant. It decided to enforce the rule of absolute liability whereby, any individual or any industry engaged in an inherently dangerous activity, was 'absolutely liable' for any harm caused to the plaintiff while carrying out the hazardous activity.

Note: My synopsis of *M.C. Mehta v. Union Of India & Ors* (The Supreme Court of India, July 8, 1996)..

plant of Shriram Industries and was not in favor of the industry being granted permission to continue. The Counsel for the defendant pleaded that the closedown of operations would result in the unemployment of four thousand employees. He argued that the Delhi Water Supply Undertaking would face a situation where chlorine and other purifying chemicals produced by Shriram Industries would no longer be available.

Pursuant to *M.C. Mehta and Anr v. Union of India & Ors* (1996), the Supreme Court of India ordered 292 industries in this Taj Trapezium Zone to use safe fuels such as propane instead of coal. It gave them an ultimatum of choosing between the use of alternative fuels or face a relocation of their industries. It also shows how the Supreme Court justices contributed to judicial activism letting their judicial decision be influenced by environmental activism. By applying the doctrine of absolute liability, evoking Article 21 of the Indian Constitution to include the right to clean and healthy environment as a part of one's fundamental rights, it provoked the creation of environmental legislation and the creation of Green Tribunals in India. Furthermore, the Supreme Court favored the rise of epistolary jurisdiction, which differs from regular writ jurisdiction, whereby the court acted, reacted to letters sent by private individuals and agencies addressed to an individual judge, and broadened the *locus standi*. It should also be noted that the Court, apart from appointing its own team of experts, also gave the activist-petitioner the right to have his own team of experts. It did not pass a blanket ban on all industrial activity in the Taj Trapezium Zone, as it was cautionary, and kept in mind the economic consequences to the economy. It acknowledged the need for industrialization, and that accidents were prone to occur in the course of such industrial activity. It emphasized the need for policies to prevent hazardous accidents and establish absolute liability in similar cases. The Precautionary Principle shows the Supreme Court's support of environmental measures that "anticipate, prevent and attack the causes of environmental degradation."[118] It applies the Polluter Pays Principle, that it is the polluter who pays, and thus places the onus of proof on the polluting industry to show that it functions in a manner that is environmentally benign. This case thus broadened the definition of the right to live, by including the right to a hygienic life.

Justice Kuldip Singh became known as the green judge after he presided over several similar PILs on environmental issues. His decision now sets a precedent both in terms of the substantive understanding of the principles of the Environmental Rule of Justice (EROL), as well as literary texts of excellence showing how law meets literature in the era of the Anthropocene.

ENVIRONMENTAL RULE OF LAW

Supreme Courts around the world have recognized the need to uphold the Precautionary Principle of protecting the rights to life, sustainability, and dignity of communities surrounding industrial project areas. In *D.G. Khan Cement Company v. Government of India* (2021),[119] the Supreme Court of Pakistan barred the construction of cement plants in environmentally fragile zones, thus ruling that "the environment needs to be protected in its own right"[120] and that "man and his environment each need to compromise for the better of both and this peaceful co-existence requires that the law treats environmental objects as holders of legal rights."[121]

In *Construction of Park at Noida Near Okhla Bird Sanctuary v. State* (2010),[122] residents in the state of Uttar Pradesh challenged the construction of a state-financed recreational park project adjacent to the Okhla Bird Sanctuary. In the construction, 6,186 trees were cut down, including 179 trees like bottle brush, bottle palm, *Ficus benjamina*, *Cassia siamia*, eucalyptus, fishtail palm, the rubber plant, silver oak, etc.[123] Trees were felled to make space for the park's commemorative plaza, national memorial, and pedestrian pathways.[124] While the petitioners argued that no environmental clearance had been obtained by the government and that the bird sanctuary's sensitive ecological balance was at stake, the government claimed that Environmental Impact Assessment (EIA) reports were redundant as the land in question was not classified as forestland.[125] Even though this case is not directly linked with climate change, it shows the willingness of the Court to consider the impact that environmental degradation can have on the fundamental right to life guaranteed by Article 21 of the Constitution of India. The Court granted permission for the project to be launched subject to conditions recommended by three expert bodies.

Similarly, in *Karnataka Industrial Areas Development Board v. Sri C. Kenchappa & Ors* (2006),[126] the Supreme Court of India ruled in favor of local farmers who opposed the government's decision to allot land for a research and development facility. The research foundation proposed to erase cattle grazing land to build a facility to house around 500 scientists, 150 staff members, and 250 technical people. The local farmers appealed to the Highest Court of the land to voice their concerns. If *gomal*, or cattle-grazing land, was transformed into an industrial park, farmers and their cattle would undergo grave hardship.[127] Deprivation of their land violated their constitutional rights to life granted in Article 21 and equality before the law.[128] In this decision, the Supreme Court of India reasoned on the urgent need for Sustainable Development in the era of climate change.[129] By applying the Precautionary Principle, the Polluter Pays Principle, and Public Trust Doctrine, the Court decided to protect ecology and environment in accordance with the provisions of the Constitution of India.[130] It concluded that the state development board would have to insist on recipients of land allotments getting a clearance certificate from the state pollution control board for the proposed development.

Likewise, in *Subhash C. Pandey v. Union of India* (2014),[131] the petitioner alleged before the National Green Tribunal (NGT) that farmers in the Indian state of Madhya Pradesh needed crop insurance after natural disasters caused by rain and hailstorms.[132] He argued that farmers needed humanitarian relief as some farmers had even committed suicide. The NGT ordered the government to take measures to protect dependent families from further trauma and suggested a revision of the scheme rules that considered the payment of compensation.[133]

In *Balachandra Bhikaji Nalwade v. Union of India* (2009)[134] the petitioner challenged the installation of a 1,200-megawatt coal thermal power station in the state of Maharashtra, arguing that it would have an adverse effect on his mango orchards.[135] He contended that the Ministry of Environment and Forests, and the National Environment Appellate Authority had relied on an incomplete Environmental Impact Assessment (EIA) and had granted approval and clearance to the project.[136] He claimed that the assessment lacked precise data and was inconclusive regarding the adverse effects of coal thermal emissions on mango and cashew plants. By reasoning that the UN Framework Convention on Climate Change (UNFCCC)[137] required parties to anticipate, prevent, and minimize the causes of climate change, the Delhi High Court directed the Expert Appraisal Committee to reexamine the approval in accordance with the Principle of Sustainable Development.[138]

In *Hanuman Laxman Aroskar v. Union of India* (2020),[139] the Court introduced for the first time the notion of the Environmental Rule of Law (EROL). The case provided safeguards for environmental protection in the Indian context.

This pioneer EROL case presented in table 2.2 set the stage for proper environmental decision making in India. It emphasized the need for good environmental governance within a Rule of Law framework to bridge the gap between theory and practice of environmental law. It insisted on the principle of a real transformative principle in environmental disputes and was opposed to the mere transferring of law into another package or the pouring of "Old Wine in a New Bottle."[140]

The Aarhus Convention (1998)[141] mandates the obligations to be respected by states and insists that governments frame policies that are transparent. As environmental law is a relatively young domain, judges may often lack expertise. Gitanjali Nair rightly sums the present *status quo* where the public is disgruntled with dissatisfaction being nailed as "an establishment-driver of environmental courts in many countries, based on public perceptions of delay,

Table 2.2: Hanuman Laxman Aroskar v. Union of *India* (2020)

M.A. No. 965 of 2019 in Civil Appeal No. 12251 of 2018
IN THE SUPREME COURT OF INDIA CIVIL APPELLATE JURISDICTION
Judgment rendered on January 16, 2020

Bench: Dr. Chandrachud; D. Y, Ajay Rastogi

Rule: Under Article 226 of the Constitution of India citing the High Court's broad powers to issue orders and writs to any person or authority; and Land Acquisition Act (1894) regarding the acquisition of land by a government authority and its use thereof.

Facts of the case: In 2015, the Government of Goa was granted Environmental Clearance (EC) from the Union Ministry of Environment to develop a second international airport in Mopa, Goa, as the Dabolim airport in Goa was not sufficient. In 2017, the petitioners, Hanuman Laxman Aroskar and the NGO Federation of Rainbow Warriors challenged the grant of an Environmental Clearance (EC) for the development of a greenfield international airport at Mopa in Goa. The Supreme Court of India suspended the environmental clearance for an airport on March 29, 2019, and directed the administration to reconsider the decision. Accordingly, additional submissions by the airport project authorities were submitted to the Supreme Court of India and in April 2019, the Expert Appraisal Committee reconsidered the recommendations and stipulated additional environmental safeguards and conditions, which were accepted by the Supreme Court on January 16, 2020, withdrawing the suspension from EC.

Issue: Whether the Indian government's approval of a new airport adequately considered environmental impacts.

Reasoning of the court: The court reasoned that the fundamental issue in the outcome of this case, was a quest for environmental governance within a Rule of Law paradigm. By citing both the Paris Agreement (2015) and India's Nationally Determined Contribution to the Paris Agreement as key aspects of India's Environmental Rule of Law (EROL), the court established that the government was required to adequately balance environmental concerns with airport development goals.

Conclusion: After analyzing the additional submissions by the government, on January 16, 2020, the Supreme Court lifted its suspension of the environmental clearance, thus permitting the airport project to go forward. The government scrutinized the additional environmental impact information, the commitment to creating a zero-carbon airport and imposed additional environmental conditions on the project. It appointed the National Environmental Engineering Research Institute to monitor compliance with the government's environmental conditions and ordered the project authority to pay the costs of oversight. The Supreme Court identified the economic significance of the airport project while exhibiting a judicial activist approach to environment and industrial development by submitting its decision to the expert advice of the Expert Appraisal Committee. The Supreme Court took into consideration the fact that the Mopa airport project involved several stakeholders who had invested huge capital. A closure of the project would result in adverse economic consequences. The Supreme Court also considered the time sensitivity of the case and directed the Expert Appraisal Committee to revisit the recommendation within a prescribed time, thus not letting the case drag intermittently in Court.

Note: My synopsis of *Hanuman Laxman Aroskar v. Union of India* (The Supreme Court of India, January 16, 2020).

lack of expertise, lack of independence and/or corruption."[142] So, specialized forums have been created in most countries like the Land and Environmental Courts in Australia,[143] the Environmental Courts and Tribunals in the UK,[144] the Land and Environment Courts in Sweden,[145] and the National Green Tribunal in India.[146] Other than the National Green Tribunals, the High-Level Committee (HLC) created by India's Ministry of Environment, Forests and Climate Change (2014), is in the process of drafting and amending six of India's major environmental laws: the Environmental Protection Act (EPA) (1986), the Forest Conservation Act (FCA) (1980), the Wild Life Protection Act (WLPA) (1972), the Water Prevention and Control of Pollution Act (1974), the Air Prevention and Control of Pollution Act (1981), and the Indian Forest Act (1927).[147]

NAVIGATING THE ANTHROPOCENE

The time is now! The Doomsday Clock ticks, awakening our awareness of near-disaster. Alerts of the disasters awaiting us in the Anthropocene are many that are voiced through diverse forms of high and low culture. The matter of climate justice has been evoked by indigenous people, poets, writer, activists, dancers, justices, orators, and craftsmen through different forms of agency and enterprise. The pressing realities of global warming and climate change have stirred debate beyond national boundaries of a country. The hyperobjects of climate change and global warming render analysis of these phenomenon possible only in a global context and is not restricted just to the policies of an individual country like India, whose court cases have been analyzed above in detail. Climate change concerns are viscous and non-local, spreading their tentacles across nations ignoring the traditional precincts of territorial space and political time. Our time is a time when ecologists in action are creating platforms with increased points of interface between movements. Activist organizations no longer work alone, but exist in tandem, sharing experiences and gaining support of other ecological networks to have their voices heard. The mode of the ecocritical science fiction in Singh's "Tales of a Starfaring Age" could be applicable to any continent on Earth, suggesting ways of navigating ecological collapse and alerting generations on how to deal with the uncanny incoherencies of our time with tsunamis, wars, and tidal waves. In *The Value of Ecocriticism*, Clark maintains that the distinguishing feature of postcolonial ecocriticism, in contrast to early strands of American and British ecocriticism, has always been its focus on environmental injustice, on an "environmentalism of the poor," on people being deprived of healthy living conditions, of migrants being driven into urban slums by the loss of the forests or wetlands that once sustained them.[148] Court cases in today's world are fashioned around both *ration decidendi* and *obiter dicta* with justices referring to literary works to draw inspiration and enlighten judicial forums on the need for the right Environmental Rule of Law (EROL). Across the world, judgments of the Anthropocene have engendered the refurbishing of legislative structures. Everyone plays a role in the polyphonic space of humans at the threshold of the Anthropocene as seen through the engagement of protest movements, political agendas, legislative action, and ecocritical science-fiction discourse.

The universal message of hope is one that can serve as a truly revolutionary global force that can rise to write the next chapter of human history. Like Singh's Tipi-Bird in the tale, "'Listen!' said the Tipi-Bird," Sudeep Sen's poem "Listen to the Stars" in *Anthropocene: Climate Change, Contagion, Consolation*, begins with this caution and the heed to listen:

> Listen to the stars—far, flung apart—elsewhere,
> nowhere, everywhere. An aural orchestra—distant
> pan-flute crackles echoing anti-gravity static,
> space-dust murmurations, galactic-sighs, crests-troughs.
> A philharmonic score—a nebula poem, a long poem,an epic—its
> unceasing ocular cadence, haunting—
> black hole's cosmic crescendo—an axiomatic trance.[149]

Sen addresses the stars in the skies, invokes the manifestation of cosmic synergy, and revels in the response from the galaxy of stars. The auditory score, styled as an interstellar, long epic poem, sets fire and rekindles life into stellar-dead black holes as in his photo captioned "Intimate Skies" in figure 2.1. Each line revels in its polyphony of notes with the panpipes' melodious woodwind notes echoing in the space devoid of human gravity. In far-off space, the space-dust murmurs as in the rumbling of drums, emits galactic brass-like sighs between radio wavelengths of crests and troughs of string instruments. The cosmic crescendo in Sen's poetry is a message of consolation and hope in the era of the Anthropocene. He shows how a flashing star, or a meteor can trigger poetic inspiration to imagine a symphony recital, the writing of a nebula poem that could evolve into an epic. Unlike the cosmic blackhole in spacetime where gravity is so strong that nothing, including light or sound or other electromagnetic waves, could build enough energy to escape; Sen's anti-gravity black hole is one filled with polyphonic tones of a cosmic philharmonic performance, throwing the listener into an unquestionable trance of hope in the Anthropocene.

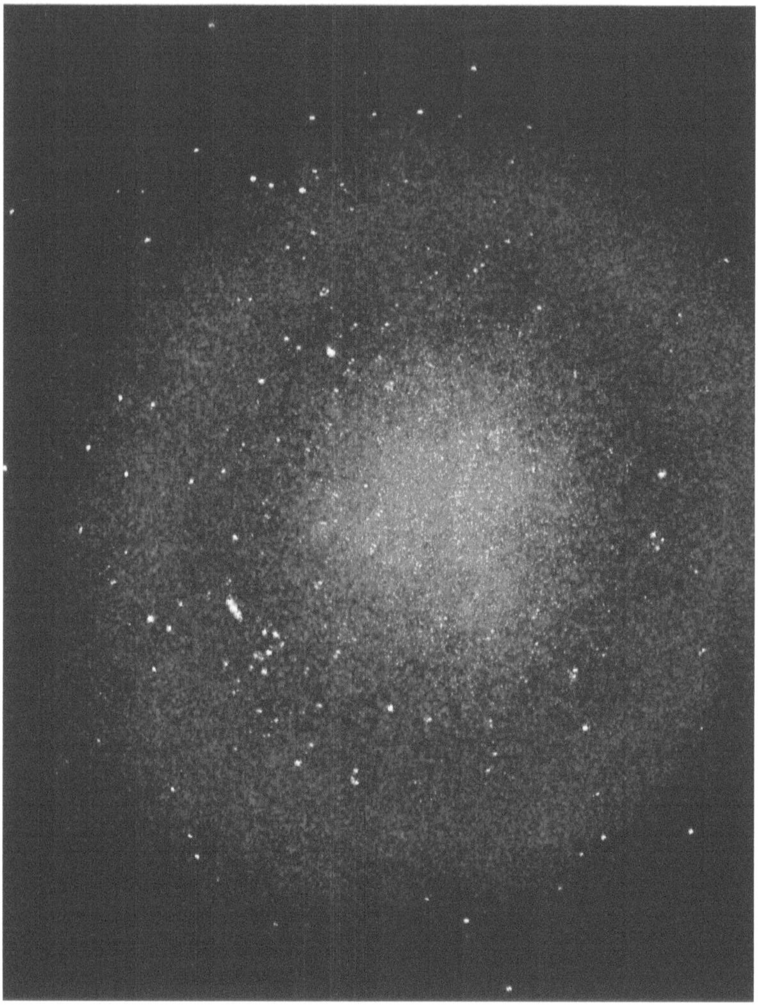

Figure 2.1. My Intimate Skies. *Source*: My Intimate Skies © Sudeep Sen.

NOTES

1. John Mecklin, "Current Time—2023," *Bulletin of the Atomic Scientists*, January 24, 2023. https://thebulletin.org/doomsday-clock/current-time/.

2. Will Millar, "Doomsday Clock: What Is It, How Close Is It to Midnight, and What Time Have Scientists Set It to in 2023?" January 24, 2023. https://www.londonworld.com/read-this/doomsday-clock-what-is-it-how-close-is-it-to-midnight-and-what-time-are-scientists-due-to-set-it-in-2023-3999447.

3. "Martyl Langsdorf, Designer of the Doomsday Clock." *Bulletin of the Atomic Scientists*, January 12, 2023. https://thebulletin.org/virtual-tour/martyl-langsdorf-designer-of-the-doomsday-clock/.

4. Prince Rogers Nelson, "1999," Prince—1999 Lyrics | Lyrics.com. Accessed March 21, 2023. https://www.lyrics.com/lyric/8706616/1999.

5. Billy Corgan, "Doomsday Clock," Smashing Pumpkins—Doomsday Clock Lyrics | Lyrics.com. Accessed March 21, 2023. https://www.lyrics.com/lyric/26597212/Smashing+Pumpkins/Doomsday+Clock.

6. Adrian Smith and Bruce Dickinson, "2 Minutes to Midnight." Iron Maiden—2 Minutes to Midnight Lyrics | Lyrics.com. Accessed March 23, 2023. https://www.lyrics.com/lyric/4937868/Iron+Maiden/2+Minutes+to+Midnight.

7. Michael Stipe, "It's the End of the World" Lyrics by R.E.M. from Blast from the Past Soundtrack. It's The End of the World Lyrics—STLyrics.com. Accessed March 23, 2023. https://www.stlyrics.com/lyrics/blastfromthepast/itstheendoftheworld.htm.

8. *Justice League*. USA: Warner home video, 2017.

9. Sam Meredith, "Boris Johnson Warns It's 'One Minute to Midnight' to Prevent Climate Catastrophe," CNBC, November 1, 2021. https://www.cnbc.com/2021/11/01/cop26-boris-johnson-says-one-minute-to-midnight-amid-climate-crisis.html.

10. "What Is Iugs?" IUGS. Accessed April 14, 2023. https://www.iugs.org/history.

11. *A Life on Our Planet. Netflix*, 2020. https://www.netflix.com/title/80216393.

12. "Welcome to the Anthropocene," *Economist*, May 26, 2011, https://www.economist.com/leaders/2011/05/26/welcome-to-the-anthropocene.

13. Ian Braddick, "'Anthropocene Monument'—Professor Lise Autogena Exhibiting at Symposium-Performance and Exhibition in Toulouse." *The CCRI Impact Blog*, July 26, 2018. https://blogs.shu.ac.uk/c3riimpact/lise-autogena-anthopocene-monument-france/.

14. "The Human Epoch: Defining the Anthropocene," *Nature*, March 11, 2015.

15. Bruno Latour, "The Anthropocene and the Destruction of the Globe," in *Facing Gaia: Eight Lectures on the New Climatic Regime* (Cambridge: Polity, 2017), 112.

16. Paul J. Crutzen, "Geology of Mankind." *Nature* 415, no. 6867 (2002): 1–23. https://doi.org/10.1038/415023a.

17. "Working Group on the 'Anthropocene.'" Subcommission on quaternary stratigraphy. Accessed March 23, 2023. http://quaternary.stratigraphy.org/working-groups/anthropocene/.

18. John Charles Ryan, "Ecocriticism. The Year's Work in Critical and Cultural Theory." 2020, October 25: mbaa018. Doi: 10.1093/ywcct/mbaa018. PMCID: PMC7665768.

19. Kensy Cooperrider, "How We Make Sense of Time," *Scientific American*, November 1, 2016. https://www.scientificamerican.com/article/how-we-make-sense-of-time/.

20. Stephen Jay Gould, *Time's Arrow: Time's Cycle. Myth and Metaphor in the Discovery of Geological Time* (Massachusetts: Harvard University Press, 1987), 2.

21. Tim F. Flannery, *The Weather Makers: The History and Future Impact of Climate Change* (Melbourne: Victoria Text Publishing, 2008).

22. Dale Dominey-Howes claims that the contemporary crisis narrative of the Anthropocene is insufficient to understand the current environmental history of hazards and disasters. Dale Dominey-Howes, "Hazards and Disasters in the

Anthropocene: Some Critical Reflections for the Future," *Geoscience Letters* 7, no. 5(1) (2018): 1–15.

23. Through letters of doomed explorers in the Scott Polar Institute, Nancy Campbell explains that archives exist in polar ice and unravels history of people and their relationship with ice. She analyzes how polar ice contains compressed narratives of all time and archives for us to decipher. Nancy Campbell, *The Library of Ice: Readings from a Cold Climate* (Bompiani: Scribner, 2018).

24. Nolan et al. analyzed documented vegetational and climatic changes at six hundred sites worldwide since the last glacial age to the present. They studied the vegetational responses to temperature variations of 4° to 7°C. They warn that in the absence of mitigation efforts, terrestrial ecosystems will disappear or transform in composition and structure. Connor Nolan et al., "Past and Future Global Transformation of Terrestrial Ecosystems under Climate Change," *Science* 361, no. 6405 (2018): 920–23.

25. Ghosh, *The Great Derangement*, 8.

26. Timothy Morton, "This Is Not My Beautiful Biosphere," in *A Cultural History of Climate Change*, edited by Tom Bristow and Thomas H. Ford (New York: Routledge, 2016), 229, 233.

27. Timothy Morton, *Hyperobjects: Philosophy and Ecology after the End of the World* (Minneapolis: University of Minnesota Press, 2013), 133.

28. Jeanette Winterson, *The Stone Gods* (London: Hamish Hamilton, 2007), 199.

29. Max Weber, "Science as a Vocation," in *Max Weber: Essays in Sociology*, edited by H. H. Girth and C. W. Mills (New York: University Press, 1958), 134–56.

30. Marc Augé writes about humanity's fears of the different forms of violence, namely economic, social, political, and technological changes. He details how they affect nature and humanity. Marc Augé, *Les Nouvelles Peurs* (Paris: Payot, 2013).

31. Chakrabarty, "Anthropocene Time," 6.

32. Chakrabarty, "Anthropocene Time," 12.

33. Morton, *Hyperobjects*, 1.

34. Idem, 81–82.

35. Idem, 81–82.

36. Idem, 83.

37. Idem, 55.

38. Konstantinos Apostolou Doxiades and J. G. Papaioannou, *Ecumenopolis: The Inevitable City of the Future* (New York: Norton, 1974).

39. "How Much Does It Cost?" ESA. Accessed March 24, 2023. https://www.esa.int/Science_Exploration/Human_and_Robotic_Exploration/International_Space_Station/How_much_does_it_cost.

40. Simonetta Di Pippo, United Nations OOSA Director Simonetta Di Pippo on Space Sustainability. Oxford University Space and Astronomy Society. YouTube, 2021. https://www.youtube.com/watch?v=cEJa2bp6nhU.

41. Nibedita Mohanta, "How Many Satellites Are Orbiting around Earth in 2022?" *Geospatial World*, January 6, 2023. https://www.geospatialworld.net/prime/how-many-satellites-orbiting-earth/.

42. These satellites are the backbone of cable and TV monitoring; ensure satellite-based navigation or Global Positioning Systems (GPS); can track future disasters like floods, earthquakes, and high dam levels; photograph images of the surface of the Earth with high resolution cameras; ensure public safety and national defense; and offer virtual classroom learning to children in remote areas.

43. NASA's Earth Observing System (EOS) coordinates a series of polar-orbiting and low-inclination satellites to observe the Earth's land surface, biosphere, atmosphere, and oceans; the National Oceanic and Atmospheric Administration Satellite (NOAA) gives a complete view of weather and environmental conditions around the world each day; the CERES (Clouds and the Earth's Radiant Energy System) project provides satellite-based observations of the Earth's radiation budget (ERB) and clouds; the Television Infrared Observation Satellites (TIROS) sends early storm warnings and televises infrared weather observations; the AURA satellite's Ozone Monitoring Instrument (OMI) instrument can provide data to detect tropospheric ozone and distinguish between aerosol types, such as smoke, dust, and sulfates, and measure cloud pressure and coverage; the Gravity Recovery and Climate Experiment (GRACE) satellite can show where gravity pull is felt the most on Earth; the MODIS satellite MODIS measures the properties of clouds such as the distribution and size of cloud droplets in both liquid water and ice clouds; and the Sentinel 6 satellite can measure the height of the ocean.

44. "Every Satellite Orbiting Earth and Who Owns Them." Dewesoft. Accessed March 24, 2023. https://dewesoft.com/daq/every-satellite-orbiting-earth-and-who-owns-them. The United States owns 2,804 satellites; China is second with 467; the UK has 349; India has launched sixty-one, including EDUSAT, the pioneer educational satellite; and France has thirty-one.

45. Arthur Scott-Geddes, "Un Space Chief Calls for Mass Action to Save Earth and Cosmos," *National*, July 4, 2021. https://www.thenationalnews.com/uae/environment/un-space-chief-for-mass-action-to-save-earth-and-cosmos-1.1085174.

46. Suniti Namjoshi, *Dangerous Pursuits* (New Delhi: Penguin Zubaan, 2022).

47. Namjoshi, *Dangerous Pursuits*, 49.

48. *Return to Space*. Netflix, 2022. https://www.netflix.com/search?q=retour%20dans%20l%27espace&jbv=81111324 (Accessed: March 31, 2023).

49. *Jeff Bezos Speaks at Amazon India Event*. YouTube, 2020. https://www.youtube.com/watch?v=jzfXlg-wyUU.

50. Grush Loren, "Virgin Galactic Says First Customers Headed to Space Soon," *Bloomberg News*, February 28, 2023. https://www.bloomberg.com/news/articles/2023-02-28/virgin-galactic-says-first-customers-head-to-space-within-months?leadSource=uverify%20wall.

51. *Don't Look Up*, 2021. https://www.netflix.com/title/81252357.

52. Idem.

53. Jamie Margolin (2001–) is an American climate activist from Seattle who founded the activist organization called Zero Hour, aimed at educating people about the climate crisis and involving them in activism.

54. John Mecklin, "Summit: Not Everything Is for Sale," *Bulletin of the Atomic Scientists*, September 17, 2018. https://thebulletin.org/2018/09/summit-not-everything-is-for-sale/.

55. Ainslie Beattie, "Pacific Climate Warriors." Transition Network, September 7, 2018. https://transitionnetwork.org/news/pacific-climate-warriors/.

56. Beattie, "Pacific Climate Warriors."

57. Lawrence Buell, *The Futures of Environmental Criticism* (Oxford: Wiley-Blackwell, 2005), 63.

58. Buell, 97.

59. Beattie, "Pacific Climate Warriors."

60. Sarah Pulliam Bailey, "The Dakota Access Pipeline Isn't Just about the Environment. It's about Religion," *Washington Post*. WP Company, October 27, 2021. https://www.washingtonpost.com/news/acts-of-faith/wp/2016/12/05/the-dakota-access-pipeline-isnt-just-about-the-environment-its-about-religion/.

61. Su T. Fitterman, "The Dakota Access Pipeline (DAPL)—Environmental & Energy Law Program." Harvard Law School, February 28, 2023. https://eelp.Law.harvard.edu/2017/10/dakota-access-pipeline/.

62. Mikhail Mikhailovich Bakhtin, *Problems of Dostoevsky's Poetics* (Minneapolis: University of Minnesota Press, 1984), 42.

63. Idem, 42.

64. Jan M. Olsen, "Norway's Government Apologizes to Sami Reindeer Herders." AP NEWS. Associated Press, March 2, 2023. https://apnews.com/article/norway-protest-wind-farm-sami-reindeer-904e83b5be17d8c4c8febf131227ef4b.

65. "Sundargarh: Why Tribals of Kharia Community Protesting against Odisha Govt?" *Ground Report*, October 22, 2022. https://groundreport.in/sundargarh-why-tribals-of-kharia-community-protesting-against-odisha-govt/.

66. "What Is Taj Heritage Corridor?" *Hans India*, March 30, 2015. https://www.thehansindia.com/posts/index/Education-and-Careers/2015-03-30/What-is-Taj-Heritage-Corridor/140716?infinitescroll=1.

67. Darko Suvin, *Metamorphoses of Science Fiction: On the Poetics and History of a Literary Genre* (New Haven: Yale University Press, 1979), 7–8.

68. Suvin, *Metamorphoses*, 64.

69. Suvin, *Metamorphoses*, 37.

70. Timothy Clark, *The Value of Ecocriticism* (Cambridge: Cambridge University Press, 2019), 9.

71. Vandana Singh is an Indian science-fiction writer who is an associate professor and chair of the Department of Physics and Earth Science at Framingham State University in Massachusetts. Her short fiction published in different reviews and journals includes *Ambiguity Machines and other stories* (2018) and *The Woman Who Thought She Was a Planet and other stories* (2009).

72. Vandana Singh, *The Woman Who Thought She Was a Planet* (New Delhi: Penguin Random House India Private Limited, 2008).

73. Suvin, *Metamorphoses*, 7–8.

74. Salman Rushdie, *Grimus* (London: Gollancz, 1975), 141.

75. Singh, 132.

76. Singh, 132.
77. Singh, 131.
78. Singh, 132.
79. Suvin, *Metamorphoses*, 7–8.
80. *Sonhali* means "golden" or "resplendent" or "gleaming" in Hindi.
81. Singh, 134.
82. Singh, 134.
83. Singh, 200.
84. Mikhail Mikhailovich Bakhtin, *The Dialogic Imagination* (Austin: University of Texas Press, 1981).
85. Bakhtin, *Problems of Dostoevsky's Poetics*, 165.
86. John Ronald Reuel, Tolkien, *The Lord of the Rings* (London: Houghton Mifflin Company, 2004), 67.
87. Singh, 136.
88. Singh, 138.
89. Bakhtin, *Problems of Dostoevsky's Poetics*, 95.
90. Singh, 134.
91. Singh, 134.
92. Singh, 138.
93. Singh, 15.
94. "Principle 10." UNEP. Accessed April 16, 2023. https://www.unep.org/civil-society-engagement/partnerships/principle-10.
95. Dipesh Chakrabarty, "The Climate of History: Four Theses," *Critical Enquiry* 35 (2009): 197–210.
96. *Massachusetts v. Environmental Protection Agency* (Supreme Court of the United States of America, April 2, 2007).
97. *Friends of the Earth, Incorporated v. LaidLaw Environmental Services* (Supreme Court of the United States, January 2, 2000).
98. *Friends of the Earth v. The Governor in Council and Others* (Federal Court of Vancouver, October 20, 2008).
99. *Urgenda Foundation v. The Netherlands* (Supreme Court of the Netherlands, December 20, 2019).
100. Idem, 3.9.
101. Idem, 31–33.
102. Idem, 71–75.
103. *R (on the application of ClientEarth) v. Secretary of State for the Environment, Food and Rural Affairs* (the High Court of Justice Queen's Bench Division Planning Court, May 1, 2013).
104. Directive 2008/50/EC of the European Parliament and of the Council of 21 May 2008 on ambient air quality and cleaner air for Europe. Queen's Printer of Acts of Parliament. Accessed April 17, 2023. https://www.legislation.gov.uk/eudr/2008/50/contents.
105. *R (on the application of ClientEarth) v. The Secretary of State for the Environment, Food and Rural Affairs* (CJEU, November 19, 2014).

106. *R (on the application of ClientEarth) v. Secretary of State for the Environment, Food and Rural Affairs* (UKSC, April 29, 2015).

107.*R v. Secretary of State* (2015), 40.

108. *Virender Gaur and Ors. v. State of Haryana and Ors* (Supreme Court of India, November 24, 1994).

109. "Constitution of India," Constitution of India | Legislative Department | India. Accessed April 23, 2023. https://legislative.gov.in/constitution-of-india/.

110. "UN Environment Document Repository Home," UNEP. Accessed April 17, 2023. https://wedocs.unep.org/bitstream/handle/20.500.11822/29567/ELGP1StockD.pdf.

111. Constitution of India, April 10, 2023. https://www.constitutionofindia.net/constitution_of_india.

112. Krishnadas Rajagopal, "There Will Be At Least One Constitution Bench in Supreme Court throughout the Year: CJI-Designate U.U. Lalit," *Hindu*, August 26, 2022. https://www.thehindu.com/news/national/there-will-be-at-least-one-constitution-bench-in-supreme-court-throughout-the-year-cji-designate-uu-lalit/article65814413.ece.

113. *M.C. Mehta v. Union of India & Ors* (The Supreme Court of India, July 8, 1996).

114. *Rylands v. Fletcher* (House of Lords, July 17, 1868).

115. *M.C. Mehta*, 12–13.

116. Idem, 2.

117. Kalyani Ramnath, "The Runaway Judgment: Law-as-Literature, Courtcraft and Constitutional Vision," *Journal of Indian Law and Society* 3 (2011).

118. *M.C. Mehta*, 11(1).

119. *D. G. Khan Cement Company v. Government of Punjab* (The Supreme Court of Pakistan, April 15, 2021).

120. Idem, 16.

121. Idem, 16.

122. *Construction of Park at Noida Near Okhla Bird Sanctuary v. State* (The Supreme Court of India, December 3, 2010).

123. Idem, 3 (ii).

124. Idem, 3 (iii).

125. Construction of Park at Noida, 1.

126. *Karnataka Industrial Areas Development Board v. Sri C. Kenchappa & Ors* (The Supreme Court of India, May 12, 2006).

127. Idem, 3.

128. Idem, 4, 36.

129. Idem, 65.

130. Karnataka Industrial Areas, 76–82.

131. *Subhash C. Pandey v. Union of India* (The Green Tribunal, August 20, 2014).

132. Idem, 1–4.

133. Idem, 4.

134. *Balachandra Bhikaji Nalwade v. Union of India* (Delhi High Court, September 18, 2009).

135. Idem, 1.

136. Idem, 1–4.

137. "UN Framework Convention on Climate Change," Unfccc.int. Accessed April 17, 2023. https://unfccc.int/.

138. Balachandra Bhikaji Nalwade, 23.

139. *Hanuman Laxman Aroskar v. Union of India* (The Supreme Court of India, January 16, 2020).

140. Himanshu AhLawat and Sujith Koonan, "Environmental Rule of Law in India: A Transformative Principle or Old Wine in a New Bottle?)" *Journal of Indian Law and Society* 13, no. 1 (2022): 133–45.

141. "Access to Justice in Environmental Matters Convention," UNECE. Accessed April 17, 2023. https://unece.org/environment-policy/public-participation/aarhus-convention/text.

142. Gitanjali Nain Gill, *Environmental Justice in India: The National Green Tribunal* (London: Routledge, Taylor & Francis Group, 2018).

143. Land and Environment Court of New South Wales. Accessed April 17, 2023. https://www.lec.nsw.gov.au/.

144. "HM Courts & Tribunals Service," GOV.UK. Accessed April 17, 2023. https://www.gov.uk/government/organisations/hm-courts-and-tribunals-service.

145. "National Specialised Courts in Sweden," European e-Justice Portal. Accessed April 17, 2023. https://e-justice.europa.eu/19/EN/national_specialised_courts?SWEDEN&member=1.

146. National Green Tribunal. Accessed April 17, 2023. https://www.greentribunal.gov.in/.

147. "Report High Level Committee to Review Various Acts Administered by Ministry of Environment, Forest & Climate Change, Government of India, November 2014." Accessed April 17, 2023. https://www.naredco.in/notification/pdfs/Final_Report_of_HLC.pdf.

148. Clark, 138.

149. Sudeep Sen, *Anthropocene: Climate Change, Contagion, Consolation* (Sutton: Pippa Rann Books & Media, 2021), 146.

Chapter 3

Animals in the Forum

In the idyllic world of Disney's animated, musical drama-film *The Lion King*,[1] each animal completes his journey through life by respecting all beasts, from the crawling ant to the leaping antelope. Mufasa, the majestic animal king of Pride Rock, counsels Simba, his lion cub, "Everything you see exists together in a delicate balance. As king, you need to understand that balance and respect all the creatures. . . . We are all connected in the great Circle of Life."[2] The web of life is interwoven, with each species depending on the other for survival. When a species goes extinct, a thread in the web is cut, leaving holes in the planet's ecological web and shaking the finely balanced systems of nature. Mufasa's dream of a delicate balance in nature based on natural laws with predators and prey coexisting within their boundaries has been rejected by scientists for decades. The Greek philosopher Herodotus who developed the idea of natural laws believed that nature exists in some sort of balance with predators letting their prey survive in the right numbers without completely erasing them from existence.[3] Likewise, the Roman politician and philosopher Cicero propagated the thought that this balanced relationship between predator and prey was the work of the gods.[4] Ancient myths of different cultures show how nature's propensity to exist is configured in circles enabling it to restore the balance among species, allowing life to continue in a never-ending loop or harmony. In Norse mythology, life is configured as a circle with generations and species being brought back to life after the great battle of Ragnarok. In the Greek creation myth, Zeus entrusts the Titan brothers, Prometheus and Epimetheus, with the task of populating Gaia. Epimetheus created the animals, endowing each kind of species with its traits and means of survival. In the myth, he however exhausts his repertoire of skills, leaving none for Prometheus's masterpiece, Man. In the biblical myth, God created Man and the Animals on the sixth day after creation. Even though great floods wipe out all species, life continues with the dawn of a new beginning. In the anthropocentric setting of creation tales and myths, humans take precedence over animals, succeeding in the struggle of the survival of the fittest, thus proving in Darwinian terms that well-tuned lifeforms are those that inherit the Earth.

The language of nature is one subdued by the human voice. The human voice needs to establish an affinity toward nature by recognizing animals as subjects and agents on the planet. The language of nature is one filled with the voices of beasts of all kinds varying from "the sounds of animals, whales, birds, insects, wind, and water: a language more ancient and basic than human speech. To hear this language requires patient, disciplined study of the natural world. But it is a language for which we have an affinity."[5] This affinity toward nature requires recognizing animals as subjects and agents and imagining the world from the other's perspective. In a ten-hour address at the 1997 Cerisy conference in Picardie, France, entitled "The Autobiographical Animal," Jacques Derrida lectured on the human, man-made right of attributing animals their names. He recalls the primal, biblical-naming ceremony in the book of Genesis, when, after having created animals on the fifth day, God, the creator, proceeded to create Man in his own image.[6] Though created after animals, it is man who gets the prerogative of naming the animal world.[7] The name-calling protocol, Derrida argues, is the way that the 'human' reserves itself "the right to the word, the naming noun (*nom*), the verb, the attribute, to a language of words, in short to the very thing that the others in question would be deprived of, those that are corralled within the grand territory of the beasts: The Animal."[8] Through reference to *animot*,[9] a word composed of the *animal* and *mot*, meaning "word" in French, Derrida proceeded to prove the intention of designating the animal as the inferior species in the hierarchy. He holds that the muteness, or the absence of language, attributed to the beast, stems from having received a name, as one thus loses "the power to name, to name oneself, . . . to answer (*répondre*) for one's name."[10] Having named the animal, Derrida reminds us that we as humanity acknowledge the fact that one will survive the other, and that human and animal lives are entangled with each other. We are subject to the animal gaze, "fully aware eyes, looking over our shoulders,"[11] as in the Derridean remark on how every animal has a "bottomless gaze, as with the eyes of the other, the gaze called 'animal' offers to my sight the abyssal limit of the human: the inhuman or the human, the ends of man, that is to say, the border crossing from which vantage man dares to announce himself to himself, thereby calling himself by the name that he believes he gives himself."[12] The animal gaze is fitted with more superior sense organs than humans, rendering them capable of far-sighted sensing of tsunamis as in 2004, when they sought higher ground before humans to escape the angry, swirling waves. Endowed with a unique bird's-eye view of the world, birds rarely collide in mid-flight; rats and other rodents have night vision and accompanying sensory whiskers that help them detect earthquakes, mud falls, and landfalls; unique somatosensory cortex neuro zones of dogs enable them to synchronize their heartbeats with their owners, giving them canine clairvoyance regarding seizures and heart attacks; both predatory and docile members of the cat family have super senses in the wild and at home to detect ultrasonic sounds and see what is invisible to the human eye; human vision is trichromatic, enabling us to see a larger part of the picture, unlike animals, which have varied degrees of vision ranging from the 360-degree-monocular eyeball of the chameleon, to the binocular vision of birds of prey.[13]

A WARNING FROM STAN THE TYRANNOSAURUS REX

A bronze replica of Stan, the Tyrannosaurus rex fossil discovered in 1987 at the Hell Creek formation in South Dakota, guards the entrance of Googleplex, Google's corporate headquarters at Mountain View, California, as in figure 3.1, captioned "Google Stan." Stan stands as a reminder of a bygone era when he reigned supreme but was relegated to extinction as he had not been innovative enough in the game of survival. Stan warns Googlers to embrace the new, the uncertain, and the uncanny. Geologists describe the Cretaceous hot period as one that ended when an asteroid struck the Earth, changing the face of the Earth by leaving debris that reduced the Sun's heat and light rays, rendering the Earth inhabitable for the dinosaur species, which could not adapt to the cooler habitat.

In the incoherent world in which we live, dinosaur bones are now being auctioned for millions of dollars. On April 19, 2023, Trinity or TRX-293, a

Figure 3.1. Google Stan. *Source*: Google Stan © Shanti Palayankottai.

hybrid T. rex skeleton comprised of 293 bones from three different T. rex specimens, was sold at an auction house in Zurich, Switzerland, for $6.1 million. Trinity, who stands at 12.8 feet high and 38.1 feet long, was displayed at the Koller auction house and was sold to the highest bidder, the Phoebus Foundation. But other T. rex specimens have fetched higher prices and have even made their presence felt in courtrooms. In 2020, the auction house Christie's displayed Stan, the reconstituted remains of the approximately sixty-seven-million-year-old T. rex skeleton in New York City. As the most complete 188-bone skeleton in the history of our time, Stan, who stands thirteen feet tall and forty feet long, was sold to a mysterious buyer for a record-breaking $31.8 million. The owner's identity was revealed a year later to be the Abu Dhabi Museum, whose launch with Stan as its main exhibit is planned for 2025.[14]

Sue, the world's most-complete T. rex species, has been the subject of legal battles regarding ownership. Named Sue, after the paleontologist Susan Hendrikson, who discovered her on the rocky landscape of Dakota, Sue was excavated by the Black Hills Institute of Geological Research (BHI), which belonged to brothers Peter and Neal Larson. The Indian ranch land where Sue was found belonged to Maurice Williams and was considered as part of Indian Trust land. Sue remained locked up as the federal government with the FBI proceeding to gather information of the BHI's illegal methods of collecting dinosaur remains. In *U.S. v. Larson* (1997),[15] it was decided that the beneficial owner of the land upon which the discovery was made, namely Maurice Williams, was the rightful owner of Sue. Williams auctioned Sue at Sotheby's Auction House in New York in 1997 for $8.3 million to the highest bidder, the Field Museum in Chicago.

Dinosaurs were back in the Federal District Court of Montana in *Black Hills Institute of Geological Research v. Fort Peck Paleontology et al.* (2010),[16] when the plaintiff, Peter Larson, president of Black Hills Institute of Geological Research, Inc., filed an $8.2 million lawsuit and alleged that that Fort Peck Paleontology Inc., a competitor, had wrongfully pirated and reproduced copyrighted portions of some of the most famous T. rex specimens in the world. Having prepared, created, sculpted, and cast museum-quality fossilized dinosaur creations and exhibits, Black Hills Institute paleontologists had the credit of having re-created both T. rexes Sue and Stan. BHI had lent incomplete portions of a T. rex skeleton, nicknamed "Peck's Rex," to the Montana-based Fort Peck Paleontology Inc., for further research. In this federal lawsuit, Black Hills Institute contended that Fort Peck Paleontology had unlawfully retained possession of some of these bone specimens and had even proceeded to make unauthorized copies of the Stan and Sue copyrights. It claimed that unauthorized copies had been incorporated into the "Peck's Rex" skeleton displayed at the Museum of the Rockies in Bozeman,

Montana. The amount of damages sought was $7.4 million, and this underscores how lucrative the trade in dinosaur bones and replicas has become in our time. This case was dismissed in 2012 with prejudice as having been fully settled on its merits, each party bearing its own costs and attorneys' fees.

In an era of unpredictable weather patterns, Stan's warning is like the prediction of the Intergovernmental Panel on Climate Change (IPCC) on the estimated increase of around 2.7°C by the end of the century.[17] Wildfires caused by rising temperatures have resulted in the destruction of habitat of forest species, forcing wildlife to stray out of their comfort zones in search of food and shelter. It is estimated that Africa's elephants will disappear due to illegal poaching in the next forty years. Wildfires that destroyed the Australian bush landscape in 2019–2020 burned 186,000 square kilometers and displaced koalas and kangaroos that can live only in this habitat.[18] In France, the strange appearance of foxes and wolves in cities have been attributed to the natural instinct of the animal to find refuge in a crowded city far away from seasonal man-hunters.[19] Similarly omnivorous coyotes have been sighted in North American cities, often traversing kilometers in search of food and unoccupied space to set up a new pack.[20] Human-wildlife conflict is on the rise, with animals intruding into human spaces and humans resisting the unwelcome animal intrusion. In India, tigers are protected species in fifty-two tiger reserves, but these predatory beasts are prone to attack neighboring villages, who often dread tiger attacks.[21] Extractive capitalism and the pursuit of limitless economic growth has resulted in countries owning huge ecological footprints. The quest for fossil fuels, the burning of forests to clear land for monoculture, and the use of non-renewable forms of energy have resulted in wildlife species heading for extinction.

CAUTIONARY TALES

In *Jurassic Park*, Michael Crichton's cautionary tale warns us that anthropocentrism is no longer the preferred mode of existence, as seen in the storyline of humans meddling with nature.[22] He warns that bringing the Cretaceous Period dinosaur to the Anthropocene through genetic re-creation only results in paleontological chaos on Earth. In the computer-generated-imagery movie by Steven Spielberg based on Crichton's book *Life Finds a Way*, Jeff Goldblum, who plays the role of Dr. Malcolm, delivers the same line—"Life finds a way"—to highlight nature's capacity to survive and reproduce despite all the odds.[23] The moral of the tale is that even if advances in science permit the re-creation of extinct species, it is humans who have the ultimate task of deciding where the boundaries lie.

In Daphne Du Maurier's 1952 novel *The Birds*, birds attack humans, aiming for their eyes, a seemingly metaphorical assault of human failure to see changes in nature. In this apocalyptic tale set in Cornwall, birds mimic World War II aerial strategies to overcome modern technologies by attacking a fighter RAF plane and causing it to crash. In the novel, war is not just a destroyer, but it is also a mobilizer of technologies that have disassociated humans from the environment. The change in the behavior of birds is linked to wartime technological developments. Alfred Hitchcock's film *The Birds* in 1963, set in the Monterey Bay area, was inspired by the mysterious attack by disoriented seabirds that had ingested a toxin or harmful algae blooms, causing them to ram themselves onto houses in the California bay.[24] In 1962, biologist Rachel Carson's scientific text on the adverse biological effects of pesticides on American farming entitled *Silent Spring* has this text on its opening pages:

> It was a spring without voices. On the mornings that had once throbbed with the dawn chorus of scores of bird voices there was now no sound; only silence lay over the fields and woods and marsh.[25]

Carson's *Silent Spring* met with opposition from a chemical corporation, Velsicol Chemical, which threatened her with lawsuits.[26] She was labeled hysterical, but she helped spark the modern environmental movement, and the pesticide DDT was banned from use. James Patterson and Michel Ledwige's science-fiction novel *Zoo*, published in 2012, is yet another cautionary tale of how the animal world is capable of an uprising and organized rebellion. In a scenario typical of the Disney adventure-comedy film *101 Dalmatians*,[27] when the dogs of London decided to launch a clarion dog-call, the Twilight Bark, to reach out to all dog species of different spots and stripes to search for the puppies who had been dognapped, in *Zoo*, dogs and wolves, lions, and other predators communicate with each other in unpredictable ways to hunt humans in cities and safari camps. As the scientific world comes up with its theories about dystopian wild behavior, the novel's cautionary warning is that human enterprise on the planet is affecting the environment and animal behavior.

But cautionary tales seem of no avail. In September 2021, Colossal Laboratories and Biosciences, in keeping with its motto "May Prehistory Thunder Forward," announced its landmark de-extinction project of resurrecting the woolly mammoth.[28] The project, launched by Harvard geneticist George Church and software-entrepreneur Ben Lamm, has received the support of the CIA.[29] With skin cells extracted from endangered Asian elephants, they aim to reprogram them with versatile stem cells that carry mammoth DNA. This genetic process involves identifying specific Asian-elephant genes that cater mammoth hair, essential for insulating fat layers and other cold climate needs of the future hybrid. It also involves a comparison with mammoth genomes of animals recovered from the permafrost in the Arctic tundra. A surrogate elephant mother will have the ultimate mammoth task of bringing into the world a woolly mammoth that will be able to inhabit once again the tundra zones. Known hybrid farmhouse animals are the hinny (horse-donkey), the beefalo (bison-domestic cattle), dzo (yak-cattle), zubron (cow-wisent), cama (camel-llama), yakalo (yak-buffalo), and chimeras (sheep-goat with two genetically distinct cells).[30] Wildlife hybrid varieties are namely, the zonkey (zebra-donkey), liger (lion-tiger), wholphin (killer whale–dolphin), leopon (leopard-lion), grolar (grizzly–polar bear), zebroid (zebra-horse), coydog (dog-coyote), jaglion (jaguar-lion), and Savannah cat (African wildcat–domestic cat).[31]

When two different species are genetically crossed, these creatures that emerge often exhibit monster-like tendencies, making them incompatible and incapable of leading an animal existence. Ligers are known to reach a height of six feet and weigh 165 kilos before their first year. They have very short lifespans and exhibit the deadly, killer instincts of two predator species. As such attacks by hybrid animals can go awry, legislation has been passed to ban illegal breeding of such animals. Coydog attacks are now classified as a class B misdemeanor in the state of Indiana (USA) under section IC 15-20-1-5.[32] Savannah cats bred as domestic cats have been known to attack fowl and livestock in Juvignac in the Herault region of France.[3334]

Some animals have metamorphized while others have succumbed to extinction. Those that have metamorphized have been labeled as shapeshifters. Birds in Australia like the gang-gang cockatoos and the red-rump parrots, which use their beaks to regulate temperature, have increased their beak sizes by 4 and 10 percent since 1871.[35] This strategy of evolution in action has been noted in the Turks and Caicos islands, where the Anole lizards survived hurricanes by increasing the size of their toepads and reducing their hind legs; the Humboldt or jumbo squid reduced their body size to half to cope with higher water temperatures in a biological process called plasticity that exists in the genome of the Chilean valleys; the little dovekies of the Arctic region have changed their feeding patterns to fly less and conserve energy.[36] According to a study conducted by the Field Museum in Chicago, migratory birds have changed their flight behavior by timing their departure five days earlier and stretching out the stay in a faraway warmer land by seventeen days.[37] The International Union for Conservation of Nature (IUCN) has classified more than forty-one thousand species in its red list, as species under the threat of extinction: the Javan rhino in Indonesia; the Amur leopard in China; the Sunda island tiger in Sumatra; the mountain gorillas of Congo, Rwanda, and Uganda; the Tapanuli orangutan in Sumatra; the Yangtze Finless Porpoise in China; the black rhinos of Kenya, Namibia, South Africa, and Zimbabwe; the

African forest elephants of Gabon and the Republic of Congo; the Sumatran orangutan in Indonesia; and the Hawksbill turtle in the tropical and subtropical waters of the Atlantic, the Indian, and the Pacific oceans.[38] Due to a warming ocean and human conflicts, like vessel strikes and entanglement with fishing gear, the North Atlantic right whale's numbers have dwindled to a mere 336, the lowest count in twenty years.[39] Other animals on the brink of extinction include the Ethiopian banana frog, whose habitat has been reduced to a mere 772 square miles after massive deforestation.[40] Extinct species that we now see on webpages and encyclopedias include the saber-toothed cat, the wooly mammoth, the dodo, the great auk, the Stellers sea cow, the Tasmanian tiger, the passenger pigeon, the Pyrenean ibex, the Baiji white dolphin, and the West African black rhinoceros.[41]

THE ANIMAL TURN

Illegal wildlife trade is the curse faced by endangered species—like the poaching of elephants for ivory; the hunting of tigers for their skins and bones; the capturing of bears to harvest their bile from gallbladders; the extraction of horns of species like rhinos, elephants, and buffalos as they are prized for their medicinal properties; the gleaning of wax from the musk deer for perfume; the skinning of alligators, snakes, leopards, minx, and buffalos for accessories and clothing; and the combing of the shores of beaches for the shells of turtles and oysters.[42] Animals are voiceless, devoid of discourse, and humans have well-established their supremacy over the animal world by being the dominant species of the Holocene. Human beings occupy land, have terraformed it to vast stretches of monoculture, and have eradicated many diseases. In the survival of the fittest, it is Man who has won over Animals.

Serpil Oppermann, in her article, "Ecocriticism: Natural World in the Literary Viewfinder," contemplates on the relationship between nature and man. She writes that, "A vision of nature as a self-articulating subject refutes nature/culture dualism inherent in our thinking towards a consciousness of humans valuing both nature and culture in diversity. However, the assumption that nature speaks for itself creates a discursive problem in literary texts, for it is again the human subject speaking for nature in a paradoxical attempt to overcome the human/nonhuman divide within the discourse itself."[43] Oppermann's proposition doubts the recognition of an animal voice as its potential is articulated by man. However, she emphasized the importance to study the relationship between man and animals from a "non-dualistic perception" and "not as the other excluded from the realm of discourse."[44]

There is a growing field of human-animal studies with scholarly interest being given to anthrozoology and the relationships between humans and other animals. This project, labeled "The Animal Turn Project," aims to collect key materials from the North Carolina State University Libraries' Animal Rights and Welfare Collections, housed in the Special Collections Research Center (SCRC), and historical records of the ASPCA (American Society for the Prevention of Cruelty to Animals).[45] Similar animal advocacy movements like the RSPCA (Royal Society for the Prevention of Cruelty to Animals), founded in 1824 in a London coffee shop, aimed at recognizing animals as sentient beings, and not just mere means for food, transport, or sport.[46] It is the world's first animal charity, and as its name suggests, it had Queen Victoria's royal patronage. France's SPA (La Société Protectrice des Animaux) was founded in 1847 by Pierre Dumont de Monteux to prevent cruelty to carriage horses.[47] The European Union Legislation on Animal Welfare (1974)[48] established a wide range of legislative provisions for its member states. It details the norms to be observed for farm animals, like poultry, calves, and pigs, as well as transport and slaughter operations for all species. It bans battery farms for laying hens and requires group housing for pregnant sows. In Asia, the AFA (Asia for Animals Coalition),[49] founded in 2001, has twenty-four animal welfare coalition members. It is the largest network with hundreds of global animal welfare organizations working together to share information and contemplate on the best strategies to improve the lives for the animals of Asia.

In the United States, currently twenty states have comprehensive bans that ban the ownership of wild or exotic animals as pets or only allow those animals to be kept under certain licenses not including pet or private possession (i.e., for educational or scientific purposes); thirteen states have partial bans on exotic pets; whereas fourteen states permit private ownership of exotic animals under a licensure or permit scheme; and only three do not have a statutory or regulatory scheme that addressed the private ownership of exotic pets, but may regulate some aspect of ownership.[50] In Europe, the European Parliament resolution of November 24, 2022, provides guidelines on improving EU regulations on wild and exotic animals to be kept as pets in the European Union.[51] The increasing growth of animal pet cafés[52] in South Korea, Thailand, and mainland China has led to a worldwide petition being signed to forbid practices that are cruel to the animal, like painting them, dyeing their fur, and earning a living from an animal.

The Animal Protection Index[53] ranks fifty countries around the world according to the protection granted to animals by each country's welfare policy and legislation. The index of A to G shows the country's commitment to and engagement in protecting animals. While no country merits an A, Iran and Azerbaijan are the only ones with a G. The UK, the Netherlands, Austria, Switzerland, Denmark, and Sweden get a B. India is ranked a C, along with Spain, France, Italy, Germany, Poland, and Malaysia. Even though

India's ranking seems to have improved in the last 2020 index, there is criticism regarding cruelty exemptions on the use of animals for scientific research and animal welfare offered by the Prevention of Animal Cruelty Act (1960).[54] This act forbids the infliction of unnecessary pain or suffering on animals; establishes the Animal Welfare Board of India (1972); and details its powers, functions, constitution, and the term of the office of members of the Board. It provides the guidelines for a committee to make rules with regard to such experiments and restricts displaying, exhibiting, and training of performing animals. NGOs, like the People for the Ethical Treatment of Animals (PETA), has established through their protests that animals are not ours to experiment on, eat, wear, use for entertainment, or abuse in any other way.[55] The International Convention for the Protection of Animals (ICPA) "urges all nations to negotiate an international convention for the protection of animals that establishes standards for the proper care and treatment of all animals to protect public health, the environment, and animal wellbeing."[56]

A three-time Green Oscars winner, Indian documentary maker Mike Pandey was featured as one of the Heroes of the Environment by *Time* magazine in its October 2009 issue.[57] The frame in his documentaries is one that that shifts "subjectivities from human to nonhuman subjects,"[58] typical of making the Animal Turn. The Animal Turn refers to means used to renew the interest in non-human species, especially animals. The first season of the *Earth Matters* television series, spanning 108 episodes, caught worldwide attention in 2001. Each frame took the viewer on a journey across India, from coral reefs to the threatened tigers in the Sundarbans forests. The documentary aimed at enhancing the viewers' understanding of the delicate balance that exists between human and non-human protagonists on the planet. It disclosed the massive destruction of natural resources and ecosystems in recent times and brought public attention to Pandey's enterprise and patience in finding the right setting, time, and season to shoot his documentary. He shifts viewers' perspective "from a narrow anthropocentric worldview to a view-centered, or eco-centric view in which the ecosphere (. . .) is taken as the 'center of value for humanity.'"[59] By framing animal encounters and stories, Pandey moves away from speciesism and prejudiced beliefs of human supremacy over animals and gives animals center stage. In the *Earth Matters* eco-media narrative frames, Pandey, the documentary producer, crosses into primarily non-human spaces, reassesses the environmental *status quo*, and presents the dialectics of existence of human and non-human collectives. His documentaries of different regions of India, with their specific flora and fauna, are shot from the perspective that the environment itself is inter-relational and continually remade, despite being physically and discursively segmented by human action and representation. The media of documentaries may be viewed as a "system driven by particular kinds of energy flows, exchanges and mutual dependencies just like a forest or a desert, a savannah or a city."[60] The setting is different in each documentary, but the documentary revels in its capacity to reunite a network that is constituted by many flows of energy that work together: human living agents like the producers, the speakers, the cameramen; non-living agents like the camera lens, the props onstage, the software and machines used in the production process. Each documentary in my study frees a different kind of energy flow, often culminating in the apex courts of justice for judicial activism.

Mike Pandey's series of conservation documentary films have led to the Indian government's enactment of laws to protect wildlife. His documentaries have sparked eco-awareness and brought about legislative protection for species, namely whale sharks, vultures, elephants, and the horseshoe crab, over the last decade in India. In *The Vanishing Vultures*,[61] Pandey shows how these birds of prey known as the scavengers of the skies are in turn prey to the veterinary drug diclofenac. Zoroastrians depend on these birds to eliminate the remains of humans in the Parsi Tower of Silence. These birds, known for scavenging dead animals, are being driven to extinction. By filming their habitat and highlighting the fact that there were only two to three thousand remaining birds of their kind, the film induced the drug controller general of India to issue a notice to all state drug controllers to stop the production and sale of this veterinary drug.[62] Since this decision in May 2006, these predatory birds have been a protected species in India. Similarly, Pandey's documentary *Shores of Silence* shows the merciless hunting of huge whale sharks.[63] The broadcast of this documentary marked its capacity to serve as a tool to bring about legislative changes for the whale shark, which is now a protected species under the Wildlife Act of 1972 in India. Likewise, the films *Last Migration*[64] and its sequel, *Vanishing Giants*,[65] showing elephants being captured in Sarguja district of Chhattisgarh state in Central India, stirred a nationwide debate and forced the Indian government to ban the brutal, archaic methods of elephant capture in India. In the *Timeless Traveller*, the horseshoe crab, the world's oldest living creatures with a history of 562 million years, is the subject of a new energy flow in this documentary.[66] The documentary highlights how the superb species, with their capacity to cure diseases like tuberculosis and regenerate bone marrow, has been practically wiped off the coastlines of India. By drawing attention to their longevity, and by lobbying for their existence, the documentary has prompted the Indian government to protect the horseshoe crab under Schedule IV of the Wildlife Act of 1972, giving the species a chance for survival.[67]

POLYPHONY IN ANIMAL FABLES

Fables have shaped the imagination of its tellers for centuries. Fables that traveled down the silk route were recited in the caravanserais of the Silk Road that linked the East to the West. The fabulist's terrain was one that was re-tilled by the new speaker, who included new nuances to the original fable. The Roman fabulist, Phaedrus, was the first Latin author to translate the works of Aesop from Greek. Phaedrus versified, in iambic trimeters or two-foot lines, the beast lore of his time by interspersing them with anecdotes drawn from daily life, history, and mythology. Far from being the master of the genre, Phaedrus declares in his fables his obligation to Aesop by declaring honestly as his artifice of remodeling Aesop's fables into casual verse. In *Aesop's Human Zoo*, Phaedrus begins with a tribute to Aesop by praising the double-game form that evokes laughter.

> He has trees talk, besides beasts of the zoo?
> Remember: I'm fun. And fables are fiction.[68]

Here multiple voices surface in the accolade to the Greek storyteller—Aesop's expression of pithy morals; trees that talk; beasts of the zoo participate in the dialogue; Phaedrus's casual verse mode of fun with its dual intention of creating laughs and voicing morals; and the reception received in the form of laughter. Understanding a fable's intent, moral, and setting is dialogic and a complex process. Each fable is passed down, carrying nuances from another's voice, and is filled with that other voice.

Aesop's world of talking animals finds its figuration in Suniti Namjoshi's feminist and beast fables. Drawing inspiration from Phaedrus's fictional artifice of creating fables with the dual intention of expressing pithy morals and evoking laughter, Indian-born British-Canadian fabulist Namjoshi[69] conjures witty and wise fables that serve as a new means for stimulating social action. Aesop in Namjoshi's *Foxy Aesop: On the Edge* shows the polyphonic nature of the fable to express the explicit or implicit voice of the fabulist: "Each time a story is told it means something different."[70] Sprite, a fabulist from the future, yells indignantly at Aesop, "Then why do you write your fables?"[71] Aesop admits that he writes fables for fun. Sprite contends that the world is a mess:

> Yes, dearth, death and famine, horrible inequalities, and strutting four-year-olds ruling the nations! Not only that, we're about to destiny the entire planet![72]

Aesop's admonishing voice to Sprite warns her not to cast fables into fixed and unalterable content, but to let the mode of the fable find free form in the ages to come. Sprite in the polyphonic world of Namjoshi's fables is capable of standing beside her creator, capable of not agreeing with the fabulist and even of voicing dissent against him.[73] Namjoshi's closing sentence in *Foxy Aesop: On the Edge* sums up how in today's postcolonial world, fables serve their purpose, but remain "repeated-mutated, fizzing with energy."[74] In her animal fables, Namjoshi configures European and Eastern fabulist traditions, retells old myths from joltingly new perspectives, creates new allusions to be passed on, subverts known forms of authority, and underscores the need for reconfiguring new worlds.

In Namjoshi's *The Conversations of Cow*,[75] a hybrid cow, called the Spindly Cow, is a product of her imagination in today's material world. The cow, a sacred one, like Kamadhenu in Indian mythology, the divine-bovine goddess, is one who is cast as a 'Cow of Plenty.' Kamadhenu in Indian myth emerged from the churning of the cosmic oceans and granted civilization the boon of prosperity. The Spindly Cow, named Spindleshanks, also bears resemblance to Nut, the 'Great Cow,' the sky goddess of Egyptian mythology, who swallowed the sun at dusk and gave birth to it anew at dawn. The hybrid Spindly Cow churned and ingested the material world each day like "pots and pans, kettles and crayfish, cabbages and turnips, articles of clothing, houses and furniture—you know, just ordinary things one sees all the time."[76] Namjoshi, the fabulist, resorts to chaotic verbiage by enumerating a list of opposing pairs comprising of kettles and crayfish, tigers, and terrapins, to highlight the chaotic state of disorder in the cow's interior. In the fable, the Spindly cow's intake of buildings and factories, humans and animals, leads to a deplorable state when the Earth loses its form and resembles a pockmarked mass. In this fable, the animals get together to address a plea to the Spindly Cow.

> "O Cow," they said, all of them at once, "you have now consumed a fifth of the planet. Is the hunger within you all assuaged? Are you satisfied?"[77]

Spindleshanks's voice emerges loud and clear when she defends her stance by stating that it was in her nature to consume the world and that it had become a habit. The voices of animals demand a casting of lots on which objects in the material world would be sacrificed to appease the material appetite of the unsatiated cow. Their arguments, disputes, discussions, and scuffles lead to world wars while the Spindly Cow continues to chomp her way through the material world until there is just one small patch of Earth for her to stand on. Unable to consume more, the Cow bursts, and a chaotic world, like the one we have today, spills out of her. The fable's closure endorses the new disordered creation as the dawn of a new world order "where the world carried on," but in a different way.[78] The fable's message is cautionary, reminding us of the need to protect our endangered planet and leave a more orderly world for our offspring. The fable's dialogic mode permits what Wayne C. Booth refers to as "a representation, at whatever time or place and in whatever genre, of human 'languages' or 'voices' that are not reduced into, or suppressed by a single authoritative voice: a representation of the inescapably dialogical quality of human life at its best."[79]

In "The Creation: Plan B," a fable featuring a parrot and a tortoise, Namjoshi starkly reminds us that there is no Planet B for humans.

> One day Parrot said to Tortoise, 'I say, let's make the world.'
> 'All right,' said Tortoise, 'and let's have continents like the patterns on my back.'
> 'And lots and lots of parrots,' put in Parrot.
> 'Ye-es,' said Tortoise, 'and an equal number of tortoises.'
> 'Of course,' said Parrot.
> For a moment or two they contemplated the world they had agreed upon.
> 'I say,' said Tortoise, breaking the silence, 'do we have to have people?'
> 'No,' replied Parrot.
> 'Phew,' said Tortoise.
> And they lived happily ever after.[80]

In the negotiation of a new world devoid of humans, there is a dialogue among Parrot and Tortoise where they both voice the dire need to protect their own species first. Tortoise envisages a continent like the patterns traced on her back, while Parrot imagines a world peopled with similar voluble parrots. The silence in the contemplation also speaks silently about their common reluctance over including people in their new world. but the fable ends with the fairy-tale closure: "they all lived happily ever after."[81] By imagining a powerful ending where everlasting happiness exists ever after, Namjoshi foregrounds the idea of 'eternal bliss' in the animal world. But what about our world, our 'Endangered Earth'?

In a fable narrated by the Blue Donkey entitled "The Purposeless Pandas," Namjoshi takes her readers to the film-shooting site where the producer is documenting an interview with the Purposeless Pandas. Pandas, in this fable, interestingly are no longer classified as "endangered," but fall under the category of "vulnerable."[82] Solely subsisting on bamboo, pandas play a crucial role in ensuring the survival of China's bamboo forests as they spread seeds and help the vegetation to grow. The mountainous regions with bamboo have rare fauna like multicolored pheasants and medicinal fauna. The panda habitat between the rivers of the Yangtze Kiang and the Yellow rivers is also home to millions of people who must live in co-existence with nature. Protected by the Wildlife Act of 1958, their species have not reached a near-stable figure of 1,800. The title of the fable, "The Purposeless Pandas," is an indication of how the 'purpose' of protecting pandas has now changed focus. It is interesting to know that the logo of the WWF with the black-and-white panda, which was adopted in 1961, draws inspiration from Chi-Chi, a giant panda, a new addition to the London Zoo in 1958. The founders considered the panda with its appealing black eyes to be an ideal mascot for their purpose, it also avoided printing in color.[83] "The Purposeless Pandas" orchestrates a polyphonic symphony of socially diverse voices. The producer tells the Pandas they are 'emblematic.' The mode of the fable enables the usually silent pandas to express reciprocal thanks in human language. The Association, called the Friends of Friends, which protects pandas in the fable's space, conveys the intent behind the camera-filmed interview.

> 'We want to help you,' their friends whispered, 'and in order to do that we've persuaded people that they wish to purge themselves of decades of guilt—that's why the cameras and the press release. You are now officially an endangered species.'[84]

The producer offers the pandas tins of protein which the pandas decide to bury and use in times of scarcity. The voices in the fable are punctured with laughter from the camera crew, the reassuring tones of the Friends of Friends and the producer as they soothe the pandas and inform them that more mass-produced tin food was available from human factories. The pandas are placed in an enclosure with palm trees to make them comfortable. But the pandas voice discomfort and claim that they do not consume palm trees. The Panda longing for bamboo is lost on the crew. The producer manages to get the pandas to smile anxiously, but not engagingly at the cameras. The Friends of Friends declare that they would be back again the next day to click photographs of pandas mating. The unappeased pandas do not return despite the offer of bamboo shoots. They leave a note stating: "We are no longer endangered. Please consider us quite extinct."[85] The fabulist finally gives the moral of the fable in the ending lines that the pandas emblematic status was uncertain as there were rumours that the pandas were "neither endangered, nor extinct, they are merely lurking."[86] The fable's open-structured ending permits further coexistence of diverse voices. This is typical of the polyphonic fable where no voice terminates the conversation with a last word, thus leaving an opening of unfinished interplay. The dialogic mode of the fable exists as in the Bakhtinian imagination of an "interaction of several consciousnesses, none of which entirely becomes an object for the other; this interaction provides no support for the viewer who would objectify an entire event according to some ordinary monologic category (thematically, lyrically or cognitively)—and this consequently makes the viewer also a participant."[87] The fable-reader is not an aloof non-participant but is one who is engaged in this dialogic world of the fable.

In a sequel to the fable "Pandas Lurking," Namjoshi, the fabulist muses on a puzzling question: "But these pandas who were lurking—what did they live on, how do they subsist?" Some scholars in the fabulistic space suggest that pandas did not require any way of subsistence and considered the discussion closed. Panda proponents state that there was a distinct possibility of pandas being everywhere in disguise and they even take to wearing badges that state "I A M N O T A P A N D A I N D I S G U I S E."[88] Those who do not wear badges are considered as those who are in pandas in disguise. The fable offers further avenues of changing factions by giving people the possibility of switching categories. The legislator also has his word in the fable, but his decision is ironically pending. But the fabulist gets to have the last word.

> But the real question now which troubles everyone is that, after all this time, should an honest-to-goodness Panda reappear, her fur burnished, her eyes glowing, her nose twitching, would she be recognised.[89]

The implicit voices of each one of the characters in the fable highlight various individual stances and even a confrontation of different, divergent ideas, but they fit into the whole fable structure. Namjoshi attempts to create fables that make a difference to both the human and the animal world. In "The Kingfisher," she compares her craft as a fabulist to that of the kingfisher: "Fish, are like poems, you catch them when they leap."[90] In the fable entitled "Dear Reader," Namjoshi includes the reader, too, in her fictional enterprise of catching fables: "We are not fighters, but fellow-travellers."[91] Unlike the critic who fails to see the inner meaning of the creative animal fables, the reader is portrayed as one who accepts the fabulist's world albeit the fictional incongruities, riddles, and enigmas.

LEGAL PERSONHOOD FOR ANIMALS

Courts around the world have discussed the issue of non-human personhood with writs of *habeas corpus* (HCW) being filed on behalf of animals in captivity in zoos and laboratories. Animal activists have voiced concerns over animal incarceration and have petitioned governments to order their transfer to safe sanctuaries or to release them back into the wild. In 2015, the Argentinian Court of Contentious Administrative and Tax Matters, in a sensational landmark ruling, *Asociación de Funcionarios y Abogados por los Derechos de los Animales y otros contra GCBA* (2015),[92] the Association of Officials and Lawyers for Animal Rights (AFADA) filed a HCW petition on behalf of Sandra, the twenty-nine-year-old Sumatran orangutan, and challenged the legality of Sandra's detention. The petitioner-association contended that Sandra, who had been born in captivity at Germany's Rostock Zoo, was now caged in a cement cell in the Buenos Aires Zoo since 1994. It claimed that the defendant, the City Zoo, had illegally and arbitrarily violated Sandra's right to ambulatory freedom, her right to be respected as a non-human person, the right to not suffer any physical or psychological harm, and the right to an environment with trees and green spaces. The zoo and the government appealed, arguing that the AFADA lacked standing and the protective action was an inappropriate course of action to examine an orangutan's situation in the zoo. Judge Berdión de Crudo rejected the writ, but the AFADA appealed to the Sixth Chamber of the Criminal Court of Appeals, which also rejected the appeal. The AFADA filed a cassation appeal against this ruling, and the Second Chamber of the Federal Criminal Cassation Court ordered the case to be sent to a competent Criminal Court. However, the court stated that the zoo and the city of Buenos Aires would continue to exercise their rights regarding Sandra, albeit in a non-abusive manner. Argentinian courts thus showed their willingness to consider animals to be sentient beings, not subjects of rights, and this judgment, even if it lacked arguments, set an important precedent. It was the first time a court in Argentina had recognized that a HCW could be filed on behalf of an animal.[93] The narrative of the court mingles with the animal activist's belief that the declaration of the entire animal kingdom, including avian and aquatic species, as legal entities have a distinct persona with corresponding rights of humans. This case has been cited in other animal rights cases around the world.[94]

But the first HCW to succeed in these animal-plaintiff courts was *Acción de hábeas corpus presentada por la Asociación de Funcionarios y Abogados por los Derechos de los Animales* (AFADA) (Tercer Juzgado de Garantías Poder Judicial Mendoza November 3, 2016),[95] the case of Cecilia, the thirty-five-year-old Argentinean chimpanzee.[96] It is the first successful case to apply the concept of the legal person to recognize an animal as a legal entity. Judge María Alejandra Mauricio granted Cecilia the HCW on November 3, 2016. She declared that Cecilia was a sentient being who deserved environmental protection.[97] She also affirmed that the rights of such animals must be determined by the state, and not by judges. Finally, the court deemed that the HCW was an adequate tool to assess the condition of incarcerated animals, as national and local Argentinean law did not provide other procedural mechanisms. The judge's acceptance of the HCW stemmed from the fact that no other legal remedy existed in the country. It is considered as a truly successful HCW as it was not reversed later by a higher court in its jurisdiction.

In the case of Chucho, the twenty-six-year-old Andean bear living in Barranquilla Zoo in Colombia, a local lawyer, Luis Domingo Gómez Maldonado, filed a HCW *Acción de habeas corpus Decision AHC4806* (2017)[98] contending that the Corporación Autónoma Regional de Caldas

(Corpocaldas) had used its authority as the entity responsible for environmental management in the region to transfer him from the Rio Blanco Nature Reserve to the Barranquilla City Zoo. He claimed that Chucho had the right to return to his natural habitat, La Planada, a reserve protecting the Andean bear. He referred to Section 3(a) of the Animal Protection law1774/2016[99] that stated that the eradication of captivity was one of the principles of animal protection in Colombia. He spoke on behalf of the bear that had to live in the scorching heat of Barranquilla instead of its natural habitat in the cold and rainy mountain ranges.[100] The petitioner drew attention to the fact that the Colombian legal system did not provide mechanisms to urgently seek the protection of animals in captivity, and hence his recourse to the human procedure of the HCW. In this case, the Civil Family Chamber of the Superior Court of the Judicial District of Manizales denied the petition on June 17, 2017, and annulled the procedure on the grounds of procedural errors.[101] The Superior Court of the Judicial District of Manizales concluded that the HCW was not the appropriate mechanism to seek the protection of animals as in Colombian law, and that there existed other mechanisms to protect animals like the *Acción Popular*, or the preventive apprehension mechanism regulated in Section 8 of law 1774 of 2016.

In 2012, in the case *Tilikum v. Sea World Parks Sea World Parks & Entertainment, Inc* (2012),[102] PETA, in conjunction with some marine mammal experts and former trainers, filed a lawsuit asking the Federal Court in California to free the five orcas—Tilikum, Katina, Corky, Kasatka, and Ulises—that lived in SeaWorld Parks. The petitioners claimed a violation of the Thirteenth Amendment of the US Constitution. PETA argued that the language of the Thirteenth Amendment, which prohibits slavery, did not refer to any type of person or a specific victim. It contended that the whales had been forcibly separated from their families and natural habitats and that they had been held captive at SeaWorld San Diego and SeaWorld Orlando. They wished to prove that the orca whales had been denied everything that was natural to them, been subjected to cruelty like artificial insemination, been bred to be performers for shows, and had been forced to perform, all for commercial profit. PETA claimed that the whale-plaintiffs had been held in slavery. Although the petition was not a petition of HCW, it resembled such a petition in many ways as it attempted to obtain the recognition of legal rights for animals on a constitutional basis. On the issue as to whether the orcas deserved constitutional protection against slavery, Judge Jeffrey Miller dismissed the case on February 8, 2012, ruling that the Thirteenth Amendment only applies to persons.

In *Naruto v. Slater* (2018),[103] Naruto, a seven-year-old crested macaque, an inhabitant in a reserve on the island of Sulawesi in Indonesia, was the monkey-plaintiff represented by PETA who filed the lawsuit as Naruto's next friend, arguing that it could not bring the action due to inaccessibility and incapacity, and thus needed a representative. In 2011, David Slater, a wildlife photographer, left his camera unattended in the Indonesian reserve. Naruto took several photographs or rather monkey selfies of itself with Slater's camera. Slater and Wildlife Personalities, Ltd., published the monkey selfies in *Wildlife Personalities*, a book that Slater published through Blurb, Inc.'s website in December 2014.[104] The book identified Slater and Wildlife Personalities as the copyright owners of the monkey selfies. However, Slater admitted in his work that Naruto took the selfie photographs itself. For instance, the book describes one of the monkey selfies as follows: "Sulawesi crested black macaque smiles at itself while pressing the shutter button on a camera."[105] Another excerpt from the book describes Naruto as "posing to take its own photograph, unworried by its own reflection, smiling. Surely a sign of self-awareness?"[106] In 2015, PETA and Dr. Antje Engelhardt filed a complaint for copyright infringement against Slater, Wildlife, and Blurb, as next friends on behalf of Naruto.[107] The complaint detailed that Dr. Engelhardt had studied the crested macaques in Sulawesi for over a decade and had known, monitored, and studied Naruto since its birth. The complaint alleged that PETA aimed to champion and establish the rights and legal protections available to animals other than their utility to human beings. The defendants filed motions to dismiss on the grounds that the complaint did not state facts sufficient to establish standing under Article III or statutory standing under the Copyright Act (1976). The California district court thus granted the motions to dismiss. On appeal, the ninth circuit court ruled in the negative holding that a monkey could not sue for damages and injunctive relief arising from claims of copyright infringement. It did not recognize Naruto, the monkey-photographer, as a legal person.

In a PIL, *Centre for Environmental Law WWF-1 v. Union of India* (1999),[108] the wildlife conservation institution brought to the notice of the Supreme Court of India, the state of rapid degradation caused to animals like the Asiatic lion in sanctuaries. It referred to the non-implementation of the provisions of Wild Life Protection Act (1972)[109] as the primary cause for this degradation. The Petitioner claimed that the Union government had the task of discharging the duty entrusted to them under Sections 19 to 25 of the Wild Life Protection Act (1972).[110] In this case, the Supreme Court of India ruled that the endangered Asiatic lion had the right to a second habitat. It emphasized the fact that human beings had the constitutional obligation to protect the environment and animal life from extinction. Through an eco-centric approach, the court reasoned that the best interest standard must be applied to protect the Asiatic lion.

In the case of *Narayan Dutt Bhatt v. Union of India & Others*[111](2014), a PIL resulted in the court ascribing legal personhood to "the entire animal kingdom including avian and aquatic," with the citizens in the State of Uttarakhand being declared "persons *in loco parentis* as the human face for the welfare/protection of animals."[112] The petitioner Narayan Dutt Bhatt requested an enquiry on the health of donkeys and other transport animals used along the fourteen-kilometre route from the Indian town of Banbasa in Uttarakhand to Mahendra Nagar in Nepal. Its mandate was expanded to include other beasts of burden. The court's legal reasoning gave animals legal personhood: "The entire animal kingdom including avian, and aquatic are declared as legal entities having a distinct persona with corresponding rights, duties, and liabilities of a living person. All the citizens throughout the State of Uttarakhand are hereby declared persons in *loco parentis* as the human face for the welfare/protection of animals."[113]

In *N.R Nair & others v. Union of India* 2000),[114] the Kerala High Court ruled that bears, monkeys, tigers, panthers, and lions should not be exhibited or trained as performing animals in circuses and fairs. It extended fundamental rights enjoyed by humans to animals, thus emphasizing the fact that the fundamental right to protection was not an exclusive human right but could be extended to animals. The petitioner decided to appeal his case, in the Supreme Court of India by citing Article 19(1)(g)[115] and argued that the Kerala High Court's decision was an infringement of his fundamental right to exercise his trade. The apex court declared that caging, training, performing, and exhibiting animals for purposes of entertainment violated the provisions of the Prevention of Cruelty to Animals (PCA) (1960) as they caused suffering to animals.

In *Animal Welfare Board of India v. A. Nagaraja & Ors (2014)*,[116] the Supreme Court banned '*jallikattu*,' a bull-fighting event during Pongal, the harvest season in South India when the participants accepted the challenge to tame the bull and retrieve the package of coins tied to its horns. This also included a ban on bullock-cart races in Maharashtra and Punjab. The inclusion of animals within the ambit of the right to human life under Article 21 of the Indian Constitution,[117] in these decisions consider the animal right to a healthy and clean atmosphere, and the animal's right to be respected and not be beaten or kicked by humans.

The Apex Court's judgment expressed the opinion that '*jallikattu*' and bullock cart racing violated India's core animal protection law, the Prevention of Cruelty to Animals Act (PCA) 1960, but also extended legal rights to animals as presented in table 3.1, by deeming that humans owed a duty of care to animals in their care. Even though, the wording of the judgment in *Animal Welfare Board of India v. A. Nagaraja & Ors* (*2014*), does not explicitly refer to legal person, the opinion of the court set a precedent for emphasizing the implicit connection between rights and personhood. The same *ratio decidendi* or rationale was considered by the High Court of Uttarakhand concerning the overloading of horses and the violation of the PCA in *Narayan Dutt Bhatt v. Union of India & others* (2018) and in *Karnail Singh & Ors v. State of Haryana* (2019)[118] when the State Court of Haryana ruled on the prohibition of cow slaughter and cow trafficking.

Table 3.1: ***Animal Welfare Board of India v. A. Nagaraja & Ors (2014)***

CIVIL APPEAL NO. 5387 OF 2014
IN THE SUPREME COURT OF INDIA
Judgment rendered on May 7, 2014

Bench: K.S. Radhakrishnan and Pinaki Chandra Ghose

Rule: Article 36 of the Constitution of India which states that the Supreme Court may, in its discretion, grant special leave to appeal from any judgment, decree, determination, sentence or order in any cause or matter passed or made by any court or tribunal in the territory of India. Provisions of the Prevention of Cruel Act (1960) that deems it is the duty of every person having the care or charge of any animal to take all reasonable measures to ensure the well-being of such animals and to prevent the infliction of unnecessary pain or suffering on it.

Facts of the case: The petitioner, AWBI, a statutory advisor body, challenged the validity of a Central Government Notification dated 11-7-2011 which banned performing bulls at *'jallikattu'* events or bullock cart races in the State of Tamil Nadu, Maharashtra or elsewhere in the country.

Issue: Whether Article 21 may be interpreted broadly to include the life of animals, who play a predominant role in the ecosystem of the planet. Whether the Central Government Notification dated 11-7-2011 is constitutionally valid.

Reasoning of the court: The court, in its reasoning, brought bulls under the protection of the human rights discourse by holding that a fight can be between animals or between human beings. It reasoned that section 5 of TNRJ [Tamil Nadu Regulation of Jallikattu] Act envisaged a fight between a bull and bull tamers, that is, between a man and an animal. Such fight is prohibited under Sections 3 and 11(1)(*m*)(*ii*) of the PCA Act. An animal's right to life guaranteed it life of existence worthy of honor, dignity, and fair treatment.

Conclusion: The Supreme Court of India banned *jallikattu*, ruled in favor of the AWBI, stating that jallikattu, bullock cart race[s] and such events per se violated Sections 3, 11(1)(a) and 11(1)(*m*)(*ii*) of the PCA Act and hence the Notification dated 11-7-2011 issued by the Central Government was valid and constitutional. Bulls could not be used as performing animals, as sections 3 and 11(1)(a) of the PCA Act, 1960, make it illegal if any person beats, kicks, overrides, overdrives, overloads, tortures or otherwise subject an animal to unnecessary pain or suffering. The court struck down the Tamil Nadu Regulation of Jallikattu (TNRJ) Act on the grounds that it was inconsistent and in conflict with Sections 3, 11(1)(a), 11(1)(*m*)(*ii*) and 22 of the PCA Act read with Articles 51-A(g) and 51-A (h) of the Constitution and hence in contradiction to the PCA Act." It held that every kind of species has a constitutional right to a healthy life and security as granted by the Constitution of India and the Prevention of Cruelty to Animals Act, 1960.

The Supreme Court struck down the practice of Jallikattu and bullock cart racing in the Indian states of Tamil Nadu and Maharashtra, respectively. By doing so, it it looked at the evolution of the rights of animals in the international context, giving examples from Germany, the UK, and a host of other countries. The Supreme Court stated, and the High Court judgment stated that since one was dealing with a welfare legislation of a sentient being, over which human beings have domination and the standard one had to apply in deciding the issue on hand was the 'Species' Best Interest.'

Note: My synopsis of *Animal Welfare Board of India v. A. Nagaraja & Ors* (Supreme Court of India, May 7, 2014).

AN ELEPHANT IN THE ROOM

In 2006, Banksy, the enigmatic street artist, claimed to have painted Tai, the thirty-seven-year-old elephant at a museum display in Los Angeles. Painted bright pink to blend in with the pink wallpaper of the display room, the "elephant in the room" symbolized people's indifference to world poverty.[119] The exhibition, though aptly titled *Barely Legal*, was labeled as "frivolous abuse" by the Los Angeles's Animal Services Department,[120] and reminds us that animal welfare is also an issue that people skirt and push to the background. The expression the "elephant in the room" comes from Mark Twain's novel *The Stolen White Elephant*, which figures detectives searching for the conspicuous elephant in the room that they had failed to see.[121] In the 1962 American musical film *Billy Rose's Jumbo*, Jimmy Durante tells Jumbo the elephant, "Easy, boy, just make yourself inconspicuous, just act natural like you were out for a stroll"; but when confronted by policemen about the presence of an elephant on the streets of Detroit, he replies, "What elephant? What elephant?" as if he had failed to notice the elephant beside him.[122] The *New York Times* article entitled "Happy the Elephant Isn't Legally a Person, Top New York Court Rules"[123] highlighted the plight of one of the seven elephants, named after the seven dwarfs in the fairy tale "Snow White and the Seven Dwarfs," who had arrived from Thailand to the United States in the 1970s.

For centuries, the Common Law writ of *habeas corpus* has been used to safeguard the liberty rights of human beings as a means to secure release from illegal custody. In an appeal brought before the Court of Appeal of New York, *Nonhuman Rights Project (NhRP), Inc. v. Breheny* (2022),[124] the *habeas corpus* writ (HCW) was used by the petitioner, an animal rights NGO, to seek *habeas corpus* relief on behalf of Happy, an elephant residing at the Bronx Zoo, to secure her safe transfer to an elephant sanctuary, to recognize Happy's legal personhood, to secure her right to free movement, and to get her an order of transfer to an animal reserve. The Wildlife Conservation Society filed a Memorandum of law expressing opposition, along with numerous documents to oppose the HCW. The NhRP highlighted the fact that it was the first time that a *habeas corpus* order has been issued to an elephant, elevating it to the status of a legal person. The use of the status of legal personhood for an animal in this case was considered as "an artificial aid to thought, a heuristic concept created by legal cognition—under the pressure of a personifying, anthropomorphic legal language—in order to illustrate the data to be dealt with."[125] Before this case, in Bronx County, such claims for a writ of *habeas corpus* had only been on behalf of prisoners on Rikers Island. On December 14, 2018, for the first time, a US court heard arguments about the elephants' legal personhood. At the preliminary conference on August 15, 2019, at the

Supreme Court of Bronx in New York, it was decided that all motions would be argued before Justice Alison Tuitt. Justice Tuitt granted the NhRP a temporary restraining order to prevent the zoo from transferring Happy out of New York State before the hearing. On February 18, 2020, Justice Tuitt issued a decision denying the HCW, arguing that she was bound to the appellate court's decisions and denied Happy's HCW. The court ruled that as the HCW was intended to protect the liberty right of human beings to be free of unlawful confinement, it has no applicability to Happy, a non-human animal who is not a 'person' subjected to illegal detention.[126] The court acknowledged the fact that elephants are intelligent beings deserving of proper care and compassion, but it granted the motion to dismiss the petition for this HCW.

The story of Kaavan, the thirty-nine-year-old elephant, labeled the world's loneliest pachyderm, hit the headlines and attracted worldwide attention to the plight of animals in zoos.[127] The one-year-old baby elephant made its voyage from Sri Lanka to Pakistan in 1985. Originally lodged at Sri Lanka's Pinnawala Elephant Orphanage, Kaavan was gifted to General Zia-ul-Haq's government as thanks for backing the Sri Lankan army during an insurgency. The general's daughter Zain Haq fell in love with elephants after viewing the Bollywood movie *Haathi Mere Saathi* (Elephants my Friends). On hearing Zain's prayer to Allah asking for an elephant to be her friend, Haq gifted his daughter the orphaned elephant cub. On reaching adulthood, the elephant was sent to the Marghuzar zoo in Islamabad. Saheli, a female elephant joined Kaavan in the early 1990s. After Saheli's death in 2012, Kaavan was left in a small half-acre enclosure, and had to stand at the fence during visiting hours, raise his trunk as a begging bowl when his mahout prodded him with a bull hook to collect money from the crowds. Elephant food was sold to the visitors, who in turn fed Kaavan. Other captive inmates, like the couple of brown bears, the marsh crocodile, wolves, and birds like ostriches, were often pelted with stones by visitors to the Marghuzar zoo. The case of Kaavan the elephant came to light when the animal activist group, Friends of Islamabad Zoo, conducted a census and brought to the notice of the public that the number of animals had dwindled drastically.[128] The pop music singer Cher co-founded the animal-rights movement Free the Wild to campaign for the release of the zoo's animals to sanctuaries in other countries. In the case *Islamabad Wildlife Management Board v. Metropolitan Corporation Islamabad & others* (2020),[129] the court had to consider the issues of whether lonesome Kaavan would have to continue to sway and bob his head against the wall of his small, dilapidated shed, displaying decades of pain and distress. The animals of the Marghuzar zoo were presented by the wildlife board as non-human living creatures with independent rights. The case raised the issue of the duty of care owed by humans through their state functionaries to protect, preserve and conserve wildlife.[130]

Table 3.2 - ***People's Charioteer Organization v. Union of India* (2023)**

Public Interest Litigation
W.P(C) No. 885/2020
IN THE SUPREME COURT OF INDIA
Judgment rendered on March 29, 2023

Bench: D Y Chandrachud, Justices P S Narasimha, and J B Pardiwala

Rule: Article 32 of the Constitution of India which states that the Supreme Court shall have power to issue directions or orders or writs, including writs like *habeas corpus, mandamus, prohibition, quo warranto* and *certiorari*, whichever may be appropriate, for the enforcement of any of the rights conferred by this Part. Article 51A(g) & 51A(h) of the Constitution of India which confers a constitutional duty on all citizens and the State to have compassion for non-human living creatures and to protect and improve wild life.

Facts of the case: The petitioner, the NGO People's Charioteer Organization, filed a PIL and claimed that recent cases of cruelty towards animals have raised questions as to how humans have shown no respect for animals' lives. The writ listed various acts of 'zoosadism' to demonstrate how humans can be devoid of sympathy. It sought an order from the court to declare all the citizens of India as persons in *loco parentis* (in place of a parent) for the protection of animals from cruelty and abuse and to ensure their welfare. The PIL referred to verdicts in two recent judgments, namely *Karnail Singh and Others v. State of Haryana* (2019) and *Narayan Dutt Bhatt v. Union of India* and others (2018), whereby all animals in the animal kingdom were recognized as legal entities and citizens were declared as "persons in *loco parentis*." It also referenced the case of *Animal Welfare Board of India v. A. Nagaraja and others* (2014) which recognized the dignity and honor of animals under Article 21 of the Indian Constitution.

In the wake of animal cruelty incidents, the petitioner painted the picture of a state of natural emergency by citing examples of animal cruelty prevalent in recent times in India like the slaughtering of cows by feeding them explosives, the lynching of the tiger species, the trading and the sale of dog meat, sexual molestation of goats and other similar incidents. It listed the Central Government of India, national ministries, all state governments, and the Union Territory of Delhi as respondents in this case, considering them as irresponsible legal guardians who had failed in their duty to protect animals. It contended that the state did not adequately protect animals and that there was a dire need for the state to set up individual emergency units, investigating independent commissions, and online portals and hotlines to report abuse. It voiced the need for Government Directives to make states prohibit animal fighting, to hold superiors in law enforcement departments accountable for their subordinates' failure to enact anti-cruelty laws, to provide animal welfare funds, to consider discontinuing animal testing and compel the National Crime Records Bureau to report and render public data and statistics of animal cruelty cases.

Issue: Whether the laws in existence are sufficient to protect animals from possible abuse and cruelty.

Reasoning of the court: The writ petition cannot be granted by this Court in its extraordinary jurisdiction under Article 32 of the Constitution of India.

Conclusion: The Supreme Court dismissed the PIL which sought declaration of the entire animal kingdom, including the avian and aquatic species as 'legal entities,' having a distinct persona with corresponding rights of a living person.

Note: My synopsis of *People's Charioteer Organization v. Union of India* (Supreme Court of India, March 29, 2023).

THE POLYPHONIC RELIGIOUS PETITION

In the wake of public attention to cases of animal cruelty, *People's Charioteer Organization v. Union of India* (2023),[131] presented in table 3.2, the petitioner, an Allahabad based NGO, filed a PIL case in the Supreme Court of India seeking *inter alia*, the inclusion of the entire animal kingdom, including avian and aquatic species, as legal entities having a distinct persona with corresponding rights of a living person. In an eighty-three-page petition, it made a plea requesting the court to make all people legal guardians who can enforce animals' rights, so that the voices of animals are heard.

To establish that animals merit a life of intrinsic worth, the petitioner included voices from religious sources varying from the Hindu religious texts of the *Vedas*, the Muslim edicts in the Koran, and the prophetic verses of the Bible. Each presented a different tone of argument to voice dissent to animal cruelty.

The Hindu religious contention in the PIL is that there was no distinction between human beings and other life forms. This argument even insisted that humans, animals, plants, insects, and tiny organisms were manifestations of God (*Pasupati*) with limited life spans.[132] It declared the existence of 8.4 million different species of living creatures with the argument from the *Vedas* that the human body is the highest of all forms with the soul inhabiting different species in the plant and animal kingdom before finally assuming a human body.[133] The argument includes the voice of Lord Krishna's sermon to Arjuna on the battlefield of Kurukshetra, "Just like man discards his old and tattered clothes and wears a new set of clothes, similarly the being discards his old and weak body in preparation for its new mantle."[134] Another voice is heard from reference to the philosophical texts of the *Upanishads* in the Vedas that state how the "entire universe (is) part of our own higher self."[135] These Hindu religious voices in the PIL expose the Vedic philosophy, that animals are also in the same chain of existence shared by man.

The secular mode of the PIL encourages the hearing of another voice from the Koran, that presents the creations of Allah as precious and that animals form communities just like humans: "There is not an animal (that lives) on the Earth, nor a being that flies on its wings, but (forms part of) communities like you. Nothing have we omitted from the Book, and they (all) shall be gathered to their Lord in the end."[136] This voice includes animals and birds as creatures connected to a larger spiritual and physical world where they are "vicegerents on Earth."[137] The Islamic tone is one that forbids the exploitation of animals and includes the voice of the Prophet Muhammad to remind the court that "One who kills unnecessarily, even a sparrow, will be questioned by Allah on the Day of Judgment.A good deed done to an animal is like a good deed done to a human being, while an act of cruelty to an animal is as bad as cruelty to a human being."[138]

The petition quotes the books from the Bible, reminding the court of the Christian belief that the Lord gave the breath of life to all living creatures from the beasts to the creeping insects.[139] Voices from the Bible enter the court's petition in the form of proverbs as "Whoever is righteous, has regard for the life of his beast, but the mercy of the wicked is cruel" and "Open your mouth for the mute, for the rights of all who are destitute."[140] As in the convening of the biblical congregation, the preacher's voice is heard in "For what happens to the children of man and what happens to the beasts is the same; as one dies, so dies the other. They all have the same breath, and man has no advantage over the beasts, for all is vanity. All life goes to the same place. All life comes from the ground, and all of it goes back to the ground."[141] The prophecy from the Bible is heard in "He who slaughters an ox is like one who kills a man; he who sacrifices a lamb, like one who breaks a dog's neck; he who presents a grain offering, like one who offers pig's blood; he who makes a memorial offering of frankincense, like one who blesses an idol. These have chosen their own ways, and their soul delights in their abominations."[142]

The PIL reminded the court that petitions to stop animal cruelty have existed in English jurisprudence since the eighteenth century. It referred to Reverend Humphrey Primatt's treatise entitled "A Dissertation on the Duty of Mercy and Sin of Cruelty to Brute Animals," written as far back as 1776, where he pleaded for the care of animals, "See that no brute of any kind . . . whether entrusted to thy care, or coming in thy way, suffer thy neglect or abuse."[143] The voice of Jeremy Bentham, is also heard in this polyphonic writ where he contends that animals are inferior beasts and "on account of their interests having been neglected by the insensibility of the ancient jurists, stand degraded into the class of things."[144] A reference is made to the bill presented on May 15, 1809, by Lord Erskine to the English Parliament in support of the bill for the protection of animals. It was the first-time an animal protection bill had been debated by a full legislative body: "They (animals) are created, indeed, for our use, but not for our abuse. Their freedom and enjoyment, when they cease to be consistent with our just dominions and enjoyment, can be no part of their natures; but whilst they are consistent I say their rights, subservient as they are, ought to be as sacred as our own . . . the bill I propose to you, if it shall receive the sanction of Parliament, will not only be an honour to the country, but an era in the history of the world."[145] The voice of Mahatma Gandhi is included in the writ: "The greatness of a nation and its moral progress can be judged by the way its animals are treated."[146] Here the essence of polyphony of this petition is obvious as in Bakhtin's polyphony where "voices remain independent and, as such, are combined in a unity of a higher order than in homophony . . . it is precisely in polyphony that a combination of several individual wills takes place . . . (and) the artistic will of polyphony is a will to combine many wills, a will to the event."[147]

The PIL also made a comparative analysis of International Animal Cruelty laws and the legal framework of foreign courts to emphasize the need for the proper implementation of Animal Welfare laws in India. It referred to the Australian Animal Welfare Act (2004) that equates the importance of animal life to that of human life with its anti-cruelty legislation that bans pet owners from cropping their dogs' ears or tails, forces farmers to stop battery farming, and seizes pets from violators.[148] The court was reminded that Switzerland's Constitution also makes a provision to protect animals' dignity; in New Zealand, all animals are recognized as sentient beings under the Animal Welfare Amendment Act, 2013;[149] the UK's Animal Welfare Act (2007) has stricter penalties for both cruelty and negligence against animals with punishments ranging from a lifetime ban from owning pets, to a fifty-one-week maximum jail term, and fines amounting up to £20,000;[150] Germany, Sweden, Denmark, and Hong Kong have animal protection acts that prevent cruelty, slaughtering, and the ill-treatment of animals.[151]

Even though the Bench of Chief Justice of India (CJI) D.Y. Chandrachud, Justice P.S. Narasimha, and Justice J.B. Pardiwala observed that it could not entertain the writ petition in its extraordinary jurisdiction under Article 32 of the Constitution, this case shows that the need for a nation-wide application of the Rights of Nature laws in India. In the Indian legal regime, animal welfare is enshrined in the Prevention of Cruelty to Animals Act (PCA) 1960 and Wildlife Protection Act 1972. Consequent bills to replace the PCA were proposed in parliament in 2011, 2014, and 2016, but they were only drafted and not approved by both Houses, the Lok Sabha and the Rajya Sabha. The bills aimed at broadening the scope of animal welfare, introducing stricter penalties, and giving a stronger foundation to animal welfare organizations.

CREATURES OF OUR TIME

With animals being heard in human forums, our time is one that that is aware of the need to preserve the species that preserve the delicate balance of bees, bats, butterflies, primates, plankton, and man. Rights of Nature laws that were initially dismissed *in limine* as frivolous have now gained legal ground. They are yet to be enforced globally and one may well wonder: Are all animals on our planet equal? Pig Napoleon in Orwell's *Animal Farm* whilst re-writing the charter of animalistic commandments wrote, "All animals are equal, but some animals are more equal than others"[152] This commandment that aimed to prevent the reproduction of the oppressive behaviour of humans seems an apt comparison to the law-making strategies in different world forums.

Forums have adapted drawing inspiration from each other. It must be borne in mind that court cases deal with just one individual form of species, or one individual animal specimen supported by a human friend. The legislative branch may also be lobbied as it has the capacity to introduce bills, approve Acts of Parliament and draft laws and statutes on the welfare of all animal species, instead of just one kind which has been the case in courts. While some forums still seem reluctant to accept HCW and embrace the new vision of all species having an equal claim to the planet, legal jurisprudence has shown that the recognition of personhood for animals was possible in the domain of copyright law where Naruto, the chimpanzee was heard in court as a legal person. With animal legal personhood being supported by activists, attorneys, academics, scientists, and philosophers, there is growing media attention to the mute and voiceless species of the planet as judges have begun to recognize the presence of the elephant in the courtroom.

Suniti Namjoshi uses the stage of Shakespeare's *The Tempest* in her fable story "The Dream Book." Ariel, the omniscient spirit-narrator has the task of making people's dreams come true; Miranda writes poetry articulating the fears of nature where trees, birds, and animals, the so-called nonentities on the planet who are plunged in a vicious circle of nightmares in which they are constantly crushed and destroyed; Prospero has the mage's privilege of calling all the shots and unstitching time to fit the present moment; and the witch Sycorax hallucinates and imagines a fair world where all species are treated alike. In "The Dream Book," the Shakespearean protagonists find that their dreams clash, mingle, and intertwine. Yet, each time they dream time and time again about creating a better world and engaging once again in the pursuit of survival of different species with equal rights to the Earth. In Namjoshi's fables, a "plurality of independent and unmerged voices and consciousnesses"[153] with equal rights to the fabulistic space combine but do not merge, showing thus their capacity to express their own directly signifying discourse that is independent of the fabulist's stance. In the final scene, the protagonists get together to embrace the notion of a "plurality of consciousness."[154]

Gonzalo: We're creatures of time.

Miranda (rapping): We eat time.

Ferdie: Secrete time.

Cal: Creep, crawl and fly through time.

Miranda: And in our dreams we flounder in time.

Ferdie: Yes, wallow in time. Shall we consent?

Miranda and Cal: Yes.

Ariel: Consent to what?

Cal: To dream a better and kinder dream.

Gonzalo: Because others have done it?

Miranda: Yes. Those are pearls that were their eyes![155]

By casting her Shakespearean protagonists in their role as creatures of time, Namjoshi's polyphonic fable serves as a new means of stimulating social action. Her fiction offers new morals for the changing times and foregrounds the need to question, rethink, and remap different ways of being creatures of our time.

NOTES

1. Roger Allers and Rob Minkoff, *The Lion King* (United States: Buena Vista Pictures, 1994).
2. Idem.
3. F.N. Egerton, "Changing Concepts of the Balance of Nature." *Quarterly Review of Biology* 48 (1973): 322–50.
4. Idem.
5. David Orr, *Ecological Literacy: Education and the Transition to a Postmodern World* (Albany: State University of New York Press, 1992).
6. Edwin H. Palmer, *The Holy Bible, New International Version: Containing the Old Testament and the New Testament* (Grand Rapids: Zondervan, 1984).
7. Jacques Derrida, "The Animal That Therefore I Am (More to Follow)," *Critical Enquiry* 28, no. 2 (2002): 369–83.
8. Idem, 372.
9. Idem, 405.
10. Idem, 388.
11. Amitav Ghosh, *The Great Derangement: Climate Change and the Unthinkable* (Chicago: The University of Chicago Press, 2017): 65–66.
12. Derrida, "The Animal," 381.
13. *The Hidden Lives of Pets*, Netflix, 2022. https://www.netflix.com/title/81318943.
14. Maya Yang, "Mystery Owner of Stan the T Rex Finally Revealed Following $31.8m Auction," *Guardian*. Guardian News and Media, March 23, 2022. https://www.theguardian.com/science/2022/mar/23/mystery-owner-of-stan-the-t-rex-finally-revealed-following-318m-auction.
15. *U.S. v Larson* (United States Court of Appeals, Eighth Circuit, April 10, 1997).
16. *Black Hills Institute of Geological Research (BHI) v. Fort Peck Paleontology et al.* (US District Court for the District of Montana, November 22, 2010).

17. "Summary for Policymakers." Global Warming of 1.5ºC. Accessed April 15, 2023. https://www.ipcc.ch/sr15/chapter/spm/.

18. "The Impact of Climate Change on Our Planet's Animals." IFAW. Accessed April 15, 2023. https://www.ifaw.org/uk/journal/impact-climate-change-animals.

19. Salomé Vincendon, "*Renards, Sangliers, Ours . . . Que Viennent Faire Les Animaux Sauvages En Ville?*" BFMTV. Accessed April 15, 2023. https://www.bfmtv.com/animaux/renard-sangliers-ours-que-viennent-faire-les-animaux-sauvages-en-ville_AN-202208210013.html.

20. David Drake, Bret Shaw, and Mary Magnuson. "Coyotes Are Here to Stay in North American Cities—Here's How to Appreciate Them from a Distance." *Conversation*, September 13, 2022. https://theconversation.com/coyotes-are-here-to-stay-in-north-american-cities-heres-how-to-appreciate-them-from-a-distance-186893.

21. *How Animals Are Rapidly Evolving Because of Climate Change | WIRED. YouTube*. WIRED, 2021. https://www.youtube.com/watch?v=uMxsflmpaYM.

22. Michael Crichton, *Jurassic Park* (New York: Random House, 1990).

23. *Jurassic Park—Life Finds a Way*. Universal Pictures, 1993.

24. Alexandra Ludka, "Hitchcock's 'The Birds': Mystery Solved." ABC News. ABC News Network, December 28, 2011. https://abcnews.go.com/blogs/entertainment/2011/12/hitchcocks-the-birds-mystery-solved.

25. Rachel L. Carson, *Silent Spring* (Boston: Mifflin, 1962), 1.

26. "Velsicol Chemical vs. Rachel Carson—the Lawsuit That Didn't Happen." Millard Fillmore's Bathtub, December 5, 2015. https://timpanogos.blog/2010/08/23/velsicol-chemical-vs-rachel-carson-the-lawsuit-that-didnt-happen/.

27. *101 Dalmatians*. Walt Disney Pictures, 1996.

28. "May Prehistory Thunder Forward: The Resurrection of the Woolly Mammoth." Colossal, October 10, 2022. https://colossal.com/mammoth/.

29. Daniel Boguslaw, "The CIA Just Invested in Woolly Mammoth Resurrection Technology." The Intercept. The Intercept, September 28, 2022. https://theintercept.com/2022/09/28/cia-extinction-woolly-mammoth-dna/.

30. Sam Brasch, "10 Farm Animal Hybrids You Didn't Know Existed." Modern Farmer, October 2, 2018. https://modernfarmer.com/2014/01/10-farm-animal-hybrids-didnt-know-existed/.

31. *15 Amazing Hybrid Animals That Actually Exist*. *YouTube*. YouTube, 2020. https://www.youtube.com/watch?v=twGnn8niQYE.

32. Hannah Fischer, "Investigating Animal Bites & Attacks." BOAH. Accessed April 15, 2023. https://www.in.gov/boah/files/9.-Presentation-Animal-Bite-Investigations.pdf.

33. "Hérault: Un Chat Savannah Confondu Avec Un Léopard Mobilise Les Gendarmes." France 3 Occitanie. Accessed April 15, 2023. https://france3-regions.francetvinfo.fr/occitanie/herault/montpellier/herault-chat-savannah-confondu-leopard-mobilise-gendarmes-1434175.html.

34. "Rhône. Villeurbanne: Un Félin Attaque Des Lapins Et Échappe Aux Recherches." Rhône. Villeurbanne: un félin attaque des lapins et échappe aux recherches. Le Progrès, January 4, 2016. https://www.leprogres.fr/rhone/2016/01/03/villeurbanne-un-felin-attaque-des-lapins-et-echappe-aux-recherches.

35. Sara Ryding and Matthew Symonds. "Animals Are Changing Their Body Shapes to Cope with Climate Change." World Economic Forum, September 13, 2021. https://www.weforum.org/agenda/2021/09/climate-change-animals-global-warming-shape.

36. *How Animals Are Rapidly Evolving Because of Climate Change | WIRED. YouTube*. WIRED, 2021. https://www.youtube.com/watch?v=uMxsfImpaYM.

37. Dana Kobilinsky, "Climate Warming Changes Bird Migration Timing and Body Size." The Wildlife Society, January 8, 2023. https://wildlife.org/climate-warming-changes-bird-migration-timing-and-body-size/.

38. "10 Of the World's Most Endangered Animals." WWF. Accessed April 15, 2023. https://www.wwf.org.uk/learn/wildlife/endangered-animals.

39. "The Impact of Climate Change on Our Planet's Animals." IFAW. Accessed April 15, 2023. https://www.ifaw.org/journal/impact-climate-change-animals.

40. "Endangered Species." Education. Accessed April 15, 2023. https://education.nationalgeographic.org/resource/endangered-species/.

41. "10 Animals That Are Now Extinct." OneKindPlanet, September 22, 2017. https://onekindplanet.org/top-10/top-10-worlds-extinct-animals/.

42. Joseph Stromberg and Sarah Zielinski, "Ten Threatened and Endangered Species Used in Traditional Medicine." Smithsonian.com. Smithsonian Institution, October 18, 2011. https://www.smithsonianmag.com/science-Nature/ten-threatened-and-endangered-species-used-in-traditional-medicine-112814487/.

43. Serpil Oppermann, "Ecocriticism: Natural World in the Literary Viewfinder," *Journal of Faculty Letters*, Hateceppe University of Ankara Turkey, 1999, 4.

44. Oppermann, "Ecocriticism: Natural World," 4.

45. "The Animal Turn." NC State University Libraries. Accessed April 24, 2023. https://www.lib.ncsu.edu/animal-turn.

46. "The Origins & History of the RSPCA." RSPCA. Accessed April 15, 2023. https://www.rspca.org.uk/whatwedo/whoweare/history.

47. "La Société Protectrice des Animaux." SPA. Accessed April 15, 2023. https://www.la-spa.fr/.

48. "The European Union Legislation on Animal Welfare: State of Play, Enforcement and Future Activities." La Fondation Droit Animal, Ethique et Sciences, February 16, 2021. https://www.fondation-droit-animal.org/proceedings-aw/the-european-union-legislation-on-animal-welfare/.

49. "Asia for Animals Coalition: Network." Asia for Animals. Accessed April 15, 2023. https://www.asiaforanimals.com/.

50. "Map of Private Exotic Pet Ownership Laws." Animal Law Legal Center. Accessed April 16, 2023. https://www.animallaw.info/content/map-private-exotic-pet-ownership-laws.

51. "Fighting the Deadly Exotic Pet Trade to Keep Wild Animals Where They Belong—in the Wild." *World Animal Protection*, March 25, 2020. https://www.worldanimalprotection.org/our-work/animals-wild/exotic-pets.

52. Johanna Rasmussen, "The Unfriendly Environment of Animal Cafés," *Forum*, December 31, 2019. http://www.theforumcuf.com/news/articleView.html?idxno=216.

53. "Animal Protection Index." World Animal Protection | Animal Protection Index. Accessed April 16, 2023. https://api.worldanimalprotection.org/.

54. "India Ranks Better in Animal Protection Index 2020, but Still Needs Improvements." *Business Standard*, March 12, 2020. https://www.business-standard.com/article/news-ani/india-ranks-better-in-animal-protection-index-2020-but-still-needs-improvements-120031200558_1.html.

55. "People for the Ethical Treatment of Animals (PETA)." PETA. Accessed April 24, 2023. https://www.peta.org/.

56. Convention on Animal Protection. Accessed April 24, 2023. https://www.conventiononanimalprotection.org/the-cap-treaty.

57. "*Time* Magazine Cover: Heroes of the Environment—Oct. 5, 2009," *Time*, October 5, 2009. https://content.time.com/time/covers/asia/0,16641,20091005,00.html.

58. Serenella Iovino and Serpil Oppermann, *Material Ecocriticism* (Bloomington: Indiana University Press, 2014), 1–2.

59. Paula Willoquet-Maricondi, *Framing the World: Explorations in Ecocriticism and Film* (Charlottesville: University of Virginia Press, 2010): 45–46.

60. Jon Dovey, "Documentary Ecosystems: Collaboration and Exploitation," in *New Documentary Ecologies: Emerging Platforms, Practices and Discourses*, edited by Kate Nash, Craig Hight, and Catherine Summerhayes (Palgrave Macmillan, 2014): 15.

61. *Vanishing Vultures—A Race Against Time*. Accessed April 15, 2023. https://www.youtube.com/watch?v=FcA0mbysRC0.

62. Docplexus, "Ban On Diclofenac Sodium Injection: DCGI Order." Docplexus. Accessed April 16, 2023. https://www.docplexus.com/posts/ban-on-diclofenac-sodium-injection-dcgi-order.

63. *Shores of Silence | The Slaughter of Whales Sharks in India*. YouTube, 2017. https://www.youtube.com/watch?v=TVMW_6_dVhE.

64. *The Last Migration*. YouTube, 2013. https://www.youtube.com/watch?v=WHVwd91pzKg.

65. *Vanishing Giants*. YouTube, 2009. https://www.youtube.com/watch?v=8bG103hHkUU.

66. Cara Tejpal, "'Not Just Films': Exploring Conservation with Riverbank Studios." Sanctuary Nature Foundation, April 14, 2021. https://sanctuaryNaturefoundation.org/article/%22not-just-films%22%3A-exploring-conservation-with-riverbank-studios.

67. Neha Banka, "In West Bengal, Marine Strandings of Endangered Horseshoe Crabs Are Increasing," *Indian Express*, August 16, 2022. https://indianexpress.com/article/cities/kolkata/west-bengal-marine-strandings-endangered-horseshoe-crabs-increasing-8091777/.

68. John Henderson Phaedrus and Thomas Bewick, *Aesop's Human Zoo: Roman Stories about Our Bodies* (Chicago: University of Chicago, 2004), vii.

69. Suniti Namjoshi is an Indian-born, Canadian and British author of collections of poems and fables as well as children's books. These include *Feminist Fables* (1981), *The Conversations of Cow* (1985), *Aditi and the One-eyed Monkey* (1986), *The Blue Donkey Fables* (1988), *Saint Suniti and the Dragon* (1993), *Building Babel*

(1996), *Goja: An Autobiographical Myth* (2000), *Sycorax: New Fables and Poems* (2006), *The Fabulous Feminist: A Suniti Namjoshi Reader* (2012), *Suki* (2013), *Foxy Aesop: On the Edge* (2018), and *Dangerous Pursuits* (2022).

70. Suniti Namjoshi, *Foxy Aesop: On the Edge* (New Delhi: Zubaan, 2018), 76.

71. Idem, 122.

72. Idem, 122.

73. Bakhtin, *Problems of Dostoevsky's Poetics*, 6.

74. Namjoshi, *Foxy Aesop*, 129.

75. Suniti Namjoshi, *The Conversations of Cow* (London: The Women's Press, 1985).

76. Idem, 80–81.

77. Idem, 81.

78. Idem, 85.

79. Wayne C. Booth, "Introduction," in *Problems of Dostoevsky's Poetics*, xiii–xxvii (Minneapolis: University of Minnesota Press, 1984): xxii.

80. Suniti Namjoshi, *The Blue Donkey Fables* (London: The Women's Press, 1988), 2.

81. Idem, 21.

82. Idem, 21.

83. "50 Years of Environmental Conservation." WWF. Accessed April 16, 2023. https://wwf.panda.org/discover/knowledge_hub/history/.

84. Namjoshi, *Blue Donkey*, 90.

85. Idem, 90.

86. Idem, 91.

87. Bakhtin, *Problems of Dostoevsky's Poetics*, 18.

88. Namjoshi, *Blue Donkey*, 94.

89. Idem, 94.

90. Suniti Namjoshi and Nilima Sheikh, *Blue and Other Stories* (North Melbourne: Spinifex Press, 2013), 23.

91. Namjoshi, *Blue Donkey*, 51.

92. *Asociación de Funcionarios y Abogados por los Derechos de los Animales y otros contra GCBA* (Juzgado No. 4 on Contentious Administrative and Tax Matters, October 21, 2015).

93. Idem, 143–44.

94. It was cited in *Islamabad Wildlife Management Board v. Metropolitan Corporation Islamabad & Others* (Islamabad High Court, May 21, 2020).

95. *Acción de hábeas corpus presentada por la Asociación de Funcionarios y Abogados por los Derechos de los Animales (AFADA)* (Tercer Juzgado de Garantías Poder Judicial Mendoza, November 3, 2016).

96. "*Presentación Efectuada Por AFADA Respecto del Chimpancé 'Cecilia' Sujeto No Humano*" ([Expte. Nro.] P-72.254/15 [Arg.]. Third Criminal Court of Mendoza, November 3, 2016).

97. Idem, 13, 19.

98. *Acción de habeas corpus Decision AHC4806* (Colombia Supreme Court of Justice, July 26, 2017).

99. "*Ley 1774 De 2016*." Animal Law Legal Center, January 1, 1970. https://www.animallaw.info/statute/colombia-ley-1774-2016.

100. *Acción de habeas corpus Decision*, 5–9.

101. Idem, 143.

102. *Tilikum v. Sea World Parks Sea World Parks & Entertainment, Inc.* (United States District Court of California, February 8, 2012).

103. *Naruto v. David Slater* (United States Court of Appeals for the Ninth Circuit, July 12, 2017).

104. David J. Slater, *Wildlife Personalities* (New York: Blurb, Wildlife Personalities Ltd, 2014).

105. *Naruto v. David Slater*, 5.

106. Idem, 6.

107. Idem, 7.

108. *Centre for Environmental Law WWF-1 v. Union of India* (1999), (Supreme Court of India, April 15, 2013).

109. "India Code: Wild Life (Protection) Act, 1972." India Code. Accessed April 16, 2023. https://www.indiacode.nic.in/handle/123456789/1726.

110. *Centre for Environmental Law WWF-1*, 45.

111. *Narayan Dutt Bhatt v. Union of India and Others* (Uttaranchal High Court, July 4, 2018).

112. Idem, 99.

113. Idem, 99.

114. *N.R Nair & others v. Union of India* (Kerala High Court, June 6, 2000).

115. Idem, 3.

116. *Animal Welfare Board of India v. A. Nagaraja & Ors* (Supreme Court of India, May 7, 2014).

117. "Article 21: Protection of Life and Personal Liberty." Constitution of India, March 31, 2023. https://www.Constitutionofindia.net/articles/article-21-protection-of-life-and-personal-liberty/.

118. *Karnail Singh & Ors v. State of Haryana* (Punjab-Haryana High Court, May 31, 2019).

119. Lawrence Wright, "The Elephant in the Courtroom," *New Yorker*, February 28, 2022. https://www.newyorker.com/magazine/2022/03/07/the-elephant-in-the-courtroom.

120. Mark Olivier, "Banksy's Painted Elephant Is Illegal, Say Officials," *Guardian*. Guardian News and Media, September 18, 2006. https://www.theguardian.com/uk/2006/sep/18/arts.artsnews.

121. Mark Twain, *The Stolen White Elephant* (London: Chatto & Windus, 1918).

122. *Billy Rose's Jumbo*. Metro-Goldwyn-Mayer, 1962.

123. Ed Shanahan, "Happy the Elephant Isn't Legally a Person, Top New York Court Rules," *New York Times*, June 14, 2022. https://www.nytimes.com/2022/06/14/nyregion/happy-elephant-animal-rights.html.

124. *Nonhuman Rights Project, Inc. v. Breheny* (Court of Appeals of New York June 14, 2022).

125. Hans Kelsen, *Introduction to the Problems of Legal Theory: A Translation of the First Edition of the Reine Rechtslehre or Pure Theory of Law* (Oxford University Press: New York, 1992), 46.

126. *Nonhuman Rights Project, Inc. v. Breheny*, 1–5.

127. Ilyas M Khan, "Kaavan, the World's Loneliest Elephant, Is Finally Going Free." BBC News, November 28, 2020. https://www.bbc.com/news/world-asia-55060433.

128. Umaima R Ahmed, "Freedom in Sight for Kaavan, 'the World's Loneliest Elephant.'" Global Voices, December 1, 2020. https://globalvoices.org/2020/10/31/freedom-in-sight-for-Kaavan-the-worlds-loneliest-elephant/.

129. *Islamabad Wildlife Management Board v. Metropolitan Corporation Islamabad & Others* (Islamabad High Court, May 21, 2020).

130. Idem, 1–4.

131. *People's Charioteer Organization v. Union of India* (Supreme Court of India, March 29, 2023).

132. Idem, 20.

133. Idem, 21.

134. Idem, 22.

135. Idem, 22.

136. Idem, 23.

137. Idem, 24.

138. Idem, 24.

139. Idem, 24–25. A quote from Genesis 1:24–25.

140. Idem, 25. Quotes from Proverbs 12:10 and 31:8.

141. Idem, 25. A quote from Ecclesiastes 3:19.

142. Idem, 25. A quote from Isaiah 66:3.

143. Idem, 26.

144. Idem, 38.

145. Idem, 28.

146. Idem, 28.

147. Bakhtin, *Problems of Dostoevsky's Poetics*, 21.

148. People's Charioteer Organization, 46.

149. Idem, 46.

150. Idem, 47.

151. Idem, 48.

152. George Orwell, *Animal Farm: A Fairy Story* (London: Secker & Warburg, 1945), 14.

153. Bakhtin, *Problems of Dostoevsky's Poetics*, 6–7.

154. Idem, 6.

155. Namjoshi, *Dangerous Pursuits*, 228–29.

Chapter 4

Water in Peril—Day Zero

In 2001, a Japanese businessman, Yasuki Takano, marketed Mahalo water as the elixir of life that had been funnelled from the Pacific Ocean depths near the Kona coast in Hawaii. He desalinated and bottled mineral water for the wealthy Japanese market. Water, a natural element, assumed the status of being pure liquid gold as exorbitantly priced Mahalo water hit the market. Today thirty to forty brands compete for shelf space in supermarkets as water has assumed the status of a lucrative commodity with multinationals vying with each other and promising health, convenience, and youth. Water is the ideal product for big businesses as it is natural, pure, and available at minimal costs. Its real value lies in its marketing and branding as giant businesses have transformed the bottled water novelty into a necessity. The customer buys freedom and revels in his capacity to make a choice while quenching his thirst. The present-day bottled water industry markets this fabulous natural resource as one filled with minerals essential for our existence. But why would one pay money for a bottle of water that one could otherwise get for free?

Geneva Lake on the north side of the Alps separates not just Switzerland and France, but also two of the world's biggest multinational corporations Nestlé and Danone. While Nestlé advertises "Good Food, Good Life,"[1] Danone's tagline targets "One Planet, One Health."[2] Their corporate rivalry is staged in the market of bottled water. Nestlé, the world's food company based in the Swiss city of Vevey, has a global turnover of $94.4 billion, with $9 billion stemming from its bottled water brand Pure Life.[3] Danone's water bottling unit situated at Évian-les-Bains on the south shore of Lake Geneva, has a turnover of $29.1 million.[4] However Evian, the company's flagship brand is marketed as a luxury product along with the boast that its pure source hails from the French Alps. Danone, on the other hand, promises natural purity, claiming that their water filters through rocks at its production site before being bottled in its purest form at its Alpine mountain base.[5] Selling nature in a bottle however generates production costs of transport, energy, shipping to ports, delivery in trucks to distribution centres around the globe, but carrying with it the implicit message that water in France is better than water available anywhere else on the planet. Nestlé's Pure Life on the other hand, that is sourced from different springs around the world at different production sites, does not incur huge transportation and logistics costs. But it uses sophisticated know-how to standardise its water as in the brewing of a coffee like Nescafé, to reconstitute the quality and taste of its water, making it an industrial product. Through the process of reverse osmosis, the same technology used by NASA to provide drinking water for astronauts, Nestlé producers use a thin membrane to remove minerals and salts, thus producing distilled water. It is consequently remineralised to add taste. Pure Life is the result when the distilled, denatured re-mineralised water is poured into a bottle. But it was the Perrier advertising 'Eau' campaign launched by Leo Burnett with puns to release the idea of French chicness—Picasseau, Sun leaution, Eau come all ye faithful, Eau-la-la, Incogniteau, Eau Pair—that resulted in water being sold like a beverage on the same lines as Coke Cola, Guinness, or even Martini.[6] Today, Martin Riese, America's first certified water sommelier, even offers his customers the different, subtle flavors of bottled water, and prepares menus pairing specific brands of water with foods.[7]

Water, the essence of light for which there is no real variety now exists in thirty to forty varieties, changing bottle shapes to cater to different water consumers ranging from the mundane to the exotic. It takes three liters to make one liter of bottled water. Furthermore, these bottles are transported in huge containers made of wood that weigh heavily on our planet's ecosystem. In September 2021, tourists and commuters who stepped out of the Reims railway station in the Champagne-Ardenne region of France, were welcomed by a 320-metre-tall giant blue penguin. Our 'fiercely hot' emperor penguin was baptized 'rudement chaud,'[8] or Rudy, the fiercely hot penguin, by its artist-creator Vincent Rahir as seen in figure 4.1.[9]

Rahir's flightless sea bird was molded out of Chilean recycled plywood. The project supported by the City of Reims and the French railways SNCF, aimed at drawing attention to our irrational behavior that can affect our planet. Why would we humans import and transport Colombian plywood from the South American continent to manufacture transport containers in another continent? What about local wood or recycling other resources at hand? Surprising too, is the fact that these transport containers were used to transport merchandise like bottles of water between factories situated within a twenty-kilometer radius. Our silent-much-photographed penguin speaks volumes of the incoherence of our times and of the ensuing global warming it engenders. What we humans do in our cities has its repercussions on vulnerable penguin colonies in Antarctica where melting sea ice from frozen ocean water has endangered their survival and breeding habitats.

Figure 4.1. "Rudement Chaud," Rudy, the Fiercely Hot Penguin.

Water, a protean element that can assume or borrow the shape of its vessel or container or bottle or physical space has the capacity to exist in its liquid state; or freeze to its crystalline form at temperatures of 0 C (32 F) or lower; and expand to the state of water vapor or its gaseous state at temperatures of 100 C (212 F) or higher. Seventy percent of the Earth's surface is covered by liquid water. The Earth's hydrosphere includes surface water in ponds, lakes, rivers, and oceans; underground water in aquifers and wells; cryosphere ice in the polar zones, glaciers, ice caps and icebergs; and water vapor in the form of fog, mist, and clouds. Water renews itself migrating into one of the three states of matter, namely solid, liquid and gas. In its trajectory through the water cycle, it moves around the planet transpiring from leaves, or melting ice that collects in rivers and lakes before it evaporates into water vapour and rises higher into the clouds, where the cool air of the atmosphere condenses and causes the vapor to turn back into liquid water or rain. Seventy percent of the Earth's surface is covered by water, our bodies are made of 70 percent of this essential, beautiful element that sustains human, animal, and plant life on our planet. However only 3 percent of the water is fresh water, and only 1 percent of that water is drinkable. Minerals in water can interact with other nutrients in our diet to nourish, hydrate and cleanse the cells in the human body. Our bodily functions are dependent on water. It is a known fact that a human being can exist without food for several weeks, but just a few days without water. Spa towns that boast of geothermal hot spring aquifers have since ancient times stored and sold water in gourds, recipients, and bottles.

The uncanny story of the Earth's water is scientific with the narrative that traces its arrival on our planet billions of years ago, when meteorites and other water-rich objects or planetesimals landed on the Earth's surface. While climate scientists debate on whether the formation of water stems from the Earth's volatile contents in its core or deep mantle, others set forth the idea of the storage of hydrogen and the resultant giant impacts that dominated the final stage of Earth's formation.[10] Individual water molecules that have been recycled through the Earth's natural systems and that are available to us in liquid form, is the water that has been recycled from time immemorial through our carbon civilization, via the atmosphere, and even through our bodies, and is thus entangled in our very being and existence.

WATER, THE SOCIAL LEVELER

In the era of the Anthropocene, water is a rare and precious commodity, as this life-giving resource has often been taken for granted. The idea that a tap is turned, and the water flows seems basic to our present-day existence in the twenty-first century. But a scenario typical of Day Zero is one with the "countervailing image—that the tap is turned, and nothing happens" thus conveying "the perilous and unpredictable nature of the new era into which society has entered."[11] In the scenario of Day Zero, both rich and poor find themselves in the same dire need for water. Non-existent water cannot be purchased by the super-rich placing them thus on the same plane as the poor who often walk miles to fetch a pot or a jerrycan of potable water in poorer countries.

In 2004, the Peruvian state-run water company, Sedapal, in Lima announced its decision to ration water to the capital city by stopping water supply for twelve hours at night. Lima's water levels in the high-altitude reservoirs at Huamantanga had fallen to 165 million cubic meters, 120 million less than in a normal year.[12] Lima relies on three rivers born in the mountain ranges of the Andes. Like the residents of Lima who depend on mountain water sources, it is estimated that by 2050, around 1.5 million people on the planet will be dependent on water from rivers that have their sources in the mountains, two hundred million more than in the 1960s.[13] The water crisis awoke the need to renovate the water infrastructure in Lima, modernize the water sector, manage persistent problems of discriminatory distribution of water to low-income groups, and face the risks of future water shortages.

On August 29, 2017, Rome faced severe drought and consequent water stress when the city's municipal water company, ACEA, decided to cut water supply during the night on peak-hot days in September. High-rise buildings were even deprived of their water supply altogether. The company plugged

1,300 water leaks and turned off one hundred fountains. The dispute over water extraction from Lake Bracciano, situated to the north of Rome, that provides the city with 8 percent of its water needs had to be resolved as the lake faced severe depletion.[14] ACEA was eventually granted access to continue using the lake on condition it cut its withdrawals from 1,100 to 400 liters per second. Poor rainfall and an old water transport system known for its leaks were identified as the cause for the shortage leading to a severe downturn in the tourism and recreation sector. The vulnerability of water resources is one that affected the whole nation irrespective of their social strata. The country continues to face water stress. Increasing drought, water scarcity, rationing of water, depleting of its resources has resulted in Prime Minister Giorgia Meloni announcing a "national water plan"[15] of seven to eight billion euros to improve infrastructures with new technologies and raise public awareness on the need to save water.

On December 7, 2017, the Bloomberg Business Report ran the headline "Will Cape Town Run Out of Water"? in the face of severe water crisis.[16] Cape Town Mayor Patricia de Lille warned the city of the rapidly decreasing water levels in the dams that supplied South Africa's second-biggest city, and on how much water its four million residents consumed daily. She predicted the possibility of "Day Zero," the day when most taps would run dry in May 2017, a couple of months before the expected onset of the winter rains. It was a water catastrophe that stirred anarchy, a scenario with city residents battling over the scarce life-dependent resource, local warlords laying their claim over water and gang leaders even controlling waterpoints extorting money from city residents.[17]

On June 19, 2019, Chennai, my home city in India, faced its Day Zero when citizens awoke to find that there was almost no more water left in the city's reservoirs. With climate change rainfall has been inadequate with groundwater levels plummeting to rock bottom. The city's ten million inhabitants drew water from their wells for their daily water consumption, and thus unwittingly depleted their groundwater resources. According to the World Resources Institute (WRI)'s Aqueduct Water Risk Atlas, 80 percent of the available water supply in Chennai is used up every year by agriculture, industries, and consumers.[18] Chennai, situated in the south-east coast of the Indian peninsula is dependent on the northeast monsoon (mid-October to mid-December) for its groundwater resources. The Chennai Metro Water Supply and Sewerage Board (CMWSSB) has a mammoth task of collecting water from the city's unpolluted lake sources, namely the lakes of Poondi, Redhills, Cholavaram, Chembarambakkam and Veeranam, whose surface water sources are situated around two hundred kilometers from Chennai city. In times of water scarcity, the city is reliant on its neighboring state, Andhra Pradesh. The Telugu Ganga project enabled water from Krishna River in the

Srisailam reservoir situated four hundred kilometers away to be diverted to the Poondi reservoir in Chennai on Day Zero. The Chennai water crisis made people question governmental reliance on vagarious monsoons.

On March 22, 2023, World Water Day, the United Nations warned nations around the globe of the looming water crisis. It is estimated that among the 7.7 billion people who have inherited the Earth, almost two billion inhabitants are struggling to survive without clean drinking water. It predicted that by 2025, 1.8 billion people, both rich and poor will be living in water stress regions.[19] The World Economic Forum's Global Risk Report of 2023 estimates that the gap between water demand and supply will be 40 percent by 2030, with a dramatic and unequal increase in demand between countries.[20] According to the WHO/UNICEF Joint Monitoring Program Report, one in four people or two billion people around the world lack safe drinking water; in 2020, only 74 percent of the global population had access to safely managed drinking water services.[21] The WRI's Aqueduct tools show that seventeen countries home to one-quarter of the world's population have to deal with extremely high levels of baseline water stress, where irrigated agriculture, industries and municipalities utilize more than 80 percent of their available water supply on average every year; forty-four countries, home to one-third of the world, face high levels of stress, where on average more than 40 percent of available supply is withdrawn every year.[22] Water will engender mass migrations with people searching for greener pastures and life-giving water. Both developed and developing countries will feel proportionately the impact of water stress. Our changing climate, pollution and poor infrastructures are the reasons for water being in peril, equalizing all and affecting people of every class and rank in all nations.

WATER BREWS WARS

Disputes around shared waters of lakes and rivers have resulted in water wars and clashes between communities and countries that depend on them. Civilization that sprang from the fertile crescent of the Tigris and Euphrates in ancient times, find mention in the Old Testament as the biblical cities of Babylon, Uruk, and Nimrud. Historical ruins of these civilizations are scattered today in the modern cities of Syria, Iraq, and Turkey that are constantly under strife in the Middle East with these same rivers being at the center of the geopolitical dispute. The Tigris and the Euphrates take their sources in the mountains of eastern Turkey, meander their way through the plains of Turkey and Syria, before converging at the Iraqi city of Al-Qurnah as the Shatt al-Arab basin in the vicinity of the Persian Gulf. Since the 1960s, these countries that share the Tigris-Euphrates basin, have engaged in unilateral irrigation projects and in the building of dams that have altered the rivers' course. Fertile silt riverbanks that once rendered farming profitable, are now the lieu of water wars. Populated by diverse peoples, including Turks, Kurds and Arabs, this spectacular wetland of 35,000 km^2 supports the livelihoods of around sixty million people and wildlife who need life-giving water for survival.[23] Various water disputes have ensued from hydro-electric projects like the dispute over the Turkish Keban dam and the Syrian Taqba dam during periods of drought; water tensions created during the Cold War, when Turkey aligned with the NATO, whilst Syria and Iraq decided to foster close ties with the USSR.[24] In 1987, water was the element under contention in signed agreements when Turkey agreed to release 500 cubic meters per second of water to Syria, whilst the latter committed to put an end to its support for the PKK, the Kurdistan Workers' Party.[25] In 1997, Turkey's refusal to sign the United Nations Water Convention (1997), further escalated the conflict and revealed how Turkey, as an upstream state, could deprive lower co-riparians of water.

The construction of the Grand Ethiopian Renaissance Dam (GERD), a non-consumptive hydropower project, being built by Ethiopia on the Nile, has led to geopolitical unrest in the Nile delta region. While Ethiopia frames the need for this project as an "existential necessity"; Egypt contends that the project is an "existential threat" to Egyptian and regional water security.[26] The Nile, the cradle of Egyptian civilization, is considered as a living being by Egyptians inextricably linked to the country's civilizational identity. Since the inception of this project in 2011, conflict has escalated as Ethiopia has diverted the river to construct the GERD, with the United Nations Security Council being solicited to intervene and resolve the geopolitical dispute.[27] Ethiopia, on the other hand, considers the building of the dam as a project to unite the Ethiopian poor population under a socially constructed "new Ethiopia-ness" with the GERD at the center.[28] Water is the resource that is much coveted by dueling countries to Africanize and Arabize the Nile.

The River Brahmaputra, Asia's trans-boundary river that has its source in the Himalayas, begins its course in Yarlung Tsangpo in China, and flows through basins in India, Bangladesh, and Bhutan. Named after Lord Brahma in Hindu mythology, it is the only Indian male river, named after the son of Lord Brahma, unlike other river bodies in India which are named after female mythological goddesses. The mighty Brahmaputra gains its force from its trans-boundary location as it affects geopolitics in Tibet, northeastern India, and Bangladesh. Its name changes during its course, namely, the Yarlung Tsangpo in Tibet, the Brahmaputra in India, and the Jamuna in Bangladesh. As the upper riparian, China wields considerable advantage over India, the lower riverbank. Despite the hydrological, data-sharing Memorandums of Understanding (MoUs) signed by India and China in 2018,[29] by the Indian Prime Minister Narendra Modi and the Chinese President Xi Jinping regarding the use of hydrological data, in November 2020; China announced plans of building a "super hydropower dam" in Tibet.[30] The strained relationship between the two countries have stirred fears of Sino-Indian water wars as the dam building has resulted in China blocking the course of the Galwan River into the Ladakh region of the Indian sub-continent. While India accuses China of weaponizing water and using the resource to gain geopolitical and strategic leverage over India; China maintains that there is no water-sharing agreement nor a joint river commission for managing their shared river resources. Border armed troupes stationed by both countries in the frontiers are proof of how the *status quo* could change at any time leading to armed conflict over water between China and India.

The River Indus that gives its name to India, has its origin in the Mansoravar Lake in Tibet, before traversing Pakistan and flowing through the Indian Plains with its five tributaries, namely Jhelum, Chenab, Ravi, Beas, and Sutlej, that water Punjab or the land of five rivers. Unlike India's river sharing with its other major co-riparians in the region, Bangladesh and Nepal, this river source is subject to a comprehensive treaty, namely the 1960 Indus Waters Treaty (IWT). The IWT granted India sole ownership of the waters of the three eastern rivers, Ravi, Beas, Sutlej, whereas Pakistan acquired complete use of the waters of the three Western rivers, Chenab, Jhelum, Indus. This water dispute on the geo-physical partition of the river system has added to the animosity between the two countries. Both river sharing countries consider that the IWT offers meagre support to the integrated or joint development of the Indus River basin. Both countries voice disaccord over the terms of the IWT signed in 1960, contending that the treaty favors one side over the other. On the one hand, Pakistan contends that it gave up more water than it gained, resulting in it suffering heavy ecological penalties coupled with the futile task of guarding its water resources against Indian poaching. India, on the other hand, argues that it gave up too much water in the 1960 treaty, and that Pakistan had rendered all its attempts at generating hydropower impossible on the western rivers. Diplomatic wrangling between the two countries over the Baglihar dam in Jammu and Kashmir has resulted in the countries approaching the International Court of Justice at the Hague. In *Islamic Republic of Pakistan v. Republic of India* (2023),[31] the Court of Arbitration at The Hague, held a first meeting in the proceedings commenced by the Islamic Republic of Pakistan against the Republic of India. At the Peace Palace, the headquarters of the Permanent Court of Arbitration (the "PCA") in The Hague, Pakistan accused India of violating rules in new dam building projects, which it contended would dry up its irrigation land. India was absent at this first meeting, and declined to participate on the grounds that the Court of Arbitration was not the competent forum to consider the questions put to it, which it argued should be decided instead by a neutral expert, or through an alternative process as stipulated under Article IX and Annexure G of the Indus Waters Treaty (1960). A second hearing was held on May 13, 2023, to decide on The Hague's competence to proceed in this arbitration and the case is still pending.

According to the UNICEF's report on water crisis in Afghanistan in 2022,[32] the country falls under the category of an extremely highly vulnerable water region, where eight out of every ten Afghan people and 93 percent of children (15.6 million) drink unsafe water. It predicts an impending collapse of the WASH (water, sanitation, and hygiene sector) that threatens children's health, development, and survival. Due to severe drought, political upheaval, economic collapse, pandemics, and multiple diseases outbreaks, it estimated that at the end of 2021, 4.3 million Afghans had migrated to greener pastures, being thus labelled as internally displaced persons (IDPs).[33] "Bone-dry Afghanistan" is on the brink of future famines without the life-sustaining element of water.[34] The transboundary water dispute between Afghanistan and Iran is a long-standing dispute over the sharing of water from the Helmand River. As Afghanistan's longest river, the Helmand has its source near Kabul in the western Hindu Kush Mountain range and takes a 1,150-kilometer trajectory through arid desert areas before emptying into Lake Hamun, which straddles the Afghanistan-Iran border. Lake Hamun, the largest freshwater lake in Iran, has in recent times dried up due to acute drought and threatens to engulf the regions with its exposed silt during dust storms.[35] It used to be one of the world's largest wetlands, straddling four thousand square kilometers between Iran and Afghanistan but is now suffering from water stress tensions. The Helmand River Treaty (1973) signed by the two countries to regulate the allocation of river water was neither ratified nor fully implemented, causing further discord. While the Iranian government voices disagreement regarding Afghanistan's agricultural expansion, dam construction activities and projects that threaten water security in its eastern and northeastern provinces; Afghanistan on the contrary, has expressed reluctance to engage in water negotiations by rejecting Iran's accusations and blaming climate change phenomena like the shortage of rainfall for the dry riverbed.[36]

The Mekong, the longest river in southeast Asia has its source on the Tibetan Plateau in China, irrigates Myanmar, Lao, Thailand, Cambodia, and Vietnam before emptying into the South China sea. It serves as the hydrologic bone supporting the livelihood of around seventy million people in five countries. Its much-coveted waters have been the bone of contention of these riparian states causing regional tensions due to disputes over dam constructions. The Lancang dam has stirred criticism among the lower riparian states who argue that these dams have generated water shortages, flow alterations, devastated fisheries, and river habitat.[37][38] The Mekong River Commission aims to coordinate sustainable management of water and related resources for the mutual benefits of the five Mekong countries and aims to resolve water wars.[39]

In a time when water waters are brewing, water consortiums have been created. In 2018, the Water, Peace and Security (WPS) Partnership which is a collaboration between the Netherlands Ministry of Foreign Affairs and a consortium of six partners—IHE Delft (lead partner), Wetlands International and International Alert, Deltares, World Resources Institute, The Hague Centre for Strategic Studies—was set up to develop innovative tools that identify and address water-related security risks.[40] As the growing water crisis looms as a formidable threat to livelihoods, ecosystems, and security, the WPS is striving to develop innovative tools and services that can help local stakeholders identify, understand, and address water-related security risks by using cutting-edge technology to increase awareness and understanding. In regions prone to water-related conflict, like Mali, Iraq, India, Pakistan, Ethiopia, Kenya, the WPS works to enhance collaboration among stakeholders, and to turn threats into opportunities for peacebuilding. With water-related competition escalating in scale due to the need for the ever-vital, civilization-supportive resource, the time has come to acknowledge the fact that the existence, sustenance, and protection of water as a resource lies in the hands of individuals, activists, legislators, and judges.

POLYPHONY IN HAIKU POETRY, THE HALF-SAID THING

Haiku, the terse, succinct, poetic artform that emerged in the seventeenth century to replace long, complex and elaborate poetic tradition in Japan was originally from *renga* or linked-verse poetry called *haikai* or *hokku*. The single *hokku* (haiku) and the longer sequences of *haikai* are polyphonic as the stanzas by haiku poets are not by one poet but by different haiku masters who added haiku verses to older or contemporary poetic endeavor of their time. The form of haiku is one that seeks to "unveil the richly layered possibilities that are embedded in the lines of these poems, . . . (as) several semantic layers are simultaneously possible and . . . each contributes to the overall expression of the poem. It is in this sense *haikai* is regarded as polyphonic."[41] The linked verse structure of *renga* sets the tone of the three-line stanza consisting of seventeen syllables. The haiku in its 5-7-5 syllable pattern contains a reference to a season, time-setting of the day, and a description of the landscape. This renders a haiku readable both independently and in polyphonic sequence. Japanese haiku poets took turns adding their voice by adopting a verse structure that was either seventeen-syllable-long verses with the rhythmical structure of 5-7-5 beats, or fourteen-syllable-double-line shorter verses with a structure of 7–7 beats. In this poetical game of the seventeenth century, voices of different haiku master were involved in the witty repartee. They crafted absurd puns on refined classical themes, highlighted the traditional limitations of the classical Japanese tradition, configured day-to-day events, and even reconfigured conventional themes by setting them in comic and vulgar situations. Haiku as a stimulant of creativity gained its present-day form from Matsuo Basho (1644–1694), who endowed it with "the traits of openness and inclusiveness."[42] The second haiku master Yosa Buson (1715–1783) placed the haiku in its polyphonic form capturing imagination from different points of view, rendering the penning of haikus as an act of empathy.

In "Thinner and Thinner," five nature-haiku stanzas figure in the *renga*, with linked verse from five haiku poets, namely, Kito, Chikugo, Buson, Banan, and Shuhitsu. Jonsson Herbert in his study of Japanese *haikai* poetry comments on the status of each one of the poets. While Kito, Chikugo, Buson and Banan are well-known haiku, contemporary masters of the eighteenth century, the last name Shuhitsu is that of the anonymous scribe, a younger poet who possessed the required awareness of the rules and conventions of the genre, and who was in the process of learning the art of haiku.[43] In his role as scribe, he recorded the verses in writing and recited them as in the oral Japanese tradition, thus enabling the poets to both visualize and listen to their poetic composition. It is interesting to see the alternating pattern of 5-7-5 and 7–7 syllables in the polyphonic haikus. A haiku generally has a *kigo* or seasonal word, *kidai* or seasonal topic and *kireji*, or cutting words that play a decisive role in its composition. The seasonal word or *kigo* of the winter season in Kito's stanza, is notably absent in the ensuing stanzas by Chikugo and Buson. Banan's *kigo* of cherries at springtime is echoed by the presence of spring herbs of honewort and speedwell. The *kidai* or seasonal topic of a passage of time creates the mood of the polyphonic haiku. Each stanza of the polyphonic haiku ensemble has commas as cutting words to offset the sequence of thought and fine movement in the structure of the verse.

Following the trend of great haiku masters, Indian poet Sudeep Sen,[44] has adopted the challenging form of the haiku to include other narrative voices that are scientific, artistic, lyrical, and photographic, to focus on the challenges faced by our time. His ecocritical haiku seeks to portray the present-day, human, climate change struggle with "pollution and co-morbidities; the sharp rise and fall in atmospheric pressures, unusual heat spikes; unseasonal rain and hailstorm; invading oceans swallowing up coastlines around the world; floods; cyclones, devastation; illnesses—physical and psychological."[45] In a haiku entitled "Climate Change 2,"[46] Sen through a typical summer landscape, shifts from visual to auditory impressions to draw attention to the climatic alterations of our time.

climate change
            the terrible beauty of
unbearable heat[47]

Sen's haiku on climate change devoid of punctuation and upper-case letters shows his inclination to exercise poetic license and liberties with the traditional form. He however configures a *kigo* or seasonal word of the unbearable heat of Delhi's summer days. The oxymoron of 'terrible beauty' expresses the *kidai or* seasonal topic of climate change. The sun is absent but remains the star at the center of the universe, performing its usual role of lighting up and warming the planet. In this *shasei* or sketch of nature, Sen as a painter depicts through both visual and tactile metaphors of the effect of the sun's scorching rays on the Earth in the period of the Anthropocene. The haiku gains its energy from the intuitive or emotional leap that occurs in the space between the poem's two parts, in the gap of what's deliberately left out, as in the absence of the protagonist, the Sun.

In *Anthropocene: Climate Change, Contagion, Consolation*, Sen's haikus are also polyphonic-structured verses. They do not gain their polyphony of structure through an addition of stanzas of other poets. The polyphony stems from the poems' nods to other works that are indicated next to the title of his haiku poems. In a six-stanza haiku entitled "Rising Sea Level" that bears a reference to the poem "The Idea of Order at Key West"[48] by Wallace Stevens,[49] Sen draws inspiration from the poetics of sky and sea. Like Stevens who portrayed the dissonance between perception and reality and the need to find order through the juxtaposition of the sounds of the ocean and the human song; Sen's haiku rekindles the memory of a sea that once beckoned both humans and birds to its shores.

RISING SEA LEVELS
The ever-hooded, tragic-gestured sea.

—Wallace Stevens

Granite outcrop
            that once jutted out
of the ebullient sea—

fifty metres
            from the shore—
is seen no more.

The lighthouse—
            our beacon,
an adventure island.

We'd swim to its base—
          shells, mussels,
striated oval stones,

seagull eggs nested
          on slippery
kelp-laced rocks.

As children, reality—
          as adults,
a submerged memory.[50]

Sen's final 5-7-5 stanza highlights the difference between a former reality and a present memory. The seasonal *kigos* are of summertime when seagulls nested, and children swam in the warm waters. The seasonal moment or *kidai* is set in the childhood past. Sen casts the sea as an ever-trespassing being which has stealthily engulfed fifty meters of shoreland, resulting in the disappearance of granite outcrop. The absent words are 'cliff' in the first stanza and 'shore' in the second one, which serve to highlight their present non-existence in the haiku's poetic space. Shells, mussels, seagulls of yesteryears that lived on beautiful stratified and lace-edged rocks are part of the *shasei*, the poetic photoshop that has been erased from sight but remain in memory that is submerged and have been rekindled by Sen, the haiku master. The polyphony emerges from Sen's reference to Steven Wallace's voice on "the ever-hooded tragic-gestured sea"[51] that is visible to the adult eye but seem inexistant to a child's perception of the world. Five stanzas have longer 'em' dashes to highlight the cutting edges of *kireji* and the jolt of discovering the receding coastline. The art of haiku lies in creating exactly that gap, in leaving something out, and in dwelling in the cut that divides the haiku into its two energizing parts of the 'said' and the 'unsaid.' The sea mentioned only in the title of the haiku, acts as a simple agent of nature performing what it usually does, washing over the shores. But the unsaid tragedy of climate change catastrophe is evident in how Sen captures the essence of a moment in time, and it is up to the reader to identify the extraordinary in the ordinary. Sen's haiku thus gains its force of being the 'half-said thing.'

Sen's haiku entitled "Climate Change"[52] may also be viewed as mounted diptych frames to contrast the events of 'yesterday' and 'today.'[53] This gives the haiku the book frame, double-page view, and hinge-like plate structure attached together or adjoining each other. This double frame is typical of the eighteenth-century Japanese-wooden sundial that traced the arrival of the seasons through the sun's circular trajectory across the galaxy. The juxtaposition of two timeframes of 'yesterday' and 'today' permit the dual viewing and listening to layered voices. The polyphonic haiku diptych as in table 4.1 permits the inclusion of voices that are meteorologic as Sen endeavours to remember and record the changing seasons and climate change phenomena for readers in the present and in the future.

The stanzas show the conventional haiku-development of a typical landscape in Delhi, in the month of February, a *kigo* of the spring season, where the sequence though the same, has a different *kidai* when the seasonal moment has changed. Instead of the sun's warming rays in the yesterday stanzas of the haiku poem, the city witnesses unpredicted rain and even snowfall. While the haiku of 'yesterday' depicts a time when people peeled off layers of clothing and stacked them into cupboards with mothballs for the next winter; in the haiku of 'today,' winter clothes damp from the unforeseen rain are filled with metaphors of awkward climate change. The shift from visual to auditory impressions as in the cracking of freshly roasted peanuts to sharp-cold winds, as well as the shift from a refined appreciation of the beauty of spring to the strange, cold season serve to highlight the starkness of climate change. The *kireji* cutting words of dashes, commas, and periods are

Table 4.1: CLIMATE CHANGE

1. YESTERDAY	*2. TODAY*
Winter is fading— Delhi's February sun slow-warming the air.	Today, there is unexpected rain here— unseasonal snow
Time to peel off the extra woollen layer. Time to shell again	amid chill-sharp wind in the northern hills. The winter clothes
freshly roasted peanuts— fingers cracking open their uneven bark-skin.	I had washed and hung out to dry, are now wet and damp again.
After the season's severe cold, we prepare for spring and summer,	Dogs are coiled around each other, birds' feathers
airing out duvets before storing them until next year—	puffed up for warmth, squirrels gone back into hiding—
rolled up in cupboard's mothball company. Yesterday—was brief.	as we stare starkly at the climate change we've helped create.

Source: Sen, Sudeep. *Anthropocene: Climate Change, Contagion, Consolation*, 32–33.

reflective of aposiopesis where sentences are purposely left incomplete to lay stress on the mood of the stanzas. They create a shift from the auditory and visual impressions to tactile sensations of a change of weather where dogs lie coiled together for warmth, birds puff up their feathers, and squirrels retreat to hibernate and await better times. The themes of 'yesterday' and 'today' serve to capture the essence of a moment in time experienced by a collective 'we.' The polyphony emerges from the use of the second person plural, where Sen, the agent of the poem, includes the reader in his haiku to engage in a polyphonic admission of regret, "as we starkly stare at the climate change, we've helped create."[54]

In the prologue of his work *Anthropocene: Climate Change, Contagion, Consolation,* Sudeep Sen quotes Japanese film maker and artist, Akira Kurosawa: "The Role of the Artist is Not to Look Away."[55] In "Undercurrents: 20 Lake Haiku"[56] dedicated to Janet Pierce,[57] Sen undertakes a poetic-artistic exercise of capturing and imagining the Annaghmakerrig Lake from the point of view of the observer. By framing a twenty-stanza-haiku poem, Sen invites the reader to engage in an act of empathy, to consider a caring relationship with nature, to stir further ecocritical thinking and not to look away. Sen captures three timeframes of the passing seasons in this haiku poem. This haiku may be viewed as a triptych of three carved panels or Japanese room partitions, where each folding screen depicts a different season.[58] This three-frame scenario facilitates the interaction between the viewer and the reader by studying the impact of climate change on the Annaghmakerrig Lake in County Monaghan, Ireland. Here the polyphonic structure of the Haiku emerges from the collaboration between Sen and the painter Janet Pierce. Peirce displayed her collection of paintings of the lake called Uisce Anam[59] with haikus as captions in each painting. Sen's haiku poem in table 4.2, "Undercurrents: 20 Lake Haiku" is subtitled "for Janet Pierce."

The highlighting of the ordinary enables an emphasis on the present moment, a moment in time where the element of water is given centre stage. The reader is drawn into the setting of the poem as it stirs feelings of empathy and the ability to identify the connection to nature. In this haiku dedicated to Janet Pierce, the reader is intrigued by the reference to the addendum in italics 'Annaghmakerrig, Ireland.' The reader-surfer navigates the web to discover artist Jane Pierce's exquisite collection of watercolors titled *Uisce Anam* (Give Me Water), painted during a three-year period in response to her daily swim in the waters near her home Annaghmakerrig Lake, Country Monaghan in Ireland. Pierce, the painter-diver is the lone swimmer, and her discovery of the lake is seen through the liquid, pure state of water. The haiku's unsaid message is one of establishing a caring relationship with nature and keeping it in its pure crystalline state. Sen's haiku is a *shase*i or a sketch of nature where

Table 4.2: UNDERCURRENTS: 20 LAKE HAIKU

for Janet Pierce

1.	2.	3.
water's mirrored sheen— swans skate, gliding on its skin— marine undertow	the dark waters, suck me in their undercurrent— the ship is sinking—	blue and green merge—still waters calling cormorants'— pure white, refraction—
boat-house wood walls creak— barque, oars, rowers—now absent— memories, slow-leak	volcanic rumblings destabilize my moorings— the Earth is shifting	freezing waters thaw an artist's skin—epsom salt hot-baths purifies—
clouds lie on water, photo-perfect and stone still— a transient frame	lake's pristine waters infected by human greed— pollution of soul	clear sky, rain, slurry— lake's blue, trees' reflected greens— soulmate's oxygen—
fish come up for air glimpsing skyscape, a moment— refracted vision	whispered murmurings eavesdrop, plot, hatch, weave—churning carefully—back-stabbed	blue-greens change slowly— orange, brown, yellow, light up— autumn colours bloom—
fall-leaves coat the lake water soaking elements— demersal debris	despite lake's leaden waters, irony's missing— misplaced, forked values	geese squeak, cormorants dive, fish summersault over— invisible waves—
a shallow swimmer— skin and water burning fat— fluid aerobics	lake's blue-black ink runs deep, piercing sinews— leaving scars, unseen	gentle breeze wavers— uneven reeds circumscribe lake's surface tension—
ice-cold swim—healing— water's conductive powers— sinews assuaged		a lone swimmer dives into the pristine sheet of water—liquid graph

Annaghmakerrig, Ireland

Figure 4.2. Lake Haiku. *Source*: Lake Haiku © Sudeep Sen.

emphasis is on the changing seasons and the color hues that change the water hues of the lake. Through the prosodic seventeen-syllable stanzas with their five-seven-five pattern, each panel has a *kigo* or seasonal word, an intermediate seasonal moment of *kidai* that eludes stamped recognition as four seasons are set on three panels: autumn/winter; no season; spring/summer; and *kirejis* or cutting words. As it is impossible to depict an actual scene in full, Sen uses these abbreviations as necessary tools to get the reader into the stream of awareness and thought. Traditionally, Japanese calligraphy or *tategaki* is set in vertical columns and the blocks are read from top to bottom and from right to left. The triptych, "Undercurrents: 20 Lake Haiku" can be read in the western style of reading from left to right, as well as in the Japanese style of appraisal from right to left. The order of reading is not upset as the mid-panel has no season attached to it. The play of seasons and the passage of time are reflected on the colors of the lake's waters. The unsaid message of climate change is voiced through liquid, glacial, pure, and impure metaphors of the element 'water.' Another interesting configuration of the haiku is seen in the index of *Anthropocene: Climate Change, Contagion, Consolation*. Instead of indexing the title of the poem, here the beginning lines of each stanza, line numbers, and page numbers figure to highlight the seasonal word or '*kigo*' through the changing sounds of nature, shades and tones of seasons and the diver's perception of Lake Haiku.

In this polyphonic index, the typeset is one that awakens auditive senses through the creaking of wood walls; water ripples as fish swim up for air and swimmers float or dive into the lake's waters; falling leaves crack gently announcing the advent of autumn; the sound of pouring rain and volcanic rumbling spell the passage of seasons; birds like cormorants and geese squeak and signal the arrival of spring. The seasons are visible on the lake's waters as the changing cumulus gets reflected on its surface. The mid-panel which eludes any reference to a particular season is one that highlights the changed temporality of our time where human presence has contributed to the irreversible damage of our biosphere. The absence of *kiregi* or cutting words serves to highlight the indeterminate timespan when the lake's blue-black and even black waters fall victim to human greed. The diver's discovery of the lake is seen through a kaleidoscopic changing of colors that vary with the seasons. In this auditive lamentation, the rumbling emerges from the lake's deep depth, but the human voices are in undecipherable murmurs and whispers, as humans eavesdrop, hatch plots and weave conspiracies against a voiceless Earth. The polyphony creates an interplay with voices from nature that is never clearly stated but retains a certain mystery of what is always hinted at.[61] Sen's haiku teases and prompts the alert reader to recognize the visual, auditory, and tactile references to nature's quite call during the ever-changing tapestry of seasons. As in the Japanese haiku, Sen adopts the style of simultaneously combining several parts, each forming an individual melody and harmonizing with each other. His style of using the Japanese poetic artifice is a form of postcolonial resistance, a mode of creating hybrid language forms that thrive on the liberty of expression, and a manifestation for the need for restorative environmental justice.

ACTIVISM FOR THE GREATER COMMON GOOD

Baba Amte,[62] an activist, lawyer, and social worker, inspired by the Gandhian way of life fought for many causes[63] including the *Narmada Bachao Andolan* (NBA) or Save the Narmada Movement lead by Medha Patkar.[64] While Amte fought for the rights of the *Gonds* in Gadchiroli in the Indian state of Maharashtra; Patkar works relentlessly to represent the rights of *Bhil*, *Bhilala*, *Pavra*, *Tadvi*, and *Vassawa* ethnic groups inhabiting the boundaries between the three states of Gujarat, Madhya Pradesh, and Maharashtra. Amte and Patkar revealed to the world how these tribal folk have been exploited. These people collected dry fruits and other non-timber forest produce for businessmen and traders from the nearby towns, who in turn offered them a pittance in exchange. After initially organizing protest marches to voice indignation regarding the Gujarat government in 1985–1986, activist Medha Patkar created the organization Narmada Dharangrastra Samiti, which in 1989 became the *Narmada Bachao Andolan* (NBA). The NBA provides project information and legal representation to the concerned hill folk and peasants of the Narmada valley.

The movement launched in 1985 voices dissent against the disastrous Narmada Valley Dam projects that threaten to displace about a million indigenous people, from their homes and habitats. While the public discourse in favor of dams stresses the need for large-scale industrialization to provide water; the activist voice advocates the need to support small-scale, democratically oriented projects that consider the needs of the voiceless. On August 9, 2015, *Adivasi* or Tribal Rights Day, Medha Patkar, organized the Jeevan Adhikar-Sanghrash *Yatra*, when the Narmada valley echoed with the slogan "Modi-Shivraj Go Back."[65] The slogan coincided with the Quit India Day[66] against the British Raj. The *yatris* or peace march protesters contended that the prime minster Narendra Modi and the chief minister Shivraj Singh Chouhan had gone back on their poll promises and constitutional legal obligations. In typical *Ghandian* style, they asked the political duo Modi-Shivraj to step down, go back and quit the Narmada project. The *yatris* asserted the rights of the *Gram Sabhas* or village councils in the scheduled *Adivasi* areas and questioned the State and National governments' decision to submerge 245 villages along the Narmada River. During the Jeevan Adhikar-Sanghrash *Yatra*, Medha Patkar visited hundreds of indigenous settlements and villages to assess their needs, and made a call to preserve India's ancient, river valley civilization, to protect fertile agricultural land, to respect their customs, and to stop dam building in the name of common good. She addressed a petition to the heads of the three branches of government in India, namely, the executive, the legislative and the judiciary on August 30, 2019. She contended that more than thirty-two thousand families were facing an unprecedented existential crisis in the Narmada Valley, and were threatened with displacement from their homes, farms, and villages, without the lawfully guaranteed rehabilitation being provided to them.[67]

In her political essay-manifesto titled "Greater Common Good,"[68] Arundhati Roy[69] defends the *Adivasi* tribal people,[70] who lost their homes and livelihood to the construction of the Sardar Sarovar Dam in the Narmada valley.[71] Roy comments on the role played by activists like Amte and Patkar. She labels the Narmada Valley Project as "India's Greatest Planned Environmental Disaster"[72] and writes of how the NBA tried to save the livelihood of the indigenous tribals.

> Under the banner of the *Narmada Bachao Andolan* (Save the Narmada Movement), they did everything that was humanly and legally possible under the Indian Constitution to stop the dams. They were beaten, jailed, abused and called "anti-national" foreign agents who wanted to sabotage India's "development." They fought the Sardar Sarovar as it went up, metre by metre, for decades. They went on hunger strike, they went to court, they marched on Delhi, they sat in protest as the rising waters of the reservoir swallowed their fields and entered their homes. Still, they lost. The government reneged on every promise it had made to them. On September 17, 2017, the prime minister of India, Narendra Modi, inaugurated the Sardar Sarovar Dam. It was his birthday present to himself on the day he turned 67.[73]

Through Roy's activist account, the reader discovers in her essays the clear lay of the land of anti-national foreign agents and Indian government officials acting in the so-called pursuit of common good. Activist polyphony surfaces not just from Roy's activist call, but also from the voices of protesters in the nationwide walk and hunger strikes. Voices are heard in the courtroom in court case petitions and arguments. The rising waters of the river are heard in background as it fills man-made reservoirs. False promises find their say in the stance taken by the government. Prime Minister Narendra Modi's birthday celebration is heard along with his inaugural dam speech on September 17, 2017. Roy alerts readers about the looming suppression of the voice of history in the event of the Narmada River submerging fossils and age-old microliths of the Stone Age. The reader's muse is palpable as he wonders if the history of the *Adivasis* is doomed in the name of the greater common good.

In *Capitalism: A Ghost Story*, Roy criticizes the building of dams in the name of common good. She ponders, "How can they stop a dam?"[74] referring to the Kalpasar project, a 30-kilometer dam being built across the sea in the Gulf of Khambhat in Gujarat State. This dam project has ambitious plans of supplying water to Special Investment Regions (SIR) and Special Economic Zone (SEZ) projects that Roy labels as self-governed corporate dystopias of "industrial parks, town-ships and mega-cities."[75] This polyphonic essay's preface is dedicated to the river "Narmada and all the life she sustains."[76] The opening lines—"If you should suffer, you should suffer in the interests of the country"[77]—are a reference to a speech given by India's first Prime Minister Jawaharlal Nehru who described dams as temples of modern India while addressing homeless villagers who had been displaced by the Hirakud dam construction in 1948.[78] India boasts of being the third largest dam builder in the world.[7980] Roy's activist discourse warns us through an ironic enumeration that the building of dams of different sizes and capacities—"Big ones, little ones, tall ones, short ones"[81]—have triggered displacement. She contends that the evacuation of villagers would be inevitable once again with the Kalpasar dam. Her voice aims to "puncture the myth about the inefficient, bumbling, corrupt, but ultimately genial, essentially democratic, Indian state."[82] In the power struggle, she accuses dam builders of resorting to "deceit, lies, false promises and increasingly successful propaganda"[83] to configure a sense of false legitimacy. The activist call clashes with the wielders of power whose discourse is marked by dishonesty, libel, fake assurances that are more powerful than the lone, honest activist voice. She implies that the "Iron Triangle"[84] composed of politicians, bureaucrats, and dams work hand in glove with consultants from developed countries to devise Environmental Impact Assessments (EIAs) that mask and hide the unavailability of water statistics, the destruction of flora and fauna, and the mass exodus of uneducated villagers. Roy accuses the Indian government of violating human rights, depriving the possibility of a normal standard of life to innocent, tribal *advisasi* people as they "stand to lose their homes, their livelihoods, their gods and their histories."[85] She states that this quest for modernity is evident in the creation of the Dholera SIR, the first planned Green Field Smart City of India.[86] She contends that this project will lead to the extinction of rare fish species and is typical of the self-seeking human decision to survive at the expense of wildlife and "exploiting nature while minimizing non-human claims to a shared Earth."[87] Roy mocks the World Bank's use of acronyms as in PAP's or Project Affected Persons arguing that such acronyms only managed to "mutate muscle and blood into cold statistics."[88] Graham Huggan and Helen Tiffin in *Postcolonial Ecocriticism* examine the relationship between humans, animals and the environment in postcolonial literary texts. They hold that human societies need to consider their relationship with non-human species with whom they share the planet. They insist on the need to imagine new ways of creating awareness of these ecologically connected groups. Roy's essay, with its hidden, environmentalist agenda of social and environmental advocacy, is imaginative and serves as "a catalyst for social action and . . . a full-fledged form of engaged cultural critique."[89] With time running out, Roy insists that words can prove to be the best arms to protect India's polluted rivers. Her activist voice reveals "a war between modern, rational, progressive forces of 'Development' versus a sort of neo-Luddite impulse—an irrational, emotional 'Anti-Development' resistance, fueled by an arcadian, pre-industrial dream."[90] Two forces that are at antipodes with each other, each voice contending to act in the name of the greater common good.[91] Her story against dams is a strong one that resists the dynamics of displacement, gives voice to "stories within stories,"[92] and struggles to preserve a whole eco-system of cropping and breeding patterns of humans and animal species.

Activist Vandana Shiva[93] has voiced concerns over the impacts of large-scale hydro-electric plants on the peasants who depend on the land, wildlife who inhabit these areas, and riparian ecology. In "Women and the Vanishing Waters,"[94] she writes of how big dam projects displace people and affect downstream flows. She points an accusing finger at government-planned excavation of limestone in the Doon Valley situated within the Sivalik Hills in the Lower Himalayas, in the state of Uttarakhand in India. Shiva takes the eco-feminist stance of contending that the displacement of people due to the building of dams meant that there was vast deforestation and the disappearance of food and fodder on which tribal women depended on to sustain their families. Her opposition to the building of dams, namely the Tehri Dam in the Garhwal Himalayas, the Koel Karo and Subarnarekha dams in Bihar, and the Inchampalli-Bhopal-Pattanam project in Maharashtra, resulted in projects being stalled. But this opposition was not just from peasants, but also from Brahman landlords whose voices were stronger. Shiva refers to a song by Daya Pawar[95] that is sung by *dalit* women in Maharashtra.

I water the vegetation with drops of my sweat
As dry leaves fall and fill my parched yard.[96]

Tribal *Adivasi* voices sing of the impact of the dam in their daily lives. Their life in the forests is one that feeds the dam's waters. They are forced as bonded laborers to build the dam that will slowly rob them of their homes and sustenance. The absence of grain is due to the dam that has taken over their agricultural land. The search of grain means separating the old husk in the futile hope of gleaning a few morsels. Women with babies hide their infants in baskets to escape the watchful eyes of the dam supervisors. They toil in the hot sun to eke a livelihood. As the dam forms shape, the song intones further despair as the waters flow feeding lucrative sugarcane fields, while the tribal women forage the forests for elusive drops of water. The dry pathway is one watered by their tears and not by rain that evades the barren landscape. In Shiva's documentary *The Seeds of Vandana Shiva*,[97] she has documented her visit to the mountain slopes of Doon Valley, where she met the tribal women of the forests. The women as guardians of the forests reveal that the issue in contention was water. Severe surface mining and scraping of the limestone on the hill slopes had resulted in water scarcity. Rainfall creates giant caves and cavities in the mountains, which are nature's aquifers. Mountain mining had robbed Doon Valleys off its water source with mining waste destroying the stream flows. Shiva conducted a six-month independent study to show how villages were being washed away, and she convinced the government that the limestone left in the mountain contributed more to the economy than the extraction of limestone from the mountain.

THE CASE AGAINST DAMS—STORIES, NON-STORIES, AND METANARRATIVES

The River Narmada, India's fifth largest river, flows through the states of Gujarat, Madhya Pradesh, Maharashtra, and Rajasthan. A multi-purpose dam to provide fresh water and hydroelectricity was started in the wake of India's independence in 1947. Seven projects on the Narmada basin to bridle the waterway and generate electricity were initially considered by the planners. Four projects at Bharuch in Gujarat, Bargi, Tawa, and Punasa in Madhya Pradesh were singled out. Out of these sites, Gora in Gujarat was chosen as it could cater to a full supply level of 161 feet (49.08 meters). The project foundation stone was laid by India's first prime minister, Pandit Jawaharlal Nehru, on April 5, 1961. In 1964, pursuant to the debate regarding the sharing of the Narmada waters, the government of India by applying Section 4 of the Interstate Disputes Act (1965), created the Narmada Control Authority Tribunal to resolve the matter. The first built dams—the Bhakra Nangal dam in Punjab, the Hirakud dam on the Mahanadi in Orissa, and the Nagarjuna

Sagar dam on the Krishna River in Andhra Pradesh—were part of the first five-year plans implemented in India to procure self-sufficiency. Jawaharlal Nehru, India's first Prime Minister, endorsed them as "temples of modern India."[98] The current Sardar Sarovar Project, benefits from World Bank funding to structure the riverbed powerhouse, the main canal, the canal powerhouse, and the irrigation network of the four states. It is interesting to view the consequences of the public litigation dispute launched by NBA in the landmark case *Narmada Bachao Andolan v. Union of India & Others* (2005) that is detailed in table 4.3.[99]

In *Narmada Bachao Andolan v. Union of India & Ors* (2000) water security, dam politics, and freshwater debates are configured as "stories," "non-stories," and "metanarratives."[100] Storylines are configured with a beginning, middle, and end. In this case, the dominant story of a beneficial dam is the one that supports the very need to provide fresh water, generate hydroelectricity, and share the waters and energy equitably among the four sharing states of Gujarat, Madhya Pradesh, Maharashtra, and Rajasthan. Parallel to the dominant story, there are the activist "counter stories,"[101] which also have a beginning, middle, and end but are not dominant. These activist narratives highlight the atrocity of the project that fails to calculate and compare the projected costs and the anticipated benefits. These activist counter arguments show how the hydro-electric project will devastate human lives and biodiversity by destroying thousands of acres of forests and agricultural land, thus depriving them of their livelihood. They highlight how the dam construction in a hilly area, would place the livelihood of forest dwellers at stake; would submerge an area of approximately 37,533 hectares of land in three states: Gujarat, Maharashtra, and Madhya Pradesh, whereby 248 villages would disappear; peasants and hill folk with no formal title to land would have to evacuate and resettle.[102] These counter stories contrast the proponents' contention on the benefits of providing drinking water to forty million people; on producing 1450 megawatts of electricity, and on irrigating 1.8 million hectares of land and on considering the displacement of 180,000 farmers as justified to gain greater common good.[103] The narratives of the opponents lay stress on the fact that the Narmada hydro-electric project would affect biodiversity harmfully, would most likely destroy acres of forests and fertile land, thus depriving thousands of people of their homes and livelihood. These counter narratives serve as "a point-by-point rejoinder to dominant arguments,"[104] signposting what went wrong. Along with the dominant story and counter stories, there exist "non-stories," critiques of the dominant story, which are cited in this case, as in the criticism of the functioning and the actions of the Narmada Control Authority (NCA), the findings of the Khosla committee,[105] and the inspection reports of the World Bank Reconnaissance Mission. Finally, there are metanarratives, which, by comparing and contrasting dominant stories to

Table 4.3: *Narmada Bachao Andolan v. Union of India & Ors* (2005)

IN THE SUPREME COURT OF INDIA
Writ Petition (civil) 328 of 2002
Judgment rendered on March 15, 2005

Bench: B. N. Kirpal, A. S. Anand, S.P. Bharucha

Rule: Article 21 of the Constitution of India, 1950 provides that no person shall be deprived of his life or personal liberty except to a procedure established by law. The right to life includes the right to health, the right to food, and the right to a pollution-free environment.

Facts of the case: The *Narmada Bachao Andolan* (NBA), a non-legislative association that has been in the front line of the resistance to the development of the Sardar Sarovar Dam, filed a writ petition contending that the environmental clearance had been granted for the dam construction without any consideration of the relief and rehabilitation of the tribal groups. They argued that Article 21 of the Constitution on environmental rights and the Indigenous and Tribal Populations Convention (1957) No. 107, that granted tribal communities governmental protection had not been respected. The NBA contended that the environmental clearance had been granted without proper examination and that further submergence would affect the livelihood of tribal and indigenous tribes of India. They contended that the project was not in accordance with the ILO convention no 107.

Issue: Whether the clearance had been granted after proper study and surveys. Whether the conditions imposed by the ministry of the environment had been respected. Whether the Narmada Control Authority had been biased in giving the award.

Reasoning of the court: The court applied the 'Precautionary Principle' reasoning that the issues concerned benefits or possible disasters on the environment were uncertain. It is possible to apply the 'concept of sustainable development' only after the construction of the dam.

Conclusion: The court issued various directions. The court *inter alia* opined in favor of the Union of India that: (i) displacement of the tribal and other persons would not *per se* result in violation of their fundamental or other rights; (ii) on their rehabilitation at new locations they would be better off than where they were; (iii) at the rehabilitation sites they will have more and better amenities than those they enjoyed in their hamlets; and (iv) the gradual assimilation in the mainstream of the society would lead to betterment and progress.

Source: My synopsis of *Narmada Bachao Andolan v. Union of India & Ors* (Supreme Court of India, March 15, 2005).

nonstories and/or counter stories, can lead to the formulation of a different policy agenda with a new approach to law and policymaking.[106] These stories give rise to new metanarratives that influence decision-makers like the issues of water security and environmental and urban water concerns, as they frame laws to present a coherent legislative framework that is amenable to all, yet flexible enough to counter and pre-empt potential opposition. For instance, in Arundhati Roy's essay "The Greater Common Good," she criticizes the 183-page judgment and ironically remarks that it is a "veritable eulogy on the virtues of Dams, which is not based on any evidence produced before the court."[107] She observes that the only dissenting justice, S.P. Bharucha, clearly stated that he was against the construction of the Sardar Sarovar dam. He detailed the reasons in favor of the dam's suspension of construction: "An environmental clearance based on next to no data in regard to the environmental impact of the Project was contrary to the terms of the then policy of the Union of India in regard to environmental clearances, and therefore, no clearance at all."[108] His minority opinion insisted on the need to frame mandatory guidelines as per the Narmada Water Disputes Tribunal requirements regarding the rehabilitation of displaced tribal people before the catchment area treatment. His minority voice was swept aside by the majority opinion of the two concurring justices, B. N. Kirpal and A. S. Anand, who were in favor of the dam's construction and stated that there was no reason to "assume that the authorities will not function properly."[109] Her activist criticism in her non-fiction or non-story does not just weaken the dominant discourse but tends to expose its absurdity in the postcolonial context.

Principle 15 of the Rio Declaration (1992) declares, "Where there are threats of serious or irreversible environmental damage, lack of full scientific certainty should not be used as a reason for postponing measures to prevent environmental degradation."[110] In *Narmada Bachao Andolan v. Union of India and Ors* (2000), the court's application of the Precautionary Principle shows how the Supreme Court of India took the weak stand of estimating that the environmental impacts of dams were neither uncertain, nor catastrophic for the environment. The court failed to consider two key facts highlighted in Justice Barucha's dissenting opinion. He firstly pointed out that at the time of the environmental clearance in 1986, two Union Ministries had voiced doubt regarding the possible environmental damage to the region; and secondly, no environmental impact assessment had been made.[111] Instead of applying the Precautionary Principle,[112] the Supreme Court of India used the principle of Sustainable Development.[113] It opted for a balancing test between the competing interests of social costs and economic development and permitted the construction of the Sardar Sarovar Dam to continue.

LEGAL STANDING OF RIVERS—POLYPHONY OF MYTH, METAPHOR AND AUTHORITY

The trend for assigning legal personality to rivers began in 2008 when Ecuador amended its constitution, whereby *Pachamama* or Mother Earth was recognized as a legal entity.[114] Similarly, in 2009, the Constitution of Bolivia was amended to recognize the rights of Mother Earth, in keeping with the heterogeneous indigenous worldviews present in the Andean region.[115] In

2011, Richard Frederick Wheeler and Eleanor Geer Huddle brought their case before the Provincial Justice Court of Loja[116] in Ecuador requesting a constitutional injunction in favor of the Vilcabamba River. They contended that the Provincial Government of Loja had destroyed the riverbanks by discarding rocks, sand, and gravel by the riverside. The Provincial Court of Loja ruled in favor of the Vilcabamba River, granting a Constitutional Injunction based on the Precautionary Principle, and acknowledged that it was the responsibility of the constitutional judges to protect nature and offer legal tutelage to a river enabling its natural course. The river was granted a legal voice. In the case *New Zealand Māori Council v. Attorney-General* (2013),[117] the Supreme Court of New Zealand granted the same legal rights as a human being to the Whanganui, the third largest river in New Zealand. This long litigation was commenced by the ancestors of the Whanganui River 140 years ago. Hundreds of tribal representatives wept with joy when their bid was successful and resulted in their river kin being awarded legal status as a living entity. In *Colorado River Ecosystem v. State of Colorado* (2017),[118] the claimants who considered themselves as guardians of the Colorado River Ecosystem filed a lawsuit against the State of Colorado. On December 4, 2017, the Federal District Court for the District of Colorado ruled that actions of the State of Colorado violated the river's rights. On February 26, 2019, Ohio voters in the city of Toledo, via a ballot initiative passed the "Lake Erie Bill of Rights" (LEBOR) to protect Lake Erie from pollution. Pursuant to the passage of LEBOR, a lawsuit *Drewes Farms P'ship v. City of Toledo* (2020)[119] was filed by the petitioner, Drewes Farms, an agricultural company. The U.S. District Court ruled in favor of the plaintiffs on the grounds that the LEBOR was unconstitutionally vague and exceeded Toledo's municipal authority. The LEBOR was, however, the first initiative in the United States to enact a law considering the rights of an entire lake ecosystem.[120] It attracted international attention to the new emerging paradigm of 'Rights of Nature' or 'environmental personhood' movements. Pursuant to a writ petition in *Human Rights and Peace for Bangladesh (HPRB) and others v. Secretary of the Ministry of Shipping and others* (2019),[121] the High Court of Bangladesh recognized the River Turag as a living entity with legal rights. It decided to accord the same rights to all Bangladeshi rivers by evoking its *parens patriae* jurisdiction, an old Common Law doctrine that makes the court act according to the best interest of its ward or child. In *Center for Social Justice Studies et al. v. Presidency of the Republic et al.* (2016),[122] Colombia's Constitutional Court declared that the Atrato River basin that had been subject to degradation from mining, possesses rights to protection, conservation, maintenance, and restoration. The court ordered steps to be taken to establish a joint guardianship for the Atrato River basin; and it stipulated that the guardians would be a representative from the national government and a representative of the indigenous people living in the Atrato river basin.[123] In February 2021, the Innu Council of Ekuanitshit and the Minganie Regional County Municipality granted the Magpie River in northeastern Quebec nine legal personhood rights,[124] in keeping with local Innu customs and practices: to flow; to have its ebb and flow cycles respected; to evolve naturally; to maintain its natural biodiversity; to fulfil its essential functions within its ecosystem; to maintain its integrity; to be safe and to be preserved from pollution; to regenerate and be restored; the legal right to sue.

Inspired by the rights regime for environmental protection in other foreign forums, India has begun to extend constitutional protections that are guaranteed primarily to citizens to rivers and water bodies. In two decisions rendered by the state of Uttarakhand namely, *Mohammed Salim v. State of Uttarakhand* (2017) and *Lalit Miglani v. State of Uttarakhand* (2018), presented in table 4.4, the rivers Ganges, the Yamuna, and their tributaries were elevated to the status of living entities with rights analogous to those of human beings, bestowing them rights to protection against harm, as if they were citizens of India.

Miglani, an advocate of the Uttarakhand High Court, submitted a polyphonic brief that drew inspiration from Hindu myths to transform and re-present these stories in his fact statements in the trial. The Ganges in Indian mythology is considered as the crossing point between Heaven and Earth. In Hindu mythology, the creation myth of the Ganges, imagines the river coming into being when Vishnu in his incarnation as a dwarf brahmin took two steps to traverse the universe. While taking his second step, his big toe accidentally creates a big void in the universe from which the holy waters of the river spill onto the Gangotri glacier of the Himalayas. The waters spilling onto the Earth has another mythical catch attached to it as it served to appease King Bhagiratha, whose ancestors had been reduced to ashes by the *vedic* sage Kapila. The king's prayers were answered, as Vishnu's unleashing of the heavenly waters permitted the purifying of the ashes of the dead and enabled them to ascend to heaven. Fearing that the immense water force may submerge the Earth, Shiva lent his help by letting the Ganges descend slowly in his hair into the Himalayan Mountain ranges through a period of thousand years, whereafter it was guided across India by Bhagiratha who split it judiciously into manageable tributaries. Miglani also refers to another sacred river, the Yamuna, which on the night of Krishna's birth, parted to enable his father Vasudeva to carry him to safety. The parting of waters in both Hindu myths, is a metaphor of how rivers need to be shared and partitioned as a resource for all to share. These creation myth stories are among the primary ways of making sense of the world, including the world of law. This understanding of metaphor helps unravel stories in law. Characters can be "entities"

Table 4.4: Lalit Miglani v. State of *Uttarakhand & Others* (2018)

W.P (MD No.140 of 2015)
IN THE HIGH COURT OF UTTARAKHAND AT NAINITAL
Judgment rendered on July 4, 2018

Coram: Alok Singh, Rajiv Sharma

Rule: Under article 21 of the Indian Constitution, the right to a clean healthy environment may be invoked. Pursuant to Article 51-A (g), it is the duty of every citizen of India to protect and improve the natural environment including forests, lakes, rivers, and wildlife and to have compassion for living creatures.

Facts of the case: Lalit Miglani, an advocate at the Uttarakhand High Court filed a public interest litigation petition detailing the deterioration and pollution of the sacred River Ganges and held the central and state governmental authorities responsible for not executing their statutory duties. The petitioner filed a miscellaneous application requesting the court to declare the Himalayas, glaciers, streams, water bodies etc. as legal entities and juristic persons having legal rights like the sacred rivers Ganga and Yamuna.

Under Article 263 of the Constitution of India, the court set up an inter-State Council for all the riparian states of the Ganges to make recommendations for the rejuvenation of the river; setting up sewage treatment plants; and closing polluting industries bordering the river. In a context of general non-compliance of authorities in environmental cases, and in the wake of the 'Rights of Nature' decision in *Mohammed. Salim v. State of Uttarakhand* (2017) that conferred legal personhood on rivers Lalit Miglani in a continuing mandamus pursued an order that would declare the Himalayas, glaciers, water bodies etc. as legal entities as juristic persons on a par with sacred rivers like the Ganges and the Yamuna.

Issue: Is there a constitutional imperative on the State Government and the municipalities to ensure and safeguard proper environment and take adequate measures to protect nature from man-made projects?

Reasoning of the court: It held that all water bodies like glaciers, rivers, lakes and all landforms like meadows, valleys, jungles, wetlands, and grasslands, were legal entities. These natural forms had the right to exist, persist, maintain, sustain, and regenerate their own biosystems. The rivers were not just unrepresented water bodies, but scientifically proved biological living species. Hence, the court reasoned that humans had a constitutional, legal, and moral duty to protect the environment and the ecology.

Conclusion: Even though, it is not the function of the court to oversee the day-to-day enforcement of the law, which is conventionally the duty of the Executive, but in the case of non-compliance or malfunctioning of the enforcement agencies, the courts may intervene and pass orders directing the enforcement agencies to implement the law. The court referred to the doctrine of *parens patriae* and named the Chief Secretary and the Advocate General of Uttarakhand as the *persons in loco parentis* or 'legal parents' of the holy rivers. It implemented the Namami Gange project to clean and rejuvenate the rivers. It directed the officials to protect the status of these biological systems and promote their health and existence.

Note: My synopsis of *Lalit Miglani v. State of Uttarakhand & Others* (High Court of Nainital, Uttarakhand, March 30, 2017).

or "abstract concepts" servings as props in a case "doing something—something that might amount to a plot."[125]

The Yamuna River has its source from the Yamunotri glacier and irrigates three Indian states, namely Uttarakhand, Uttar Pradesh, and Haryana. From its source in the Himalayan Yamunotri glacier, the slowly melting ice descends into the north Indian plains and joins the Ganges in Triveni Sangam. In Hindu mythology, the Yamuna is the daughter of the sun god Surya and the sister of Yama, the god of death. Hindus believe that a dip in the waters of the Yamuna can free them from the fears of death. Miglani draws on this mythical story to narrate the emergency of climate change action in the courtroom. The present-day connection between myth and the present, serve as settings in the courtroom. Miglani contends that as Gangotri and the Yamunotri glaciers are both receding due to pollution as well as climate change, urgent remedial steps are required to be taken to ensure that the receding of these glaciers is stopped. As in all mythical stories, there are different voices in this legal narrative, one of the plaintiff-protagonist who draws on creation myths to preserve the River Ganges, to highlight the pollution caused to it by industrial activity, and to reveal the inadequate situation to resolve the problem. The antagonist is the industrial polluter who exists to manifest progress thanks to industrial permits and licenses. Myth as "an archetype or master story"[126] emerges in the legal narrative as a story that is "simply cultural, soaked up by living in a particular place and time, or . . . may be encoded at birth."[127]

In the backdrop of the *Mohammed Salim v. State of Uttarakhand* (2017) orders, that introduced the concept of personhood of rivers into Indian law, the stage was set for Miglani to submit his miscellaneous, polyphonic application. The application sought for an order declaring "the Himalayas, Glaciers, Streams, Water Bodies, etc. as legal entities as juristic persons at par with pious rivers Ganga and Yamuna."[128] The petitioner pled the plight of not just the river Ganga but voiced the concerns of all forms of natural geographical features all over the country. The court noted that it is unusual for such an application to be entertained after disposal of the main application, but it went on to accept the application in accordance with the principle of "continuous mandamus"[129] for securing the compliance of its judgment passed in a PIL case. The court accepted the polyphonic appeal by acknowledging the presence of local inhabitants living on the banks of rivers and lakes and let their voice be heard in the forum.

However, the decision raises debate on other issues as it does not precisely define the personhood principle, and only vaguely states, "The rights of these legal entities shall be equivalent to the rights of human beings and the injury/harm caused to these bodies shall be treated as harm/injury caused to the human beings."[130] It does not clearly stipulate the compensation, duties, and liabilities. One wonders if rivers can be ordered not to flood or if they can be held liable for flooding. The case sets a precedent for future cases regarding the conferral of personhood. It is important to understand that the mere grant of legal personhood may not be sufficient without the necessary community-based stewardship of humans offering protection to these voiceless natural entities.

The allocation and sharing of water have always been controversial issues since India's independence in 1947 due to various reasons: increasing population, India's irrigation-based agriculture, industrialization, and the consequent need for thermal power. The Constitution of India does not have specific provisions to resolve water disputes. The legislative branch has the power to legislate and implement laws; and these laws are often disputed in courts. Like the Narmada Water Disputes Tribunal, there are other inter-state river water disputes tribunals constituted under Inter-State River Water Disputes (ISRWD) Act (1956), namely the Ravi and Beas Water Tribunal to resolve the dispute between Punjab and Haryana over the Ravi and Beas rivers; the Vansadhara Water Disputes Tribunal to hear the river water sharing wrangle between Odisha and Andhra Pradesh; the Mahadayi Water Disputes Tribunal to adjudicate river water sharing disputes between Karnataka, Goa and Maharashtra; the Mahanadi Water Disputes Tribunal to decide on the sharing of the waters of the Mahanadi between the states of Odisha and Chhattisgarh; and Krishna Water Disputes Tribunal to settle the Krishna river water disputes between Maharashtra, Andhra Pradesh, and Karnataka.[131] The ISRWD Act provides for the adjudication of disputes relating to the sharing of rivers and thermal force, whereby a state government may request the central government to allocate an inter-state river dispute to a Tribunal for adjudication. The *Narmada Bachao Andolan* case refers to another case, *State of Andhra Pradesh v. State of Karnataka* (2022),[132] where the court had ordered the discontinuing of the Krishna River project until the resolution of the water disputes under the provisions of the Inter-State River Water Disputes Act, 1956 and adjudicated nineteen years later in 2022. This shows the slow passage of a case through the judiciary process.

This case also shows how justices rely on constitutional protections like writs of continuing mandamus to safeguard the environment. In Indian Court jurisdiction, it is quite atypical for any application to be reheard after the main petition has been concluded, but in accordance with the principles of continuing mandamus and in larger public interest, it was decided in *Lalit Miglani v. State of Uttarakhand & Others* (2015) to hear the case. By questioning the concept of sustainable development, on whether they enabled development and conservation to be complementary without affecting the other adversely, the court noted that in view of the depleted state of natural resources, it was clear that they were no longer complementary despite the attempts at using Precautionary and Polluter Pays Principles. The court thus decided to allow

Lalit Miglani's writ of continuous mandamus enabling the protection of legal entities or juristic persons to rivers, glaciers, and other natural entities. It showed how an insightful decision extended further protection to other ecosystems and has co-benefits for climate action.

INNOVATIVE BLUE PLANET PROJECTS

Our Earth, the 'Blue Planet' as seen from outer space, owes its name to water as the sun's radiation is absorbed by the oceans and reflected as blue light. Seventy-one percent of the planet is covered by water; 96 percent is held in the oceans; 3 percent is freshwater; 1.2 percent is drinking water; and the rest is either found deep in underground water or is locked up in glaciers, permafrost and ice caps.[133] Clean water activists contend that water scarcity is not just engendered by climate change, but is also due to human error, inadequate planning, insufficient use of the right technologies and failure to react and prevent this truly daunting crisis. Water visionaries and innovators are at work trying to reimagine and reinvent water systems that generate, supply, and clean the water we all depend on for our very lives. They have attempted different ways of facing these water challenges of water scarcity by building resilient infrastructure against climate change, and by making water an affordable commodity that is accessible to all.

In May 2018, Sebastien Tilmans, the civil engineer who founded the Stanford Codiga Resource Recovery Centre, launched a new water treatment plant in Redwood Shores to clean wastewater and produce the biogas methane. He wisely advocates the idea that the concept of waste does not exist in nature. He states, "Every by-product of some natural process is an input for another. All the things we flush down the toilet or into sewers—water, energy, fertilizer—can be recovered as valuable by-products of the anaerobic purpose."[134] His project relies on bacteria that eschews oxygen while producing burnable methane. Climate science has shown that billions of years ago, the Earth's atmosphere contained unbreathable gases with microbes evolving in the absence of oxygen. As Earth matured, it slowly assumed its present nitrogen-oxygen atmosphere, resulting in these anaerobic, or oxygen-averse bacteria retreating into the lower ocean hydrosphere and the ozone layers of the stratosphere. Tilmans used the anaerobic-oxygen-averse bacteria to clean the wastewater and produce methane, the natural gas that can be burned as fuel or even used as a chemical feedstock to make biodegradable plastics.

In 2019, Beth Koigi was awarded the Africa Prize for Engineering Innovation founded by the Royal Academy of Engineering. Her innovative water ATM-like box was considered as a scalable engineering solution to local challenges. The industrial town of Thika in Kiambu, Kenya, is a drought-prone region that faces severe water stress and lacks safe drinking water. In 2016, Koigi came up with an innovative water filtration system to provide clean drinking water for the locals. As a student, studying Community Development, she developed a water filtering device made from low cost, easily available materials such as an ordinary peanut butter jar and charcoal. Through rigorous testing, Koigi created a filter that was surprisingly robust capable of removing amoebas from the local water supply. She launched her innovative water producing machine called Majik Water that like the Namibian beetle draws its water needs from the atmosphere. Her machine extracts clean water from the atmosphere and works on the same principle as a refrigerator and an air conditioner. The air is pulled in by a fan and then passed through a condenser coil. After condensation the water is displaced to a collecting tank. Koigi propagates the innovative idea that as long as we have air to breathe in the atmosphere, it is possible for humanity to have clean drinking water.[135]

In 2019, the Innovation by Design awards was awarded to the Water Box project launched by actor Jaden Smith and Drew Fitzgerald.[136] In 2014, Flint city in Michigan faced severe water stress when the city's water source was switched from the Detroit River to the Flint River. This change in river source, resulted in a city-wide lead contamination of public drinking water. Though aid was offered to the city in 2018 through the free bottled water program, it was the innovative water project launched by Smith and Fitzgerald called JUST water that saved the city of Flint. They created the Water Box in Flint to provide clean drinking water to its community. This water box filtrates lead and gives ten gallons of clean water every sixty seconds. This Water Box was engineered with proven components that reduce heavy metals like lead and eliminates harmful bacteria.

Actor Matt Damon contends that innovation is not enough, and he wisely reminds us, "When the well is dry, we know the worth of water."[137] After a trip to Zambia in 2006, he discovered that people walked about a mile every day to fetch water in pots and jerrycans. His humanitarian project collected $27 million that was used to unleash $1.1 billion in micro credit permitting people to install affordable water filters in their homes. He believes that people need to be treated with dignity, not as charity cases, but as people worthy of economic citizenship. Through water.org, Damon breaks down the barriers by providing water filtration systems for sixty dollars in ten instalments to give people access to safe water instead of walking miles for it.

James Elser, a lake ecologist, has developed phosphorus recycling practices by treating wastewater, removing phosphorus that contaminates lakes, and disposing the sediment in landfills.[138] Climate scientists consider that the phosphorus cycle is like the water cycle. Like water molecules brought to our planet by meteoroids, phosphorus molecules found in phosphate rock was formed over millions of years in the Earth's crust. Phosphorus atoms accumulated in sedimentary rock deposits are biological accelerants necessary for plant existence. Like water, phosphorus is necessary for life on Earth, but too much of phosphorus can upset the planet's ecosphere. James Elser warns us, "Phosphate is a biological accelerant. . . . It's like spraying gasoline on a forest fire. It just makes life go crazy."[139] His project of mining human and animal waste, processing them and using phosphorus has given life to a new project at the largest water treatment plant in Chicago. Since 2013, the Stickney Water Reclamation Plant (WRP)[140] that extracts large deposits of phosphorus from 750 million gallon of water per day, removes this finite resource to unearth an agricultural fertiliser that assures in revenue stream from waste.

In 2019, Frank Rogalla, a maverick thinker in Andalusia in southern Spain, came up with another innovative idea to completely rethink the concept of waste. While Elser's project in Chicago aimed at preventing the massive overgrowth of algae by removing phosphorus from the city's wastewater, Rogalla advocated the idea of one man's trash, being another man's treasure. He deliberately encouraged the idea of the formation of algae to harvest it for the creation of the biogas methane. Like water and phosphorus, algae are also one of the oldest organisms on Earth having the innate propensity to survive with elements available in nature namely, sunshine, nutrients, and the water. He created algae in a few hours in canals by feeding them wastewater. Through the process of flotation, he separated the algae from the water, and pumped it into a digester where it was converted into biogas or methane after gas purification. His production principle stems from the fact that algae can produce oxygen, and that oxygen from algae has the capacity to clean wastewater. So, Rogalla's All-Gas project[141] does not merely clean water, but it also harvests algae to produce biofuel used in cars in the city of Chiclana in the southwest coast of Spain. If implemented all over Andalusia, Rogalla hopes that thirty million cars may run one day on just bio-methane.

In the Danish capital of Copenhagen, Peter Holme Jensen developed a new method of purifying water with the aid of aqua protein present in the human body.[142] He drew inspiration from Nobel Prize winning laureate and molecular biologist, Peter Agre, who in 2003 was lauded for his discovery of the Aquaporin water channel. By combining the Aquaporin protein with artificial membranes, Jensen developed innovative new forward osmosis that taps the human body's thirty to forty different variations of aqua protein. By using biotechnology, he integrated this biological protein into a membrane to filtrate 700 litres of water every second. He coated the surface of a membrane with aquaporin protein and extracted water by forward osmosis. His research has opened the doors for an entirely new range of filtration products and the creation of his company AquaPorin that aims to speed up and cut the waste from reverse osmosis and other membrane-based processes.

DEFERRING DAY ZERO

Arundhati Roy in her essay "The Greater Common Good" writes that we may have run out of heroes for the twentieth century, and it is time now to inspire "shiny new ones"[143] to come along and save the Earth's inhabitants.

> We have to fight specific wars in specific ways. Who knows, perhaps that's what the twenty-first century has in store for us. The dismantling of the Big. Big bombs, big dams, big ideologies, big contradictions, big countries, big wars, big heroes, big mistakes. Perhaps right now, this very minute, there's a small god up in heaven readying herself for us.[144]

Through an enumeration of the 'big' she highlights the need to dismantle wars, bombs, mistakes, and dominant ideologies that show case the 'big' often leaving small issues untended and small people ignored. Her activism against dams that annihilate nature and indigenous ways of life also encourages the idea of changing the planet through a step-by-step process of small actions where people in the fringes and edges can take part. To defer Day Zero, the conservation of water is not one to be implemented only in the scale of city and nation planning. It should be scaled down to individual actions like residential reusing of water, recycling, petitioning governments to take tangible action, supporting grassroots movements, and coming up with innovative new ideas to create a brave new world where water regains its regenerative capacity. The water we have on Earth has always existed. It is all the water that we will ever possess. Though we may never run out of water, the problem lies in keeping this water potable and in storage for purposeful use. If all the water stored in glaciers melt due to global warming, climate scientists have predicted that ocean levels will rise by 230 feet, thus erasing many coastal cities. It is in our hands to manage water. Through the battle between potable water versus polluted water, these water visionaries have managed to address an issue by considering ways that go against the grain of traditional ways of existence. Like the fog-basking Namibian bee that harvests and collects fresh water in the deserts by capturing moisture from fog in the ridges through the tiny grooves on its body, it is time for biomimicry and innovative ideas to recycle every drop of water on the planet.

NOTES

1. "'Good Food, Good Life': Célébration des 150 Ans de Nestlé." Nestlé. Accessed June 9, 2023. https://www.nestle.ch/fr/media/newsandfeatures/150-ans-de-nestl%C3%A9.

2. "One Planet. One Health." Danone, November 4, 2019. https://www.danone.com/fr/stories/one-planet-one-health.html.

3. "Nestlé Reports Full-Year Results for 2022." Nestlé Global. Accessed June 9, 2023. https://www.nestle.com/media/pressreleases/allpressreleases/full-year-results-2022.

4. Danone. "Danone: A Solid Set of Full-Year 2021 Results; a Strong Finish to the Year." GlobeNewswire Newsroom, February 23, 2022. https://www.globenewswire.com/news-release/2022/02/23/2389984/0/en/DANONE-A-solid-set-of-Full-Year-2021-results-A-strong-finish-to-the-year.html.

5. "Evian—Danone Eaux." Danone, March 20, 2023. https://www.danone.com/fr/brands/waters/evian.html.

6. "Eau La La!" Perrier History | Perrier UK. Accessed June 9, 2023. https://www.perrier.com/uk/since-1863/history/eau-la-la.

7. *Meet the Water Sommelier*. *CBS Sunday Morning*. YouTube, 2021. https://www.youtube.com/watch?v=7YKbeh3cKpY.

8. *Rudement chaud* means "fiercely hot" in French.

9. "Un Manchot Géant Se Dresse Devant La Gare de Reims." Actus—Champagne FM, January 11, 2022. https://www.champagnefm.com/un-manchot-gant-se-dresse-devant-la-gare-de-reims#:~:text=Il%20s%27agit%20d%27une,aux%20dangers%20du%20réchauffement%20climatique. Rudy now stands in Rahir's hometown Dormans in the Grand Est region in France.

10. "Where Did Earth's Water Come From?" *Earth & Planets*. Accessed June 3, 2023. https://epl.carnegiescience.edu/news/where-did-earths-water-come.

11. Nick Shepherd, "Making Sense of 'Day Zero': Slow Catastrophes, Anthropocene Futures, and the Story of Cape Town's Water Crisis." *Water* 11, no. 9 (2019): 1–19. https://doi.org/10.3390/w11091744.

12. Hannah Hennessy, "Americas | Andes Drought Leaves Lima Thirsty." BBC News, May 9, 2004. http://news.bbc.co.uk/2/hi/americas/3697647.stm.

13. Erica Gies, "Why Peru Is Reviving a Pre-Incan Technology for Water." BBC Future, May 11, 2022. https://www.bbc.com/future/article/20210510-perus-urgent-search-for-slow-water.

14. "Italy Drought: Rome Forced to Cut Water Pressure at Night." BBC News, August 29, 2017. https://www.bbc.com/news/world-europe-41081066.

15. Antonella Cinelli, "Italy's Water Crisis Exacerbated by Leaky Pipes, Data Shows." Reuters, March 21, 2023. https://www.reuters.com/business/environment/italys-water-crisis-exacerbated-by-leaky-pipes-data-shows-2023-03-21/.

16. Michael Cohen, "Will Cape Town Run out of Water?" Bloomberg.com, December 8, 2017. https://www.bloomberg.com/news/features/2017-12-08/will-cape-town-run-out-of-water.

17. Shepherd, "Making Sense of 'Day Zero,'" 4.

18. Raj Bhagat Palanichamy, "How Does a Flood-Prone City Run out of Water? Inside Chennai's 'Day Zero' Crisis." World Resources Institute, June 25, 2019. https://www.wri.org/insights/how-does-flood-prone-city-run-out-water-inside-chennais-day-zero-crisis.

19. "World Water Day." United Nations. Accessed June 8, 2023. https://www.un.org/en/observances/water-day.

20. "Global Risks Report 2023." World Economic Forum. Accessed May 17, 2023. https://www.weforum.org/reports/global-risks-report-2023, 57–58.

21. "Progress on Household Drinking Water, Sanitation and Hygiene, 2000–2020: Five Years into the Sdgs." UNICEF DATA, June 16, 2022. https://data.unicef.org/resources/progress-on-household-drinking-water-sanitation-and-hygiene-2000-2020/.

22. Rutger Willem Hofste, Paul Reig, and Leah Schleifer. "17 Countries, Home to One-Quarter of the World's Population, Face Extremely High Water Stress." World Resources Institute, August 6, 2019. https://www.wri.org/insights/17-countries-home-one-quarter-worlds-population-face-extremely-high-water-stress.

23. "Tigris-Euphrates Alluvial Salt Marsh." One Earth. Accessed May 18, 2023. https://www.oneearth.org/ecoregions/tigris-euphrates-alluvial-salt-marsh/.

24. Aysegül Kibaroglu, "An Analysis of Turkey's Water Diplomacy and Its Evolving Position Vis-à-Vis International Water Law." *Water International* 40, no. 1 (2014): 153–67. https://doi.org/10.1080/02508060.2014.978971.

25. Gleick, Peter H. "Water, War & Peace in the Middle East." *Environment: Science and Policy for Sustainable Development* 36, no. 3 (1994): 6–42. https://doi.org/10.1080/00139157.1994.9929154.

26. Gashaw Ayferam, The Nile dispute: Beyond water security—Carnegie endowment for . . . , January 19, 2023. https://carnegieendowment.org/sada/88842.

27. "Egypt Addresses UN Security Council over Ethiopia's Continued Filling of Gerd." *Egypt Independent*, August 4, 2022. https://egyptindependent.com/egypt-addresses-un-security-council-over-ethiopias-continued-filling-of-gerd/.

28. "Tensions over Nearly Finished Gerd Rooted in National Identity, Experts Say." Africa Defense Forum, April 18, 2023. https://adf-magazine.com/2023/04/tensions-over-nearly-finished-gerd-rooted-in-national-identity-experts-say/.

29. "India, China Sign Two Mous on Sharing of Brahmaputra River Data, Rice Supply." *The Wire*, June 9, 2018. https://thewire.in/uncategorised/india-china-sign-two-mous-on-sharing-of-brahmaputra-river-data-rice-supply.

30. Genevieve Donnellon-May, "China's Super Hydropower Dam and Fears of Sino-Indian Water Wars." *The Diplomat*, December 12, 2022. https://thediplomat.com/2022/12/chinas-super-hydropower-dam-and-fears-of-sino-indian-water-wars/.

31.*Islamic Republic of Pakistan v. Republic of India*—Press Release (The Hague, May 17, 2023).

32. Wash on the brink—UNICEF. Accessed May 17, 2023. https://www.unicef.org/media/118356/file/%20UNICEF%20Afghanistan%20WASH%20on%20the%20Brink%202022.pdf.

33. Nasrat Sayed and Said Hashmat Sadat. “Climate Change Compounds Long-standing Displacement in Afghanistan.” migrationpolicy.org, June 29, 2022. https://www.migrationpolicy.org/article/climate-change-displacement-afghanistan.

34. Charlie Faulkner, “Water Crisis Heightens the Risk of Famine in Afghanistan.” The Third Pole, August 17, 2021. https://www.thethirdpole.net/en/food/bone-dry-afghanistan-stares-at-future-famines/.

35. “A Dry Lake Hamun Means More Dust Storms.” NASA. Accessed June 8, 2023. https://earthobservatory.nasa.gov/images/150941/a-dry-lake-hamun-means-more-dust-storms.

36. Kumar, Ruchi. “Iran and Afghanistan Face off over Sharing Helmand Waters.” The National, May 28, 2023. https://www.thenationalnews.com/mena/2023/05/28/iran-and-afghanistan-face-off-over-sharing-helmand-waters/.

37. Alex Liebman, “Trickle-down Hegemony? China′s ‘Peaceful Rise’ and Dam Building on the Mekong.” *Contemporary Southeast Asia* 27, no. 2 (2005): 281–304. https://doi.org/10.1355/cs27-2f.

38. “Requiem for a River.” *Economist*, January 26, 2016. https://www.economist.com/news/essays/21689225-can-one-world-s-great-waterways-survive-its-development.

39. “Mekong River Commission (MRC).” (MRC). Accessed June 10, 2023. https://www.mrcmekong.org/.

40. “Water, Peace & Security Partnership.” World Resources Institute, August 29, 2022. https://www.wri.org/initiatives/water-peace-security-partnership.

41. Herbert H. Jonsson, Reading Japanese Haikai Poetry: A Study in the Polyphony of Yosa Buson’s Linked Poems (Boston: Leiden, 2016), 1.

42. Jonsson, Reading Japanese Haikai Poetry, 3.

43. Idem, 25.

44. Sudeep Sen, an Indian poet’s poetry collections include The Lunar Visitations (1990), Postmarked India: New and Selected Poems (1997), Lines of Desire (2000), Distracted Geographies (2003), Rain (2005), Aria (2011), Anthropocene: Climate Change, Contagion, Consolation (2021), and Red (2023). He has translated poetry and worked as an editor on many anthologies, including The HarperCollins Book of English Poetry by Indians (2012) and Midnight’s Grandchildren: Post-Independence English Poetry from India (2004). His prose collection entitled Postcards from Bangladesh (2002), won the UPL Excellence Award, BodyText: Dramatic Monologues in Motion (2009), and EroText (2016), winner of the Global Literary Festival Award for Literary Excellence.

45. Idem, 23.

46. Idem, 34.

47. Sen, *Anthropocene*, 34.

48. Wallace Stevens, *Collected Poems of Wallace Stevens* (New York: Alfred K. Knopf, 1971), 128.

49. Wallace Stevens (1879–1955) was an American modernist poet who won the Pulitzer Prize for *The Collected Poems of Wallace Stevens*.

50. Sen, *Anthropocene*, 31.

51. Stevens, *Collected Poems*, 128.

52. Sen, *Anthropocene*, 32–33.

53. The diptych, double-page view is my idea of studying this haiku duo poem. It has been typeset as a diptych with permission from its haiku master Sudeep Sen.

54. Sen, *Anthropocene*, 33.

55. Idem, 17.

56. Idem, 126–28.

57. Janet Pierce (1947–), a contemporary Scottish-born painter, based in Ireland who has has spent many years of her life near the Annaghmakerrig lake in County Monaghan. Uisce Anam is Irish Gaelic for soul water. This is the title of the series of water colour paintings she did whilst swimming every day in the lake beside her home.

58. The triptych, three-frame view is my idea of studying this three-part haiku poem. It has been set as a triptych with permission from its haiku master Sudeep Sen.

59. Janet Pierce a contemporary spiritual artist working on canvas, paper . . . , accessed September 13, 2023, http://janetpierce.com/uisce-anam.php. See figure 4.2 that is captioned Lake Haiku by poet-photographer Sudeep Sen.

60. Sen, Anthropocene, 9.

61. Jonsson, Reading Japanese Haikai Poetry, 252.

62. Baba Amte (1914–2008) organized peace and justice marches across India and is the recipient of the Padma Shri Award (1971), the Ramon Magsaysay Award (1985), the Padma Vibhushan Award (1986), the United Nations Prize in the Field of Human Rights (1988), the Gandhi Peace Prize (1999).

63. Baba Amte's social work include the rehabilitation and empowerment of the poor suffering from leprosy. He organized long protest marches for causes including environmentalism, religious tolerance, peace, and justice. He fought for the well-being of India's indigenous tribes.

64. Medha Patkar (1954–) is an Indian social activist who works to support people displaced by the Narmada Valley Development Project, a plan to create a dam across the Narmada River. She founded the *Narmada Bachao Andolan* or Save the Narmada Movement and her campaigns underline the two basic tenets in the Indian constitution, the rights to life and to livelihood.

65. "On Quit India Day, Modi-Shivraj Asked to Quit Narmada Valley." TwoCircles.net, August 9, 2015. http://twocircles.net/2015aug09/1439131493.html. Shivraj Singh Chauhan has served as the chief minister of Madhya Pradesh (2005–2018 and since 2020) and is the longest serving chief minister of this state. He is a partisan of the same political party, as the Indian Prime Minister Narendra Modi, the Bharatiya Janata Party.

66. The Quit India Movement was launched by the All India Congress Committee (AICC) by Mahatma Gandhi on August 9, 1942, to protest against British rule and to ask the British to quit India. This day is celebrated every year as August Kranti Day/Diwas or the Quit India Day. On this day tribute is paid to freedom fighters.

67. Patkar, Medha. "Narmada: Petition for President, CJ, PM, Saying 2 Lakh People May Face Submergence—Counterview—30.8.19." *Narmada Bachao Andolan*, August 31, 2019. https://narmadaandolan.org/narmada-petition-for-president-cj-pm-saying-2-lakh-people-may-face-submergence-counterview-30-8-19/.

68. Roy, "The Greater Common Good," 43–141.

69. Arundhati Roy (1961–) is an Indian author, actress, and political activist-writer who was awarded the Booker Prize in 1997 for her semi-autobiographical debut novel *The God of Small Things*. Her second novel is *The Ministry of Utmost Happiness* (2017). Arundhati Roy's political essays have been compiled into the following collections: *The End of Imagination* (1998), *The Algebra of Infinite Justice* (2001), *Power Politics* (2002), *War Talk* (2003), *An Ordinary Person's Guide to the Empire* (2005), *The Shape of the Beast* (2008), *Listening to Grasshoppers: Field Notes on Democracy* (2009), *Broken Republic* (2011), *My Seditious Heart* (2019) and *Azadi: Freedom, Fascism, Fiction* (2020).

70. The *Adivasis* are the earliest inhabitants of the Indian sub-continent. They are considered as the indigenous tribes who occupied the hill and mountainous regions of India. The term *Adivasi* was coined in the 1930s to give a sense of identity to the various indigenous tribes of India. In *Hindi* '*adi*' means 'of earliest times,' and '*vasi*' means 'inhabitant.'

71. The Sarvar Sarovar Project across the Narmada is being built at an estimated cost of Rs. 392.4 billion (approximately 8 billion USD). It is the world's second largest concrete gravity dam, with the world's third highest spillway discharging capacity of 87,000m3, and will be the largest irrigation canal in the world after its completion, irrigating Kutch and Saurashtra. The government of India calls it an 'eco-friendly' indigenous hydropower reservoir. More detail is provided in the court case *Narmada Bachao Andolan v. Union of India & Ors* (2000) that follows this section.

72. Arundhati Roy. "The Greater Common Good." In *The Algebra of Infinite Justice* (New Delhi: Penguin Books, 2001), 86.

73. Arundhati Roy, "Arundhati Roy Extract: 'The Backlash Came in Police Cases, Court Appearances and Even Jail.'" *The Guardian*, May 31, 2019. https://www.theguardian.com/books/2019/may/31/my-seditious-heart-arundhati-roy.

74. Arundhati Roy, *Capitalism: A Ghost Story* (London: Verso Books, 2015), 15.

75. Idem, 16.

76. Roy, "The Greater Common Good," 46.

77. Idem, 47.

78. The Hirakud dam was India's first river valley project after independence from British rule on August 14, 1947. It is India's largest dam and the world's fourth largest barrage that harnesses hydroelectricity to power villages along the River Mahanadi.

79. Arundhati Roy, "The Greater Common Good," 56.

80. "Top 20 Countries with the Most Number of Dams." Numerical.co.in. Accessed June 11, 2023. https://numerical.co.in/numerons/collection/60e1d4b6ef7874158890333f.

81. Arundhati Roy, "The Greater Common Good," 56.

82. Idem, 69.

83. Idem, 52.

84. Idem, 77.

85. Arundhati Roy. "On Citizen's Rights to Express Dissent." In *My Seditious Heart: Collected Non-Fiction* (Gurgaon: Hamish Hamilton, 2019), 155.

86. "Smarthomes Infrastructure." Dholera SIR—India's first Industrial Greenfield Smart City in Dholera City. Accessed June 11, 2023. https://www.smart-homes.in/dholera-sir/. The Dholera Special Investment Region (DSIR) covers approximately 920 sq kilometers and covers twenty-two villages that are strategically situated between the industrial zones of Ahmedabad, Baroda, Rajkot, and Bhavnagar in Gujarat State. This industrial hub will have a six-lane access-controlled expressway, metro rails and an international airport.

87. Graham Huggan and Helen Tiffan, *Postcolonial Ecocriticism* (London: Routledge, 2006), 5.

88. Arundhati Roy, "The Greater Common Good," 80.

89. Graham Huggan and Helen Tiffan, *Postcolonial Ecocriticism*, 12.

90. Arundhati Roy, "The Greater Common Good," 52.

91. Idem, 65.

92. Idem, 109.

93. Vandana Shiva (1952–) is an eco-feminist, physicist, and the founder of the Research Foundation for Science, Technology, and Natural Resource Policy (1982). She advocates food sovereignty, anti-globalization, and sustainable methods of agriculture. She works with grassroots campaigns to prevent deforestation and the construction of large dams.

94. Shiva, Vandana. *Staying Alive: Women, Ecology, and Development*. Berkeley: North Atlantic Books, 2016.

95. Daya Pawar or Dagdu Maruti Pawar (1935–1996) was an Indian Marathi language author and poet known for his contributions to *dalit* or tribal literature.

96. Shiva, *Staying Alive*, 186. The poem is in italics as in the author's text.

97. *The Seeds of Vandana Shiva*. CORE, 2022. core.live/movies/the-seeds-of-vandana-shiva-movie.

98. "When the Big Dams Came Up." The Hindu, March 19, 2015. https://www.thehindu.com/news/national/when-the-big-dams-came-up/article7012590.ece.

99. Narmada Bachao Andolan v. Union of India & Ors (Supreme Court of India, March 15, 2005).

100. Nora Lanari and John Overton, "Dam Stories: Using Narrative Analysis to Understand the Debate over Water Security and the Waimea Community Dam." *New Zealand Geographer* 78, no. 1 (2022): 51–62. https://doi.org/10.1111/nzg.12329.

101. Idem, 54.

102. Narmada Bachao Andolan v. Union of India & Ors (2005), 11:1–3.

103. Idem, 11:4.

104. Nora Lanari and John Overton, 54.

105. Narmada Bachao Andolan v. Union of India & Ors (2005), 10, 12–13.

106. Nora Lanari and John Overton, 55.

107. Arundhati Roy, "The Greater Common Good," 138.

108. Idem, 139.

109. Narmada Bachao Andolan v. Union of India & Ors (2005), 283: (9)

110. The Rio Declaration on Environment and Development (1992). Accessed June 12, 2023. https://www.iau-hesd.net/sites/default/files/documents/rio_e.pdf.

111. Narmada Bachao Andolan v. Union of India & Ors (2005).

112. In *Vimal Bhai & Others v. Ministry of Environment & Forests* (National Green Tribunal, New Delhi December 14, 2011) the NGT found the forest clearance for dam building to be in line with the precautionary principle and the principle of sustainable development as the EIA was carried out properly and the Forest Advisory Committee had carried out studies pertaining to the impact of the dam.

113. Similarly in *Alaknanda Hydro Power Company Ltd v. Anuj Joshi and Ors* (Supreme Court of India, August 13, 2013), the Supreme Court of India noted the importance of comprehensively assessing the impacts of multiple hydroelectric projects.

114. En ejercicio de sus atribuciones constitucionales y legales, expide la siguiente caso no. 1149-19-jp/20 (el pleno de la corte constitucional del ecuador 10 November 2021).

115. Bolivia (Plurinational State of)'s Constitution of 2009. Accessed June 15, 2023. https://www.constituteproject.org/constitution/Bolivia_2009.pdf.

116. Richard Frederick Wheeler y Eleanor Geer Huddle c/ Gobierno Provincial de Loja, juicio 11121-2011-0010 (30 March 2011).

117. *New Zealand Māori Council v. Attorney-General* (New Zealand Supreme Court, August 29, 2013).

118. *Colorado River Ecosystem v. State of Colorado* (Colorado Federal District Court, December 4, 2017).

119. *Drewes Farms P'ship v. City of Toledo* (United States District Court, N.D. Ohio, Western Division February 27, 2020).

120. "Federal Judge Strikes Down 'Lake Erie Bill of Rights.'" Animal Legal Defense Fund, March 29, 2021. https://aldf.org/article/federal-judge-strikes-down-lake-erie-bill-of-rights/.

121. Human Rights and Peace for Bangladesh (HPRB) and Others v. Secretary of the Ministry of Shipping and Others (High Court of Bangladesh, January 30, 2019).

122. Center for Social Justice Studies et al. v. Presidency of the Republic et al. Judgment T-622/16 (Constitutional Court of Colombia, November 10, 2016).

123. Center for Social Justice Studies et al. v. Presidency of the Republic et al. section 9.32.

124. Joy Green, "Quebec's Magpie River Granted Legal Personhood." The Futures Centre, March 24, 2021. https://www.thefuturescentre.org/signal/quebecs-magpie-river-granted-legal-personhood/.

125. Linda H. Edwards, "Once Upon A Time in Law: Myth, Metaphor, and Authority." *Tennessee Law Review* 77: 889.

126. Idem, 889.

127. Idem, 889.

128. Lalit Miglani, 1.

129. Idem, 1.

130. Idem, 2.

131. Inter-state River Tribunals. Accessed June 13, 2023. https://pib.gov.in/Pressreleaseshare.aspx?PRID=1541735#:~:text=There%20are%20currently%20five%20existing,and%20Krishna%20Water%20Disputes%20Tribunal.

132. *State of Andhra Pradesh v. State of Karnataka* (Supreme Court of India, September 28, 2022).

133. "Earth's Freshwater." *Education*. Accessed June 12, 2023. https://education.nationalgeographic.org/resource/earths-fresh-water/#:~:text=Only%20about%20three%20percent%20of,buried%20deep%20in%20the%20ground.

134. "New Water Treatment Plant Tests Stanford Technology for Cleaning Wastewater While Creating Energy." *Stanford News Service*, May 11, 2018. https://news.stanford.edu/press-releases/2018/05/11/new-plant-tests-treat-wastewater/.

135. Koigi, Beth. "Majik Water." Beth Koigi: Majik water | TED Talk. Accessed June 9, 2023. https://www.ted.com/talks/beth_koigi_majik_water.

136. The Water Box: Jaden Smith's ambitious plan to provide clean water in Flint—and the rest of America. Accessed June 9, 2023. https://www.fastcompany.com/90400006/the-water-box-jaden-smiths-ambitious-plan-to-provide-clean-water-in-flint-and-the-rest-of-america.

137. Alejandro de la Garza, "Matt Damon Wants You to Care about Water." *Time*, March 29, 2022. https://time.com/6160927/matt-damon-water/.

138. Lara Herrington Watson, "James Elser Hopes Phosphate Recycling Can Solve Two Environmental Problems." American Association for the Advancement of Science (AAAS). Accessed June 9, 2023. https://www.aaas.org/james-elser-hopes-phosphate-recycling-can-solve-two-environmental-problems.

139. Dan Egan, "The Wizard of Phosphorus: One Man's Quest to Turn Sewage into Eco-Gold." *Big Think*, March 8, 2023. https://bigthink.com/life/capture-phosphorus-sewage-wastewater/#:~:text="Phosphate%20is%20a%20biological%20accelerant,process%2C%20and%20apply%20chemical%20fertilizer.

140. "One Water Spotlight: Stickney Water Reclamation Plant." One Water Spotlight: Stickney Water Reclamation Plant | US Water Alliance. Accessed June 9, 2023. https://uswateralliance.org/resources/one-water-spotlight-stickney-water-reclamation-plant.

141. Paul Callaghan, "Visiting the Algae All-Stars in Spain." *Brave Blue World*, June 25, 2019. https://www.braveblue.world/blog/2019/5/20/visiting-the-algae-all-stars-in-spain-6xnse.

142. Jonathan Smith, "This Biotech Uses Bacterial Proteins to Purify Water Faster." Labiotech.eu, June 24, 2022. https://www.labiotech.eu/startup-scout/water-purification-aquaporin-osmosis/.

143. Roy, "The Greater Common Good," 53.

144. Idem, 53.

Chapter 5

The Flame of the Forest

In the spring months from January to April, the sub-tropical forests of India and southeast Asia are ablaze with flowering-vermillion-colored palash flowers. The dry, deciduous plant species *Butea monosperma*, known as Flame of the Forest or palash or dhak or bastard teak, shed their leaves to let their flowers blossom to their full glory, thus spreading the color of fire across the forest land. These thirty- to fifty-foot-high trees bloom in forests; insects and bees thrive on their nectar permitting cross pollination; and their seeds are picked and tossed by the wind. Its ungainly crooked trunk and branches are hidden

Figure 5.1. Flame of the Forest. *Source*: Flame of the Forest © Sudeep Sen.

from view under the crown of orange-red flowers. Palash flowering trees figure in Hindu mythology as a form of *Agni*, the God of Fire. Its tri-foliate leaves represent the Hindu Holy Trinity of *Brahma* (the Creator), *Vishnu* (the Preserver), and *Shiva* (the Destroyer). Its leaves are used in *Hindu* religious ceremonies to bless calves, render them fertile, and enable them to mature as milk-yielding cows of plenty. Palash twigs are used to light sacred fires, while its wood serves to shape ladles to pour ghee into the sacred flame. The palash leaves contain a dye that is used to toss red-colored powder at *Holi*, the *Hindu* spring festival of color. It is an ingredient in *Ayurvedic* medicine, with the various parts of the tree serving as remedies for various ailments ranging from sore throats to snake bites. These palash forests thrive in the Indian state of Jharkhand in eastern India and has been aptly chosen as this state's emblem. Forests splashed in red serve as a canopy in Kipling's works: *The Jungle Books* with Mowgli leading "the buffaloes for the ravine by the dhak-tree";[1] and in his short story "Beyond the Pale" when the widow delivers him a love note accompanied with a single *dhak* synonymous of "'desire,' 'come,' 'write,' or 'danger.'"[2] Rabindranath Tagore, the bard of India, was inspired by the Palash trees in his hometown, Santiniketan in West Bengal.

> The intoxicating red of 'palash,' blend with fragrance of *champa*
> I weave with music into a net of color and fervor[3]

Palash in India spreads a riot of color through forests and even cities in India inspiring verses of poetry and nostalgic thought. Sudeep Sen writes, "Forests full of redolent, fire-bright, orange palash flowers flood my mind. I imagine I am walking in Bengal's Purulia groves surrounded by red, and more red. It is the color of my memory now, lit in passion."[4] The Flame of the Forest, a flame that lights the forests is kept alive through oral narratives of its jungle folk, the *Adivasi* tribes of India whose lives are sustained by the forests. These forests are prone in our time to catch fire, set the trees ablaze, thus destroying hectares of forests as in the May 2023 forest fires that spread through the forests of Goa in the south-western coast of India.[5] Deficient rainfall, continued dry seasons, extreme weather conditions, low humidity, and unusual high temperatures have been suggested as causes for the wildfires.

Greenpeace warns that species go extinct when the biosphere changes; our Earth is dying and is on the verge of collapse with only 15 percente of the world's forests and 3 percent of the planet's oceans being free from the pressures of human extraction.[6] David Attenborough's documentary *Life on Our Planet* (2020) traces the metamorphosis and evolution of our planet during the last century. He calls existence at the time of the Holocene as a life in the "Garden of Eden," a period when temperatures remained stable by not exceeding 1°C.[7] After dinosaurs and 75 percent of the species were erased off the face of our Earth by the killer meteoroid, nature has been constantly reconstructing herself by building new life forms. Phytoplankton of the seas and immense forests in the northern hemisphere have locked carbon reserves for centuries. Attenborough documents how rising sea temperature, alarming temperature swings, melting poles, changes in rainfall patterns have upset the natural balance resulting in an Earth on fever. The Amazonian tropical forests occupy 1 percent of the Earth's area, contain 10 percent of the world's species with seventy-six billion tons of carbon being stored in its natural green house.[8] It releases twenty billion tons of water into the atmosphere per day, thus permitting the functioning of global and regional carbon and water cycles. Climate scientists warn that the deforestation of the Amazonian rainforests is the cause for longer spells of dry seasons. With a shrinking forest giving way to savannahs, they believe that the tipping point will arrive at 20 to 25 percent of deforestation, representing a rise in global temperatures by 4°C, with central, eastern, and southern Amazon regions facing the threat of becoming barren scrubland.[9] Similarly, Borneo's rainforest ecosystem has lost 50 percent of its lowland rainforests between 1973 and 2015.[10] Forests have been wiped out to permit large-scale palm tree plantations, thus resulting in the terraforming of the landscape. Decades of logging and land clearing has resulted in the loss of habitat of orangutans and elephants. Forests that sustain life on our planet are in danger.

THE FORESTS SPEAK, FEEL, AND CRY

In *The Glass Palace*,[11] Amitav Ghosh gives voice to the teak forests in Burma. Teak forests were erased to make way for rubber plantations in colonial times. The ground underfoot in the forests of Burma in *The Glass Palace* has a carpet of dead leaves shed by the mighty teak tress. The slopes bear "the shadows of thousands of trunks, all exactly parallel, like scratches scored by a machine."[12] The portrayal of the landscape shows the agony undergone by the imperial teak tree in the era of British colonization. The mighty teak assumes the status of a tree that had "felled dynasties, caused invasions, created fortunes, brought a new way of life into being."[13] Ghosh describes how the chopped trees were left to rot and die as timber yards began to sprout, and local timber lords worked hand in glove with the British, to exploit the forests for lucrative gain, reap huge profits, and thus participate in what William Rueckert calls "the self-destructive or suicidal motive that is inherent in our prevailing and paradoxical attitude towards nature."[14] As the girdles cut thin incisions into the imperial teak trees at a height of four feet and six inches of the ground, the assassinated trees voice agony by emanating "great tocsins of protest as they fell, unloosing thunderclap explosions that could be heard miles away, bringing down everything in their path, rafts of saplings."[15] The wanton felling results in co-existing species of flora being destroyed as the land turns barren. In his article "Nature and Science," Christopher Manes contends that nature is devoid of speech, as the human voice is essentially a human prerogative in our culture. Ghosh endeavors to give voice to the voiceless forests, thus assuming what Manes calls the "humbler status of homo sapiens: one species among millions of other beautiful, terrible, fascinating and signifying forms."[16] By giving voice to the teak trees, Ghosh participates in what Manes refers to the transmission of ecological knowledge and thoughtfulness where one is involved in "metaphorically relearning the language of birds—the passions, pains, and cryptic intents of other biological communities that surround us and silently penetrate our existence."[17] In the fictional space, the River Irrawaddy with its timber-laid cargo rumbles like a furious-seething waterway as it is forced to participate in the process of ecological destruction with trees being dislodged through its water. The voices of the forest sound like war zone cries of distress amid detonations.

> The river was now a swollen angry torrent, racked by clashing currents and pock-marked with whirlpools. When the feeder streams slammed head-on into the river, two-ton logs were thrown cartwheeling into the air; fifty-foot tree trunks were sent shooting across the water like flat bottomed pebbles. The noise was that of an artillery barrage, with the sound of the detonations carrying for miles into the hinterland.[18]

Through metaphors of war and distress, Ghosh describes a warzone where the torrents crash and whirl creating fatal death undercurrents that catapult and thrust the logs into the river streams like a cannon. The gentle Irrawaddy becomes the zone of river warfare as its waters echo with the sound of log explosions that are broadcast on sound waves into the deserted forest landscape. By giving voice to forest logs, forest river streams, teak trees, and portraying them as being eloquent and intelligible entities, Ghosh participates in the postcolonial eco-critical endeavor of suggesting the need to "contemplate not only learning a new form of ethics, but a new language free from the directionalities of humanism, a language that incorporates a decentered, postmodern, post-humanist perspective."[19] To hear the voice of the forests, it is necessary for humanity to be tuned to the strains of deep ecology and create a link between nature, the silenced subject, and reverse the environmentally destructive practices modern society pursues.[20]

The forest is not just the home for flora and fauna, but also a Mother Goddess who offers a home and shelter to tribal folk who hunt her animals and depend on the forest mother for sustenance. In *The Book of the Hunter*, Mahasweta Devi documents the oral histories of the *Shabars*, the tribal hunters to remember forgotten voices. In this oral narrative, Devi relates the *Hindu* creation myth of the primal *Shabar* to trace the tribe's nomadic style of existence. The first *Shabar* forest inhabitants, Kalketu and Phullora are brought to life by the forest goddess Abhayachandi who crushed a rock into a lump of clay to blow the breath of life into them. The forest goddess Abhayachandi in Hindu mythology is the consort of Lord Shiva. Filled with mirth, the generous forest mother grants the *Shabars* one of the five streams of the Shilai river: "She gave them *abhaya* or reassurance against all fears; she kept all her wild creatures, trees, and forest children—the *Shabars*—safe in her lap, covered by her sari."[21] She grants the *Shabars* the boon of an empire, gives them the role of guardians of the forest, guides them through the forests by manifesting her presence through the blossoming of blue *gandharaja* flowers, and crowns them as King Meghaban and Meghabati of Gujarat. But these forest guardians disappoint the forest goddess Abhayachandi when they let a *brahmin* trespass her forests to steal her image. The goddess curses them to a life of constant upheaval. She punishes the worldly city by crushing it with ferocious earthquakes, thus condemning the *Shabars* to a life of perpetual displacement and destroying the voiceless beings of the forests. The forests voice agony as they transform into an unyielding terrain where no flowers bloom and no birds sing. The cautionary tale explains the origin of existence as understood by the *Shabar* culture, the reasons for their scattered existence and hardships faced as "children of the forest."[22]

In the novella *Pterodactyl, Puran Sahay and Pirtha*, related from the perspective of an urban journalist, Puran Sahay, is a cautionary tale. The famine-stricken village of *Nagesia* is covered by the shadow of the pterodactyl, a mythical pre-historic creature, that serves as a bad omen presaging ecological changes and disasters. The pterodactyl represents the spirit or soul of the ancestral tribal people of India who have been pushed out of their land.

> Alas! In pain we are stone, mute. We failed to give peace to the ancestors. We are coming to an end, rubbed off the soil. And the quiet soul casts its shadow and hovers. We didn't know how it would look. This is surely the ancestors' spirit![23]

The inclusion of a large-flying-carnivorous-Jurassic reptile, the Pterodactyl, in the oral tale serves to voice the despair of the tribal *Nagesias's* ancestors who have suffered from loss of land, identity, and community.

> This man-made poverty and famine is a crime, this widespread thirst is a crime, it is a crime to take away the forest and make the forest-dwelling peoples naked and endangered?[24]

Through metaphors of hunger and thirst, Puran Sahay highlights how anthropogenic, deliberate, and negligent destruction of the forests could leave a tribe unprotected and prone to extinction.

Another etiological myth is narrated in the short story, "Little ones," to explain the reasons for the stunted growth of the *Aagariya* tribe. In this tale of the *Aagariya* tribe miners in Lohri, they are the entitled demon *asur* clan who forged iron, ingested flames, bathed in rivers of fire, and were capable of descending into the netherworld to forge and smelt iron. In this explanatory oral tale of the *Aagariyas* passed down from generation to generation, King Logundih, the *Aagariya* sovereign is burned to death by the sun's scorching rays along with his eleven brothers for having dared to rival the sun god. The *Aagariya* consort escapes by hiding herself in a pot of curds and cooling herself from the punishing rays of the sun. The clan survives as she gives birth to her son, Jwalamukhi, who on reaching adulthood wages a war with the sun god to avenge the death of his ancestors. The battle leads to an exchange of curses.

> During the battle, Jwalmukhi cursed the sun god—only when the moon is full will you be able to mate with her. The sun god said—As for you *Aagariya* folk, all the wealth you earn from iron will turn to ashes. From that time, the *Aagariya* has been poor.[25]

Dispossessed of their right to iron, these ironmongers of old, are now relegated to a life in the jungles, where lack of sustenance resulted in their former majestic bodies shriveling into stunted-pygmy forms. Reduced to their present-day nomadic existence, the *Aagariyas* in this oral tale roam the forests, plundering villages at night to sustain themselves. By tracing the mythical past Devi shows how misrecognition can lead to inequity in the distribution of resources, exclusion from society to *Adivasi* communities, and continued misrecognition.

POLYPHONY IN ORAL TRIBAL NARRATIVES

In the wake of independence in 1947, dams or temples of modern India as visioned by Jawaharlal Nehru started sprouting in post-Independence India. Building dams in the name of establishing equity and distribution of water, resulted in monstrous development programs encroaching into forests, the habitat of the indigenous *Adivasi* tribes of India. Lush green forests were replaced with asphalt roads that in Mahasweta Devi's oral narratives figure as sinister graveyards of the tribal ancestors, who lie underfoot roads, houses and hospitals built for a modern existence. It is interesting to refer to Walter

Ong's assertion that language as an articulated sound, is paramount and that writing transcribes articulated speech into graphlets, and thus expands its potentiality.[26] Writing can never exist without orality and Devi's stories of the difficulties faced by the tribal folk reveal how mainstream settlements have elbowed the tribes into the obscurity of the forests.

In *The Book of the Hunter*, Devi pens and transcribes the tales of the *Shabars* whose illiterate and simple way of life is evident in their existence in forests without any deeds of landownership. Devi in the preface of *The Book of the Hunter* documents how the government has exploited, pauperized, and usurped tribal lands in West Bengal.[27]

> In present-day India, the tribes known as 'criminal' are the ones in greatest distress, whether they are the *Sansis* of Punjab and Delhi, the *Parhaiyas* of Bihar, or the *Lodha Shabars* and *Kheria Shabars* of West Bengal. It is with regard to these tribes and their rehabilitation in history that it is necessary to seek out the oral lore which once existed and is no longer available. In the process of suffering atrocious cruelties and becoming uprooted, they have lost their oral traditions.[28]

Polyphony in oral lore resides in recognizing the existence of many voices contributing towards the story. While rendering an oral narrative, the master narrator has the task of impersonating different voices or unique speech acts typical of Bakhtinian polyphony. Each utterance is either declarative, assertive, imperative, or acts of speech that draws its listener or audience onto the setting of the story, thus building on the plot. Devi aims at giving a voice to those who speak a nameless dialect that does not figure in the official list of known languages and dialects in India. Unlike educated, mainstream settlements who possess the power of the pen, tribal folk must depend on the indigenous knowledge transmitted to them by customs and oral accounts passed down to them from their ancestors.

In the preface to *Pterodactyl, Puran Sahay and Pirtha*, Gayatri Chakravorty Spivak, the translator, notes that in the quest of building modem India, planners have invaded and defiled land belonging to *Adivasi* tribes.

> As far as the tribal is concerned, the road, the big road is the enemy. It will take away whatever crop he grows, whatever vegetable he grows, and in times of famine and natural disorders like rain failures or flood they will come in lorries and trucks and take away their children to be sold in other places as bond labor.[29]

Bridges, dams, and roads are evidence of development and growth in our modern times and are built in the name of equity and distribution. In present times, it is usual to see lorry and truck loads of *Adivasi* folk being transported to cities by labor contractors as bonded laborers. Devi exposes certain problems for discussion as in the distinct reporting voice of the reporter, Puran Sahay. As the author, she remains the spectator and onlooker who remarks and writes on the lay of the forest space. As in Mikhail Bakhtin's polyphony where there is a plurality of voices and multiplicity of independent, unblended stances, the author's voice as the "consciousness of the creator" is not entirely absent but is consciously present.[30]

In the polyphonic fictional space, Devi's voice is constantly heard, and "does not transform others' consciousness . . . into objects and does not give them second hand and finalizing definitions."[31] She re-creates and voices these other consciousnesses, granting them authenticity, and dialogical interaction. Through the juxtaposition of two antipodal time-spaces of the mythical past and the present, in *Pterodactyl, Puran Sahay and Pirtha*, Devi highlights the *Adivasi* lament on how development has led to ecological disequilibrium.

> Once there was forest, hill, river, and us. We had villages, homes, land ourselves. Then there was game to hunt. It rained, peacocks danced, we lived. . . . The souls of the ancestors were at peace. Blessed us. We lived. And now? Why did the foreigners come? . . . We were kings. Become subjects. Were subjects become slaves. Owed nothing. They made us debtors. Alas, they enslaved and bound us. . . . Our land vanished . . . the forest disappeared; they made the four corners unclean. Oh, we had our ancestors' graves! They were ground underfoot to build roads, houses, schools, hospitals. We wanted none of this.[32]

Adivasi tribes who reigned supreme in their jungles find that they have been stripped off their rights to forest land. Through the rhetorical device of a contrast, their plea emphasizes the differences between two different epochs in time. A time of ample produce is in stark contrast with the present time where poverty reigns supreme as once sacred forestland disappears and is confiscated in the name of equity and distribution. The polyphonic utterance of the collective voice remains at the lyrical axis of the collective consciousness. This 'other' voice is marked by the presence of the pronoun 'you' or the collective marker 'we.' The collective 'we' are the participants in this act.

In "Little Ones," the village Lohri is cast as the bitter Earth where nothing thrives nor lives. Oppression reigns supreme with the *Aagariyas* trying to till a soil that is hard to plough.

> Nothing grew. Not paddy, not *jowar*, not *maroa*, not *bhutaa*. Strike the earth with a plough, and it's as if you hit iron beneath the surface. A cursed land. You can tell as soon as you set eyes on it.[33]

The anaphoric enumeration of negatives in 'nothing' and 'not' serves to highlight the starkness of the landscape and the frugality in their lifestyle where there are no life-giving crops. The use of assonance in striking the Earth and ploughing it highlights how the once strong *Aagariyas* who mined iron in the netherworld, are now devoid of the strength to till the soil.

TRACING IMAGINARY MAPS OF RECOGNITION

In *Bitter Soil*, Mahasweta Devi's preface gives an account of the purpose behind her enterprise of writing. She states that her penning of the narratives of the tribals was with the aim of giving an audible voice to the exploited and of denouncing "the faces of the exploiting agencies: The feudal-minded landowner, his henchmen, the so-called religious head of the administrative system, all of whom, as a combined force, are out for lower-caste blood."[34] Her call for social and environmental justice is to give recognition to the unrecognized who suffer both social and environmental inequity. She makes a call for an equitable distribution of power and resources to all.

In the novella, *Pterodactyl, Puran Sahay and Pirtha* in the collection entitled *Imaginary Maps*, Devi traces imaginary maps of the tribals that do not exist in the postcolonial map of India. Gayatri Chakravorty Spivak, the translator writes in her preface about the choice of the word 'imaginary.' She advances the idea that the word 'imaginary' refers to those geographical boundaries that remain untraced and unestablished in the broader map of the world. Including the *Adivasis* in the political and geographical map of India needs the acknowledgement of their existence. Devi in her oral lore tales of the *Adivasis* attempts to trace the maps of both the geographical existence of these tribes, as well as imagine their trials in the face of socio-economic progress in postcolonial India.[35] In the preface to *The Book of the Hunter*, Devi states that the aim of the book was to re-discover tribal identity and the lost glory of the *Shabar* tribe.

> Such is my goal, but I don't know whether I will accomplish it. This is however a beginning. The encroachment of towns and non-*Adivasis* upon their territory, *Adivasis* abandoning their lands and going away, the heartless destruction of forests, the search of the forest children for a forest home, and the profound ignorance of mainstream people about *Adivasi* society—these are all truths about our own time.[36]

By imagining new boundaries, Devi gives recognition to these indigenous groups by moving beyond the boundary and enabling a discovery of national and international politics of cultural and economic systems. The imaginary map on the cover of the book as well as in the opening chapter of the novella is an attempt at cartography and situating the little narratives among the larger configuration of the grand narrative of the nation. The little narratives of caste-ridden discrimination, exclusion of *Adivasi* tribes labelled as 'criminal,' need a new map of recognition where the tribal population of *Oraons*, *Mundas*, *Santals*, *Lodhas*, and *Baigas* figure. Through the inclusion of the extinct flying reptile, a pterodactyl, in the novella *Pterodactyl, Puran Sahay and Pirtha*, Devi portrays the dark shadow of global capitalism on indigenous groups who are exploited as cheap, bonded laborers. Through the voice of the ancestors, the reader hears the incessant call for action. Puran Sahay's voice as the reporter engages in revealing the lifestyle of the *Nagesia* tribals, their habits and rituals, their belief in the gods and goddesses of the forests and rivers, their customs of honoring dead values and ancestors. In his pursuit of unveiling the truth, Puran Sahay, like Devi the master narrator lives with the *Nagesias* to learn and discover more about their tribal ways of life. Faced with initial resistance and hostility as a representative of the mainstream culture of capitalist India, the persistent reporter's voice triumphs over tribal resilience as he convinces them to relate their tales. The *Nagesias* reveal their history through their tales passed down to them from their ancestors. Puran Sahay's report becomes a historical treatise where he documents forgotten history. He launches on a quest to situate Pirtha and its mythical past on the world map. From the role of a reporter, he slowly transforms into an envoy for the tribals as he unveils the corruption that is affecting the forests, its resources, and its people. He draws a survey map of "Pirtha Block," describing it as "some extinct animal of Gondwanaland. . . . It is as if some prehistoric creature has fallen on its face. . . . Such are the survey lines of Pirtha Block."[37] His picturesque duplication of the survey map of Pirtha as a pterodactyl, serves to connect the myth of the extinct animal with the plight of the *Adivasis*. While the *Adivasis* voice their pleas for recognition, government officials resort to lies as "government proclamations are only on paper, they do nothing when it comes to the reality."[38] Puran Sahay's news of Pirtha attracts world media attention resulting in teams of welfare and foreign aid groups descending in Pirtha to "determine the 'why and how.'"[39] Devi draws attention to the fact that the dialect of the *Nagesias* does not contain the word "exploitation,"[40] but she contends that its absence in their vocabulary meant that the tribals were unaware of how they merited a place in the list of languages and dialects spoken in India. The quest for the recognition of tribal land is typical of the postcolonial enterprise engaged in the "authentication of histories of exploitation and the evolution of strategies of resistance"[41] in the fight for "new narratives of equality and human community."[42] In the postcolonial quest for development and capitalist gain, *Adivasis* once oppressed, continue to suffer as in colonial times from oppressive technologies, lack of governmental support, and uneven distribution and division of labor. The neglect of the area over centuries makes Pirtha and its population a space of intervention and a narrative of capitalism where the tribals struggle to earn "human recognition, respect."[43] Devi's accounts of the oral narratives of indigenous tribes has resulted in these groups figuring on the collective imaginary map of India that recognizes their existence. By penning their tales in her fiction, Devi has shown how their identity, history, culture ideology, culture, language, and literature are integrally related to their close, symbiotic relationship with nature. Eco-justice to the *Adivasis* thus means including their claims into "a broad call for justice"[44] and showing a "commitment to ecological and environmental justice, in addition to social justice."[45] As in Benedict Anderson's assertion that all nations are "imagined communities, that are distinguished by the style in which they are imagined,"[46] Devi's portrayal of the indigenous communities moves them into the broad discourse of environmental and ecological justice in India. Her eco-critical texts have enabled the transition of eco-justice from the local to the global by providing the necessary activist narrative to implement such change.

ECO-FEMINIST ACTIVISM FOR THE FORESTS

Women have spurred grass-roots Earth Movements that are dedicated to protecting the forests. Wangari Maathai's The Green Belt Movement (GBM)[47] has planted fifty-one million trees since 1977 to empower women through trees and thus addresses the problem of global deforestation. In the first Chipko Movement in 1973, tribal Indian women embraced trees to prevent logging of the Himalayan forests. The Chipko Movement got its name from the *Hindi* word '*chipko*' meaning 'to hug' or 'to cling to' when indigenous women of India exhibited their close ties of existence with nature. Launched by Sunderlal Bahuguna,[48] this non-violent social and ecological movement encouraged tribal women to hug and cling to the forest trees to prevent them from being logged down. This movement believes that "*Prakriti* lives in stone or tree, pool, fruit or animal, and is identified with them."[49] When the Chipko women embraced trees to protect them, they exhibited the close ties that exist between women and nature and asserted how the forests merited representation, support, and a voice. Women in the postcolonial world are often more involved than men in food production, be it in the plucking of tea leaves, or in the search for daily means of sustenance as in the case of the tribal communities like the *Adivasis* and *Shabars* in the forests of India.

> "We just live wherever ma puts us at any time . . . some call her Abhayachandi, and others call her a desolate forest. The forest itself is our mother, what d'you say? . . . She gives us fruits, flowers, tubers, leaves, wood, honey, resin,

> medicine, herbs, barks, leaves and roots, even animals to hunt. She gives us everything, keeps us alive—doesn't that make her our mother?[50]

The idea of the forest as a mother who offers the forms of sustenance necessary for existence like fruits and herbs as well as wood for fire and shelter is typical of eco-feminism. The primeval forests made by the creator at the beginning of the world serve as the basis to show how Mother Earth has always had to contend with masculine forces like lawmakers who wish to deprive her tribal forest children of the gift of hunting.

In her essay "Walking with the Comrades,"[51] Arundhati Roy's activist narrative traces her journey across the thick forests of Bastar in east-central India. Accompanied by *Adivasi* rebel minorities hailing from the *Gond*, *Halba*, and *Muria* tribes for more than two weeks, she describes their armed struggle in their fight against big corporations and the Indian government to regain their tribal lands that are rich in minerals, iron ore, and coal. Roy contends that the economic policies like the structural adjustment programs since Indian independence have enabled the effective usurpation of tribal land and minerals by state governments. In an essay entitled "Mr Chidambaram's War," Roy contends that the governments of Chhattisgarh, Jharkhand, Orissa, and West Bengal have signed hundreds of MoUs with corporate houses, worth several billion rupees, for steel plants, sponge-iron factories power plants, aluminum refineries, dams, and mines.[52] The reference is to P. Chidambaram, India's home minister in 2010 and a former non-executive director for Vedanta, India's leading natural resources conglomerate. He is referred to as the "CEO of Operation Green Hunt" by Roy.[53] As *Adivasi* towns and villages get occupied by multinational mineral companies and state-backed armed forces, it has been recorded that between 2005 to 2008, around three hundred thousand people from 644 *Adivasi* villages in the Bastar region of Chhattisgarh state were subjected to atrocities committed by Salwa Judum, a government-supported vigilante group acting to vacate mineral-rich lands.[54] In 2007, it is estimated that nearly fifty thousand *Adivasis* were forcefully relocated into makeshift camps operated by paramilitary groups, and many fled to adjoining states.[55] Roy describes how the government of India launched its military attack called Operation Green Hunt to target the *Naxalite*[56] rebels opposed to the expansion of mining in Bastar's thick forest belt.[57] Roy links the Indian government's military crackdown in Bastar to the Chhattisgarh state government's trend of signing MoUs with multinational companies to boost the extraction of iron ore, bauxite, and other precious mineral resources like uranium, limestone, and dolomite.[58] Roy describes how the forests of Dandakaranya that spread over the Indian States of West Bengal, Jharkhand, Orissa, Chhattisgarh, and Andhra Pradesh, home to the *Adivasis*, now possesses a new name of the "Red Corridor" or the "Maoist corridor" with big mining and steel companies like "the Mittals, Jindals, Tata, Essar, Posco, Rio Tinto, BHP Billiton, and, of course, Vedanta"[59] vying with each other to grab rare resources. By presenting *Adivasi* resistance to the take-over of their forests and farmlands in the context of resource grabs by government agencies and private corporations, Roy's essays portray indigenous activists and Naxalite insurgents as "resource rebels."[17] The walk with the Maoist comrades is one filled with meetings, nightly walks, brief pauses for rest in huts, camps and jungle-villages, including the centenary celebration of the 1910 *Bhumkal* celebration, remembering the famous *Adivasi* rebellion against British colonial. Women of the Bastar tribe sing songs at the *Dada log* enumerating the various atrocities committed to tribal women: forced marriage, abduction, sequestration, bigamy, and domestic violence.[60] Roy's activist presence as a traveler-narrator speaks of her attempt at recording the stories of the Dandakaranya forests, its people, the *Naxalite* insurgency, and the various itineraries of conflict both feminist and tribal. The essay is written in the first-person plural where Roy resorts to the use of "we" in her activist narrative. The plural voice and tone serve to highlight the common point of view.

> We're walking in pitch darkness and dead silence. I'm the only one using a torch, pointing down so that all I can see in its circle of light are Comrade Kamla's bare heels in her scuffed, black chappals. . . . It turns out to be a long walk. . . . We are privileged because Comrade Leng, the master of ceremonies, is walking with us. In Gondi *leng* means 'the voice.'

Comrade Leng who renders a song at the *Bhumkal* celebration also bears a name that means 'voice.' He is the voice of the *Adivasis* as he sings their songs, lamenting their loss of land. Here the polyphony stems from the voicing of Leng's song through the activist voice which describes the struggle to be heard. During the walk in the jungle, there is no sign of camaraderie or chatter, but the sound is one of silenced talk accompanied by the sound of walkers in *chappals* through the forests. On arrival at the camp Roy describes how the hundred comrades lined up in two rows to sing.

> Everyone has a weapon. And a smile. They begin to sing: *Lal lal salaam, lal lal salaam, aane vaaley saathiyon ko lal lal salaam.* (Red salute to the comrades who have arrived). It was sung sweetly, as though it was a folk song about a river, or a forest blossom. With the song, the greeting, the handshake and the clenched fist. Everyone greets everyone, murmuring *Lalslaam, mlalslaa mlalslaam.*[61]

In her activist narrative, Roy transcribes the voices of many as evident in the pronouns 'they' and 'everyone.' The voices resound in unison as they salute the red Maoist flag, each voice has an accompanying 'weapon' and a 'smile,' oxymorons of conflict and peace. Graham Huggan and Helen Tiffin have however pointed out that Roy's privileged status as a "cosmopolitan elite" makes her an unfit "representative" of tribal movements in India.[62] They argue that Roy's essay "The Greater Common Good" appears to usurp the *Adivasi* voice behind the *Narmada Bachao Andolan* (Save the Narmada Movement). Arundhati Roy's political non-fiction has often been viewed with a disdainful eye[63] and considered as "objectionable writings."[64] Huggan and Tiffin contrast Roy's activist authorship with Ken Saro-Wiwa, the Nigerian author who campaigned extensively for the Ogoni people fight to protect their Niger Delta homeland from oil leaks and resource grabs. Huggan and Tiffin argue that while Saro-Wiwa writes on behalf of the Ogoni people as an Ogoni himself; Roy, a celebrity writer resorts to journalistic writing and that her activist non-fiction does not necessarily constitute an act of representation. Their scholarly view is no doubt pertinent, but any reader of Roy's nonfiction will agree that Roy's activist narrative highlights and manages to make voices heard in the debate regarding the deforestation of the forests and the displacement of indigenous forest folk.

Another Indian eco-feminist Vandana Shiva has expressed the view in *Staying Alive: Wood, Ecology and Development*, that food in postcolonial countries is 'gendered' and that subaltern tribal women's knowledge on the preservation of forests was often ignored by the 'men of the forests,' as the forest preservation experts in postcolonial countries were usually men.[65] The *Chipko* or tree hugging movement to protect life-giving trees in the 1970s, sprang when tribal women hugged food-giving trees to prevent logging activity in the Himalayan ranges. This idea of non-violent resistance stems from Mahatma Gandhi's 24-day *Dandi* March or Salt *Satyagraha* in 1930 when he made life-essential salt from seawater to protest peacefully over the British monopoly of salt production. Shiva draws inspiration from the Indian cosmic myth that all existence stems from primordial energy which is the essence of all matter and pervades everything. She explains that tribal women in rural India believe in the manifestation of this energy as nature or '*Prakriti*.'[66] Shiva considers modern science and technology as a western, patriarchal, and colonial project, which is basically violent and perpetuates this violence against women and nature. She accuses this model of development of being a shift away from traditional Indian philosophy, which sees *prakriti* as a living and creative process, the feminine principle, from which all life arises. She argues that in the name of development, nature has been exploited mercilessly and that the feminine principle was no longer associated with activity, creativity, and sanctity of life, but was considered passive and as a resource. She attributes this exploitation as the cause for marginalization, devaluation, displacement, and ultimately the dispensability of women.

She contends that women's special knowledge of nature and their dependence on it for sustenance, were systematically marginalized under the onslaught of modern science. Shiva, however, notes that Third World women though victims of the development process, also possess the power for change. In Save the Western Ghats Movement, a '*padayatra*' or a march was organized across 1,300 kilometers covering the States of Maharashtra, Goa, Karnataka, Tamil Nadu, and Kerala to draw attention to the environmental problems in the hills of the Western Ghats. The Movement consisting of twenty local and regional grassroots associations, opposed the felling of trees, forced the government to recognize these ranges as a global diversity spot, ban the felling of trees and cancel the launch of the Silent Valley National Park. These grassroots environmental non-violent movements are concerned with both environmental preservation and issues of economic equity and social justice. In her documentary *Seeds of Vandana Shiva*,[67] Shiva speaks on how when women gathered to protest ecological destruction of life on Earth, they found ample proof of the link between patriarchal domination and violence against women especially in postcolonial countries. She contends that ecofeminism is about the liberation of women that cannot be achieved in isolation. While ecofeminism contends that patriarchal ideology denies women rights, women need to reconfigure the underlying structural relations inherent in one's culture. The focus is thus on the process of achieving equality, through non-violent, non-hierarchical forms of protest and engagement. She criticizes the entire model of development and relegates it to a mode of thinking that is a Western "reductionist world view"[68] where forests, land, resources, and people are manipulated to increase the production of pulpwood, thus consequently decreasing the output of water from forests, and reducing the diversity of different life forms both human and non-human that constitute the community of the forest.[69] Contending that the reductionist paradigm is responsible for having created this disparity between nature and women, she argues that the dominant patriarchal structures reduce women to the role of mere consumers.

> Women in sustenance economies, producing and reproducing wealth in partnership with nature, have been experts in their own right of a holistic and ecological knowledge of nature's processes. But these alternative modes of knowing, which are oriented to social benefits and sustenance needs, are not recognized by the reductionist paradigm, because it fails to perceive the interconnectedness of nature, or the connection of women's lives, work, and knowledge with the creation of wealth.[70]

Through her analysis, Shiva points out the critical links between the different development perspectives, the process of change brought about by development, and its impact on the environment and the people dependent on it for their subsistence. She argues with Maria Mies that whenever women have protested to stop ecological destruction or nuclear annihilation, they were "aware of the connections between patriarchal violence against women, other people and nature."[71] However, Vandana Shiva's arguments have been refuted by scholars like Gabriel Dietrich who points out that Shiva's theory of the philosophy of '*prakriti*' is too general and not representative of all women in India; and argues that the *Hindu* feminine principle cannot be applied to all religious communities in India like Muslims, Christians, Sikhs and other minority communities.[72] Meera Nanda voices the idea that judging other cultures from the vantage point of modern science, would be "epistemic violence" against the other.[73] The term *epistemic violence* was used by Gayatri Chakravorty Spivak in her essay, "Can the Subaltern Speak?"[74] Spivak voices the idea that oppressed minorities characterized as Other are restricted by their linguistic competences, are denied the access to hegemonic power, and do not have the opportunity of self-representation. Spivak's contention that "epistemic violence" obstructs, undermines non-Western methods, or approaches to knowledge and that "the subaltern has no history and cannot speak, the subaltern as female is even more deeply in shadow."[75] Nanda considers Vandana Shiva's brand of eco-feminism as that of a neo-populist scholar, who has tried to cast the West as vicious and the Third World as virtuous. She rebukes Shiva for branding modern science as western, inherently masculine, thus looking at India with her face backwards. Different voices highlight different issues on how environmental feminist activism can address their concerns for the forest and its people.

PARTICIPATION AND PROCEDURAL JUSTICE

David Schlosberg in *Defining Environmental Justice: Theories, Movements, and Nature*[76] posits that the quest for equity in the distribution of resources like water or forests is the cause for the inequity in the distribution of the profits that projects in the name of equity and distribution engender. Schlosberg's paradigm argues that recognition and respect for indigenous practices and land rights is central to the demand for social and environmental land rights. He contends that there is also "inequity in terms of who receives the bads—the pollution, waste, lack of resources, and theft of intellectual property related to local environmental knowledge."[77] This is typical of Schlosberg's paradigm on recognition where he identifies the need of recognition for not just individuals, but to whole communities.[78] Though unfeatured on world cartography, the *Adivasi* tribals have their voices inscribed in the story's narrative that can be heard and read time and time again, thus granting them recognition. The notions of equity, recognition, and participation are all linked as demonstrated through the Schlosberg model. His paradigm also considers the dimension of participation by those suffering "injustice of the lack of cultural recognition."[79] David Schlosberg's paradigm argues that recognition and respect for indigenous practices and land rights is central to the demand for social and environmental land rights. He refers to the Sixth International Indigenous Peoples' Forum on Climate Change, which calls upon the United Nations Framework Convention on Climate Change (UNFCCC) to recognize, protect, promote Indigenous Peoples' rights, and thus secure the future of humanity and social and environmental justice for all (International Indigenous Peoples' Forum on Climate Change). Courts around the world agree on the increasing necessity to have specialized environmental courts with special expertise in environmental matters and sustainable development. Australia was pioneer in setting up its first specialist comprehensive Land and Environment Court of New South Wales in 1680, a "one-stop shop" for environmental planning and land matters.[80] It set up its specialized tribunal to be a means to an end; capable of delivering consistency in decision-making; decreasing delays through its expertise in environmental disputes; and facilitating the development of environmental laws, policies and principles).[81] In Sweden, since May 2011, the country has established five Land and Environment Courts that are part of the district courts in Nacka, Vänersborg, Växjö, Umea, and Ostersund and one superior environmental court as the Svea Court of Appeal.[82] In the United Kingdom, the Environmental Tribunal came into existence in 2010 becoming a part of His Majesty's Court system. It is a part of the General Regulatory Chamber of the First-tier Tribunal, initially entrusted with limited jurisdiction, and was restricted to hearing appeals on matters pertaining to civil sanctioning powers of environmental regulators; but its jurisdiction has slowly grown to include appeals concerning civil sanctions under eco-design regulation and appeals under Welsh plastic-bag regulations. In India, the creation of Public Interest Litigation (PIL) in the 1980s paved the way for an era of judicial activism aimed at protecting the human rights of marginalized sections of society. PIL enabled citizens traditionally excluded from courts by virtue of illiteracy, poverty, ignorance, isolation, or caste to be able to enforce their fundamental human rights through law, either in person or through a court-recognized 'friend.' The use of PIL as a broad-based, people-oriented approach envisioned access to justice as a 'wheel of transformation' through judge-fashioned processes and remedies.

Jurisdictions around the world are all developing some form of specialized environmental court or tribunal, which permits a flexible mechanism for dispute resolution. Due to general dissatisfaction with the general court system regarding the delay in decision-making, and lack of expertise in environmental law and climate science, India has also enacted laws permitting the creation of the specialized court structure of National Green Tribunals.[83] Judges in ordinary courts may lack sufficient experience of the practicalities of environmental law and may be comfortable dealing with expert testimony and the task of balancing anticipated environmental harm and economic benefits" (19). India thus set up the National Green Tribunal in 2010, which is a specialized judicial body that adjudicates environmental cases in the country. The idea of justice being rendered through a fairer distribution of environmental harm has resulted in an active democratic engagement with courts, taking resistance against environmental harm from the social domain to the legal. In *Anirudh Kumar v. Municipal Corporation of Delhi* & Ors (2015) stated that it was in favor of judicial activism

> Our current processual jurisprudence is not of individualistic Anglo-Indian mould. It is broad-based and people-oriented and envisions access to justice through 'class actions,' 'public interest litigation' and 'representative proceedings.' Indeed, little Indians in large numbers seeking remedies in courts through collective proceedings, instead of being driven to an expensive plurality of litigations, is an affirmation of participative justice in our democracy. We have no hesitation in holding that the narrow concept of 'cause of action' and 'person aggrieved' and individual litigation is becoming obsolescent in some jurisdictions.[84]

In *State of Uttaranchal v. Balwant Singh Chaufal & Ors* (2010), the court began to entertain cases concerning the enforcement of the fundamental rights of marginalized and deprived sections of the society.[85] The rule of *locus standi* was amended to include 'aggrieved persons' who were previously excluded legal access. In a writ petition filed in 2008, Wildlife *First and Ors v. Ministry of Forest* (2019),[86] Wildlife First, the Wildlife Trust of India, and other conservationists petitioned the Supreme Court of India to assess the constitutional validity of the Forest Rights Act (FRA) (2006).[87] The petitioners sought to recover forest land encroached upon by people who had their claims to land rejected under the FRA. According to the FRA forest dwellers needed to document a case with state governments to safeguard privilege to their territories. Indigenous, illiterate people who had dwelt for more than one hundred years were suddenly asked by authorities to show proper documentation regarding entitlement of the land. Cases were thus dismissed without proper reasons or were attributed to the wrong translation of the Other Traditional Forest Dwellers (OTFD) definition, or basically for the absence of proof or nonappearance of GPS overview. According to the FRA, categories of person could claim rights if they (i) resided in forests or forestland, or, if they were (ii) dependent on forest manufacture for their support and if they were (iii) Forest scheduled regular Tribes and Other traditional Forest Dwellers (OTFDs) or communities sustained on forests for a minimum of seventy-five years. On February 13, 2019, the Supreme Court ordered all States to evict indigenous tribals who had had their claims rejected under the Act by July 24, 2019. Further, it directed the Forest Survey of India to conduct a satellite GPS survey and place on record encroachment positions before and after evictions. It directed the Chief Secretaries of various States to submit affidavits explaining why they had up until now failed to evict individuals who had had their claims rejected. On February 28, 2019, the Court decided to place a stay on its own order, directing States to submit whether due process had been followed in rejecting claims. This is not the first time that forest dwellers have been deprived of their homes in the forests by the Ministry of Forests (MoEF). In 2014, around 450 families from indigenous *Baiga* and *Gond* people group were evicted from the forests to secure tigers in the Kanha Tiger Reserve. They were not awarded any recovery benefits as guaranteed by the administration. Even though the FRA (2006) aimed at respecting and recognizing the rights of forest dwellers, it has not succeeded in achieving this goal. This is the battle between tribal dwellers who call themselves the guardians of the forests and the forest ministry who are encroachers not just to their dwelling spaces, but also to their fundamental right to life and equality guaranteed by the Constitution. The decision is pending.

LEGAL CUSTODIANS OF THE FORESTS

The Madras High Court in the case *A. Periyakaruppan v. The Principal Secretary & Anr* (2022)[88] ruled that nature merited the same legal status as a human being, thus enabling the forests to have the same rights, duties, and liabilities as a person. This case was inspired by the 18-year legal wrangle between Ecuador and Chevron/Texaco in *Chevron Corporation and Texaco Petroleum Corporation v. Republic of Ecuador* (2018).[89] In 2020, the Permanent Court of Arbitration (PCA) in the Hague passed a verdict, under which Ecuador would have to pay a penalty of $96 million to the U.S. energy firm Chevron regarding the oil-export dispute cases filed in the early 1990s. As this legal dispute was being enacted in the courtroom, the legislative branch of government in Ecuador decided to include Rights to Nature laws in its Constitution on September 8, 2008. It declared that "Nature or Pachamama, has the right to exist, persist, maintain, and regenerate its vital cycles, structure, functions, and its processes in evolution. Every person, people, community or nationality, will be able to demand the recognition of Rights for Nature before the public bodies."[90] Ecuador's rich oil reserves had greedy oil companies coveting the lay of the land. The context was ripe for the passage of laws called the Rights of Pachamama or Mother Earth. Similar laws to give ecosystems, animals, and elements of the natural world legal rights akin to those of humans were enacted in Bolivia, New Zealand, Bangladesh, Ecuador, Brazil, Colombia, and Mexico. Spreading like a wave across continents. Today, many 'Rights of Nature' cases are pending in courtrooms around the planet.

During the Copenhagen Summit in 2009 on Climate Change, Bolivia's President, Evo Morales refused to sign The Copenhagen Climate Change Deal. Instead, he passed the law for the Defense of Mother Earth that recognizes the rights of Mother Earth, as well as the obligations and duties of the Plurinational State to guarantee that these rights are respected.[91] This law consequently received approval in the World People's Conference on Climate Change and the Rights of Mother Earth in Cochabamba in Bolivia in April 2010. Columbia has also protected its part of the Amazon, giving the rainforests the same legal rights as humans. In 2018, in response to a petition, the Supreme Court of Colombia recognized that fundamental rights of life, health, the minimum subsistence, freedom, and human dignity are substantially linked and determined by the environment and the ecosystem. It declared that the Colombian Amazon forests were entitled to protection, conservation, maintenance, and restoration, and it ordered the government to develop and implement action plans to address deforestation.

In the United States Supreme Court case, *Sierra Club v. Morton* (1972),[92] the petitioner claimed a special interest in the conservation and sound maintenance of the national parks, game refuges, and forests of the country. He filed a lawsuit seeking a declaratory judgment and an injunction to restrain federal officials from approving an extensive skiing development project in the Mineral King Valley in the Sequoia National Forest. Sierra Club relied on § 10 of the Administrative Procedure Act, which grants judicial review to a "person suffering legal wrong because of agency action, or [who is] adversely affected or aggrieved by agency action within the meaning of a relevant statute."[93] In a four-to-three decision, the U.S Supreme Court's majority opinion delivered by Justice Potter Stewart, decided that the Sierra Club did not have standing to sue under the Administrative Procedure Act as it had failed to show that any of its members had suffered or would suffer injury as a result of the defendants' actions. In his dissenting opinion, Justice William O. Douglas argued on the contrary that the standing doctrine should allow environmental organizations such as the Sierra Club to sue on behalf of inanimate objects such as land. This case though unsuccessful, set a precedent suggesting the possibility for inanimate objects to have legal personality for the purpose of lawsuits, and that those who had "an intimate relation with the inanimate object about to be injured, polluted, or otherwise despoiled are its legitimate spokesmen."[94]

In *A. Periyakaruppan v. The Principal Secretary and Anr* (2022),[95] the case in southern Indian state of Tamil Nadu came before the Madras High Court on the petition of a government official, A. Periyakaruppan, who had been

Table 5.1: ***A Periyakaruppan v. The Principal Secretary and Anr*** **(2022)**

W.P (MD) No. 18636 of 2013, W.P (MD) No. 3070 of 2020 and No. 2614 of 2020
IN THE MADRAS HIGH COURT
Judgment rendered on April 19, 2022

Coram: S. Srimathy

Rule: Application of the Preamble and Articles 38, 39 and 39A of the Constitution of India regarding the application of the doctrine of '*parens patriae*' and the duties and obligations of the state towards vulnerable citizens incapable of exercising their rights.

Facts of the case: During his term of service as a *tahsildar* or tax collector in the Revenue Department of the Government of India, A. Periyakaruppan, granted *pattas* or land deeds on land classified as protect forests. On reaching retirement age in 2006, he was not allowed to retire but was placed under suspension as disciplinary proceedings were still pending. The Government decided to impose a penalty of ⅓rd of his eligible retirement pension.

Arguments by the petitioner: The petitioner argued that he had been unjustly punished for merely carrying out the orders of his hierarchical superiors, the Madurai Assistant Settlement Officer (ASO) and the Chennai Director of Survey and Settlement (DSS), who on the contrary had gone scot-free. As the *patta* or land deed had been cancelled, the petitioner contended that there had been no monetary loss and that the punishment was too harsh on a civil servant who had dedicated 35 years to government service.

Arguments by the respondent: The respondents contended that the petitioner had illegally granted *pattas* of the Government land. They stated that the petitioner had granted the land deeds despite knowing that forestlands were protected land. They insisted that the petitioner had failed to apply any factual test and had not performed his duty to protect the forests. The respondents pleaded that the petitioner should not have acted upon the orders of his superior as such an act contravened the law. The petitioner, being a *tahsildar* or tax collector, had the duty to protect the lands of the government and not implement the orders of his superiors without proper contemplation.

Issue: Whether the petitioner could be granted the same relief as his co-petitioners.

Reasoning of the court: The doctrine of *parens patriae* that is invoked to recognize the inherent authority of the state to provide protection and ensure the welfare of persons *non sui juris*, such as minors, insane, and incompetent persons, was extended to include Nature that was voiceless and in need of protection.

Conclusion: The court noted that the proceedings could not be equated to other cases while considering the period of delinquency. It ruled that the petitioner's case was different from that of his superiors, but as there had been no monetary loss, it reduced the punishment to a six-month suspension for the act done against nature. The court observed that Mother Nature must be protected and preserved as indiscriminate destruction or change was leading to an endangered ecosystem. It considered that the destruction was due to anthropogenic influence and that the natural environment must not be harmed in the name of sustainable development. The Court required governments to act as guardians of Mother Nature by favoring a 'right of nature' approach that offered higher degree of protection than conventional 'Polluter Pays' or 'Precautionary' Environmental Principles. By invoking *parens patriae* jurisdiction, the court declared Mother Nature to be a living being having the status of legal entity and thus possessing corresponding rights, liabilities, and duties. Mother Nature was thus accorded rights akin to human fundamental, legal and constitutional rights.

Note: My synopsis of *A. Periyakaruppan v. The Principal Secretary & Anr* (Madras High Court, April 19, 2022).

forced to retire and had lost part of his pension for having granted a deed for a tract of land in a protected forest to a private individual. The land located in the Megamalai area is known as the 'green peak' and 'high wavy mountain' due to its dense evergreen forests and cardamom plantations.

In this landmark case presented in table 5.1, Justice Srimathy invoked the power of the court to act as a guardian or custodian of those who cannot care for themselves. In her opinion, she observes that Mother Nature must be protected and preserved and that "Indiscriminate destruction or change is leading to several complications in the ecosystem, ultimately is endangering the very existence of the animals, flora and fauna, forests, rivers, lakes, water bodies, mountains, glaciers, air, and of course humans. Strangely the destruction is carried on by few humans."[96] She referred to a precedent ruling in *Lalit Miglani v. State of Uttarakhand* (2018) that declared the court justices as persons in *loco parentis* as they lent a human face to protect, conserve and preserve all the water systems like streams, rivulets, lakes, air, meadows, dales, jungles, forests wetlands, grasslands, springs, and waterfalls in the state of Uttarakhand.[97] She observed that the natural environment must not be abused and expressed skepticism regarding judicial jargon like 'Sustainable Development,' 'Polluter Pays,' 'Precautionary Principle' shall not be allowed anymore.[98] By adopting the public policy narrative of granting 'nature' the '*parens patriae*' status, she has paved the terrain for expanding the legal doctrine of 'rights' and 'duties' of 'nature as a legal being' into existing bureaucratic and effective frameworks. She insisted that nature merited fundamental rights, legal rights, and constitutional rights for its survival, and sustenance. Justice Srimathy's judgement provides a new opportunity for the FRA to reconsider ways and means of protecting indigenous communities and forest zones. Seen through an eco-feminist lens, Justice Srimathy's judgment offers protection to tribal women selling the fruits of the forests in village and city markets. The court acting as custodian directed the State Government and the Central Government to take appropriate steps to protect Mother Earth in all possible ways. The court in its role as a custodian extended its judicial arm to protect tribal inhabitants of the forests. A creative application of the judgment would enable better usage of scientific data, proper implementation of ecosystem policies like carbon offsets, and nature-based solutions for disaster management. The judgment sets a precedent and will be quoted in Environment Impact Assessments (EIAs) and Environmental Clearances (ECs), thus showing how the judiciary can influence the legislative in decision making. The granting of '*parens patriae*' jurisdiction to forests can spawn a nexus linking policy makers and climate scientists.

It is interesting to trace how India recognizes the Rights of Nature in its Constitution. After the British colonial victory in the Sepoy Mutiny (1857–1859), the Indian Forest Act of 1865 was enacted by the British, and amended later as the Indian Forest Act of 1927. Both acts failed to protect the forests of India and its people as they aimed to safeguard the interests of British colonizers. After independence, the Forest Conservation Act 1980 was passed, restricting the use of forests for non-forest means. The Forest Conservation Act 1980 was introduced by the Indian Parliament to control deforestation and conserve forests and their resources. Article 48A under the Directive Principles of State Policy demands the State to "protect and improve the environment and safeguard the forests and wildlife of the country,"[99] while Article 51A (g) imposes a fundamental duty upon citizens to "protect and improve the natural environment, including forests, rivers, and wildlife, and to have compassion for all living creatures."[100] The Forest Resources Act (2006) is currently in force and aims to undo the historical injustice towards forest dwelling communities; ensure land tenure, livelihood and food security to indigenous forests; and finally, to strengthen, sustain, and conserve the biodiversity of the forests.[101]

NATIONAL GREEN TRIBUNAL FOREST CASES

The National Green Tribunal was set up on October 18, 2010, pursuant to the National Green Tribunal Act (2010).[102] It is a specialized judicial body equipped with environmental and climate science expertise solely for the purpose of adjudicating environmental cases in India. It is composed of both technical members and judicial members on the bench represented on equal parity, thus offering multi-skilled cognizance of both scientific and technical expertise in adjudicating environmental cases. The National Green Tribunal Act provides for the presence of an epistemic community like recognized forestry experts in environmental engineering, environmental management experts, and climate scientists, capable of providing appropriate solutions on technical or complicated environmental problems, free from corporate or organizational associations or biases. The NGT can deliberate and render judgment on the determination of who is an 'aggrieved party' and who has 'standing' as a litigant. This is in keeping with the precedent set in Supreme Court decisions that analyzed environmental issues within a broader human rights framework and used the concept of 'standing' applicable to PILs as in *Amit Maru v. Ministry of Environment and Forest* (2014),[103] *The Goa Foundation Anr v. Union of India and Ors* (2013),[104] *Vimal Bhai & Others v. Ministry of Environment and Forests* (2011),[105] and *Ms. Betty C. Alvares v. The State of Goa and Ors* (2014). The NGT itself has expanded on this by pointing out that the results of environmental degradation are not restricted to individuals and rather felt by everyone. Any order issued by NGT supersedes all forms of executive action by any ministry or government agency. The

NGT has even passed judgement on the validity and legality of policy action under the legislations covered by the NGT Act. In *Society for Protection of Environment and Biodiversity v. Union of India*,[106] the NGT quashed the December 2016 Environment Impact Assessment (EIA) notification issued by the MoEF that was determined to be diluting substantive provisions of EIA Notification of 2006.[107] In *Wilfred J. v. Ministry of Environment & Forests* (2014),[108] the NGT decided that the Act grants it powers of judicial review in a limited scope pertaining to all matters related to the environment. The clearance given to a port was challenged in this case, as it was situated in an ecologically sensitive area. However, the NGT rejected the petitioner's claim as it gave weight to the economic importance of the port. In *Punamchand v. Union of India & Ors* (2014), the petitioner challenged the clearance granted to a hydroelectric project requiring around one hundred thirty-three thousand trees to be felled. As the applicant was absent during the hearing, the NGT accepted the government plan to plant two million seedlings which exceeded the NGT's mandated ratio of 1:8.[109] However, in *Tamil Nadu Pollution Control Board v. Sterlite Industries (I) Ltd.* (2019), the Supreme Court of India held that the NGT had no general power of judicial review, and that government orders could not be judicially reviewed by the NGT unless there existed an appeal under Section 16 of the NGT Act, which permitted an appeal of decision on environmental clearances.[110] As in the principles of separation and a balance of powers, the legislature can amend the rules under the NGT Act, through the passage and approval of both houses of parliament and the presidential assent. In *Indian Council for Enviro-Legal Action v. Union of India And Ors* (2014), the applicant requested the Green Tribunal to take action to reduce the unregulated emissions of H acid produced by a chemical plant, a greenhouse gas that is thousands of times more potent than carbon dioxide (CO_2). The NGT directed the Ministry of Environment and Forests and the appropriate bodies to implement and install the write machinery for waste disposal and the regulating of H acid emissions and waste.[111]

India witnessed a 115 percent increase in forest fires in March 2023 aggravated by the absence of rain in February and abnormally high temperatures for the season.[112] And 42,799 forest fires were detected in the beginning of March by the satellite-based forest fire monitoring systems of the Forest Survey of India (FSI); it estimates that the number has increased by 19,929 when compared to 2022.[113] According to the Indian Meteorological Department (IMD) which forecasts monsoon and records rainfall data for India, India received 7.2 mm rainfall in February, the sixth lowest recorded data for the month since 1901.[114] Low rainfall means dry forests that are prone to wildfires that can spread easily and release carbon dioxide (CO_2) emissions and other greenhouse gases (GHG) that are harmful to climate change. The Ministry of Environment and Forests has been summoned to court in cases where petitioners have challenged Environmental impact Assessments (EIAs) and Environmental Clearances (ECs) that do not consider the ecological impact on forests.

In *Jan Chetna v. Ministry of Environment & Forests* (2011),[115] the petitioner, Jan Chetna, a social and environmental group, challenged the Environmental Clearance granted without a public hearing to Scania Steel and Power Ltd. for the expansion of its existing Sponge Iron Plant in the forest area of Chhattisgarh. The National Green Tribunal of New Delhi suspended the clearance and issued a judgment ordering the Ministry of Environment & Forests (MoEF) to develop proper mechanism and check the authenticity of environmental data reported in the EIA/EMP report. While considering the issue of *locus standi*, the Tribunal ruled that the petition satisfied the definition of a 'person aggrieved' and had the required locus standi to file the appeal. It ruled in favor of the petitioner as it held that since no environmental clearance had been granted for the existing Sponge Iron plant under the EIA Notification (2006). Thus, the concession not to hold public consultation was not extended to Scania Steel and Power Ltd.[116]

In the case *Rajiv Dutta v. Union of India* (2019)[117] presented in table 5.2, the petitioner Rajiv Dutta, an environmental lawyer, referred to the large scale and uncontrolled forest fires that had ravaged the States of Uttarakhand and Himachal Pradesh resulting in enormous ecological damage to the pedosphere of this already endangered biological zone. In this case, the respondent, the Union of India confirmed that that since May 6, 2016, no active forest fire had been detected by satellites, and no forest fire points information had been submitted by the Forest Survey of India (FSI). The respondent's submission thus matched the petitioner's contention that almost all the recent fires incidents were incidents of surface fire, and that these fires had been tackled and doused by the forest fire services.

The litigant contended that the forest fires had had a devastating effect on the glaciers of Uttarakhand, which had resulted in Indian rivers being enveloped with black carbon soot causing them to melt faster than usual. He also stated that the government had the obligation to curb existing fires, prevent future fires, and restore forest ecology. The respondents, States of Uttarakhand, and Himachal Pradesh, argued that extremely low temperature had been recorded in the year 2016, thereby causing a serious moisture deficit in the soil and in the forest areas, making conditions conducive to the spread of forest fires. They also claimed that 97 percent of the fires had occurred due to human negligence.

This landmark decision established the critical role played by legislative and judicial bodies in protecting the forests. There are two climate change scientific narratives in this case, presented by both the petitioner and the respondent. Rajiv Dutta, the petitioner, enumerated the various emissions

Table 5.2: ***Rajiv Dutta v. Union of India*** **(2019)**

Original Application No. 216 of 2016
BEFORE THE NATIONAL GREEN TRIBUNAL, NEW DELHI
Judgment rendered on May 2, 2019

Coram: S. Kumar, M.S. Nambiar, DR. D.K. Agrawal, A.R. Yousuf, B. S. SAJWAN

Rule: Under sections 14 and 15 of the National Tribunal Act, a citizen can have his case heard at the tribunal when it relates to a substantial question relating to environment, including enforcement of any legal right relating to environment. The claimant can claim relief and compensation for any environmental damage arising under the enactments specified in the Schedule.

Facts of the case: The petitioner, a senior environmental lawyer, filed a case before the National Green Tribunal (NGT) claiming that the government needed to take more action to control the large scale and uncontrolled forest fires ravaging the States of Uttarakhand and Himachal Pradesh. He contended that these fires had largely been caused by humans, local land mafia and other individuals who were engaged in the enterprise of cutting wood for commercial purpose. He accused forest officials of turning a blind eye to the fires and requested the court to act. He elaborated on how large areas of virgin forest lands, along with diverse biological species had gone extinct due to anthropogenic intrusion. He warned the government that if no urgent steps were taken, there would be further devastation to the flora and fauna of the states of Uttarakhand and Himachal Pradesh which are considered as part of the wealth of the Indian nation. He supplemented his wildfire storyline with annexes of news reports from the *Times of India*, dated May 1, 2016, and May 3, 2016, to prove the extent of loss which had occurred due to wild forest fires. He argued that these forest fires degraded the ecological sustainability of a highly endangered biological zone. He listed the emissions released by forest fires as carbon dioxide CO2, carbon monoxide (CO), and methane (CH4), organic aerosols and black carbon, non-methane organic compounds, nitrogen oxides, and Sulphur dioxide (SO2). He detailed how the emissions of these gases adversely affected both atmospheric and surface absorption of solar energy and resulted consequently in marked cool or warm air currents.

Issue: Whether emissions from forest fires contribute to climate change. Is there a need to develop forest fire management plans?

Reasoning of the court: The court reasoned that even though the respondents defense regarding low moisture as the cause for dryness and the spread of forest fires was plausible. It articulated the view that the States of Himachal Pradesh and Uttarakhand had been slack, in dealing with this serious environmental issue that had resulted in ecological damage. It had failed to implement the national forest policy and related forest fire management plans. Such failure had resulted in the loss of forest biodiversity, degradation of environment and air quality, thus affecting the citizen's right to a healthy environment.

Conclusion: The Tribunal directed the central and the state governments of Himachal Pradesh and Uttarakhand to formulate national policy and guidelines for forest fire prevention and control. The respective States must prepare and implement forest fire management plan for effective prevention and control of forest fire. It laid out steps to be taken like the mapping of the forest areas which were considered as vulnerable areas; to ensure that adequate resources and manpower were placed at the disposal of the forest department to manage and implement action plans for controlling forest fires.

Note: My synopsis of *Rajiv Dutta v. Union of India* (National Green Tribunal, New Delhi May 2, 2019).

released by forest fires and cited the example of the Indonesian forest fire in 1997 that had released between 0.81 and 2.57 giga-tons of CO_2 into the atmosphere, which ranges from 13 to 40 percent of the global carbon emissions caused by burning of fossil fuels.[118] He also contended that forest fires in forested ecosystems are one of the primary mechanisms that played a role in regulating patterns of carbon storage and release. The storyline also draws on the reasoning that wildfires in forested regions are a critical link in the global carbon cycle, with forests having the capacity to store about 45 percent of terrestrial carbon and sequester around 25 percent of annual anthropogenic carbon emissions.[119] He narrates how in the event of wildland fires, a large release of carbon takes place causing black carbon deposits to settle on the glaciers of Uttarakhand, which are the lifeline of major north Indian rivers like the Ganges and the Yamuna. The respondent, the Union of India acknowledged that general meteorological conditions in the year 2016 for the State of Uttarakhand had been erratic when compared to previous years, as inferred from Indian Meteorological Department (IMD) data pertaining to temperature and rainfall. According to the IMD, rainfall had been sparse. Heat waves had left the forest extremely vulnerable to fires across the country, and many incidents of forest fires had been reported during the forest fire season by both the media and the forest fire services. The respondent, the Union of India also contended that the main reason for forest fires was the quality of forest floor litter in Uttarakhand, that had majorly pine needles that were highly inflammable and conducive to forest fires. It argued that it used sufficient scientifically managed fire prevention practices every year during the winter season, preceding the forest fire season every year. It explained that the weather conditions of forests in Uttarakhand were monitored for fire sensitivity, detection, and control of forest fires. The Green Tribunal issued a direction to the State of Himachal Pradesh and Uttarakhand to submit before the MoEF the Crisis Management Plan for forest fire, prevention, and control, as prepared by them. According to the ministry this matter has been pending since 2010, and the MoEF was directed to file the details to the States which have not responded to their reminder and not submitted the crises management plan. Furthermore, they were directed to file the causes for such fire which they have found as a result of their studies as well as the action plan prepared for prevention and control of forest fire in the country, as disclosed by them by a public declaration on May 10, 2016.

PROTECTING THE FORESTS

All attempts to protect the forests need to be done on both local and global scales as forests sustain multiple forms of life and have the capacity to sequester carbon emissions that have been pumped into the atmosphere by human activity. Forests can thrive only when everything else around it thrives too. The forests house people, animals and trees who have equal claim to it. Chopping down the forests reduces the rainfall, causes increases in temperatures, and results in a drier climate that triggers forest wildfires. Ecocritical narratives have inspired activism and have resulted in Green Tribunals that serve as polyphonic forums of discussion for parliamentarians, judges, lawyers, activists, academicians, environmentalists, climate scientists, and other stakeholders. The idea of legal personhood for forests has not been embraced by all forums around the globe, nor has the idea of legal custodianship of forests. But increasing awareness of the climate science has resulted in governments operating by considering the three dynamics—cognizance, the need to take appropriate action, and take preventive measures to prevent further damage and curb such preventable fires. World summits aim to establish a balance in nature and protect the forests. In the sixth edition of the One Planet Summit held on March 1, 2023, at Libreville in Gabon, thirteen heads of state and government, twenty-seven ministers, international NGOs, representatives from the private sector, think tanks, and indigenous peoples' organizations joined together to renew their collective ambition on preserving and sustaining the forests, and tackling the interrelated global challenges of climate change and biodiversity loss. Similar collective action to protect the Mahan forest in the Indian state of Madhya Pradesh with its oldest forests from coal mining, more than one million people signed a petition on Greenpeace India's Junglistan campaign.[120] The campaign showcases and highlights legal cases and reports, includes celebrity endorsements called Fools for Forests, and even hosts a show on MTV.

In an ancient story from the Quechua people in Peru, a little hummingbird tires to extinguish a forest fire by fetching drops of water from the lake.

> One day in the jungle a fire broke out in the jungle
> All the animals ran out of the jungle fearing for their lives.
> Suddenly the Jaguar saw a little humming bird head (q'inti)
> The Jaguar asked him what he was doing and the Q'inti said
> 'I am flying to the lake to get water to help put out the fire'
> The jaguar laughed at him and said, 'You're crazy, you can't put out this fire!'
> The Q'inti replied, 'At least I am doing my part.'[121]

Like Q'inti, the hummingbird, we need to do our mite in extinguishing forest fires and preserve the biodiversity of forests that provide the lifeline for people and the planet.

NOTES

1. Rudyard Kipling, *The Jungle Books* (Oxford: Oxford World's Classics, 1996), 55.

2. Rudyard Kipling, "Beyond the Pale," in *Plain Tales from the Hills* (Oxford: Oxford University Press, 1996), 128.

3. Reba Som, "Ektuku Chhoya Lage," in *Rabindranath Tagore: The Singer and His Song* (New Delhi: Penguin, 2017), 34. 2017. Rabindranath Tagore (1861–1941) wrote, "Jana Gana Mana" and "Amar Sonar Bangla," the national anthem of in Bangladesh. He was awarded the Nobel Prize for literature for his book of songs, *Gitanjali*. His songs are sung and transmitted from one generation to another.

4. Sudeep Sen, *Red* (Gauteng: Nirox Foundation, 2023), 54. Figure 5.1 is a photo shot and captioned by Sen as "The Flame of the Forest."

5. Pavneet Singh Chadha, "Why Did Goa See a Spate of Forest Fires in March?" *Indian Express*, May 8, 2023. https://indianexpress.com/article/explained/explained-climate/goa-forest-fires-in-march-2023-explained-8596719/.

6. Marie Bout, "5 Reasons We Need Wildlife in Order to Survive." Greenpeace Aotearoa, March 8, 2021. https://www.greenpeace.org/aotearoa/story/5-reasons-we-need-wildlife-in-order-to-survive/.

7. *A Life on Our Planet*, Netflix, 2020. https://www.netflix.com/title/80216393.

8. "Learn about the Amazon Rainforest." WWF. Accessed April 15, 2023. https://www.wwf.org.uk/where-we-work/amazon.

9. Sandy Matt, "Why Is the Amazon Rain Forest Disappearing?" *Time*. Accessed June 19, 2023. https://time.com/amazon-rainforest-disappearing/.

10. Natalia Ocampo-Peñuela, John Garcia-Ulloa, Itto Kornecki, Christopher D. Philipson, and Jaboury Ghazoul. "Impacts of Four Decades of Forest Loss on Vertebrate Functional Habitat on Borneo." *Frontiers*, April 9, 2020. https://www.frontiersin.org/articles/10.3389/ffgc.2020.00053/full.

11. Amitav Ghosh, *The Glass Palace* (London: HarperCollins, 2000).

12. Idem, 199.

13. Idem, 71.

14. William Rueckert, "Literature and Ecology: An Experiment in Ecocriticism," in *The Ecocriticism Reader: Landmarks in Literary Ecology*, edited by Cheryll Glotfelty and Harold Fromm (Athens: University of Georgia Press, 1996), 107.

15. Amitav Ghosh, *The Glass Palace*, 69.

16. Christopher Manes, "Nature and Silence," in *The Ecocriticism Reader: Landmarks in Literary Ecology*, edited by Cheryll Glotfelty and Harold Fromm (Athens: University of Georgia Press, 1996), 26.

17. Idem, 25.

18. Amitav Ghosh, *The Glass Palace*, 120.

19. Cheryll Glotfelty, "Introduction: Literary Studies in an Age of Environmental Crisis," in *The Ecocriticism Reader: Landmarks in Literary Ecology. Athens: University of Georgia Press*, edited by Cheryll Glotfelty and Harold Fromm, xv–xxxvii (Athens: University of Georgia Press, 1996), 17.

20. Christopher Manes, 17.

21. Mahasweta Devi, *The Book of the Hunter*, trans. Sagaree Sengupta and Mandira Sengupta (Calcutta: Seagull, 2002), 58.
22. Idem, 58.
23. Devi, "Pterodactyl, Puran Sahay and Pirtha," in *Imaginary Maps*, trans. Gayatri Chakravorty Spivak (New York: Routledge, 1995), 120.
24. Idem, 158.
25. Devi, "Little Ones," in *Bitter Soil* (Calcutta: Seagull Books, 1998), 5.
26. Walter J. Ong, *Orality and Literacy: The Technologizing of the Word* (London and New York: Routledge, 2002).
27. Devi, *The Book of the Hunter*, ix.
28. Idem, viii.
29. Devi, *Imaginary Maps*. Trans. Gayatri Chakravorty Spivak (New York: Routledge, 1995), xi.
30. Wayne C. Booth, "Introduction." In *Problems of Dostoevsky's Poetics*, edited by Mikhail Mikhailovich Bakhtin (Minneapolis: University of Minnesota Press, 1984), xxiii.
31. Bakhtin, *Problems of Dostoevsky's Poetics*, 165.
32. Devi, "Pterodactyl, Puran Sahay and Pirtha," 119–200.
33. Devi, "Little Ones," 7.
34. Devi, *Bitter Soil*, trans. Ipsita Chanda (Calcutta, Seagull Books, 1998), viii.
35. Devi, *Imaginary Maps*, xiii.
36. Gayatri Chakravorty Spivak, "Introduction," in *Imaginary Maps*, trans. Gayatri Chakravorty Spivak (New York: Routledge, 1995), viii.
37. Devi, "Pterodactyl, Puran Sahay and Pirtha," 99.
38. Idem, 192.
39. Idem, 144.
40. Idem, 144.
41. Homi K. Bhabha, "The Location of Culture," in *Literary Theory: An Anthology*, edited by Julie Rivkin and Michael Ryan (Oxford: Blackwell, 1998), 937.
42. Edward Said, *Culture and Imperialism* (London: Chatto and Windus, 1993), xiii.
43. Devi, "Pterodactyl, Puran Sahay and Pirtha," 177.
44. Schlosberg, 96.
45. Idem, 116.
46. Benedict Anderson, *Imagined Communities: Reflections on the Origin and Spread of Nationalism* (London: Verso, 1991), 6.
47. Wangari Maathai (1940–2011) was the founder of the Green Belt Movement (1977), which encourages people, particularly women, to plant trees to combat environmental degradation. A scholar and an environmental activist, she was the first woman to obtain a Ph.D. in East and Central Africa, and the first African woman to receive the Nobel Peace prize (2004).
48. Sunderlal Bahuguna Ji (1927–2021) was one of India's first environmentalists. He was the founder of the Chipko movement to preserve the forests in the Himalayas and opposed the construction of the Tehri dam across the Bhagirathi dam, India's tallest dam, in the 1980s.
49. Vandana Shiva, "Women in Nature," 39.

50. Mahasweta Devi, *The Book of the Hunter*, 62.

51. Arundhati Roy, "Walking with the Comrades," in *Broken Republic: Three Essays* (New Delhi: Hamish Hamilton, 2011), 37–146.

52. Arundhati Roy, "Mr Chidambaram's War," in *Broken Republic: Three Essays* (New Delhi: Hamish Hamilton, 2011), 24–25.

53. Idem, 27.

54. Aruna Kashyap, Becker, Jo, and Ganguly, Meenakshi, "'Being Neutral Is Our Biggest Crime': Government, Vigilante, and Naxalite Abuses in Chhattisgarh State" (New York: Human Rights Watch, 2008), 8.

55. Idem, 8.

56. Naxalites are partisans of Naxalism or the growth of militant communism in India that came into being with the the creation of the Communist Party of India–Marxist-Leninist (CPI-ML) in 1969, and the consequent emergence of rebel groups such as the Maoist Communist Centre (MCC) and the Peoples' War Group (PWG). Naxalites claim to represent the poor tribal people and believe in the Maoist doctrine of sustained peasant-led revolution.

57. Arundhati Roy, "Mr Chidambaram's War," 2.

58. Idem, 24.

59. Idem, 25.

60. Arundhati Roy, "Walking with the Comrades," 102.

61. Idem, 61–62.

62. Huggan, Graham, and Helen Tiffin, *Postcolonial Ecocriticism: Literature, Animals, Environment* (New York: Routledge, 2010), 53, 72.

63. In a legal affidavit entitled "On Citizens' Rights to Express Dissent" in her work *My Seditious Heart*, Roy quotes an extract from the Supreme Court Order dated October 15, 1999, that accuses Roy's writing of violating the dignity of the court and polluting the stream of justice.

64. Arundhati Roy, "On Citizens' Rights to Express Dissent," in *My Seditious Heart: Collected Nonfiction* (Toronto: Hamish Hamilton, 2019), 156.

65. Vandana Shiva, "Women in Nature," in *Staying Alive: Women, Ecology and Development* (New Delhi: North Atlantic, 1989), 40.

66. Idem, 39.

67. *The Seeds of Vandana Shiva*, *Core.Live/Movies/the-Seeds-of-Vandana-Shiva-Movie*, 2022.

68. Vandana Shiva, "Science, Nature, and Gender," in *Staying Alive: Women, Ecology and Development* (New Delhi: North Atlantic, 1989), 24.

69. Idem, 24.

70. Idem, 24–25.

71. Maria Mies and Vandana Shiva. *Ecofeminism* (New York: Zedbooks, 1993), 14.

72. Gabriel Dietrich, *Reflections on the Women's Movement in India: Religion, Ecology, Development* (New Delhi: Horizon India, 1992).

73. Meera Nanda, *Prophets Facing Backward: Postmodern Critiques of Science and Hindu Nationalism in India* (New Brunswick: Rutgers University Press, 2003).

74. Rosalind C. Morris and Gayatri Chakravorty Spivak. *Can the subaltern speak? Reflections on the history of an idea* (New York: Columbia University Press, 2010).

75. Idem, 25.
76. David Schlosberg, *Defining Environmental Justice: Theories, Movements, and Nature* (Oxford: Oxford University Press, 2007).
77. Idem, 83.
78. Idem, 89.
79. Idem, 89.
80. Usha Tandon, "Environmental Courts and Tribunals: A Comparative Analysis of Australia's LEC and India's NGT," in *The Indian Yearbook of Comparative Law* 2016, 477–502. Doi.org/10.2139/ssrn.3693408.
81. Tandon, 477–502.
82. "National Specialised Courts in Sweden." European e-Justice Portal. Accessed April 17, 2023. https://e-justice.europa.eu/19/EN/national_specialised_courts?SWEDEN&member=1.
83. Gitanjali Nain Gill, *Environmental Justice in India: The National Green Tribunal* (Earthscan from Routledge: New York, 2017), 19.
84. *Anirudh Kumar v. Municipal Corporation of Delhi & Ors* (Supreme Court of India, March 20, 2015), section 63.
85. *State of Uttaranchal v. Balwant Singh Chaufal & Ors* (Supreme Court of India, January 18, 2010), section 33.
86. *Wildlife First and Ors v. Ministry of Forest* (Supreme Court of India, February 13, 2019).
87. Dhanush Samvaad, "Ministry of Tribal Affairs, Government of India," Ministry of Tribal Affairs—Government of India, accessed July 12, 2023, https://tribal.nic.in/FRA.aspx.
88. *A. Periyakaruppan v. The Principal Secretary & Anr* (Madras High Court, April 19, 2022).
89. *Chevron Corporation and Texaco Petroleum Corporation v. Republic of Ecuador* (PCA Case No. 2009–23, Second Partial Award on Track II) (30 Aug. 2018).
90. Ecuador's Constitution of 2008—constituteproject.org. Accessed June 16, 2023. https://www.constituteproject.org/constitution/Ecuador_2008.pdf.
91. "Defending Mother Earth in Bolivia." Cultural Survival. Accessed June 16, 2023. https://www.culturalsurvival.org/news/defending-mother-earth-bolivia.
92. *Sierra Club v. Morton*, U.S. 727 (U.S. Supreme Court, April 19, 1972).
93. Idem, section 1.
94. Idem.
95. *A. Periyakaruppan v. The Principal Secretary & Anr* (Madras High Court, April 19, 2022).
96. Idem, section 18.
97. Idem, section 21.
98. Idem, section 20.
99. "The Constitutional Scheme of Animal Rights in India." Animal Law Legal Center, January 1, 1970. https://www.animallaw.info/article/constitutional-scheme-animal-rights-india#:~:text=Article%2048A%20lays%20down%20the,and%20wildlife%20of%20the%20country.

100. "Article 51A: Fundamental Duties." Constitution of India, April 21, 2023. https://www.constitutionofindia.net/articles/article-51a-fundamental-duties/.

101. Dhanush Samvaad, "Ministry of Tribal Affairs, Government of India." Ministry of Tribal Affairs—Government of India. Accessed June 16, 2023. https://tribal.nic.in/FRA.aspx.

102. National Green Tribunal. Accessed June 22, 2023. https://greentribunal.gov.in/about-us.

103. *Amit Maru v. Ministry of Environment and Forest* (National Green Tribunal, Pune October 1, 2014).

104. *The Goa Foundation Anr v. Union Of India Ors* (National Green Tribunal, New Delhi July 18, 2013).

105. *Vimal Bhai & Others v. Ministry of Environment and Forests* (National Green Tribunal, New Delhi December 14, 2011).

106. *Society for Protection of Environment and Biodiversity v. Union of India* (National Green Tribunal, December 8, 2017).

107. Idem, sections 51–52.

108. *Wilfred J. v. Ministry of Environment & Forests* (National Green Tribunal, New Delhi July 17, 2014).

109. *Punamchand v. Union Of India & Ors* (National Green Tribunal, Pune April 16, 2014), section 8.

110. *Tamil Nadu Pollution Control Board v. Sterlite Industries (I) Ltd.* (Supreme Court of India, February 18, 2019), section 124.

111. *Indian Council for Enviro-Legal Action v. Union of India and Ors* (Supreme Court of India, February 13, 1996), section 7.

112. Jayashree Nandi, "115% Rise in Forest Fires This Month." *Hindustan Times*, March 13, 2023. https://www.hindustantimes.com/india-news/115-rise-in-forest-fires-this-month-101678733527908.html.

113. Dehradun, Webline Infosoft Pvt. Ltd. "FSI Activities & Services." Welcome to Forest Survey of India. Accessed June 18, 2023. https://fsi.nic.in/.

114. India Meteorological Department. Accessed June 18, 2023. https://mausam.imd.gov.in/imd_latest/contents/rainfallinformation.php.

115. *Jan Chetna v. Ministry of Environment & Forests* (The National Green Tribunal, New Delhi, May 11, 2012).

116. Idem, section 4.

117. *Rajiv Dutta v. Union Of India* (National Green Tribunal, New Delhi May 2, 2019).

118. Idem, 69.

119. Idem, 12–15.

120. Greenpeace India. "Mahan Forests Inviolate—No Go for Mining Says MoEF." Greenpeace India. Accessed June 22, 2023. https://www.greenpeace.org/india/en/press/2353/mahan-forests-inviolate-no-go-for-mining-says-moef/.

121. "Q'inti the Hummingbird—A Quechen Story." *The Flight of the Hummingbird*. Accessed June 22, 2023. https://www.hummingbird.vancouveropera.ca/story.

Chapter 6

Solastalgic Earth Emotions

Through *Solastalgia*,[1] a lyrical film about climate grief released in 2019, Vancouver-based cinematographers Sean Stiller and Pascal Tremblay explore the dislocation, anguish and longing humanity feels from the climatic changes happening on our shared home, our planet Earth. The film, shot in Tofino, Tla-o-qui-aht land on Meares Island in British Columbia in Canada, incorporates dance, poetry, and audio-visual recordings of the natural surroundings. The film embodies responses to the term coined by Glenn Albrecht, 'Solastalgia,'[2] for the eco-affect or Earth emotion, the homesickness engendered by environmental catastrophe. It explores the grief one feels on viewing on media or reading news reports or on visiting the site of the Amazonian region afflicted by the 2019 wildfires that swept the forests leaving the landscape barren and desolate. The film makes the viewer wonder if one can find healing in acknowledging and accepting the sorrow and pain one experiences from climate catastrophe. The film also explores the brighter angle of climate change by nudging viewers to consider the lived experience, accept the invitation to find solace in difficult times, and express one's deep respect and appreciation for the living planet that houses all life forms. Crashing waves, foggy-logged forests, epic old growth of wild vegetation, night shots of dark and mysterious beaches with its sea life, thorny unkept bushes, bare-rocked cliffs, and mushrooms of smoke bombs contribute to the portrayal of Solastalgia or environmental despair in the film. *Solastalgia*, the Stiller-Tremblay award-winning film, inspired further cinematic creativity.[3]

In 2023, an exhibition at the Kalmar Konstmuseum in Sweden, entitled "Solastalgia—Climate & Future" exhibited Dutch artist, Eline Kersten's solastalgic paintings accompanied by her film entitled *Solastalgia*.[4] The paintings reveal how people were affected by the closure of a limestone quarry in the Netherlands. The film adds more value to its accompanying painting by showing the transformation from a natural reserve area to an industrial area. It enables voices of affected people to be heard, thus offering solace. Kersten highlights the fact that the voices are many, as many memories surface from this moment in time and place. The Solastalgia experienced by every individual in the film, differs depending on the perspective of each stakeholder. The Kalmar Museum makes the visitor muse on "What will the landscape of the future look like?"[5] Other solastalgic paintings displayed by Swedish artists like Ella Tillema[6] and Nils Kreuger[7] in the same Konstmuseum exhibits, highlight the human bond with nature, and show how humanity pales in comparison to nature's grandiosity. The works of Solastalgia are not restricted to the sense of solace and desolation encountered in one's home space, as seen in the Swedish artist, Catrin Andersson's depiction of climate catastrophe. Andersson in her painting entitled "Glaciär Sara Ugma"[8] uses a color combination of magenta and violet to depict the increased temperature between 51–54°C engendered by the forest fire that ravaged the glacier Sara Ugma in the Himalayas in the spring of 2022. A climate catastrophe in the far-off Himalayas, invisible to the human eye in Sweden, becomes visible through the artist's visualization of the forest fire that depicts its soot, a mass of impure, carbon particles on the life-giving rivers of India.

The term *Solastalgia* owes its existence to Australian farmer-philosopher Glenn Albrecht who, in *Earth Emotions: New Words for a New World*, coined the term *Solastalgia*[9] to capture the feeling of chronic distress caused by negatively perceived changes to one's home and landscape.

> Solastalgia, in contrast to the dislocated spatial and temporal dimensions of nostalgia, relates to a different set of circumstances. It is the pain experienced when there is recognition that the place where one resides and that one loves is under immediate assault (physical desolation). It is manifest in an attack on one's sense of place, in the erosion of the sense of belonging (identity) to a particular place and a feeling of distress (psychological desolation) about its transformation. It is an intense desire for the place where one is a resident to be maintained in a state that continues to give comfort or solace. Solastalgia is not about looking back to some golden past, nor is it about seeking another place as 'home.' It is the 'lived experience' of the loss of the present as manifest in a feeling of dislocation; of being undermined by forces that destroy the potential for solace to be derived from the present. In short, solastalgia is a form of homesickness one gets when one is still at 'home.'[10]

Albrecht describes feeling acute desolation on seeing a large-scale open pit coal mine in the Upper Hunter Valley of New South Wales. Upper Hunter Valley, once renowned for being a valley of immense beauty, had even been named as "the Tuscany of the South."[11] Even though the colonized people of the Hunter Valley had known a history of coal mining, the former colonial mining was nothing compared to the "gaping open-cut wounds"[12] to the land inflicted by the newer, modern forms of mining. He refers to the modern mining companies as "new leviathans"[13] engaged in terraforming the landscape into ravaged hills with pocked marked pockets of toxic water. The terraformed landscape with its disturbed landscape of power stations ejecting toxic steam filled him with a feeling of intense despondency and emptiness that evaded any existing word term or definition. Even though the feeling was close to the melancholia of nostalgia (*nostos*—to return home), it had negative tinges of desolation of having lost a loved home environment. His contention with dual feelings of desolation and nostalgia, resulted in his naming the experience as an Earth Emotion of Solastagia. The term *nostalgia* has its origins from the Greek *nostos*, meaning return to home or native land—and the New Latin suffix *algia*, meaning suffering pain, or sickness, from the Greek root *algos* and refers to "the sickness caused by the intense desire to return home when away from it, and the reason for interrelated mental and physical distress."[14]

Like water, the amount of carbon on Earth remains the same as it was in the Mesozoic era millions of years ago when dinosaurs roamed the Earth. Carbon is stored in water bodies like oceans and reservoirs, as well as in the pedosphere in rocks and sediments, while the rest is stored in living organisms and the atmosphere. Through the carbon cycle, carbon the basic building block of life is present in all living organisms. Compounding from solids, liquids, and gases, carbon exists in both organic and inorganic forms as living and dead organisms, fossil fuels, rock deposits, dissolved water, and carbon dioxide (CO_2) in the atmosphere. While inorganic carbon is extracted from ores and minerals and have different allotropic forms with differently arranged atoms including diamonds, fullerene, and graphite due to their chemical and physical properties; organic carbon is oxidized by atmospheric oxygen as in human respiration and is also present in the soil. Carbon in the ocean floor stem from the remains of skeletons and shells of marine creatures containing calcium carbonate. These deposits form limestone, thus a carbon atom could spend millions of years traversing the planet in different forms during the carbon cycle.

Greenhouse gases like CO_2, methane (CH_4), nitrous oxide (N_20), and halocarbons that absorb and release heat into the atmosphere are produced during the carbon cycle. They are stored or sequestered in the Earth's soil or pedosphere; in the cryosphere where water exists as snow, ice, and permafrost; in the lithosphere or the rock structure; in carbon sinks like peatlands, forests, or seagrass beds; and in the hydrosphere like oceans, rivers, and reservoirs. During the day, the sun's ray warms the planet, at night the Earth cools releasing heat back into the air. Some of the heat is stored as greenhouse gases in the atmosphere. Our planet remains at a constant 14°C (58°F) on average thanks to this greenhouse effect. If released in large quantities, these greenhouse gas molecules in the atmosphere absorb light, preventing some of it from escaping the Earth. This heats up the atmosphere resulting in a planet on fever.

CARBON OFFSETS: A PLEDGE, OR A HOAX?

As governments around the globe are striving to deal with the urgent climate crisis by implementing policies to reduce greenhouse gases and are encouraging companies to be carbon neutral. The strategy of companies to be 'carbon neutral' refers to the approach of calculating and taking stock of their total carbon emissions and trying to compensate for any unavoidable emissions, through carbon offsetting projects. Such a strategy implies that a company's carbon dioxide output has a net neutral impact on the environment, whereby a corresponding same amount of CO_2 released into the atmosphere is removed, leaving a 'zero-carbon balance.' According to the report published by the International Energy Agency (IEA) in 2023, CO_2 emissions are unevenly distributed across income groups and regions. The IEA report compared both the developed and the developing world by considering differences in income and wealth, and the corresponding lifestyles and consumption patterns. It reported that during the year 2021, the average North American emitted 11 times more energy-related CO_2 than the average African; among the top 1 percent of emitters, each had carbon footprints of over fifty tonnes of CO_2, that were one thousand times larger than those of the bottom 1 percent of emitters; the global average energy-related carbon footprint was approximately 4.7 tonnes of CO_2 per person—the equivalent of taking two round-trip flights between Singapore and New York, or of driving an average SUV for eighteen months.[15] While around 85 percent of the top 10 percent of emitters have advanced economies like Australia, Canada, the European Union, Japan, Korea, New Zealand, the United States, the United Kingdom, and China, some countries from the Middle East, Russia, and South Africa, are classified as countries with relatively high income and wealth inequality that use emission-intensive fuel mixes, and the bottom 10 percent of emitters globally live in developing economies in Africa and Asia, where they consume relatively small amounts of goods and services, but lack basic amenities of the developed world. The term *carbon majors* refers to the global leading producers of oil, natural gas, coal, and cement—public investor-owned companies such as ExxonMobil, Shell, BP, Chevron, Peabody, Total, and BHP Billiton; and state-owned entities such as Saudi Aramco, Gazprom, National Iranian Oil, Coal India, Pemex, CNPC and Chinese coal, of which Shenhua Group & China National Coal Group are key players.[16]

The Intergovernmental Panel on Climate Change (IPCC)'s sixth annual assessment report suggests ways of mitigating climate change and warns that it is imperative and essential to meet goals and preconizes 10 Gt of carbon removal annually by 2050.[17] Today, we are at just 0.003 Gt far below this recommended standard. With the effects of climate change becoming increasingly evident, companies are now under the obligation of cutting down their environmental footprint. Corporate agendas focus on making claims of being 'carbon neutral' before a certain date. Purchasing patterns of customers is one influenced by a company's green claims of being carbon neutral, environmentally friendly and on commitments to protect the environment. Interestingly, there are two overlapping carbon markets: a voluntary market where individuals and entities can purchase carbon offsets and make a commitment to certain causes of their choice; or opt for compliance policies in keeping with standards of national government or regulatory bodies. Keen to profit from the eco-trend, companies that fall under the category of the voluntary carbon market resort to Green Washing and sometimes even resort to making false environmental claims. More than 1,500 companies like TotalEnergies, Shell and BP, to multimillion-dollar corporations, like Amazon, British Airways, Coca Cola, and Nestlé, have made 'net zero' commitments.[18]

Corporate 'net zero' pledges of greenwashing are evident in the carbon-offset policies of airline companies. The German airline Lufthansa announced its "Green Fares" policy giving passengers the option of booking more sustainably whereby they paid a little more money to reduce the climate impacts of their flights.[19] British Airlines along with its claims of flying zero emissions aircrafts that use hydrogen-electric fuel cells, also suggest the use of an online calculator to calculate per-passenger carbon-emission and the means to buy offsets to balance it.[20]American airlines has resorted to a "Cool Effect" strategy for its carbon offset program, by proposing customer participation in projects like "See the Forests," for "Peat's Sake," and "Mirador Clean Stoves."[21] While Southwest Airline woos its passengers with a program called "Wanna offset carbon?" and the possibility of earning ten Rapid Rewards bonus points for every dollar spent helping the airline offset its carbon emissions, Ryanair, the low-cost, Irish flight carrier, invites passengers to contribute €2 to support environmental projects in Bulgaria, Portugal, and Nepal, purporting the idea of compensating an equivalent of 50 percent of emissions based on the flight's average route distance and fuel burn.[22] While the claims sound exaggerated, these airline companies claim to prevent, avoid, or reduce emissions or contribute to projects that aim to remove CO_2 from the atmosphere. Passengers are cast as primary players in the offset programs to reduce their carbon footprints. These carbon offset projects pledge to avoid emissions claim to stop deforestation or restoring hectares of peat swamps and creating local jobs in poor countries.

The aviation industry is not the only sector that entices customers to participate in carbon offsets projects. Internationally renowned companies have labelled their products as 'carbon neutral' persuading their customers that buying their products would sustain the planet and not make the climate crisis worse. According to an investigation led by the *Guardian*, these forestry and nature-based offsets approved by the world's leading certifier Verra, and purchased by the aviation industry, and other big corporations like Disney, Shell, and Gucci are mostly worthless as they are likely to be "phantom credits" and not genuine pledges to trigger carbon offsets.[23] Verra, with its headquarters in Washington, D.C, has managed since 2007 the world's leading voluntary carbon markets program, the Verified Carbon Standard (VCS). On the one hand, Verra boasts of its capacity to incubate new ideas and channel billions of dollars into the vital preservation of the forests.[24] On the other hand, the *Guardian*'s nine-month investigation denounced eighty-seven Verra's offset programs as disappointing as 94 percent of the Verra offset credits had no benefit to the climate; the threat to forests had been overstated by about 400 percent on average for Verra projects; and that there was evidence of human rights issues of forced eviction in one of its offset projects in Peru.[25] The United Nations Environment Program (UNEP) stated in 2019 that carbon offsets are not our get-out-of-jail-free card, and that such offsets were being used by polluters as a free pass for inaction and that it was imperative to act.[26] Greenpeace has denounced carbon offsets programs as "scams" or "book-keeping tricks" of climate villains with "the hallmarks of a classic con"[27] by contending that greenwashing programs are driven by greed, feigned compassion, and exploit the climate impact fears of people.

There is also a new wave of companies pledging to be 'carbon neutral' by 2030 to mitigate climate change. Microsoft strongly speaks of becoming 'carbon negative' by 2050 and aims to remove from the environment all the carbon the company has emitted either directly or by electrical consumption since it was founded in 1975.[28] Amazon pledges to reduce carbon emission to zero by 2040, a decade ahead of the deadline set by the Paris Climate Agreement (2015), and to power all its operations with 100 percent renewable energy by 2025 as part of its goal to reach net-zero carbon.[29] While 'carbon neutrality' signifies that an organization has engaged in removing the same amount of CO_2 from the atmosphere as it is emitting; net zero, also implies that the organization is removing an equal amount of all greenhouse gasses (GHGs) it releases. Steelcase, the global innovative design furnishings company announced having reached carbon neutrality and net zero in 2020 and its goal of taking its commitment further with a goal to become 'carbon negative' by 2030 through a good understanding of climate science.[30] IKEA in another twist to the term, has announced its intention of being 'climate positive' by 2030 by drastically reducing GHG emissions from its entire value chain by making sustainable choices.[31] These claims will take time to concretize, and the veracity of these climate commitments can be tested and verified only with time. Are they genuine pledges or mere hoaxes? Not all companies intend to be deliberately misleading, not are all commitments genuine. The problem is evident in the fact that there exists no singular standard guideline for achieving carbon neutral emissions and companies have decided to name, label, and create their own definitions.

MINING THE MATERIAL LAY OF THE LAND

On a visit to Doon Valley situated within the Shivalik Hills in the Lesser Himalayas, in the Indian states of Uttarakhand, Himachal Pradesh, and Haryana, eco-activist Vandana Shiva discovered that surface mining for limestone had resulted in the scarring of the mountain slopes. The valley situated in the mountain-protected zone receives rainfall only during the monsoon season between July to October. The water for the remaining months of the year is stored in the rich humus of oak trees in the higher slopes, and in the mixed natural forests of the lower slopes. Limestone deposits on the mountain slopes also have the capacity to serve as natural aquifers and store water that trickles through their fissures and cracks in natural storage cavities. Water from these cavities feed thousands of springs and streams that form the Ganges and the Yamuna rivers in Northern India. In her essay, "Women and the Vanishing Waters,"[32] Shiva gives a solastalgic account of the devastation caused by mining in the Doon Valley.

> A few decades ago, maldevelopment came to the Doon. Mountains were mined for chemical grade limestone, forests were uprooted, debris was thrown down the slope, and nature's system of water storage was destroyed. Now, when the rains come, 3,000 mm of water run off the slopes immediately, creating floods carrying topsoil and boulders eroding river banks and filling up flood plains—after that the land is parched, the streams and rivers dry. In mining the limestone, nature's water reservoir has been mined too; the reductionist mind fails to see the non-commercial economic functions that minerals perform in their linkages with other elements of nature.[33]

She evokes the distress caused by environmental change. The once lush mountain slopes of her childhood showed scars of industrial mining. Limestone, natural aquifers that absorbed and stored mountain rain had vanished. With no more natural storage tanks, monsoon rain ran down the slopes and caused massive floods in a region that had never known floods. Shiva conducted an independent study on the impact of mining on limestone in Doon Valley, Uttarakhand. She took on the challenging task of overturning the dominant narrative of decision makers who mined in the name of progress. As mining activity exploited the villagers, waste destroyed the stream flows, and villages were washed away. Shiva's scientific background prompted her to conduct an independent study to estimate the amount of water that flowed from the limestone belt and compare the approximate cost of pumping water from the Ganges and the Yamuna to mountainous villages. She proved that forests left standing in the mountain contributed more to the economy than their conversion into timber. Activist voices raised to protest, resulted in the case culminating in the Supreme Court of India, *Rural Litigation and Entitlement Kendra & Ors v. State of U. P. & Or*s (1985).[34] This decision related to earlier decisions by the Supreme Court in the matter of limestone extraction. In this case, the apex court heard a writ petition from the petitioner, Rural Litigation and Entitlement Kendra, regarding the unauthorised and illegal extraction of limestone from quarries in the Mussoorie Hill ranges in India.[35] The petitioner held that the quarries caused a hazard to healthy environment and affected the perennial water springs that gave water to the villages.[36] As in the scientific study conducted by Shiva, the court appointed committee, the Bhargav Committee, concluded after inspecting the lime stone quarries that the limestone left in the mountain contributed more to the economy than its extraction from the mountain.[37] On March 12, 1985, the Court in *Rural Litigation and Entitlement Kendra & Ors v. State of U. P. & Or*s (1985) passed a judgment emphasizing the fact that even though industrial development was necessary for economic growth of the country, haphazard and reckless working of the mines could result in loss of life, property, and basic amenities like supply of water. It ruled that ecological imbalance produced by mining, would result in a situation of no real economic growth and no real prosperity.[38] It insisted on the need to strike a proper balance by considering adequate safeguards.[39]

Arundhati Roy comments on power politics in the Indian postcolonial context: "People—communities, castes, races and even countries—carry their tragic histories and their misfortunes around like trophies, or like stock, to be bought and sold on the open market."[40] In her essay "Power Politics," Roy asserts that the ruling elite in India, bureaucrats and multi-national companies, welcome foreign dignitaries, and showcase India as an investment conducive haven. She describes how Delhi, India's capital was prepared for Bill Clinton's visit to India in 2000, "Whole cities were superficially spruced up. The poor were herded away, hidden from the presidential gaze. Streets were soaped and scrubbed and festooned with balloons and welcome banners."[41] Through metaphors of cleansing, Roy describes how Delhi was transformed, scrubbed, and cleaned to welcome the American presidential contingent. In *Capitalism: A Ghost Story*, Roy criticizes this stance of creating an appearance of a "Good Investment Climate"[42] and describes how Rand and Enron coveted ownership of Indian Earth, air, and water. Delhi was once again spruced up for the Commonwealth Games when once again efforts were made to beautify the capital.

> Street vendors disappeared, rickshaw pullers lost their licenses, small shops and businesses were shut down. Beggars were rounded up, tried by mobile magistrates in mobile courts, and dropped outside the city limits. The slums that remained were screened off, with vinyl billboards that said DELHIciously Yours.[43]

Delhi was purged of unwanted elements, street vendors, and beggars were swept away from obvious view, whereas slums were hidden from view with vinyl boards. In short, Delhi was the perfect haven for investment and deliciously so. Furthermore, Roy remarks on how mining conglomerates like Vedanta Resources, the UK-Indian diversified mining company, mines the arts, through its hosting of film, art, and literary festivals to assume popularity as patrons of artistic and literary enterprise. She writes on how Vedanta sponsors a film competition called 'Creating Happiness' to encourage the youth to make films themed on Sustainable Development;[44] similarly, the Jindal Group,[45] the stainless-steel giant, runs a contemporary art magazine to support artists who work with the same medium of stainless steel; Indian energy giant Essar was also involved in a mining scandal when it flooded farming land with refuse-ash water, reaping a fine of Rs. 50 lakhs or approximatively $70,275 from the Pollution Control Board of the State of Madhya Pradesh,[46] but it was ironically the principal sponsor of the Tehelka Newsweek Think Fest in 2012–2013, known for its mind-stirring discussions by major writers and activists; corporate giants like Tata Steel and Rio Tinto host the five-day Jaipur Literary Festival where the right to free speech is lauded.[47] Roy's activist tirade contends that despite the public display of embracing the arts, these miners of resources both natural and creative exploit India for material gain.

Vijay Rathod, an environmental activist reports on the illegal mining conducted in the Thriveni Sangam, located at Prayag, Allahabad, in India.[48] The Ganges, the Yamuna, and the Saraswati rivers meet and merge in this sacred place before flowing into the Arabian Sea. Hindus meet at Prayag for festivals to take a dip in the holy waters that they believe would wash away sins and free them from the cycle of rebirth, thereby achieving *moksha* or freedom. Prayag's undulating silt-sand dunes used to attract tropical birds of different feathers, until industrialists in the area decided to mine, quarry, and transport the sand for commercial gain. The removal of sand and rock meant that fishing shelters of the fishing community was fast disappearing. Rathod, an environmental activist, cited the Coastal Regulation Zone (CRZ) notification of 2011 that prohibited activities in a five-hundred-meter radius from the High Tide Line (HTL). He campaigned for action to be taken to ban illicit mining and the District Level Coastal Committee (DLCC) intervened on March 25, 2015, and removed the access road to the illegal extraction site of the riverbed.[49]

Bavdi Bander in the Kutch District of Gujarat has a foreshore or intertidal zone of two hundred kilometers where land is visible at low tide and is submerged at high tide. Inhabitants in this region with a coastline of 405 kilometers have depended on fishing and salt production for generations. Mangroves forests exist on the coastal border with fisherfolk spawning prawns, and salt producers engaged in the activity of bundling and drawling water for large saltpans. The two communities were often in conflict over where the boundaries lay in the inter-tidal belt especially in recent times. Neelkanth, a large-scale producer of salt began expanding its inter-tidal area at Bavdi Bander, which restrained the access of fishermen into the harbor. Despite a notice issued by the Principal Secretary of the Department of Environment of Forests of the Government of Gujarat on February 27, 2013, citing the Coastal Regulation Zone (CRZ) notification of 2011, Neelkanth continued its salt production and submitted a revised application to the Gujarat Costal Zone Management Authority (GCZMA) for clearance to continue their activity. The CRZ lays out clearly the regulatory procedures for activities to be carried out on the four-zone coastlines of India. Vimal Kalavadiya, an eco-activist representing Namati Environmental Justice Program petitioned the GCZMA to not grant this approval on the grounds of illegality as the activity in question was under *sub judice* in the Gujarat High Court. Google Maps helped to pinpoint the area and photographs provided ample proof, leading to a rejection of the application and halting further salt invasion. Nature proved her ability to survive as the sea washed over the coastline bringing back the old biodiversity to Bavdi Bander.

In *Animal's People*,[50] Indra Sinha, an Anglo-Indian writer,[51] describes the Solastalgia he experienced after the Bhopal Gas Tragedy on December 2, 1984. Thick-white mist of toxic gas from the American multinational corporate Union Carbide India Limited enveloped the city of Bhopal in the Indian state of Madhya Pradesh in the dead of the night. Three thousand sleeping inhabitants lost their lives; eight thousand residents died in the month consequent to the disaster; 520,000 people were exposed to the gases with one hundred thousand of them sustaining permanent injuries.[52] The catastrophe was labelled as the worst industrial disaster in history, as forty-two tons of a legal gas methyl isocyanate (MIC) evaporated from the Union Carbide India Ltd and formed an eight-kilometer-wide noxious cloud with people waking up in the dead of night gasping and showing symptoms of ocular irritation. It led to an era of still-born foetuses and deformed babies. After independence in 1947 with the implementation of five-year plans aimed at development in the industrial and agricultural sectors, the time was conducive for companies like Union Carbide to set up huge pesticides manufacturing factories in India.[53] India's massive agricultural plan that aimed at food self-sufficiency attracted foreign investors like Union Carbide to set up pesticide units in

India. Though initially set up in 1934 to produce light, industrial, and commercial utility goods, it slowly began the production of the pesticide Sevin, using MIC as an intermediate. Sevin's liquid carbamate had the chemical properties to kill multiple pests that tended to hamper food production. In India, the monsoon rains that bring moisture-laden winds from the Indian Ocean into the subcontinent play a decisive role in the growth of crops. The southwest Monsoon's arrival prompts farmers to sow seeds in July. It wets the parched landscape and enables crops to sprout. Indian farmers depend on the second downpour of the northeast Monsoon in October as it permits the arrival of insects and consequent cross-pollination. To prevent the pests from completely eradicating their crops, farmers used Sevin to control the insects. This climatic picture permitted large American corporates like Union Carbide to flourish in India. On the night of the Bhopal gas disaster, due to the overfilling of MIC tanks and over-amplified tank pressures, safety systems in the Union Carbide factory malfunctioned, resulting in a deathly, runaway chemical reaction. As a result of the gas leakage, trees died, animal carcasses piled up in the streets of city of Bhopal, families lost their dear ones and those who survived were left with permanent genetic disorders. In his work of fiction, Sinha records events through an act of perception where he captures the present desolate state of the Union Carbide Factory.

> Eyes imagine you're in the factory with me. See that thing rising above the trees, those rusty pipes and metal stairs going nowhere? That's the place where they made the poisons. It used to be bigger, but bits kept falling out. Each big wind pulls more iron sheets loose. We hear them banging like angry ghosts. All that's left now is a skeleton. Platforms ladders and railing are corroding. Its belly is a tangle of pipes like rotting guts. Huge tanks have split, stuff's fallen out that looks like brown rock. How often did Zafar warn that if the dry grasses inside the factory ever caught light, if fire reached these brown lumps, poison gases would gush out, it will be that night all over again.[54]

Through metaphors of decay and neglect, Sinha describes the presence of disintegrating pipes, rotten railing, corroded guts, open tanks, and decomposing lumps. The voices of angry ghosts are heard through the falling bits of corroded iron sheets that bang in the wind. He evokes the possibility of fire, should the poison ignite and unleash another replay of environmental catastrophe. Solastalgia, the human response to negative environmental change is evident in Sinha's account of the loss of an endemic sense of place. The place being his homestead transformed by anthropogenic influence. The negative Earth Emotion of Solastalgia is one that has connotations that relate to both psychological and physical contexts, highlighting "a personal feeling of abandonment (isolation), and to a landscape or structure that has been devastated."[55]

ANTI-COAL MINE ACTIVISM

In October 2014, thirty Pacific Climate Warriors arrived in Australia to dramatize the dangers of climate change. They arrived in their kayaks or traditional canoes to blockade Newcastle's coal port to highlight the stress caused by Australia's coal industry to their homes. They wished to broadcast a message to King Coal that the coal industry's mining for profit was destroying their island homes. Accompanied with the sound of chants and singing, the Pacific Warriors launched their kayaks to block the port beginning by surrounding the massive 226-metre bulk carrier, the Rhine, a giant, rusting coal ship. As police forces on jet skis and in boats towed the protesters away, the warriors chanted their slogan, "We are not drowning. We are fighting!"[56] Canoes versus coal ships is like David versus Goliath when tiny warriors decided to affront the mighty coal industry, but the message to the world is evident in their stance to denounce the coal industry's quest for profit.

In 2014, Vattenfall, the state-owned-Swedish coal mining company decided to restructure and to put its lignite power plants and mines in the Lausitz region of eastern Germany up for sale. It aimed to raise around three billion euros ($3.8 billion).[57] Its operations had been affected by the economic downturn and Germany's renewable energy drive. The solastalgic landscape at Vattenfall's lignite mines in Germany is dotted with deep craters as enormous excavators have clawed at mounds of brown coal, tearing off chunks with giant scooped teeth. Its tender note to sell received an expression of interest from Martina Krueger, the director of the Nordic arm of Greenpeace. Her intent was to shut down the mine and leave the coal sequestered underground.[58] After extensive calculations Krueger and her team of Greenpeace activists decided that Vattenfall would have to make an offer to fund for the clean-up as the mine would no longer make money. Greenpeace's bid was however rejected.

In 2015, the Yes Men Duo, Andy Bichlbaum and Mike Bonanno pulled one of their elaborate pranks and media hoaxes to discuss the relationship between corporations and climate change. In *The Yes Men Are Revolting*,[59] they highlight corporate greed of companies like Shell who are involved in Arctic oil drilling. They targeted the negligent behaviour of oil companies to show how "we're screwed up"[60] because of corporation greed. Their video showed balloon men dressed up as polar bears walking in the streets of cities and even in beaches trying to find Arctic snow. The duo impersonated Shell workers and distributed snow-cones made of "the last iceberg in existence"[61] to raise the alarm on the Anglo-Dutch company sailing its oilrig, the Polar Pioneer, into the Arctic. As in their eponymous 2004 film, *The Yes Men*,[62] the fake news pranksters insisted on making a stand, embracing change and voicing the idea that "it is stupid not to address climate change."[63] Exposing and voicing dissent against the twisted logic of corporate capitalism is typical of the Yes Men's activist enterprise that condemns the absurdities of the economic system that ruthlessly rules the planet.

The #StopAdani campaign in Australia has campaigned actively since 2014 to stop Adani Mining Pty Ltd and Carmichael Rail Network Pty Ltd, wholly owned subsidiaries of Adani Australia, part of the Indian Adani Group from mining coal in Aboriginal land and "ripping the heart out of Wangan and Jagalingou country."[64] Through creative methods of protest, the #StopAdani campaign has alerted the international community on stopping Adani getting one billion dollars from Australian taxpayers. Through a campaign called "People Power," they have raised the question "one billion dollars for a billionaire? Yeah, no thanks."[65] Its creative community actions during the Queensland state election resulted in the government veto of the billion-dollar handout for Adani. When Adani lost its case in *Adani Mining Pty Ltd v. Pennings* (2020),[66] #StopAdani campaigners pulled out placards with the words "There is a Planet B."[67]

The mass climate justice movement *Ende Gelände*, which means 'here and no further,' in its online activists' guide *Shut Shit Down*, shows how its organigramme is structured as affinity groups, comprising of "fingers" or activist groups with hundreds of activists who are engaged in mass activism of blocking railways and coalmines in the Rhineland mining area in 2011.[68] In keeping with its slogan, "Stop Coal, Protect the Climate," Ende Gelände activists in 2022 shut down key points of coal infrastructure in the east of Germany, thus successfully blocking train tracks that take coal from the open-cast coal mines to the power stations in the region, namely Jaenschwalde-Ost, Welzow-Sued and Vereinigtes Schleenhain as well as the port of Hamburg.[69] Other similar non-violent activist groups include Hambacher Forst, and Extinction Rebellion Deutchland. Instead of just blockading city streets, they voiced protest at the frontlines of the ecocide by storming and occupying mines that bear the scars of coal mining. In 2023, Ende Gelände is campaigning to clean gas asserting that it is a dirty lie?[70] It aims to create a climate of justice that is "colorful, noisy and queer" as it aims to construct a camp where LGBTQIA (Lesbian, Gay, Bisexual, Transgender, Transexual, Queer, Intersex, and Asexual) people will find safer spaces and get the opportunity to fight for climate change. On January 17, 2023, activists like Greta Thunberg[71] were carried out of the Garzweiler II opencast lignite mine site by police.[72] Activism to sequester carbon by occupying coalmines sends out the message that the carbon needs to stay well sequestered in the ground for our planet's survival.

AFFECTIVE ECOCRITICISM: ANECDOTAL POLYPHONY AND EARTH EMOTIONS

The word *anecdote* has its origins from the sixth-century scholar Procopius of Caesarea's accounts of the Byzantine court of his time. These tales were given the name Anekdota (*an* and *ekdotos*), or Hidden or Secret Histories. True to the secrecy of its form, the mode of the anecdote remained unknown until Procopius's work was published by a Greek humanist, Niccolò Alamanni in 1623. Sean Cubitt in *Anecdotal Evidence* writes on the reception of anecdote and how it gains life from the "Publication of the unpublished, the self-contradiction of giving out the things not given out, is perhaps the origin of our distrust of anecdotes, with their sly air of conspiracy and unattributable briefings in the corridors of power."[73] Anecdotes express truth about real events that have occurred and have the capacity to portray different points of views of the same situation. The occurrence or event in time in an anecdote is usually the result of an incident. The teller of the anecdote possesses the capacity to direct the telling by halting it, delaying its delivery, "reframing and recontextualising, so that the situation it recounts cannot be taken simply as itself."[74] As a result of confluences, anecdotes are usually told, heard, retold, and reheard by different people at different points of time. Each teller adds his own grain of experience and wisdom into the tale. The telling and the reception remain different at each recital of the anecdote. The anecdotal polyphony gains new strength each time from the manner and occasion of its telling and reception. The secret element of anecdotes is that the interconnection is not simple. Many forces, in harmony or conflict, produce the anecdote's unique situation, where "Retellings and reconsiderations inflect and disturb the passage of the anecdote, which has never completely given or completely withheld itself. The anecdote unpicks the stability of the given, the fait accompli."[75] In Indra Sinha's *Animal's People*, the self-conscious narrator captures and records moments of the Bhopal Gas Tragedy through anecdotal tape recordings to record a moment of time in history and transmit environmental awareness to future generations. Sinha's work of 'Solastalgia' is a portrayal of the anguish caused by the loss of solace and the sense of despair linked to the author's nostalgic portrayal of his homeland India. The meeting or "encounter of a listener with the telling of an event is itself an event, and it is in that encounter that the anecdote begins to deliver its full freight."[76] The self-conscious narrator opens the anecdote with the lines, "If you want my story, you'll have to put up with how I tell it."[77] As all points of view are subjective and not objective, the self-conscious narrator voices how the "possible, imagined, regretted, or wished for inhabits not only the future and the past but the non-identical present in its dialectic of actuality and potential."[78] The third-person omniscient view enables the anecdotes to assume large dimensions as "stories of small people in this world can achieve big things."[79] The polyphony in Sinha's *Animal's People* stems from the anecdotal re-manoeuvring of content whereby the telling though "identical in content would take on another meaning and tone,"[80] when related by the different characters in the fictional space. Not only do the different voices from the anecdote's space get their say; other voices from the external world contribute to the polyphony in the novel. As in Bakhtin's premise, external voices also have their say, thus resulting in "the conflict of historical forces and voices of the epoch—social, political, ideological."[81] In *Animal's People* anecdotal polyphony is evident in the interaction of the ecocritical text with materialism, ecologies, communities, governmental policies, environment, and social phenomena in the Anthropocene. These discursive anecdotal formulations constitute the stories of matter or a material web of meanings, in which "human and non-human players are interlocked in networks that produce undeniable signifying forces."[82]

> Jarnalis, there's a lot to tell, it wants to come out. Like rejoicing, the world's unspoken languages are rushing into my head. Unusual meanings are making themselves known to me. Secrets are shouting themselves into my ear, seems there's nothing I cannot know.[83]

The polyphony of voices is one that is orchestrated so that each voice gets its turn to relate its tale. Typical of the 'secretive'[84] story mode of the anecdote, the omniscient, all-knowing, self-conscious narrator has the task of letting all voices be heard in dialogic sequence, as each voice clamours to be heard. The anecdote serves as the ideal form to voice unspoken languages, unusual meanings, and unusual secrets in the fictional space.

> 'In this very court,' I say to break the fucking spell, 'I used to be a mystery defendant.' So, then they want to know how, why, etcetera, and I've done the voices.
>
> —*Case against boy known as Animal, section chaar sau bees*
> —*Where is the accused?*
> —*You honour he is here.*
> —*Where? I don't see him.*
> —*Right here, your honour, in the dock.*
> —*Don't be silly. I am looking at the dock, there's no one there.*
> —*Your honour accused is of unusual stature.*[85]

Though ridiculed in the courtroom as a defendant of unusual stature, Animal breaks the spell by imitating the voices of all the victims in the Bhopal gas tragedy case. His anecdote is typical of an act of translation and transcription where he identifies the topic to be related, narrates, completes incomplete sentences, and seeks out multiple interpretations to generate further encounter of voices.[86] Though invisible in court due to his animal-four-foot stature, structure and gait, Animal's voice carries in court as he renders his dialogic anecdote with its many points of view rendered in different voices.

In *Animal's People*, affective ecocriticism is revealed through the "environmental affect"[87] of Solastalgia that sparks other positive Earth Emotions[88] or environmentalist affects like Hope, Love, Optimism, and Resilience; as well as negative Earth Emotions, such as Anxiety, Disappointment, and Homesickness. Voices in the fictional space express positive emotions to combat those forces that threaten Biophilia or the love of life and the innate affinity of human beings with the natural world. The expression of a negative Earth Emotion of Dread is evident in Animal's negative apprehension of sorrow, extreme anxiety, and deep sadness in the description of the city of Khaufpur[89] as one in the enumeration of "open sewers, garbage everywhere, poisoned wells, poisoned babies, doctors who don't do their jobs, corrupt politicians, thousands of sick that no one seems to care about."[90] Solastalgia stems from the "transformation or destruction of the physical environment (home) by forces that undermine a personal and community sense of identity and control. Loss of place leads to loss of sense of place experienced as the condition of Solastalgia.'"[91] Dread of the apocalypse, a negative psychoterratic (psyche-Earth) emotional state is caused by the destruction of the environment, toxic pollution, and climate warming."[92]

> Look inside, you see something strange, a forest is growing, tall grasses, trees, creepers that shoot sprays of flowers like fireworks. Once inside, in the grass, it's careful feet. Fucking place is full of cobras. Dogs too. . . . Sometimes I'd bring other kids in to play marbles and spin tops when we didn't want the grown-ups to know where we were. To make sure they didn't come back on their own I'd tell them stories of children who had wandered into the factory and were never seen again.[93]

The anecdote carries with it voices of both humans and nature. Metaphors that spell danger serve to highlight the uncanny. Cobras silently lurk in tall grass, their hisses unheard; unattended, gigantic creepers shoot flowers like fireworks in the eerie setting; spaces far from adult supervision tinkle and whir with the sound of marbles and spin tops. The old factory is alive with stories that express, "Topaversion," which is a feeling that "one does not wish to return to a place that one once loved and before it was irreversibly changed for the worse."[94] Animal's stories also resound with emotions of "Topophobia," that serve to instill the fear of a place that might prevent one from entering into it.[95]

The anecdotes reveal the *status quo* of poisoned wells, pesticide infected soil, genetically deformed babies as nature and her creatures mourn remaining mute, as evident in the negations of "No birds sing. No hoppers in the grass. No bee humming. Insects can't survive here."[96] In the polyphonic space, silent nature gets her say as the anecdote includes the birds' silenced-sad song, the crickets' hushed-cracking hops, and the muted-humming of bees. The polyphonic anecdote includes headlines from broadsheets and tabloids, thus figuring published formal anecdotes, thus serving as catapulting "systems for generating anecdotes, systems to be read and interpreted in the same way as texts and events."[97]

> The city's anger blazes up like a huge fire. On the same day as the Gazette article is published, small presses in the Claw and Jyotinagar are working overtime printing posters, WE WON'T LET YOU BURY JUSTICE, plus LIFE POISONED IS LIVING DEATH, plus NO SELL OUT. Nisha wants one to say LAW DIES, HELL IS BORN, but Zafar says that the court case is still alive, to say that law is dead is to accept in advance that the Kampani has won.[98]

The killing of ecosystems, the demise of law and order, the birth of chaos and confusion compound further proof of Solastalgia, the profound sense of isolation and intense desolation. The news article from the official Law Gazette fires "Terrafurie" with tabloids rushing to print posters that presage an apocalyptic terrifying vision of chaos reigning over Law and Order. Through the oxymoron of a 'living death,' the antitheses of 'law dies, hell is born,' the juxtaposition of contrasting ideas, Animal's anecdote presents Earth Emotion of "Terrafurie,"[99] or protective and hopeless anger toward authorities who maintain the social and political *status quo*, but do not engage in protecting the Earth from destruction. This feeling is generally heightened by the community's lack of power in the face of State and corporate might, the pain of being unable to console in times of great distress and the loss of homeland.

In the fictional court scene *Khaufpur v. Kampani*, like the real-life case, *Union Carbide Corporation v. Union of India* (1991), proponents for climate change voice an urgent plea for action to bring solace to the victims, opponents voice strong support for the existence of giant corporates like Union Carbide.

> My people are the poorest on the planet, those we fight against are the richest. We have nothing, they have it all. On our side there is hunger, on theirs greed with no purpose but to become greedier. Our people are so poor that thirty-three thousand of them together could not afford one Amerikan lawyer, the Kampani can afford thirty-three thousand lawyers. So my second wish is that you go back to my first and make the impossible possible . . . and third . . . I would like to see the face of my enemy.[100]

The polyphonic anecdote with its contrasting opposites of the superlative in 'poorest' and 'richest'; the comparative difference in 'greed' and 'greedier'; opposing poles of the substantive forms of 'hunger' and 'greed'; conflicting camps of lawyers and litigants; serves to highlight the different voices where the dialogue of ideas is never "closed-off" or "finalized" but transform and renew themselves through a constant interaction with other ideas.[101] Finally, meaning cannot be abstract or neutral because all words are shot through with context, polemic and intention.[102] The dialogic space of the polyphonic anecdote is rife with eco-anxiety that is typical of the Anthropocene, a time when anthropogenic influence has contributed to the severity of environmental crises. This negative Earth emotion of "ecoanxiety" is evident as one that occurs in "those who still have an element of concern left in them for the state of the environment."[103] Negative Earth Emotions can evoke positive Earth Emotions, thus displacing apocalyptic perceptions of the future filed with feelings of eco-fear, Terrafurie, Global Dread, Eco-anguish, and Despair. The anecdotal transmission and recording of the catastrophe for future generations is an expression of Eco-concern over the biophysical health of the planet. By expressing Eco-concern, he awakens positive Earth Emotions of Hope. Animal enunciates the need to hope for a better future through an acceptance of his fate. He enunciates his last anecdotal words of human speech in a polyphonic rendering in three languages: English, French, and Hindi.

> Under all the signatures and crosses, I write:
> *Je ne suis pas un homme, mais un animal*
> *dans cet hôpital je ne trouve rien de mal*
> There Elli, I've made you a poem.'
> Growls the blood-tuskery voice before I can stop it:
> *Mere munh se nikli insanna ki zubaan,*
> *Qurbanni ke jaanvar ki aakhri qurbaan.*[104]
> My lips have uttered human speech,
> the last sacrifice of the slaughtered beast.[105]

Despite being a beast that has been beaten, defeated, and thrashed by society, at court and in daily life, he tries to speak, only to discover that he has begun to emit the growls of a savage beast. Having lost the gift of human speech, he comes to terms with his four-legged form and enumerates his animal-like agility of climbing trees, roaming jungles, and performing animal like feats that upright humans are incapable of executing. He contends, "If I'm an upright human, I would be one of millions, not even a healthy one at that. Stay four-foot, I'm the one and only Animal."[106] The positive Earth emotion of Biophilia, living life with love and difference overcomes the negative

Earth emotions of 'Terrafuie' and Eco-anxiety, with Animal rejoicing in his unique state of being.

> *I am Animal fierce and free*
> *in all the world is none like me*
> Eyes, I'm done. . . . Go well. Remember me. All things pass, but the poor remain. We are the people of Apokalis. Tomorrow there will be more of us.[107]

He makes a call for "Soliphilia" or the "process of converting the negative into the positive . . . removing the causes of Solastalgia," considering it to be the right antidote for the people of the apocalypse.[108] The anecdote serves as the right mode of address to awaken positive Earth emotions that will favour an exit from the Anthropocene to the Symbiocene, a period of re-integration between humans and nature, where the planet will be "the ideal home in which our positive emotions can thrive."[109]

THE DANCE OF THE CORPORATE VEILS

In *Animal's People* Indra Sinha configures the dance of the corporate veils, where the defendant shareholders hide behind the corporate veil[110] claiming that their liability does not extend beyond the value of their shares. Once a company is incorporated, the company may be held liable for corporate fraud; but if it was "set up to save its members from being held liable, the court can decide to lift or pierce the corporate veil."[111]

> 'My lord,' says Zafar, 'there are two sets of defendants in this case, first there are the local accused, employees of the Kampani, their personal defence lawyers are here before you. Then there are the Amrikan accused, ergo the Kampani itself plus the big bosses who took the crucial decisions. For the past eighteen years these Amrikan defendants have not shown up in this court. They have not even bothered to send lawyers. They sit in Amrika claiming this court has no jurisdiction over them, yet nothing can be achieved without them being here, thus these proceedings drag on and on, for the people of this city justice continues to be delayed and denied.[112]

In *Animal's People*, Zafar, the lawyer highlights how Union Carbide Corporation was ordered to attend court, but evaded court hearings on many occasions.[113] In *Union of India v. Union Carbide* (1991), the case against Union Carbide was fought both in American and in Indian courts. Both parties wanted their claims to be heard in different forums, while Union Carbide Corporation favoured American soil, the Union of India, which first presented its petition in American courts, had to approach Indian forums when the federal court of the United States ruled that the right forum was India. In the long wait, and during the court hearings, Zafar in *Animal's People* muses, "Must all perish before these Amrikan defendants appear? . . . I think in no other country would the law be allowed to become such a farce."[114] The court guffaws as lawyers inform the learned judge that one had lost count of the number of petitions presented to the court to predecessor judges and that each plea had been "deemed devoid of merit."[115] Through the narrative of court case proceedings, Zafar reveals both ethical and aesthetic dilemmas posed by man-made environmental crises, as well as highlights the need to petition courts to lift the corporate veil.

In the case *Life Insurance Corporation of India v. Escorts Ltd. & Ors* (1985),[116] the Supreme Court deemed it neither necessary nor desirable to enumerate cases where the lifting of the veil was permissible.

> Generally, and broadly speaking, we may say that the corporate veil may be lifted where a statute itself contemplates lifting the veil, or fraud or improper conduct is intended to be prevented or a taxing statute or a benevolent statute ought to be evaded or where associated companies are inextricably connected as to be in reality, part of one concern. It is neither necessary nor desirable to enumerate the class of cases where the lifting the veil is permissible, since that must necessarily depend on the relevant statutory or other provisions, the objects sought to be achieved, the impugned conduct, the involvement of the element of public interests, the effect on parties who may be affected etc.[117]

The petitioners in *Union of India v. Union Carbide* (1991) contended that the lifting of the corporate veil was justified in the circumstances as Union Carbide had evaded being present in court. Under the statutory scheme, the Bhopal Gas Leak Disaster (Processing of Claims) Act 1985, set up by the Government of India for the registration and processing of claims, around 487,000 claims were brought to its attention. The resulting American litigation involved around 145 actions representing approximately two hundred thousand citizens with "the legal wrangle over accountability and compensation" exposing the radically different views in the global north and south.[118]

Union Carbide Corporation ignored all summons sent to appear for trial in India, as it refused to accept India's jurisdictional forum. The cases cast light on the "dance of the corporate veil"[119] led by big corporations like Union Carbide. In June 2001, Dow Chemicals and Union Carbide merged in a deal,[120] whereby it was agreed by the two entities that all business conducted under the name of "Dow business" dissolved any former connection with Union Carbide Corporation. The launching of the new corporate entity meant that all shares "shall no longer be outstanding, shall be cancelled and retired and shall cease to exist."[121] After the merger all Union Carbide products were renamed as Dow products. Dow Chemicals alleged that it had to appear for a suit where there was "an erroneous assumption that Union Carbide Corporation has merged into Dow."[122] Even though, Union Carbide claimed to be principally a Texan business to India's courts, the New York Registrar of Corporations, where the company has been listed for almost a hundred years, reveals its nerve center to be Midland, Michigan, where Dow Chemicals also happens to have its corporate head office. Furthermore, tax filings in Texas detailed the company's officers as board directors, and press articles revealed that Union Carbide board directors who were listed since the merger were either based in Midland or they were acting Dow Chemicals's manager, or both. Union Carbide's CEO also held the same post at Dow Chemicals. Shareholders in Dow Chemicals also figured as United Carbide Corporation and vice versa. In 2005, when the Indian court issued a summons to Dow Chemicals Michigan, Dow Chemicals India applied for a freeze on the summons, arguing that Dow Chemicals Michigan had "no nexus" with Union Carbide.[123]

The obvious pooling of interests has made plaintiffs like Bano and Sahu to entreat the courts to lift the corporate veil behind which companies hide their business activities.[124] The Bhopal Medical Appeal begins with "Now you see Carbide, now you don't"[125] to explain the difficulty in piercing the corporate veil. The Bhopal Medical Appeal highlights how since the signing of the $8.1 billion merger between Union Carbide Corporation and Dow Chemicals, the latter had increased its sales by 150 percent to a sum of $57 billion annually.[126] Campaigners allege that in the 1990s Union Carbide Corporation marketed its products through a third-party distributor, called Everyready India due to the unresolved legal dispute and public disapproval. Labeling the corporate cover-up as the "dance of the corporate veils" the appeal alleges Union Carbide of being a fugitive concealed and sheltered by Dow Chemicals: "If Dow is not Carbide, then Dow is harbouring a fugitive, a distinct offence under Indian law. If Dow is Carbide, Dow is also a fugitive."[127]

SOLASTALGIA IN THE COURTROOM

Glenn Albrecht's concept of Solastalgia was presented to the Land and Environment Court of New South Wales in the case *Bulga Milbrodale Progress Association Inc. v. Minister for Planning and Infrastructure and Warkworth Mining Limited* (2013)[128] when plaintiffs contested the ten-year permit and approval of a mining project that would expand Mount Thorley-Warkworth coal mine into areas previously designated as "non-disturbance areas."[129] The court overturned the approval on the grounds that the expansion of the mine would have a negative impact on the environment and that economic benefits were negligible in comparison.[130] In assessing biodiversity concerns, the court considered vulnerability to climate change. The petitioner, the Bulga Milbrodale Progress Association referred to Albrecht's concept of Solastalgia to articulate the psychological effects of this land transition to the region.[131] Albrecht who had conducted research on the phenomenon in the Bulga community was called to the witness stand. He had interviewed seventeen residents and he noted that ten of the interviewed residents had experienced feelings of Solastalgia.[132] Even though the court was open to consider the idea of Solastalgia as a cause for distress, it noted that the methodology used by Albrecht had specific language prompts that may have influenced the residents to answer accordingly.[133] Chief justice Preston also added that the sample size was too low and not reflective of the whole community.[134] The appeal was upheld and the approval to expand the mining project was denied.

The case *Union of India v. Union Carbide Corporation* (2023) presented in table 6.1, the court order begins with a solastalgic account of events that led to the court case: "A horrendous tragedy occurred on the night of 2nd and 3rd December 1984, due to the escape of deadly chemical fumes from the factory owned and operated by M/s Union Carbide India Limited."[135]

Consequent to the gas disaster seven individual Bhopal survivors and five organizations representing survivors filed a civil action lawsuit in *Bano v. Union Carbide Corporation* (1999) in the Federal Southern District Court of New York.[136] The plaintiffs sought a comprehensive cleanup of the Bhopal site, as well as compensation and medical monitoring for victims. The Hon. John F. Keenan, the same judge who had ruled in the original 1986 lawsuit against Union Carbide about the American court lacking forum *non-conveniens*, presided in the Banu case. On October 17, 2003, nine members of the US Congress submitted an *amicus curiae* letter to the court stating that the 'polluter pays' principle applied in this case because the polluter, Union Carbide, had abandoned its site, had transferred its shares to a subsidiary and had conducted a change of ownership. A bill was even introduced in the US House of Representatives on September 29, 2004, by US Congressman Frank Pallone to ensure that Union Carbide provides environmental rehabilitation in Bhopal. Similarly, Amnesty International released a press report on November 29, 2004, entitled "Clouds of Injustice: Bhopal Disaster 20 Years On,"[137] to draw attention to the ongoing violation of human rights in Bhopal. The report cites Judge Weeramantry, in the International Court of Justice in The Hague, who said: "The protection of the environment is . . . a vital part of contemporary human rights doctrine, for it is a *sine qua non* for numerous human rights such as the right to health and the right to life itself. It is scarcely necessary to elaborate on this, as damage to the

Table 6.1: *Union of India v. Union Carbide Corporation (UCC)* (2023)

IN THE SUPREME COURT OF INDIA ORIGINAL JURISDICTION
Curative Petition No.345–347 of 2010
Judgment rendered on March 14, 2023

Bench: Sanjay Kishan Kaul, Sanjiv Khanna, Abhay S. Oka, Vikram Nath, J.K. Maheshwari

Facts of the case: On 2 December 1984 an accident at the Union Carbide Industries Limited in Bhopal resulted in a leak of 40 tons of methyl isocyanate into the air, along with other poisonous gases. It is estimated that 3,000 inhabitants died, 15,000 people died prematurely in its aftermath.

Rule: Article 142 provides a unique power to the Supreme Court, to do complete justice between the parties, when the law or statute may not provide a remedy.

Issue: The Court had to rule on whether increasing the settlement amounts was in keeping with Article 142 of the Constitution of India.

Court cases and compensation: On February 1985, the Indian Government filed a suit in the Federal District Court of New York claiming that Union Carbide Corporation in the USA owed $3.3. billion as reparations to the victims. On March 29, 1985, the Indian Parliament passed the Bhopal Gas Leak Disaster (Processing of Claims) Act granting the Government of India, the legal status to act as a representative for the victims of the catastrophe. On May 12, 1987, the US Federal Court dismissed the suit filed by the Indian government on the grounds that the proper forum was a court in India and the not the USA. Legal proceedings began in India only on September 5, 1986, when the Union of India filed a suit against Union Carbide Corporation in Bhopal District Court seeking compensation for the victims of the gas leak. The Bhopal District Court ordered the defendant to pay an interim compensation of $3.3bn to the victims. On appeal at the Madhya Pradesh High Court, the compensation was reduced to $2.7bn. This decision was challenged by both Union Carbide Corporation and the Union of India on February 15, 1989, with the apex court ruling and settling the dispute by ordering Union Carbide to pay $470 million to the Union of India as a full and final settlement of all claims. In May 1989, due to country-wide public protests in India regarding the settlement amount, the Supreme Court of India decided to review and increase the settlement. The Supreme Court one again rejected the Union of India's petition regarding the interim compensation of $3.3bn under Article 142 that enables it to issue or pass any order that it feels is necessary to provide complete justice in a case before it. In 2010, the Union Government filed yet another curative petition regarding the 1989 settlement seeking additional compensation of $1.1bn. This was the last chance petition available to a claimant to request the Supreme Court to review its own decision even after a review petition is dismissed.

Reasoning of the court: The Bench said the government's request to the court to use its extraordinary powers under Article 142 of the Constitution to order enhancement of compensation was not the appropriate course of action.

Conclusion: The Supreme Court rejected the plea on the grounds with the five-judge constitution bench ruling that the issue could not be raked up, three decades consequent to the settlement. The Bench highlighted the fact that the government had never filed a review petition but had sought reparation at the apex court invoking the limited jurisdiction of a curative petition, with private parties hoping to "ride on the coattails of the Union."

Note: My synopsis of *Union of India v. Union Carbide Corporation* (Supreme Court of India, March 14, 2023)

environment can impair and undermine all the human rights spoken of in the Universal Declaration and other human rights instruments."[138] OnAugust 28, 2000, Judge Keenan dismissed the Bhopal residents' claims at the trial court on the grounds that the injury had occurred too long ago to present a claim. He concluded that the organizations that had filed the suit could not represent the victims, and that an order to Union Carbide concerning a clean up of the plant would be difficult to enforce. So, the District Court did not address the question of whether Union Carbide had caused the pollution. On March 17, 2004, in *Bano v. Union Carbide Corporation*, the US Second Circuit Court of Appeals reversed Judge Keenan's dismissal in part.[139] It held that while the plaintiff's personal injury claims were time-barred, the stated property damage claims were not. The Court decided to apply the Polluter Pays principle to order Union Carbide to clean up the Bhopal site.

The Polluter Pays Principle has been applied in many court cases as *Vellore Citizens' Welfare Forum v. Union of India* (1996),[140] the Indian Supreme Court ruled that, "Once the activity carried on is hazardous or inherently dangerous, the person carrying on such activity is liable to make good the loss caused to any other person by his activity irrespective of the fact whether he took reasonable care while carrying on his activity. The rule is premised upon the very nature of the activity carried on."[141] Similarly in *MC Mehta v. Union of India* (1997) the Supreme Court ruled that the Polluter Pays Principle ensured that the absolute liability for harm to the environment extended not only to compensate the victims of pollution but also of restoring the environment degradation caused by the polluter.[142]

In *Sahu v. Union Carbide Corporation* (2004),[143] a group of the Bhopal catastrophe survivors joined forces with EarthRights International to file a class action lawsuit in the Federal Southern District Court of New York. The plaintiffs brought their personal injury claims under a common umbrella of victims who were seeking relief for tort caused by Union Carbide's indiscriminate dumping of toxic waste. They sought damages for personal injury, medical monitoring of survivors, a court order obliging Dow Chemical, hiding under a corporate veil to clean up the Bhopal site and supply drinking water supplies to affected residents. As in *Bano v. Union Carbide Corporation* (1999), the case *Sahu v. Union Carbide Corporation* (2004) was dismissed and reinstated and reheard in November 2006, when the Southern District Court of New York's trial court granted a summary judgment in favor of the defendant finding Union Carbide Corporation not liable for the alleged damages. On appeal in 2008, the Second Circuit Court of Appeals, vacated the judgment of the trial court on the grounds that the summary judgment did not adequately show ample proof for a dismissal. The case was remanded back to the district court for further proceedings. Judge Keenan summarily dismissed Sahu on June 26, 2012, by referring to the fact that the Union Carbide

Corporation was not the right defendant-entity to bring litigation against as there existed a distinct separation between Union Carbide India Ltd (UCIL), which was the Bhopal plant subsidiary, and the Union Carbide Corporation (UCC). In *Sahu v. Union Carbide Corporation* (2013),[144] Sahu and other co-plaintiffs appealed to the U.S. Court of Appeals for the Second Circuit once again, which heard oral arguments on June 17, 2013, that contended that the pollution stemmed from technology provided by UCC, and that there existed ample proof under the law to hold UCC liable for its own tortious acts. The Second Circuit Court of Appeals affirmed the District Court's order granting summary judgment to the Union Carbide Corporation.

Consequent to the dismissal of the Sahu case, human rights lawyers like the British human rights lawyer, Louise Christian expressed the opinion that the US appeals court had failed to take into consideration compelling evidence about the central role played by the US-based Union Carbide Corporation in "equipping, overseeing and enabling the Indian offshoot of the company to produce UCC's own product."[145] Rachna Dhingra of the Bhopal Group for Information and Action highlighted the fact that the federal court judges had voted in favor of American corporations accountable for crimes committed outside American territory.[146] While Nawab Khan, president of the Bhopal Gas Peedit Mahila Purush Sangharsh Morcha, reminded the victim plaintiffs that it had taken survivors of the Nazi Holocaust fifty years to obtain redress through the judicial forums and the same could be the case for Bhopal gas victims; Balkrishna Namdeo, president of the Bhopal Gas Peedit Nirashrit Pension Bhogi Sangharsh Morcha, stated that the US judges' clarification that the decision to absolve the parent corporation should not be cited as a precedent for other cases, "is the best illustration of how unsure the judges themselves are about the legal validity of their decision."[147] In *Union of India v. Union Carbide Corporation* (2023), the Supreme Court however observed that careful consideration had been given to pleadings, data, and all material relating to proceedings in both US and Indian courts, to aptly consider "the enormity of human suffering occasioned by the Bhopal Gas disaster and the pressing urgency to provide immediate and substantial relief to victims of the disaster."[148]

THE COALGATE COURT CASE

In the mediatized coal allocation scam, or 'Coalgate' political scandal, that engulfed the United Progressive Alliance (UPA)[149] government in 2012, the Comptroller and Auditor General of India (CAG) alleged that the exchequer had suffered huge loss because of the government's opaque policy of allocating coal blocks to certain private players, instead of a transparent tender bid.[150] Justice R.M. Lodha began his judgment with an ode to coal, the black diamond. He highlights the potential of coal as a feedstock liquid transport fuels representing significant economic growth for India.

> 'Coal is king and the paramount Lord of industry' is an old saying in the industrial world. Industrial greatness has been built up on coal by many countries. In India, coal is the most important indigenous energy resource and remains the dominant fuel for power generation and many industrial applications. A number of major industrial sectors including iron and steel production depend on coal as a source of energy. The cement industry is also a major coal user. . . . Coal is an extremely important element in the industrial life of developing India. In power, iron and steel, coal is used as an input and in cement, coal is used both as fuel and an input. It is no exaggeration that coal is regarded by many as the black diamond.[151]

The coal allocation scam, popularly known as 'Coalgate' in the media is a political scandal that involved the UPA government in 2012. Coal blocks in India are under government control with the government retaining the control to allocate coal blocks to public and private individuals or enterprises for use. According to the proper procedure of allocating these blocks, the highest bidder is granted use of the coal block. But in this scam, the government allocated 194 coal blocks overlooking the bid procedure. It came to light when the Comptroller and Auditor general of India (CAG) accused the government of not having held auctions to allocate the 194 coal blocks to private individuals or enterprises for captive use. This scam is considered as the biggest scam in India and many high profile people were involved. It was criticized in the press as "crony capitalism."[152] The facts of the case *Manohar Lal Sharma v. The Principal Secretary & Ors* (2014) as seen in table 6.2, shows the scope of the Indian Supreme Court to enquire into the decision passed by the executive branch.

While the CAG argued that the Centre's role was merely confined to the granting of 'allocation letters' to companies, which he asserted were 'letters of intent' and could not be viewed as an attempt to circumvent the powers of the State under the Mines and Minerals Regulation and Development Act 1957 (MMDR Act);[153] the petitions alleged that sections 3 and 4 of the MMDR Act had not been respected as the State governments had not been consulted by the Centre.[154] The CAG's argument was based on the premise that the exchequer had suffered a huge loss and public and private entities had profited from windfall gains, because of the government's opaque policy of allocating coal blocks. Due to the absence of the process of competitive bidding, corrupt politicians had lobbied for allotment to certain private players, thus raising debate on "crony capitalism."[155] The CAG contended that

Table 6.2: ***Manohar Lal Sharma v. The Principal Secretary & Ors* (2014)**

IN THE SUPREME COURT OF INDIA ORIGINAL JURISDICTION WRIT PETITION
(CRL.) NO. 120 OF 2012
Judgment rendered on August 5, 2014

Bench: Chief Justice R.M. Lodha, Madan B. Lokur, Kurian Joseph

Rule: Under article 13 of the Indian Constitution, the State or the Union shall not make such rules that takes away or abridges the essential rights of the people.

Facts of the case: In India, coal has vast potential as a feedstock for processing liquid transportation and electricity generation. In 2012, the Comptroller and Auditor General of India (CAG) accused the government of India of having allocated 194 coal blocks to public and private enterprises during the period 1993 to 2010 in an unlawful and unconstitutional manner. The CAG contended that the non-compliance with the Mines and Minerals Development and Regulation Act (1957) required legal action. At the same time, a group of writ petitions were filed in the form of a Public Interest Litigation. M.L. Sharma, a lawyer, and an NGO called Common Cause separately filed petitions before the Supreme Court, challenging the allocation. The petitions were clubbed together and heard jointly by the Court. The Court served a notice on the Union of India, instructing it to file a counter-affidavit via the Secretary of the Ministry of Coal, addressing the details of guidelines for allocation of coal blocks and the process adopted for their allocation of a large segment of coal blocks made between (1993–2010) by the Central Government. They argued that these allocations were arbitrary, lacked transparency and should be deemed unconstitutional.

Issue: Whether the guidelines for the allocation of coal mines contain inbuilt mechanisms to ensure fair distribution of coal blocks to private companies. Whether the guidelines had been strictly followed and if the objectives of the policy had been achieved. What the reasons were for not opting for tenders or competitive bidding for the allocation of coal blocks. What steps had been considered to ensure that allottees had not breached the terms of their contracts.

Reasoning of the court: The court observed that auctioning was not necessarily the best procedure as it would increase the cost of input thereby triggering a cascading effect; furthermore, it reasoned that the process of auction would also favour bigger corporations which would in turn hinder the growth of smaller contenders in the market.

Conclusion: While exercising powers of judicial review of the government's distribution of natural resources, the Supreme Court was not concerned with the ultimate decision but the decision-making process. It declared all allocations of capital coal blocks since 1993 as illegal, arbitrary, and quashed 42 out of 46 allotments. However, as no challenge had been made regarding competitive bidding for the lowest tariff for power, as in the case of Ultra Mega Power Projects (UMPPs) the allocations were not cancelled.

Note: My synopsis of *Manohar Lal Sharma v. The Principal Secretary & Ors* (Supreme Court of India, August 25, 2014).

some private players had been allocated more coal blocks than needed for their mining operations, and that several companies had sold coal meant for internal use in the open market. The petitioners claimed that the State government had not been consulted as per due procedure. The three-bench panel of justices after seeking feedback from the Central government and the concerned states (Jharkhand, Orissa, Madhya Pradesh, West Bengal, Maharashtra, and Andhra Pradesh) ruled that the allocation of coal blocks by Screening Committees reflected arbitrariness and bias towards the companies which had been allocated contracts. Chief Justice R.M. Lodha who authored the judgment laid emphasis on the fact that the whole process undermined the spirit of Article 14 of the Indian Constitution that provides for equality before the law or equal protection of the laws within the territory of India.

In a federal system of government in India, there is also the question on whether the Central Government or the State governments must legislate on the control and allocation of resources. The role played by the Central government in the Coalgate scandal may be perceived as an act of federal overreach by the States, the idea that the federal government had exerted power inappropriately. While the judgment rejected the argument that the cancellation of licenses might weaken the economy, it reasoned that the inconvenience caused by the termination of contracts would be a warning on the need for better management of the mining sector in future. The judgment unleashed a nationwide debate on how courts should be increasingly aware of the potential economic consequences of their decisions. Thus, in the Coalgate scandal, the companies that had been all set to fire their mining operations had to let go. Following the decision, power stocks fell to 7 percent after the Supreme Court's orders on coal allocation and nearly a million people lost their jobs.[156] But *Manohar Lal Sharma v. The Principal Secretary & Ors* served as a catalyst for the amendments to the Mining Policies of the Centre, that culminated in the Mineral Mining Policy Act (2016). The case showed the power of the Judiciary to check Executive actions.

SEQUESTERING CARBON TO SAVE THE PLANET

"Earth Song" from Michael Jackson's album *HIStory*[157] was composed in 1995 after the singer experienced Solastalgia, feelings of despair and loss at the state of the planet while on a concert tour in Austria. The film was shot in four different geographical locations: the Amazonian forests with natives showing anguish at its disappearance; the desolate war zone of Croatia; illegal poaching in Tanzania; and a simulated forest fire at Warwick in New York. The solastalgic song framed as a wake-up call has a series of questions asking the listener to contemplate on elements in nature that are taken for granted like sunrise, rain and fields that have been affected by climate change. Jackson muses:

> Did you ever stop to notice
> This crying Earth, these weeping shores?[158]

The images of a weeping Earth that is crying in pain are followed by the song evoking a rhetorical question—"what about us?" The listener to the Earth Song is filled with Solastalgia, the growing sense of psychological distress over the destruction of our environment, when he imagines the lamenting cries of animals, plants, and people. Each cry is punctuated with the question "what about us?" Jackson interrogates and muses on what we can do to save the planet. Offsetting carbon is not just in the hands of big corporations and big businesses. In today's world, activist engagement of opposing coal mining and convincing climate change billionaires to invest in closing mines has brought carbon-engaged issues to the forefront. As lawyers bring carbon emission cases and coal scams to the courtroom, the judiciary in various forums around the world has set up climate science committees to weigh and balance the carbon emissions catastrophe and contemplate the needed legislative action, thus paving the way for new policies to be enacted. Upsetting the carbon cycle is disastrous for the planet as more CO_2 in the atmosphere will result in further global warming. To save the planet, humanity must consider how to sequester and contain the CO_2 in the hydrospheric depths of the ocean, and in the pedospheric strata of the soil. All humanity needs to be aware of one's presence in the carbon cycle. To find an alternative situation to the existing catastrophism and rhetoric caused by the negative Earth Emotion of Solastalgia, we need to consider ways and means of transitioning to a new era of the Symbiocene filled with positive Earth Emotions.

NOTES

1. *Solastalgia* (Stiller/Tremblay), *Solastalgia*, 2019, https://www.solastalgia.ca.
2. Albrecht A. Glenn, "Solastalgia: A New Concept in Human Health and Identity," *PAN (Philosophy, Activism, Nature)*, 3 (2005): 44–59.
3. Similar 'Solastalgia' theme-based films were produced by Marina Hufnagel in 2022 and Violeta Mora in 2023. Earlier in 2009, the English musical duo group, Zero 7—Henry Binns and Sam Hardaker—released a song entitled "Solastalgia" in their album *Yeah Ghost* to capture the essence of hopelessness and powerlessness faced by humanity in the face of environmental loss and climate change.
4. "Solastalgia—2016–2019," Solastalgia—Eline Kersten, 2023, https://elinekersten.com/selected-works/solastalgia/.

5. "Solastalgia." Kalmar Art Museum. Accessed June 24, 2023. https://www.kalmarkonstmuseum.se/en/exhibition/solastalgia/.

6. Ella Tillema (1983–) is a Swedish artist who works with figurative oil painting, though she has also experimented with music and screen-printing.

7. Nils Kreuger (1858–1930) was a Swedish painter who specialized in landscapes and rural scenes.

8. Catrin Andersson (1974–) breaks down details from scientific research, visualising both the visible and the invisible to the human eye in the series of drawings.

9. Glenn A Albrecht, *Earth Emotions: New Words for a New World* (Ithaca: Cornell University, 2019).

10. Albrecht A. Glenn, "Solastalgia: A New Concept in Human Health and Identity," 45.

11. Glenn A. Albrecht, "Public Heritage in the Symbiocene," in *The Oxford Handbook of Public Heritage Theory and Practice*, ed. Angela M. Labrador and Neil Asher Silbermann (New York: Oxford University Press, 2018), 355–70.

12. Idem, 359.

13. Idem, 359.

14. Albrecht, *Earth Emotions*, 30.

15. Laura Cozzi, Olivia Chen, and Hyeji Kim, "The World's Top 1% of Emitters Produce Over 1000 Times More CO2 than the Bottom 1%," IEA, February 22, 2023, https://www.iea.org/commentaries/the-world-s-top-1-of-emitters-produce-over-1000-times-more-co2-than-the-bottom-1.

16. Paul Griffin, "Carbon Majors Report 2017," CDP, July 2017, https://www.cdp.net/en/articles/media/new-report-shows-just-100-companies-are-source-of-over-70-of-emissions.

17. "Climate Change 2022: Mitigation of Climate Change—Sixth Annual Assessment Report," IPCC, accessed June 25, 2023, https://www.ipcc.ch/report/ar6/wg3/.

18. Jean-Bernard Pierini, "Carbon Offsetting—Greenwashing the Climate Disaster," Greens/EFA, January 9, 2023, https://www.greens-efa.eu/opinions/greenwashing-the-climate-disaster/.

19. Green Fares: Fly More Sustainably | Lufthansa, accessed June 24, 2023, https://www.lufthansa.com/us/en/green-fare.

20. "Planet: BA Sustainability, Carbon Reduction & Net Zero," Planet | BA Sustainability, Carbon Reduction & Net Zero, accessed June 25, 2023, https://www.britishairways.com/en-gb/information/about-ba/ba-better-world/planet.

21. "American Airlines," *Cool Effect*, September 1, 2021, https://www.cooleffect.org/american-airlines.

22. "Customer Carbon Offsetting: Ryanair's Corporate Website," Customer Carbon Offsetting | Ryanair's Corporate Website, accessed June 24, 2023, https://corporate.ryanair.com/sustainability/customer-carbon-offsetting/.

23. Patrick Greenfield, "Revealed: More than 90% of Rainforest Carbon Offsets by Biggest Certifier Are Worthless, Analysis Shows," *Guardian*, January 18, 2023, https://www.theguardian.com/environment/2023/jan/18/revealed-forest-carbon-offsets-biggest-provider-worthless-verra-aoe.

24. "Verra Reviews Improved Forest Management Methodologies," *Verra*, June 16, 2023, https://verra.org/verra-reviews-improved-forest-management-methodologies/.
25. Idem.
26. "Carbon Offsets Are Not Our Get-Out-Of-Jail Free Card," UNEP, June 10, 2019, https://www.unep.org/news-and-stories/story/carbon-offsets-are-not-our-get-out-jail-free-card.
27. Chris Greenberg, "Carbon Offsets Are a Scam," Greenpeace International, May 10, 2023, https://www.greenpeace.org/international/story/50689/carbon-offsets-net-zero-greenwashing-scam/.
28. Brad Smith, "Microsoft Will Be Carbon Negative by 2030," The Official Microsoft Blog, July 23, 2020, https://blogs.microsoft.com/blog/2020/01/16/microsoft-will-be-carbon-negative-by-2030/.
29. "The Climate Pledge," The Climate Pledge—Amazon, November 17, 2021, https://www.aboutamazon.eu/planet/the-climate-pledge.
30. "Steelcase Announces Carbon Neutrality and Goal to Be Carbon Negative by 2030," Steelcase, October 14, 2020, https://www.steelcase.com/press-releases/steelcase-announces-carbon-neutrality-goal-carbon-negative-2030/.
31. "What Does Being Climate Positive Mean for Ikea?" What is climate positive. Accessed June 25, 2023. https://about.ikea.com/en/sustainability/becoming-climate-positive/what-is-climate-positive.
32. Vandana Shiva, "Women and the Vanishing Waters," in *Staying Alive: Women, Ecology and Development* (Berkeley: North Atlantic, 2016).
33. Idem, 197–98.
34. *Rural Litigation and Entitlement Kendra & Ors v. State of U. P. & O*rs (Supreme Court of India, March 12, 1985).
35. Idem, section 1.
36. Idem, sections 1–4.
37. Idem, section 5.
38. Idem, sections 8–9.
39. Idem, section 9.
40. Arundhati Roy, *The Ministry of Utmost Happiness* (New Delhi: Penguin, 2017), 195.
41. Roy Arundhati, "Power Politics," in *The Algebra of Infinite Justice* (New Delhi: Penguin, 2002), 147.
42. Arundhati Roy, *Capitalism: A Ghost Story* (London: Verso, 2015), 13.
43. Idem, 2.
44. Ironically Vedanta's tagline is 'Mining Happiness.' It is a subsidiary of the British-based parent company Vedanta Resources.
45. In 2014, the Jindal Group Jindal was under investigation in connection with the allocation of coal mining rights in a scandal labelled 'Coalgate' by India's media.
46. A lakh is 100,000 Indian rupees.
47. Arundhati Roy, "There's No Escape from the Corporations That Run India | Arundhati Roy," *Guardian*, March 19, 2012, https://www.theguardian.com/commentisfree/2012/mar/19/corporations-india-arundhati-roy.

48. Vijay Rathod, "Saving Sangam from Mining," in *Making the Law Count: Ten Environmental Justice Stories by Community Paralegals in India* (New Delhi: Namati, 2018), 8–10.

49. Vijay Rathod, "Saving Sangam from Mining," 10.

50. Indra Sinha, *Animal's people* (London: Simon and Schuster, 2009), 151.

51. Indra Sinha's *Animal's People* won the 2008 Commonwealth Writer's Prize for the Eurasia region and was shortlisted for the 2007 Man Booker Prize. Sinha was born in Mumbai but resides in France. His father was an Indian naval officer, and his mother was a British writer.

52. Ingrid Eckerman, *The Bhopal Saga: Causes and consequences of the world's largest industrial disaster* (Hyderabad: Universities Press, 2005).

53. India's first prime minister, Jawaharlal Nehru, launched on the implementation of Keynesian modelled five-year plans. The first five-year plan (1951–1956) aimed to use India's resources efficiently and maximize India's per capita income; the 2nd quinquennial (1956–1961) revolved around the idea of developing the public sector and achieving rapid industrialisation; while the third scheme (1961–1967) laid stress on agricultural development and the improvement of wheat plantation and production in India.

54. Sinha, *Animal's People*, 30.

55. Albrecht, *Earth Emotions*, 38–39.

56. "Canoes vs Coal Ships—Blockading Newcastle Harbour—Stories & Images," Stories & images, December 18, 2020, https://storiesandimages.net/cases/climate-movement/pacific-warriors/blockade/.

57. "Update 3-Vattenfall Eyes Sale of German Lignite Assets after Posting Huge Loss," Reuters, October 30, 2014, https://www.reuters.com/article/vattenfall-results-idUKL5N0SP1XE20141030.

58. Richard Fisher, "The Environmental Case for Buying a Coal Mine," BBC Future, March 18, 2022, https://www.bbc.com/future/article/20220118-the-environmental-case-for-buying-a-coal-mine.

59. *The Yes Men Are Revolting*, 2015, https://i-d.vice.com/en/article/bjnqk5/the-yes-men-turn-their-media-spoofing-stunts-to-tackling-climate-change.

60. Idem.

61. *Watch the Yes Men Impersonate Shell, Make "Last Iceberg" Snow Cones*, *YouTube* (YouTube, 2015), https://www.youtube.com/watch?v=nkqO-qOHFT8.

62. *The Yes Men* (United Artists—MGM, 2003).

63. Idem.

64. "Online Rally: Respect Wangan and Jagalingou," Stop Adani, accessed July 13, 2023, https://www.stopadani.com/respect_wangan_and_jagalingou_online.

65. Idem.

66. It is a major dispute at the Land Court of Queensland over the Carmichael Coal Mine or the Adani Mine concerning the proposed Galilee Basin of central Queensland. In *Adani Mining Pty Ltd v. Pennings* (2020), the respondent headed a group of political activists, called the "Galilee Blockade," whose object was to prevent the development of the mine and the railway. Adani Mining applied for an *ex parte* Anton Piller order against Galilee Blockade.

67. "Online Rally: Respect Wangan and Jagalingou," Stop Adani, accessed July 13, 2023, https://www.stopadani.com/respect_wangan_and_jagalingou_online.

68. Shut Shit Down—An Activist's Guide to Ende Gelände, accessed June 28, 2023, https://www.ende-gelaende.org/wp-content/uploads/2021/02/Basics-Ende-Gelaende-online-version.pdf.

69. "Ende Gelände," Ende Gelände, accessed June 28, 2023, https://www.ende-gelaende.org/en/news/ende-gelaende-ends-a-successful-week-of-action-major-gas-consumers-and-liquefied-natural-gas-terminal-construction-site-blocked-port-of-hamburg-paralyzed-for-nine-hours/.

70. "Rhineland 2017: We Are Creating a Climate of Justice—Colourful, Noisy and Queer," Ende Gelände, 13AD, https://www.ende-gelaende.org/en/news/rhineland-2017-we-are-creating-a-climate-of-justice-colourful-noisy-and-queer/.

71. Greta Thunberg (2003-), child climate activist was featured on the cover of *Time* magazine as the 2019 Person of the Year. She began with a school strike on Fridays and has succeeded in bringing planet-wide attention on the need to act on climate change.

72. Le Monde with AP and AFP, "Greta Thunberg Detained at German Coal Mine Protest," Le Monde.fr, January 17, 2023, https://www.lemonde.fr/en/germany/article/2023/01/17/greta-thunberg-detained-at-german-coal-mine-protest_6011960_146.html.

73. Sean Cubitt, *Anecdotal Evidence: Ecocritique from Hollywood to the Mass Image* (New York: Oxford University Press, 2020), 14.

74. Idem, 14.

75. Idem, 14.

76. Idem, 18.

77. Idem, 1.

78. Cubitt, *Anecdotal Evidence*, 21.

79. Sinha, *Animal's people*, 3.

80. Mikhail Mikhailovich Bakhtin, *Problems of Dostoevsky's Poetics* (Minneapolis: University of Minnesota Press, 1984), 55.

81. Idem, 83.

82. Serenella Iovino and Serpil Oppermann, *Material Ecocriticism*, (Bloomington: Indiana University Press, 2014), 1–2.

83. Sinha, *Animal's people*, 11.

84. Cubitt, *Anecdotal Evidence*, 14.

85. Sinha, *Animal's people*, 51.

86. Cubitt, *Anecdotal Evidence*, 25.

87. Kyle Bladow and Jennifer Ladino, "Introduction," in *Affective Ecocriticism: Emotion, Embodiment, Environment*, edited by Kyle Bladow (Lincoln: University of Nebraska Press, 2018), 13.

88. Glenn A Albrecht, *Earth Emotions: New Words for a New World* (Ithaca: Cornell University, 2019).

89. The fictional ghost city Khaufpur is a carbon copy of the city of Bhopal.

90. Sinha, *Animal's People*, 11.

91. Albrecht A. Glenn, "Solastalgia: A New Concept in Human Health and Identity." *PAN (Philosophy, Activism, Nature)*, 3 (2005): 46.
92. Albrecht, *Earth Emotions*, xi.
93. Sinha, *Animal's People*, 29.
94. Albrecht, *Earth Emotions*, 79.
95. Idem, 79.
96. Sinha, *Animal's People*, 29.
97. Cubitt, *Anecdotal Evidence*, 25.
98. Sinha, *Animal's People*, 261.
99. Albrecht, *Earth Emotions*, 201.
100. Sinha, *Animal's People*, 228.
101. Bakhtin, *Problems of Dostoevsky's Poetics*, 18.
102. Idem, 183.
103. Albrecht, *Earth Emotions*, 37.
104. Word in *hindi* meaning—"My lips have uttered human speech, the last sacrifice of the slaughtered beast."
105. Sinha, *Animal's People*, 167.
106. Idem, 366.
107. Idem, 366.
108. Albrecht, *Earth Emotions*, 37.
109. Idem, 129.
110. The concept of lifting the veil or piercing the veil was first held in *Salomon v. A. Salomon* (House of Lords, November 16, 1897), when the House of Lords decided that as an absolute principle that a corporation or company has a legal and separate entity of its own.
111. Anne Brunon-Ernst, Armelle Sabatier, Suhasini Vincent, Justine Beplate, *Glossaire de Droit Anglais: Méthode, Traduction et Approche Comparative*, ed. Géraldine Gadbin-George (Paris: Dalloz, 2019), 62.
112. Sinha, *Animal's People*, 52.
113. "Court Postpones Hearing against Dow Chemical for the 37th Time." Down to Earth. Accessed May 28, 2023. https://www.downtoearth.org.in/news/court-postpones-hearing-against-dow-chemical-for-the-37th-time--38949.
114. Sinha, *Animal's People*, 53.
115. Idem, 53.
116. *Life Insurance Corporation of India v. Escorts Ltd. & Ors* (Supreme Court of India December 19, 1985).
117. Idem, 90.
118. Pablo Mukherjee, "'Tomorrow There Will Be More of Us': Toxic Postcoloniality in Animal's People." In *Postcolonial Ecologies: Literatures of the Environment*, edited by George B. Handley and Elizabeth M DeLoughrey (New York: Oxford University Press, 2011), 217.
119. The Bhopal Medical Appeal. "The Dow Carbide Corporate Veil." THE BHOPAL MEDICAL APPEAL, May 26, 2022. https://www.bhopal.org/union-carbide-2/the-dow-carbide-corporate-veil/.

120. Nitin Sethi, "Dow Re-Labelled, Sold UCC Products to Evade Law: India News—*Times* of India," *Times of India*, January 29, 2012, https://timesofindia.indiatimes.com/india/dow-re-labelled-sold-ucc-products-to-evade-law/articleshow/11669179.cms?utm_source=contentofinterest&utm_medium=text&utm_campaign=cppst.

121. The Bhopal Medical Appeal.

122. Idem.

123. Idem.

124. *Bano v. Union Carbide Corporation* (Southern District Court of New York, November 15, 2001), and *Sahu v. Union Carbide Corporation* (Southern District Court of New York September 22, 2009).

125. Bhopal Medical Appeal.

126. Idem.

127. Idem.

128. *Bulga Milbrodale Progress Association Inc. v. Minister for Planning and Infrastructure and Warkworth Mining Limited* (Land and Environmental Court of New South, Wales April 15, 2013).

129. Idem, section 2.

130. Idem, section 15.

131. Idem, section 404.

132. Idem, section 423.

133. Idem, section 426.

134. Idem, section 423.

135. *Union of India v. Union Carbide Corporation* (Supreme Court of India, March 14, 2023), 1.

136. *Bano v. Union Carbide Corporation* (2001).

137. "India: Court Decision Requires Dow Chemical to Respond to Bhopal Gas Tragedy," Amnesty International, August 17, 2021, https://www.amnesty.org/en/latest/news/2013/07/india-court-decision-requires-dowchemical-respond-bhopal-gas-tragedy/.

138. Idem, 32.

139. *Bano v. Union Carbide Corporation* (US Second Circuit Court of Appeals, March 17, 2004).

140. *Vellore Citizens' Welfare Forum v. Union of India* (Supreme Court of India, August 28, 2006).

141. *Vellore Citizens' Welfare Forum v. Union of India*, section 12.

142. *M.C. Mehta v. Union of India & Ors* (The Supreme Court of India, July 8, 1996), section 31.

143. *Sahu v. Union Carbide Corporation* (Southern District Court of New York, September 22, 2009).

144. *Sahu v. Union Carbide Corporation* (U.S. Court of Appeals for the Second Circuit, June 17, 2013).

145. International Campaign for Justice in Bhopal, accessed June 27, 2023, https://www.bhopal.net/what-happened/contamination/court-cases-environmental-liability/.

146. Ibid.

147. Ibid.

148. *Union of India v. Union Carbide Corporation* (2023), 5.

149. It is a coalition formed by all left-leaning parties of India in 2004. Its founder is Mrs Sonia Gandhi, the wife of late prime minister Rajiv Gandhi.

150. "What Is Coal Scam?" *Indian Express*, May 22, 2017, https://indianexpress.com/article/what-is/manmohan-singh-cbi-coalgate-coal-block-allocation-cag-report-what-is-coal-scam-4668265/. This amount in Indian rupees represents approximately around US$ one billion.

151. *Manohar Lal Sharma v. The Principal Secretary & Ors* (Supreme Court of India, August 25, 2014).

152. Sagnik Dutta, "Mines of Scam," *Frontline*, September 19, 2014.

153. Idem, section 81.

154. Idem, section 57.

155. Sagnik Dutta, "Mines of Scam," *Frontline*, September 19, 2014.

156. "Power Stocks Fall up to 7 P.C. on SC Order on Coal Allocation," *Hindu*, November 16, 2021, https://www.thehindu.com/business/markets/power-stocks-fall-up-to-7-pconscorderoncoalallocation/article6353862.ece?utm_source=RSS_Feed&utm_medium=RSS&utm_campaign=RSS_Syndication.

157. Michael Jackson, *Earth Song* (YouTube, 2015), https://www.youtube.com/watch?v=gbAd62jzrNI.

158. Michael Jackson, "Michael Jackson—Earth Song," *Genius*, accessed June 29, 2023, https://genius.com/Michael-jackson-earth-song-lyrics.

Chapter 7

The Seeds of the Future

In *The Great Derangement: Climate Change and the Unthinkable*, Amitav Ghosh explores whether present generations are deranged[1] with how they look at the scale of climate catastrophes. Ghosh sees that such consequences remain in the hands of populations who have varying recognitions of how to address these environmental issues. Ghosh contends that "the climate crisis is also a crisis of culture, and that of the imagination."[2] He warns us that in an ever-changing world with sea level rising to swallow the Sundarbans, and the increasing possibility of submerged cities such as Kolkata, New York, and Bangkok. Ghosh paints an apocalyptic scenario of a world where cities and forests like the Sundarbans would be replaced by seascapes; major urban cities would become uninhabitable and that future generations would try to find answers in literature and art for the damaged world they had unwittingly inherited. He imagines future generations concluding that our present generation is rather 'deranged' and oblivious to the hazards, risks, vulnerabilities, and perils of climate change.

Throughout human history, artists have often combined their narratives with nature. These forms have ranged from mythology, mapping, documentation, conquering, general landscape imagery—as well as all the technical developments that have allowed art to change and respond to modern cultural commentary. Since cave paintings and stacking stones, humans have shown through art their interests in working with and documenting interactions with their environments. Globally, in recent generations, there has been growth in the content and use of art to help address the human experience during environmental change. Art of our time reflects the zeitgeist, feeding from politics, social values, identity issues, and environmental change. Unlike Italian Renaissance painters such as Michelangelo and Raphael who were commissioned by powerful patrons such as popes or kings; art today depends on social media and an increased focus on technology with many artists utilizing digital tools for creating works that reflect the cultural time of flux and change. Art has responded to war, ecological catastrophe, and crises of the new millennium in different forms.

The Tate Museum defines *environmental art* as "art that addresses social and political issues relating to the natural and urban environment."[3] Herewith below are artists, with their own methods and mediums, who add to the continued and growing movement for recognition surrounding environmental issues, offering examples for how art can be a tool to connect with human value systems. Forty-one years ago in 1982, Agnes Denes, the Hungarian visual artist, who is one of the first pioneers of environmental art, cleared two acres of land in lower Manhattan to fill it with two hundred truckloads of soil to create a wheatfield she tilled by hand.[4] The photo of her in *Wheatfield—A Confrontation*[5] was shot with Denes in the middle of the wheat field with New York's financial district in the background. The Twin Towers figure in the background and the wheat field, planted in a space of global financial trade, is symbolic of an act of protest aimed at Wall Street bankers, and big businesses who misuse space and thrive on the inequity of global trade. In 2014, the Danish-Icelandic environmental artist Olafur Eliasson presented *Ice Watch*,[6] a large-scale art installation outside the Tate Modern Art Museum that had the artist working with geologists to transport blocks of Greenland ice to London. Visitors to the museum walked around the ice blocks, touched, and witnessed it melt completely and disappear as water vapor. The ephemeral display sent a message to the world about the dangers of melting snow in the Arctic regions, and the resultant increase in the planet's temperature. In 2021, in his project entitled "Life,"[7] Eliasson decided to flood Switzerland's Fondation Beyeler, by raising the pond outside the museum, removing the museum's southern glass façade to allow it to flood and enter the museum. The water allowed visitors to wade through the different displays and see the interplay of colors in the changing settings of each display room. Water dyed a fluorescent green was filled with pond flora such as water lilies and shellflowers. Eliasson remarks, "Together with the museum, I am giving up control over the artwork, so to speak, handing it over to human and non-human visitors, to plants, microorganisms, the weather, the climate—many of these elements that museums usually work very hard to keep out."[8] The display paid apt homage to nature and the environment.

In her tapestry weaving called *The Black Gold Tapestry*, Sandra M. Sawatzky,[9] a Canadian visual artist and embroiderer, has woven a sixty-seven-meter hand-embroidered piece relating the saga of oil, global societal change, and energy transition through the power and beauty of embroidery.[10] The slides or panel sections measuring approximately thirty inches by forty inches detail the uncertainty of the present age. Likewise, Andy Goldsworthy,[11] a British sculptor and photographer in his latest environmental craft *Three River Works*[12] taps water sources, cuts stones, and grinds rock, and maneuvers the flow of water to show the elusive nature of water with its changing, meandering paths penetrating rocks and strata, and being eternally rejuvenated. He works with objects of nature, namely stones, twigs, leaves, plant stalks, clay, ice, and snow, to create an appreciation of the natural world, to highlight the ephemerality of the natural world and to highlight the importance of preserving it.

The collaborative duo Christo and Jeanne-Claude is often referred to as the work of 'Christo' in the realm of art. With the "L'Arc de Triomphe, Wrapped,"[13] a temporary artwork at Paris for sixteen days from September 18 to October 3, 2021, the historical Napoleonic monument that glorified the great army of 1806, was wrapped in twenty-five thousand square meters of recyclable polypropylene fabric in silvery blue, and was held in place with three thousand meters of red rope. During its installation, the eternal flame in honor of the unknown soldier continued to burn as a tribute to the environmental artistic creation of Christo. In keeping with the trend of Nouveau Réalisme, these partners set out to question the death of art's preciousness by considering reality as a primary medium. Their land-art pieces set out to encompass and wrap architectural and landscape elements in fabric, canvases, ropes, and metal structures to conceal world-famous architectural sites like the Reichstag in Berlin, the Pont-Neuf in Paris, The Gates in New York's Central Park, the thirty-nine-kilometre-long Running Fence down the California coast, and the Australian coastline. A relevant portion for these temporary textile imaginations were aimed at revealing the beauty of nature and human experience through concealment, challenging visitors to their works, to consider what was not seen, but perhaps had values. As part of allowing on a more-dramatic scale for such an explanation from artists, this method of 'temporary' in exhibitions highlighted that lifeforms in nature are ephemeral, but also filled with a capacity to be brought back to life again.

In 2006, mysterious-British artist Banksy's work "Trolley Hunters"[14] shows three crouching hunters stalking their ludicrous prey of supermarket trolleys to cast light on the absurd world we live in where consumers are game to supermarket tactics of buying one and getting one free. In *Show Me the Monet*, another trolley painting, which sold at Sotheby's in October 2020 for £7,551,600, Banksy reconfigures the iconic masterpiece of the Japanese bridge with discarded shopping trolleys and a traffic cone in the pond's waters.[15] In our time, the shopping trolley is not just a physical object, but one that fills virtual, digital baskets found on online websites. Banksy's *The Girl with the Balloon* sold for a whooping £16 million bounds when it shredded itself at a Sotheby's auction.[16] The art piece gained instantly more value and was renamed as "Love in the Bin" as nine bidders battled to win possession over the shredded piece, which instead of finding its place in the rubbish dump, assumed new significance for its environmental message. As Ghosh aptly writes, the "Anthropocene presents a challenge not only to the arts and the humanities, but also to our commonsense understandings and beyond that to contemporary culture in general."[17] Environmental artists, and the works they produce, offer a lens for both scholars and thoughtful observers to look further into environmental issues, creating opportunities for both consideration and concern. Artistic descriptions about the environment, be them past, present, and future, remain a work in progress as people question outcomes, or possible outcomes. That does not always produce a change in behavior. With that recognition in place, art remains a method of communication surrounding environmental themes.

HASHTAG MOVEMENTS OF GENERATION Z

The voices of Zoomers or Generation Z teenagers have moved governments into action by bringing climate change global conversations to the forefront through Hashtag-Twitter activism. The sign # preceded by a noun or a phrase commonly used on social media sites and applications to identify digital content on a specific topic, was declared as the Children's word of the year by Oxford University Press in 2015.[18] In 2019, sixteen-year-old Greta Thunberg shook the World Economic Forum conference at Davos in Switzerland with her fiery speech, "Our house is on fire. I am here to say, our house is on fire."[19] Through the rhetorical device of repetition, she delivered her wake-up call to the financial representatives of nations around the globe. Armed with statistics from the IPCC, Thunberg warned the international community that humanity had less than twelve years to undo its mistakes. She contended that financial success had come with an unthinkable price tag with unprecedented release of greenhouse gases like methane (CH_4) from the Arctic permafrost into the atmosphere. Resorting to pathos and accusative facial expressions, she insisted on the need to reduce CO_2 emissions by at least 50 percent. Her tirade is typical of Generation Z teenagers who are voicing the need for action on climate catastrophe, who use the tools of social media to relay climate change online content, and who are involved relentlessly in volunteering and attending rallies and protests. Studies conducted in 2020 reveal that 32 percent of Gen Zers (born between 1997 and 2012) and 28 percent of Millennials (born between 1981 and 1996) and the next generation, Alpha (born after 2012 through perhaps 2025), have been involved either in donating money or contacting an elected official or volunteering or attending a rally, to help address climate change in the last year, compared with smaller shares of Gen X (23 percent) and Baby Boomer and older adults (21 percent).[20] Gen Z expects governments to solve problems, rather than businesses and individuals. Twenty-nine percent of Gen Z contend that the government had to engage more to solve problems; 64 percent of Millennials are of the opinion that the government should do more to solve problems; while 53 percent of Gen Xers, 49 percent of Boomers, and 39 percent of Silents do not think so.[21]

In 2018, Greta Thunberg, who was fifteen at that time, decided to skip school to squat outside the Swedish Parliament to attract the government's attention to the lack of action on climate crisis. Her 'Skolstrejk för klimatet,' or 'School strike for the Climate,' led to the creation of #FridaysForFuture,[22] an organized, youth-led movement with teenagers from all over the world engaging through posts on Instagram and Twitter. At the COP 24 in Poland in 2018, convened under the United Nations Framework Convention on Climate Change (UNFCCC), she accused world leaders of being not mature enough to voice the inevitable, and asked them to act as responsible instead of behaving like children. She admonished them asking them to take the responsibility they should have taken a long time ago. She asserted, "you are never too small to make a difference."[23] In January 2019, at the round-table discussions of the Davos Economic Forum, once again Thunberg addressed a speech to the global energy industry and its financiers to end all fossil fuel investments. She warned that the fossil fuel industry will if, "they can get away with it they will continue to invest in fossil fuels, they will continue to throw people under the bus."[24] Thunberg's stance is typical of Z Gen climate activists who are acutely conscious of the relevance of time and have addressed calls to climate change villains to stop producing fossil fuels.

In 2018, the #4ocean campaign[25] organized by 4ocean youth campaigners highlighted through social medial that there are 8 million pieces of plastic entering into the ocean every single day. They have organized ocean clean-up operations, have harnessed the power of businesses to fund a global cleanup operation and have been responsible for recovering millions of pounds of plastic and trash from the world's oceans, rivers, and coastlines. #4ocean campaign also convinces activists to wear bracelets made with recycled glass bottles and post-consumer recycled plastic bottles to fund its ocean cleanup operations. POPs (persistent organic pollutants) that are ingested by dolphins and porpoises are toxic organic compounds that are break-down resistant and can even take a century to degrade. Plastics micro shred in the oceans and mix with plankton that are consumed by fish that humans consume. Due to biomagnification, those lower down in the food chain are less affected than bigger cetacean species like dolphins or porpoises and even humans.

On November 8, 2021, *Time* magazine's cover carried the photo of Vanessa Nakate, and her article entitled "Vanessa Nakate Wants Climate Justice for Africa."[26] As a child activist she headed the #FridaysForFuture Movement in Uganda. Her #Riseupmovement is a social media platform that is dedicated to empowering communities and amplify the voices of activists from Africa, is one that is alive with discussion and now operates on an international scale to voice support for the Congo Basin. Known as the "lungs of Africa,"[27] the Congo Basin hosts the largest carbon sink in the world, as it spans across six countries with its rainforests that provide food security to the region. Since September 2022, she has been appointed as the UNICEF goodwill ambassador for the African sub-continent.

The construction of the Dakota Access Pipeline sparked clamorous online debate about oil, the environment, and Native American sovereignty. Hashtag activism of #NoDAPL tweets highlighted the international community of the construction of the pipeline underneath Lake Oahe near the Standing Rock Reservation in North Dakota. While the US Army Corps of Engineers insisted on the growing demand for petroleum products and framed a narrative of the pipeline being necessary for consumers and their standard of living; #NoDAPL activists, on the contrary, used the conflict frame by including a tweet by prominent anti-fracking activist actor Mark Ruffalo on January 23, 2018. Ruffalo tweeted vociferously, "DAPL and #Keystone would be disastrous for the people and the environment. Let's keep fighting brothers & sisters. #NoDAPL."[28]

On June 5, 2023, Côte d'Ivoire hosted the 50th World Environment Day with the hashtag #BeatPlasticPollution. The largest global platform for environmental reach, millions of people participated online and through in-person activities, events, and actions around the world. Jean-Luc Assi, Côte d'Ivoire's Minister for the Environment and Sustainable Development welcomed participants by tweeting, "The scourge of plastic pollution is a visible threat that impacts every community around the world. As host of World Environment Day 2023, we welcome all sectors, from governments and businesses to civil society, to come together to find and champion solutions."[29] Côte d'Ivoire banned the use of plastic bags in 2014, thus supporting a shift to reusable packaging and setting example for other countries to follow likewise. Abidjan is now a hub for start-ups looking to beat plastic pollution.

In 2020, Licypriya Kangujam, an eight-year-old girl from Manipur in India attracted public attraction when she snubbed the Indian prime minister Narendra Modi by asking him not to feature her in his #SheInspiresUs campaign, if he did not want to hear her voice. Her hashtag tweets include #StopAdaniJivi to stop the corporate giant from mining more coal.[30] Child activism on Twitter highlights a story of broken trust and deception of adult indifference to issues that really matter to the Earth. As the brave Generation Z decides to tackle the bull by its horns, corporate villains lie exposed to public disapproval. Twitter's Unicode Glyphs of 140 characters gather instant responses with posts including videos, images, texts generating further multimodal stories, which are woven into narratives through a networked structure that includes further feeds, likes and hashtags.

MAKING THE MATERIAL TURN THROUGH ECO-MEDIA

Ecomedia and ecological crisis are closely entangled systems that coexist in ecological webs of connectivity whereby "human culture is connected to the physical world, affecting it and [is] affected by it."[31] Adapted to eco-media, Glotfelty's dictum might claim that as a critical gaze, ecocriticism results in a stereoscopic view that reveal in Serenella Iovino's terms the "Material Turn . . . the existence of material forces and substances—the agency of things and their role in materialistic societies."[32] This is evident in the way media infiltrates the human and the non-human world. Unlike colonial narratives that assume that human existence is superior with its domination over the natural environment, the postcolonial narrative is one that recognizes this fallacy and identifies the need to coexist with nature. Based on the premise that media is ecologically entwined, it is untenable to make an absolute division between human society and our environment. There is an immense "material mesh of meanings, properties and processes, in which human and non-human players are interlocked in networks that produce undeniable signifying forces."[33] Through social media networks environmental disasters are given agency in postcolonial India through documentaries and animated films. As humans never act alone and tend to interact in networks that include both environmental features and technologies or non-human actors, it is possible to identify three phases of representation, 'frames,' 'flows,' and 'convergence.'[34]

Humans never engage alone as they are involved along with non-human actors or 'actor networks' like technologies in the fight to preserve the environment.[35] *The Seeds of Vandana Shiva,*[36] is an autobiographical documentary on the life of the eco-activist, produced by Camilla Becket and James Becket,[37] that showcases Shiva's global impact campaign. The frame set is one of the two conflicting visions for feeding the world: big corporate giants who speak in favor of chemically dependent monoculture; and activists who advocate biodiversity, sustainability, and indigenous modes of cultivation. Through the one-and-a-half-hour documentary, the producers capture Shiva's alliance with human and non-human entities. Shiva shares her eco-feminist views; makes a call to the international community to preserve the forests and its indigenous tribes; reports on the *status quo* of slow governmental intervention typical of postcolonial governments; reveals the statistics behind her studies; and persuades the viewer through eco-media on the need to change. By figuring ten frames of reference or episodes, Shiva shows her ability to re-configure themes like ecofeminism, carbon footprints, water crisis, and seed patenting. Known in India as the 'Gandhi of Grain,' Shiva advocates the idea that the answer to feeding a hungry world, lies in encouraging local, small-scale agriculture and micro enterprises. Relying on statistical data she denounces the 1 percent model of philanthrocapitalism, "an economic model based on the illusion of limitless growth,"[38] whereby big corporations divert unaccountable money to bypass democratic structures. She contends that big agri-businesses, in their pursuit of profit, force small farmers to a cultivation of monoculture. Through the eco-media mode of a documentary, she reveals the politics of food and the existence of big Goliaths like Monsanto, Cargill, and Archer Daniels Midland who generate immense surpluses but create real scarcity in poor countries that produce food. While countries in the developing world like India and Africa are rich in natural resources, they rate as poor countries on the world index as 70 percent of children in these countries do not even have a square meal per day. Shiva's call to move beyond monocultures, to sow and harvest biodiverse crops, can be viewed as a form of non-human space where environmental narratives meet and mingle with humans and provide the context to make scientific data feel personally and culturally relevant.

The flows of energy can be understood through the lens of an environmentally motivated approach that engages all intersections of media, society, and the environment. The expert, statistical and didactic documentary is eco-activist in tone and shows Shiva lobbying in Ghana in 2014 against the plant breeders act or the Monsanto Takeover Act. In another episode in *The Seeds of Vandana Shiva* entitled "Battle in Seattle" (1999), similar flows of energy are exhibited by protestors outside the WTO venue, as they decide to use Gandhi's non-violent *satyagraha*. In Seattle, young people joined hands to prevent delegates from participating in the conference and was proof of how ordinary people at the grassroots had the power to confront multinational corporations. Monsanto is known for its trend of winning every single intellectual property lawsuit filed in the United States and Canada since 1997. Shiva's documentary draws attention to the legal battle with Monsanto in *Vandana Shiva and Ors. v. Union of India and Ors.* (1994),[39] where the Supreme Court of India dismissed the writ petition in favor of abiding with the terms of international treaties. Siva posits that genetically modified BT cotton marketed by Monsanto, has created super pests, and contributed to farmers' debt in India. By portraying the problems of conserving biodiversity in the mountains and forests of India, Vandana Shiva partakes in making a Material Turn by conjoining media and activism. Without falling into the mindset of dichotomous thinking of humans versus nature, she has shown through the media of the documentary that life on our planet is possible only if humans protect nature. The documentary with its episodes on the cutting down of mountain trees, water wars between states, the plight of the poor farmer, have alerted viewers on the need for collective action.

In *Priya and the Twirling Wind*,[40] cartoon and documentary producer Ram Devineni, who is the recipient of the Tongues on Fire Flame Award 2022 for the Best Animated Film, *Priya and the Twirling Wind*, uses the technology of augmented reality to stir further energy flows. Murals in Delhi and Mumbai with augmented reality features, viewable through the free Blippar app, enabled viewers to see special animation features on their smart phones. The movement of media content expands the agency of activists whereby different flows of content converge across multiple media platforms with media audiences awaiting new kinds of media experiences.[41] While Vandana Shiva invites audiences to engage in a process of viewing, interpreting, and lobbying; Devineni's creation of images through a combination of digital art, painting, graphic design, collage, and photography are more participatory, interactive, and collaborative. The comic book *Priya and the Twirling Wind* when scanned transforms into a pop-up book to reach young teenagers. The technology of augmented reality triggers links to other collaborative projects like the puppet interviews with climate scientists and environmentalists, like Vandana Shiva, Chris Rapley,[42] Simon Lewis,[43] Alexandria Villaseñor,[44] and Ridhima Pandey.[45] The collaboration with climate activists who speak on related topics like the *Chipko Andolan* or the tree-hugging movement shows the power of the image to converge with activism and participate in a project of 'Art meeting Activism.' The technology of augmented reality enables participation of its user community and produces data for the platforms that house its content, such as YouTube, Google, Facebook, Vimeo, and Daily Motion. In the process of collaboration, extraction, and framing, there is a dialogue between collaborators, participants, contributors, and viewers who inhabit this shared world of the Postcolonial Animated Cartoon. At the New York film festival, visitors viewed the augmented reality pop-ups. They liked, tagged, shared their experiences and entered into a discursive dialogue with their peers on social media. The series that were first released in December 2014, went viral with five hundred thousand downloads of the comic worldwide, half of them were in the Indian sub-continent, and four hundred news stories sprang all over the world.[46] Ram Devineni's animated films, the *Priya Series* have educated the younger generation on the importance of protecting the forests like the women of the *Chipko* Movement. The puppets with their pop-up-story frames have generated new flows of energy where the cartoon gets liked, tagged, shared, and viewed multiple times. Through different frames of reference, the documentary makers reveal how individuals can contribute to bringing about changes locally, nationally, and globally.

POLYPHONIC SEED PARABLES

The didactic form of the parable is one that can provide an alternative source of knowledge about the world. Through a story-frame, it teaches, presents ideas and morals in retainable picture frames that are reconfigured from various historical, biblical, or folkloric sources. Parables transmitted from one generation to another can "create vivid pictures in one's mind, stories that enable us to experience profound truths in often deceptively simple ways, stories that challenge us to respond and act—not only to do better, but also to be better."[47] While some parables seem simple and straightforward, others contain vast insight and hidden meaning. Though configured with implied analogy, parallels are often elusive in context as the parallels and comparisons are often not made explicitly. This elusiveness actively engages audiences to voice their interpretation and participate in the polyphonic space of the parable. Therefore, parables by their analogical nature are prone to encourage both tellers and spectators to "imagine new possibilities as they explore the hermeneutical potential of these brief narratives."[48] Biblical parables of Jesus related to his disciples are known to be not just simple stories, but dialogic enigmatic recitations drawing listeners and readers into ongoing discussions. These often-challenging biblical parables were framed with the intention of evoking questions and furthering debate. These parables were retold, written by the disciples in the gospels and rewritten in different versions of the Bible, thus reveling in its polyphonic capacity to include various voices. In the "Parable of the Mustard Seed," Jesus preached, "The kingdom of heaven is like a mustard seed, which a man took and planted in his field. Though it is the smallest of all seeds, yet when it grows, it is the largest of garden plants and becomes a tree, so that the birds come and perch in its branches."[49] This parable gains its polyphonic structure from yet another parable, "The Parable of the Sower,"[50] that explains the plight of those seeds that survive and flourish, as they suffer immense damage because of the weeds or the fiend plants in the field. In this parable the ever-questioning disciples ask Jesus, "'Why do you speak to the people in parables?' Jesus replied, 'Because the knowledge of the secrets of the kingdom of heaven has been given to you, but not to them. Whoever has will be given more, and they will have an abundance. Whoever does not have, even what they have will be taken from them. This is why I speak to them in parables.'"[51] The parable thus contains the seed of enlightenment, and the dialogue contained within the parables serves to argue, deepen, and enrich the reader-listener's understandings of what Jesus's parables connote. The parable is a fertile terrain not just for its didactic value, its dialogues are not circumscribed to texts or speech, it can encompass other genres like music, art, poetry, and create further polyphony. Thus hearers, readers, re-tellers, interpreters of the past, the present and the future participate in the discursive formation of meaning.

Amitav Ghosh in his fiction uses the mode of the parable by mining his own experience when he retells it, linking together moments and scenes that are in some way distinctive or different thus emphasizing that "these are, of course, nothing other than instances of exception. . . . It is through this mechanism that worlds are conjured up, through everyday details, which function 'as the opposite of narrative.'"[52] It is interesting to refer to Mikhail Bakhtin's assertion on the dialogic nature of the veracity of a narrative and that "Truth is not born nor is it to be found inside the head of an individual person, it is born between people collectively searching for truth, in the process of their dialogic interaction."[53] Ghosh's parables with their didactic messages serve as epistemological knowledge capable of conveying the preoccupations of postcolonial literature of our time that is "writing that emerges from peoples who were colonized by European powers, (that) now have some form of political independence but continue to live with the negative, economic, and cultural legacy of colonialism."[54]

In *The Glass Palace* (2000), Ghosh relates the parable of the Teak Tree in Burma, a story that is partly known and partly guessed as it has been altered in form during its various retellings. The River Irrawaddy is the setting in this parable and is the lieu of colonial trade as it is transformed into a commercial watercourse by the British colonists for the teak trade. The Burmese *chaungs* or rushing mountain streams that join the River Irrawaddy metamorphose into teak trade winds carrying huge teak branches and trunks down the river. In this parable, Ghosh recalls the existence of a teak tree in Pegu (Bago), a historical port city in Southern Myanmar. He relates the parable of an imperial teak tree that from a little seed sprouts to become a 106-foot-long-trunked structure that is chopped into pieces for colonial trade. He draws a comparison between the teak (*Tectona grandis*) and its close relative the perennial mint herb (*Mentha*) and imagines what a mint leaf would look like if it grew to be a similar gigantic plant species. Further contrasts between the two botanical species in the parable reveal the mint to be the mere size of a human thumb, whereas the teak leaf spans an elephant's footprint. While the seeds and leaves of the mint plant flavor soups and stews, the mighty teak had the notoriety of having "felled dynasties, caused invasions, created fortunes, (and) brought a new way of life into being."[55] The tenuousness of the parable's narrative is due to the fact that nobody holds a monopoly on truth, which is a vital element of reception history as the search for meaning in a parable is reliant on the hearer "listening to and interacting with a wide range of voices, including those usually not heard."[56] The parable that draws similarities ends with the parable teller admitting that "between the faint hairiness of the one and the bristling, coarse-textured fur of the other, there was an unmistakable kinship, a palpably familial link."[57] It establishes the tangible tie between the seeds of the teak tree and other related flora like verbena, sage, thyme, lavender, rosemary, and basil. It weaves in the didactic truth on the necessity of protecting all kinds of seeds to ensure their survival, be it the valuable teak tree, the humble mint, or the sacred basil.

In *The Hungry Tide* (2004),[58] Ghosh recounts the parable of *Bon Bibi* and the Fishermen in the tidal land of the *Sunderbans*. Fokir, the fisherman, sings of the time of *Bon Bibi*, the guardian of the forests, an epoch when the deity rendered the Sundarbans fit for human habitation. In this river parable "passed on from mouth to mouth and remembered only in memory,"[59] Dokhin Rai takes the form of the Ganges tiger with an insatiable craving for human flesh and stalks Dhukey, a fisher boy. This parable exists in diverse forms, varying from era to era, as it is retold according to the context, and is dependent upon the medium's capacity to retain its dialogic nature. Parables thrive as "enigmatic stories (that) continue to engage and indeed challenge our hearts, minds, and imaginations."[60] The parable set in an indefinite time space is related by the fisherman in *The Hungry Tide* who reveal the hostilities between humans and tigers. *Bon Bibi*, the forest mother wages battle against the demon-tiger-king Dokhin Rai and emerges triumphant. She divides the Sundarbans into two harmonious spaces separating humans and tigers, thus showing the reasons for the present *e*. The parable recounts how primordial laws of the 'survival of the fittest' were replaced by a newfound 'law of the forest,' where tigers and humans live in harmony. The parable's polyphony stems from the various retellings, interpretations that can be attributed to division of land between humans and beasts. As tigers roar, humans engage in battle cries; the demon-tiger-king Dokhin Rai snarls while the forest guardian *Bon Bibi*'s voice spreads an aura of peace. Through the inclusion of the parable of *Bon Bibi*, Ghosh portrays the Sundarbans as an area capable of cherishing 'human' and 'animal' protagonists who assert the right to equal space and territory thanks to an entitlement granted by the forest guardian that can be traced back to roots in time. The parable is a didactic story for our present times, as it insists on the need to protect the ever-dwindling tiger species in India by relegating them to protective reserves and sanctuaries far away from human harm; but also insists on the need to protect the forests, thus enabling the seeds of its different species to thrive in their natural environment. Ghosh, the anthropologist traces the origins of the parable, and casts it as one involved in a dialogic relationship with language, legends, and scripture.

> For this I have seen confirmed many times, that the mudbanks of the tide country are shaped not only by rivers of silt, but also by rivers of language: Bengali, English, Arabic, Hindi, Arkanese and who knows what else? Flowing into each other they create a proliferation of small worlds that hang suspended in the

> flow. And so it dawned on me: the tide country's faith is something like one of its great mahonas, a meeting not just of many rivers, but a circular roundabout people can use to pass in many directions—from country to country and even between faiths and religions.[61]

The parable propagates the seeds of harmony, mingles, and spreads it message thanks to its polyphonic propensity of blending with languages of the different parable tellers. Each parable is a world by itself with each didactic tale bearing multiplying connotations with each teller implicitly or explicitly offering his interpretations of the parables. The dialogic nature of the parable permits its propagation as different tellers continue to nurture its existence, by developing its structure, and expanding its reception as listeners over the centuries add their own interpretations and voices to the ongoing dialogues.

In the biblical "Parable of the Growing Seed," Jesus said, "This is what the kingdom of God is like. A man scatters seed on the ground. Night and day, whether he sleeps or gets up, the seed sprouts and grows, though he does not know how. All by itself the soil produces grain—first the stalk, then the head, then the full kernel in the head. As soon as the grain is ripe, he puts the sickle to it, because the harvest has come."[62] Like the biblical parable on the survival of seeds and their successive sprouting as plants, in *The River of Smoke*,[63] Ghosh's parable of a Botanical Babel is an account of how nature survives despite material exploitation. The Western plant hunter in the parable is on a botanical expedition searching for rare plants like the golden camellia and to find new varieties of plant genus in the East. His booty is in the form of seeds, saplings, plants, and horticultural-rare species that he ships from the East to the West. The parable is set in the famed Botanical Gardens of Pamplemousses, near Port Louis in the Mauritius Islands. Here the parable as a fictional story has all the attributes of a similitude, where "'the reference' in the parable refers readers to an external reality; it is different from a similitude in that the parable is a story that takes place in the past."[64] The garden of Eden in the parable, is cast as neglected, and left in a shabby state of disorder "where African creepers were at war with Chinese trees, (and) one where Indian shrubs and Brazilian vines were locked in a mortal embrace. This was a work of Man, a botanical Babel."[65] Ghosh in this parable refers to founders and curators of botanical history who helped preserve seeds, transplant saplings, and propagate rare flora in other parts of the world, like eighteenth-century French horticulturists Pierre Poivre,[66] who identified the true black pepper, and Philibert Commerson,[67] who discovered the bougainvillea. Here the polyphony emerges from the description of the botanical garden as a 'botanical babel' where flowers of different kinds manifest their presence in the parable, with Chinese, Indian, and Brazilian vines and shrubs voicing their dialogic presence though metaphors of entwinement. During the passage by ship, the flora from the East meets its counterparts in the West. The sea-borne horticultural garden thrives with rare plant species like antirrhinums, lobelias, and georginas from the Americas to medicinal plants from the Far East like camellias.

> If botany was the Scripture of this religion, then horticulture was its form of worship: tending a garden was, for Pierre Lambert, no mere matter of planting seeds and pruning branches—it was a spiritual discipline, a means of communicating with forms of life that were necessarily mute and could be understood only through a careful study of their own modes of expression—the languages of efflorescence, growth and decay: only thus he had taught Paulette, could human beings apprehend the vital energies that constitute the Spirit of the Earth.[68]

The parable refers to the biblical scriptures to grant Botany the entitlement to be included in the polyphony. As in the biblical parables of seeds, Botany is elevated to the status of a spiritual discipline that tends and nurtures plant forms. It also puts forth the idea that nature speaks and has its own voice. Nature is not mute in this parable as it demonstrates different modes of expression through its life cycle from its inception as a seed, to a consequent state of efflorescence growth, and then its final decay when it goes back to the soil like other life forms on the planet. In the parable, the plant hunter Penrose, and his aide the orphaned Paulette, sow seeds, and keep the plants alive despite bad weather at sea. While Penrose gathers rare flora, Paulette who had been taught by her father Pierre Lambert to love nature, strives to understand the expressive form of each plant species. Ghosh's parable depicts the work of Penrose as the "handiwork of a diligent nurseryman—not a man who was a speculative thinker, but rather a practical solver of problems, someone who looked upon nature as an assortment of puzzles, many of which, if properly resolved, could provide rich sources of profit."[69] Like the horticulturists Poivre and Commerson, Paulette names un-named flora giving them an identity despite their muteness and absence of human speech, and thus engages in a "creative endeavor"[70] of giving them new identity. The parable features nature's aptitude of survival thanks to its seeds, its capacity to flourish if nurtured, and the need to protect the flora of our time for the generations to come.

In *Gun Island*,[71] Ghosh writes that stories passed on through the oral tradition have life cycles when they are active or dormant due to the times of turmoil and colonial disruption. He refers to the seventeenth century, when European explorers discovered the East and established their first colonies.

> Some stories, like certain life forms, possess a special streak of vitality that allow them to outlive others of their kind. . . . And in public memory too the legend seems to go through cycles of life, sometimes lying dormant for centuries only

> to be suddenly rejuvenated by a fresh wave of retellings, in some of which the familiar characters appear under, new names, with subtly changed plot lines.[72]

Ghosh's description is typical of the mode of the parable which can be dormant or rejuvenated to life. Its vitality is evident in the changing plotlines, its history of interpretations and its capacity "to be inaccessible to monologic discourse."[73]

SEED PATENTING—DAVID VERSUS GOLIATH

In 2016, a big Goliath, $15-billion-worth Monsanto Company, labelled by *Fortune* as "the world's vilified company," decided to take the carbon pledge of saving the planet with its version of greenwashing.[74] Monsanto's CEO, Hugh Grant conceived this idea of going green in 2008, when the National Geographic Society and other groups invited billionaire CEOs like Google's Larry Page, Meg Whitman head of Hewlett Packard, former Secretary of State Madeleine Albright, former US president Jimmy Carter, and CNN's billionaire founder Ted Turner, on an Arctic expedition to examine the flora, the fauna, and the melting ice pack.[75] While watching flocks of black-and-white barnacle geese make their seasonal appearance at Svalbard in the Norwegian archipelago, they witnessed how the melting ice affected the blooming of grass, the much-awaited food of these geese species. In recent years, as the Arctic temperature has warmed, the timing of the first bloom of grass has become erratic, limiting the birds' food supply. After witnessing this climate change phenomena, Grant decided to sign the 'carbon pledge' and make Monsanto 'carbon neutral.' Newspapers around the world were quick at naming the Goliath Monsanto's greenwashing gimmick, as the "Big Bad Wolf" attempt to distract consumers from its ongoing seed poisoning of the planet.[76]

Monsanto, the American agrichemical giant, founded in 1901 is known for slipping out of the nets of legal battles through out-of-court settlements and arbitration. Since 2018, it has been become part of the Bayer group. The Bayer acquisition resulted in Monsanto's shareholders being paid 128 dollars per share as Monsanto ceased to exist on the New York Stock Exchange.[77] Out of the 147 patent violation suits filed by US farmers, only nine cases have reached the trial stage, and Monsanto has succeeded in all of them.[78] In *Bowman v. Monsanto Co.* (2013),[79] the US Supreme Court backed the agribusiness firm on its soybean patents by ruling in Goliath's favor and concluding that the appellant Vernon Hugh Bowman, the little David, had violated the company's intellectual property rights when he refused to pay royalties on unlabeled soybeans. Bowman had bought seeds from another distributor that contained genes patented by the company. In this much debated case, the court ruled that Monsanto's patents cover not just genetically engineered seeds distributed by Monsanto and its agents, but also included seeds circulating in the market that contain Monsanto's genes. However, Bowman's contention did not concern Monsanto's patents that involve genes that make soybeans resistant to the herbicide glyphosate; his claim was that Monsanto's right to charge royalties had been exhausted because the unlabeled seeds he had planted were the progeny of plants grown from previously purchased Monsanto seeds. Bowman argued that his seed purchases were not covered by Monsanto's patent license. Although Bowman had previously been a patentee paying extra fees to Monsanto, he had in the course of time begun to buy commodity beans from a local granary. He sprayed glyphosate on the beans and through this experiment he discovered that these local beans flourished, which was no doubt an indication that the anonymous seeds contained Monsanto's genes. His letter to Monsanto seeking information on its patent license rules, resulted in the giant taking him to court for violating its license.

Since the commercial introduction of genetically modified organisms (GMOs) in the 1990s, Monsanto has aggressively pursued its commercial interests on the market at home and abroad. Monsanto not only filed for patent protection for its GM plant varieties in various jurisdictions, but also devised and implemented unprecedented systems for the collection of royalties and the surveillance of farmers. It has not shied away from suing farmers, including its own customers for patent infringement, and has had an "uncanny record of winning lawsuits."[80] The trend of winning every single intellectual property lawsuit filed in the United States and Canada since 1997, is also seen in the Indian lawsuit *Monsanto Technology LLC v. Nuziveedu Seeds Ltd* (2019), set in table 7.1.[81] Monsanto's trump card has always been its contention that patent rights extended to any seed containing its patented trait, beyond the first generation and irrespective of how the seeds had been acquired.

Monsanto, the appellant-plaintiff sought permanent injunction against the defendant, Nuziveedu Seeds Ltd from using its trademark "BOLGARD" and "BOLGARD II" brand cotton technology. It claimed that defendant had violated the registered patent no. 214436 and it petitioned the Supreme Court of India to restrain the defendants from selling, and/or using its hybrid seeds bearing the patented technology, as it infringed the registered patent of the plaintiffs.[82] The defendant Nuziveedu Seeds Ltd in their written statement *inter alia* contended that their rights were protected under the Protection of Plant Varieties and Farmers' Right's Act (2001). Justice N. Sinha, the single judge concluded in favor of Monsanto by stating that the Division Bench ought not to have disposed of the suit in a summary manner by relying on documents only, that had been extracted from the public domain, and there was no gain saying that the issues raised were complicated requiring

Table 7.1: *Monsanto Technology LLC* v. Nuziveedu Seeds *Ltd* (2019)

[Civil Appeals Nos :189–190, 191–192 of 2019]
IN THE SUPREME COURT OF INDIA
Judgment rendered on January 8, 2019

Bench: N. SINHA

Rule: Article 27 of the TRIPS Agreement defines which inventions governments are obliged to make eligible for patenting, and what they can exclude from patenting. Section 3 of The Patents Act (1970) states that an invention whose primary or intended use or commercial exploitation could cause serious prejudice to human, animal or plant life or health or to the environment, cannot be patented.

Facts of the case: In 2004, Monsanto, one of the world's largest agri-chemicals and agri-technology companies based in the USA, licensed Nuziveedu Seeds Ltd, a Telangana-based seeds company, to use its patented Bt cotton-seed technology. Under the agreement, Indian companies received 50 grams (50 seeds), at 100,000 Indian Rupees, an equivalent of approximately $120 per seed of transgenic Bt. cottonseeds containing patented Nucleic Acid Sequence (NAS) of invented Bacillus thuringiensis, for a one-time payment 5,000,000 Indian Rupees, an equivalent of approximately $120000. Indian companies were entitled under the terms of the license to develop genetically modified hybrid cotton seeds. Monsanto claimed that Nuziveedu had failed to settle its dues of trait and license fees, while Nuziveedu contended that that Monsanto has illegally terminated their sub-license agreement. There was also the matter of whether trademarks of Bollgard and abbreviations like "BGII" could be used by Nuziveedu.

Case history: At first instance, the Delhi High Court, in *Monsanto Technology LLC v. Nuziveedu Seeds Ltd* (2017) ruled that an invented Nucleic Acid Sequence (NAS) is a result of human intervention and ingenuity and is not a product of nature, and thus is patentable. Whereas, in *Nuziveedu Seeds Ltd v. Monsanto Technology LLC* (2018), the appellate court cited the provisions of Section 3 of The Patents Act (1970) to state that an invented NAS after being inserted into a seed becomes part of the seed; hence, it is not patentable. The Supreme Court of India set aside the answer of the appellate court, remanded the case for expeditious trial and disposal to the court of first instance.

Issues: Whether an invented Nucleic Acid Sequence after being inserted into a seed or plant becomes part of the seed or the plant. Whether the patent granted by the Indian Patent Office to Monsanto Technology LLC on transgenic variety of cottonseeds, containing the invented Bt. trait is valid or not.

Reasoning of the court: The court highlighted the lacunae in the Division Bench's pronouncement on patentability of a genetic sequence, where the summary adjudication failed to address the questions of law and facts on patentability. It reasoned that the Division Court should have analyzed whether the nucleic acid sequence trait once inserted could be removed from that variety or not, and whether the patented DNA sequence was a plant or a part of a plant.

Conclusion: Monsanto succeeded in this case as the Supreme Court set aside the order of Division Bench. The single judge bench did not consider the counter claim of Nuziveedu Seeds on the issue of patentability. The Court held that the Division Bench's judgement declaring the patent of Monsanto was subject to patent exclusion under Section 3 of The Indian Patents Act, invalidated the patent, and thus made the defendants counter claim succeed.

Note: *Monsanto Technology LLC v. Nuziveedu Seeds Ltd* (Supreme Court of India, January 8, 2019).

technological and expert evidence with regard to issues of chemical process, biochemical, biotechnical and microbiological processes, and more importantly on whether the nucleic acid sequence trait once inserted could be removed from that variety or not and whether the patented DNA sequence was a plant or a part of a plant, etc. are again all matters which were required to be considered at the final hearing of the suit.[83]

While news narratives claimed that Monsanto had won a patent-related legal battle on patents of GM cotton seeds; environmental Organisations like the Navdanya and the Alliance for Sustainable and Holistic Agriculture (ASHA) voiced the opinion that the apex court had only invalidated a previous order by a division bench of the Delhi High Court, which had dismissed Monsanto's appeal with respect to patent exclusion under Section 3(j) of the Patents Act.[84]Activist Vandana Shiva contends that under India's patent law, seed were not inventions. In her documentary *The Seeds of Vandana Shiva*, she relates how big Giants like Monsanto function with the goal of doubling yield by 2030 and feeding the world population with genetically modified food.[85] She announces the dawn of a new form of Earth possession by big Goliaths who wish to stifle the small farmer with their mass industrial farming endeavors. In the documentary, she reminds viewers that during colonization when the British Raj controlled cotton production to send raw cotton to its factories in Great Britain, Gandhi after deep thought and reflection picked up the spinning wheel as a mode of resistance. The Gandhian idea of making one's own cloth, was a way of freeing the Indian from cloth dependency on the colonizer. To avoid a pyramid-shaped-societal class existence where the top crushes the bottom, Gandhi offered the tool of the spinning wheel to women, as it was small enough to be held by every woman, thus making the Indian woman a freedom fighter against British monopoly. Just as Gandhi used the spinning wheel to boycott foreign goods, Shiva contends that the seed would serve as the spinning wheel of modern times. Shiva has launched a project of saving seeds and visiting farmers to convince them to start saving seeds, to conserve and distribute these seeds and turn to organic farming practices that did not depend on hybrid seeds and pesticides. She collected seeds like *jowar*, *bajra*, white maize, cowpea, *navarangi*, *black bhat*, *urd dal*, *moong dal*, *jhangora*, *okra*, *ragi*, *til*, and 260 varieties of rice varieties ranging from black rice, red rice, brown rice, golden rice, long grain rice, and short grain rice to stock in a seed bank. Today Shiva's Navdhanya Seed Bank serves as a granary that speaks of how biodiversity and native seeds can feed the world. For Shiva seed saving is not a museum, as she calls them seeds that can save the future. She contends that the best scientists for seeds are the farmers who know how and when to sow their seeds depending on the changing weather, be it drought or flood. She is of the view that farmers as scientists can assess the quantity and quality of the grain.

Even though Monsanto-Bayer was successful in its intellectual property cases, it lost in cases concerning its flagship herbicide Roundup. For instance, in *Dewayne Johnson v. Monsanto* (2016),[86] a San Francisco jury ordered Monsanto to pay $39.25 million in compensatory damages and $250 million in punitive damages to the petitioner, a former groundskeeper who alleged that exposure to Monsanto's herbicides had resulted in him developing terminal non-Hodgkin lymphoma.[87] Subsequently in *Dewayne Johnson v. Monsanto Co* (2020), Monsanto and Johnson's cross-appeals were heard at the California's Court of Appeal. Even though the appeals court declared Monsanto's arguments unconvincing, it reduced the damages to $20.5 million.[88] On August 4, 2020, both parties, Monsanto and Johnson requested a review of the verdict by the California Supreme Court, but both petitions were denied. Similarly, *Hardeman v. Monsanto Company* (2016) resulted in an $80 million unanimous jury verdict in favor of the plaintiff, Edwin Hardeman who had sued Monsanto arguing that his cancer was caused by Roundup, and by Monsanto's failure to warn of the known dangers of its product.[89] In *Pilliod et al. v. Monsanto Co.* (2019),[90] Alva and Alberta Pilliod, both suffering from non-Hodgkin's lymphoma after years of using Roundup, filed a complaint against Monsanto. On June 22, 2022, the Supreme Court rejected Monsanto/Bayer's request for reconsideration and ordered 'the giant' to pay $87 million to the victims.[91] These few wins by the small man stirs hope that there is still room to right the balance in David v. Goliath legal battles for environmental justice.

REVERSED BURDEN OF PROOF

The coastal areas in India have mangrove swamps or *mangals* that support coastal aquatic ecosystems. These coastal intertidal zones are productive wetlands that play an important role in strengthening climate resilience and carbon capture, thus preventing the emission of CO_2 into the atmosphere in these coastal areas. India's mangrove saline woodland has rich shrimp farms. In *S. Jagannath v. Union of India & Ors* (1996),[92] the petitioner, the chairman of Gram Swaraj Movement, a voluntary organisation working for the upliftment of the weaker section of society, sought the enforcement of the Coastal Zone Regulation Notification dated (1991) issued by the Government of India. The petitioner sought the enforcement of a prohibition to use wet lands for Prawn farming and the constitution of a National Coastal Management Authority to safeguard the marine life and coastal areas. He argued that an Environmental Impact Assessment (EIA) should be an imperative procedure for shrimp farms. Under Article 32 of the Constitution of India, all Indian citizens have the right to file a public interest petition in the Supreme Court when they feel that their right has been unduly deprived.[93] Under the Coastal Zone Regulation Notification (1991) issued by the Government of India, all intensive and semi-intensive type of prawn farming in the ecologically fragile coastal had to be stopped. The Court opined that shrimp farms, ponds and industries must pass a strict environment test and assessments before being granted permission to carry out their operations in the ecologically fragile coastal area.[94] It ordered the Central Government to constitute an authority to oversee the protection of coastal areas and deal especially with the shrimp culture industry in the coastal states as provided for under the Environment Protection Act, 1986 for the protection of coastal areas, and thus apply the 'Precautionary Principle' and 'the Polluter Pays' principle.

Vapi, an industrial town in the state of Gujarat has witnessed decades of damage to its ecosystem. Situated at the confluence of the River Kolak and the River Daman Ganga, life in this area is dependent on these waterways. But sadly, fishing communities have lost their livelihoods because of the rapidly developing chemical industries that are situated in a 270-mile belt called the 'Golden Corridor of India.' The industrial stretch from Gujarat to Mahesana is the longest chemical industry corridor in Asia but is also one of the most polluted industrial zones where both air and water are contaminated. In 1967, a four-phase plan was enacted by the Gujarat Industrial Development Corporation (GIDC) to industrialize this zone. 1,500 industries producing a variety of chemicals like dyes, paper, pesticides, pigment, plastic, and pharmaceuticals came into being. A pollution management plant, a Common Effluent Treatment Plant (CETP), was set up only in 1993 after Vapi had been categorized as a critically polluted area. In *Research Foundation for Science v. Union of India & Anr* (2012)[95] presented in table 7.2, the respondent Research Foundation for Science, Technology and Natural Resources, an NGO directly filed a writ petition in the Supreme Court of India over water contamination issues in Gujarat and Madhya Pradesh. This NGO, which is devoted to developing sustainable methods of agriculture, was founded in 1982 by eco-activist Vandana Shiva.

The judiciary in India, has inconsistently applied the Precautionary Principle in environmental cases. This principle considers the possibility of environmental harm and considers anticipatory action to prevent it. In the event of reasonable harm, the Precautionary Principle of the Rio Declaration (1992) applies. It states, "where there are threats of serious or irreversible damage, a lack of scientific uncertainty shall not be used as a reason for postponing cost-effective measures to prevent environmental degradation."[96] It is interesting to consider the two sides of the coin, both its weak and strong application in law. The weak element being one of uncertainty, as the Precautionary Principle applies only in the event of irreversible harm to the environment. So, if the damage is not irreversible, then the Precautionary

Table 7.2: *Research Foundation for Science v. Union of India & Anr* (2012)

[Writ Petition (C) No.657 of 1995]
IN THE SUPREME COURT OF INDIA CIVIL ORIGINAL JURISDICTION
Judgment rendered on July 6, 2012

Bench: Y Sabharwal, S Kapadia

Rule: Without adequate protection to the workers and public and without any provision of sound environment management of disposal of hazardous/toxic wastes, the Hazardous Wastes (Management & Handling) Rules (1989) are violative of Fundamental Rights and, therefore, unconstitutional.

Facts of the case: This writ petition was filed by the Research Foundation for Science Technology and Natural Resource Policy, through its Director, Ms. Vandana Shiva, for the following reliefs: banning all imports of all hazardous/toxic wastes by the Union of India; amending rules in conformity with the Basel Convention (1992) and Article 21, 47 and 48A of the Indian Constitution; and establishing the violation of the Hazardous Wastes (Management & Handling) Rules (1989). The petitioner challenged the decision of the Ministry of Environment and Forests permitting the import of toxic wastes in India under the cover of recycling, making India a dumping ground for toxic wastes. Shiva, the Director of the Petitioner Foundation, highlighted some related tragedies such as the gas leaks in the Union Carbide factory at Bhopal (1984), groundwater contamination in Gujarat's Vapi Industrial area, the ship-breaking industry in Alang, Gujarat, and the consignments of hazardous waste at different Indian ports. She referred to the Basel Convention on the Control of Trans-boundary Movements of Hazardous Wastes (1992) and their disposal.

Issue: Whether only a direction was required to be issued for the destruction of the consignment to protect the environment and, if not, in what other manner could the consignments be dealt with. Whether and to what extent the hazardous wastes listed in the Basel Convention have been banned by the Government. What the framework for reducing risks to environment and public health should be.

Reasoning of the court: The Court analyzed the Hazardous Wastes Management and Handling Rules (1989) and as per the Precautionary Principle of the Vienna Declaration (1985) regarding the polluter-pays principle, thought it feasible to dispose of the oil by incineration under the supervision of a Monitoring Committee which would have no impact on the environment.

Conclusion: The Supreme Court of India considered the provisions of the Basel Convention on the Control of Trans-Boundary Movement of Hazardous Wastes (1989) and their disposal, and the report of the Monitoring Committing recommending destruction of the consignments by incineration, but also studied the fact that import of waste oil was permitted for the purpose of recycling. It decided that in those cases where the consignment was found fit for recycling, the consignment would not be destroyed, but the recycling would be done under the supervision of a Monitoring Committee. However, if deemed unfit, the consignment in question would be destroyed by incineration, and the cost of incineration would be borne by the Government.

Note: My synopsis of *Research Foundation for Science v. Union of India & Anr* (Supreme Court of India, July 6, 2012).

Principle is not applicable. But its strength lies in its premise that the absence of scientific certainty does not merit inaction. Here, the onus is on the proponent of the dangerous environmental activity to show that his activity does not endanger the environment.

In *Subhash Kumar v. State of Bihar and Ors* (1991),[97] the petitioner filed a public interest litigation claim against two iron and steel companies for having triggered health risks to citizens by emptying waste from their factories into the River Bokaro river, a tributary of the Ganges. Once again, the Supreme Court of India held that the constitutional right to life granted by Section 21, included a right to pollution-free water, which was a prerequisite for the full enjoyment of life. Activists, Bharat Patel and Manisha Goswami detail how the the CPR-NAMATI Environment Justice program adopted an evidence-based legal empowerment approach and the Right to Information applications (RTI) to seek remedies for the river pollution and fish contamination problems in both Kolak and Daman Ganga rivers.[98] Environmental court room cases are dependent on factual evidence offered by witnesses and experts, so invariably the role and status of science and technical expertise are increasingly important factors in decision-making by the court. Patel's and Goswami's activist rhetoric reflect on both past and future environmental issues as they question: "Where does the liability really lie? Who is responsible for all fishing livelihoods lost due to an illegality and disregard of law? Even as the efforts towards legal empowerment can achieve an important step ahead for the people dependent on the Daman Ganga river, how can these situations be prevented?"[99]

Similarly, in *A.P. Pollution Control Board v. Prof. M.V. Nayudu (Retd.) & Other* (1999),[100] it was ruled on whether a hazardous activity could be set up in the proximity of a reservoir used for drinking water. As the court did not possess the necessary expertise of technical personnel well versed in environmental laws in addition to judicial members, it emphasized the fact that widespread toxic pollution was a major threat to essential ecological processes and that it was vital to respect the Precautionary Principle in environmental law.[101] It deemed it appropriate to reverse the burden of proof on the industrialist proposing the activity that was potentially harmful to the environment.[102] He had to discharge this burden by showing the absence of a reasonable ecological or medical concern. If he presented insufficient evidence to alleviate concern regarding the level of uncertainty, then the presumption would operate in favor of environmental protection where the Polluter Pays Principle applies.

As a result of activism and precedents set in cases, the Indian Supreme Court began to form green benches to protect the environment by making the polluter pay. In *Sukhdev Vihar Welfare Residents Association v. Union of India* (2017),[103] the National Green Tribunal rejected the challenge of operating a waste-to-energy (Clean Development Mechanism) plant in a densely populated area because it emitted GHGs. However, the NGT fined the plant for past breaches and issued guidelines and directions for future operations. In *Gaurav Bansal v. Union of India* (2015),[104] the applicant brought to the NGT's attention that many states had not prepared State Action Plans on Climate Change as they were supposed to under the National Action Plan on Climate Change. Though it did not rule on the jurisdiction or the NGT's power, the NGT directed all the states to make a State Action Plan on Climate Change as soon as possible. In *Hindustan Zinc Ltd. v. Rajasthan Electricity Regulatory Commission* (2015),[105] the Supreme Court upheld the High Court's decision stating that companies having captive generation power plants would have to purchase a minimum percentage of energy from renewable resources as they fell within the purview of the Rajasthan law. In *re Court on its own motion v. State of Himachal Pradesh & Others* (2016),[106] the NGT, on its own motion, issued directions to curb black carbon emissions around the ecologically sensitive Rohtang pass and directed the Himachal Pradesh government to undertake measures to ensure curbs on black carbon emissions.

The Factories Act (1948) was the first act in independent India on environmental waste that governs the health, safety, and welfare of workers in factories. It was amended in 1987 to include elements of occupational health and safety, and prevention and protection of workers employed in a hazardous process. Court cases that ensure that the polluter pays have been instrumental in the passage of Acts of Parliament like the Energy Conservation (Amendment) Act 2022, which amends the 2001 Energy Conservation Act, and entered into force on January 1, 2023.[107]

THE PUBLIC TRUST DOCTRINE FOR YOUTH-LED LITIGATION

Youth activism is on the rise due the rise of platforms on social media that are conducive for propagating resources in real time. Young activists are sharing petitions, organizing protests, creating templates for e-mailing authorities, listing racist practices, highlighting black-owned businesses needing support, prompting Google to change its Black Friday Doodle to Black Owned Friday,[108] and sharing videos documenting instances of police brutality at protests. Youth have moved to challenge adult decisions at different moments in history. At the Greensboro sit-ins in 1960, four young teenagers refused to leave after being denied a meal at a segregated Woolworth's lunch counter in Greensboro in North Carolina. Their sit-in contributed to the passage of the Civil Rights Act (1964), which outlawed segregation in public spaces. In the 1970s to 1980s, university student uprisings began when students protested on multiple continents against social injustices like poverty. The Apartheid Divestment Campaigns began with students objecting to a law that mandated Afrikaans-language education, but it triggered a global movement against apartheid. Student protested at Beijing's Tiananmen Square on June 5, 1989, when Chinese troops violently cleared protesters by opening fire on protesters and onlookers, thus showing how the regime could stifle dissent. During the Velvet Revolution in December 1989, Czech students inspired by the toppling of the Berlin Wall and the end of East Germany's communist government, followed dissident playwright and future President Vaclav Havel to topple the country's Communist Party of Czechoslovakia. July 1999 saw the beginning of student activism in Iran when students at the University of Teheran set fire or tore images of Ayatollah Ali Khamenei to condemn Iran's totalitarian regime. The 2013 Black Lives Matter Movement was also shaped by student activism when students expressed dissent against racial profiling by Minneapolis police following George Floyd's murder.

The present socio-political climate is one that has instigated young climate petitioners to petition the courts for action. In a two-page judgment order in *Ridhima Pandey v. Union of India* (2019),[109] the National Green Tribunal (NGT) dismissed the case against the government of India. On March 22, 2017, a nine-year-old girl, Ridhima Patel, filed a petition in the National Green Tribunal of India, represented by her legal guardian, and was supported by Our Child's Trust, a nonprofit public interest law firm. She alleged that the Indian government had failed to fulfill its duties to the citizens of India by not taking adequate science-based action to mitigate climate change. She argued that the Paris Agreement (2015) had not been respected and that the term *environment*, as used in the Environment Protection Act (1986), necessarily encompasses the climate, and that it was the task of the government to enact policies to mitigate climate change.[110] The Green Tribunal dismissed the case on the basis that the authorities under the purview of the EPA functioned as per statutory scheme, which was not challenged by the petition. It concluded that the issue of climate change was a matter that had been dealt with in the process of impact assessment. It did not consider it necessary to issue any steps to be taken under sections 14 and 15 of the National Green Tribunal Act (2010).[111]

In another instance, in *Juliana v. United States* (2018),[112] twenty-one young citizens, along with other environmental agencies filed a complaint against the president of the USA and federal agencies. They used a rights-based argument to state that the government's policy permitted authorized usage of fossil fuel despite knowing the risks and various kinds of harm to the plaintiffs like psychological harm, impairment to recreational interests, exacerbated medical conditions, and damage to property. They claimed that their Fifth Amendment Due Process and Equal Protection rights, and the Ninth Amendment's Public Trust Doctrine had been violated. The District Court of

Oregon held that the plaintiffs had the required standing to bring a case to court that raised justiciable questions regarding green gas house emissions. The court dismissed the claim that the president was a defendant, denied the government's motions, finding that the plaintiffs had presented sufficient evidence of personalized and concrete injuries, such as the loss of income for a ski resort employee and adverse effects to a family farm, that could be linked to the GHG emissions resulting from US fossil fuel production. The petitioner's case survived the summary judgment. However, the federal appellate court in California held that the plaintiffs did not have standing to sue the Government of the United States as they had failed to show how the relief would substantially redress their injuries and that they lacked standing to bring their claims to court. It was concluded that the plaintiffs' case would have to be resolved in a more democratic fashion and be addressed to the political branches or to the electorate at large.

In *Ali v. Federation of Pakistan & Another* (2016),[113] Rahab Ali, a seven-year-old girl from Karachi in Pakistan, opposed the government's plan to exploit untapped coal reserves in the Thar Desert in the region of Sindh. She argued that air pollution was imminent due to the exploitation of the Thar coalfields which were estimated to release around 327 billion tons of CO_2, approximately a thousand times Pakistan's annual greenhouse gas emissions. She brought the problem of displacement to the attention of the Court, whereby people were forced to leave their land. She voiced the need to protect the mangrove forests as they had the natural means of offering blue carbon solutions of sequestering carbon and protecting the country against rising sea levels. She voiced doubts over the implementation of the China-Pakistan Economic Corridor which is the source of $1.2 billion investments for multiple coal-fired power plants in Pakistan. She cited the doctrine of Public Trust, claiming that the Government had a duty to help reduce atmospheric CO_2 levels to restore the energy balance to Mother Earth. She contended that Pakistan was bound by the UN Framework Convention on Climate Change (UNFCCC) and the Paris Agreement (2015) to protect the environment.

Young environmental changers are increasingly aware of political decisions and express their views through social media. The plaintiffs in all three cases mentioned above have campaigned for recognition of their rights to a livable climate and a court-ordered prescription of the massive legal, technological, and administrative requirements needed to avert a catastrophic 2°C overheating of the Earth. It should however be remembered that the Public Trust Doctrine is largely a judge-made concept where the government has a duty to preserve certain natural resources for the benefit of the public. Courts have so far generally engaged in a limited application of the Public Trust Doctrine to rivers, beaches and are yet to expand this doctrine to encompass the atmosphere.

THE PARABLE OF THE NUTMEG PLANET

Unlike the monologic novel that seeks to present its unitary voice, in *The Nutmeg's Curse: Parables for a Planet in Crisis*,[114] Ghosh's polyphonic nonfictional space has voices with various stances that get to air their own perspectives. Each voice expresses its stance or individual melody engaging in dialogic discourse, without being subject to the ideology of the author. There is also my postcolonial voice that chooses to speak and interpret the parable, thus adding to the dialogic discursive mode of Ghosh's parable. It is true that "The riddle-like nature of parables inherently includes some ambiguity,"[115] thus making different kinds of cogent interpretation possible, sowing seeds of interest, the desire to gain insight, wisdom, clarity, and thus favoring the active perusal of dialogue.

Ghosh's parable of the nutmeg (*Myristca fragrans*) is framed like a parable where multiple voices both human and non-human relate their tales. These voices speak about colonial history, the spice trade, the quest for the Earth's resources like spices, tea, sugarcane, opium, and fossil fuels. The hilly mountainous volcanic chain called the Ring of Fire rumbles, expresses protests and spits fire enveloping the Banda Islands with swirls of steam and smoke. The volcanic eruptions though vociferous in their eruptions, bestow the land with rich-earthly-alchemical minerals that enable the dense foliage to thrive on tropical soil. Stories of nutmegs have rolled out of the tongues of Venetian travellers like Marco Polo and navigators like Christopher Columbus who wrote stories of the spices in their travelogues and rendered oral accounts for royal ears. The tales of the much-coveted spice with medicinal properties that could even cure the plague is still chanted by the Bandas in the Banda Islands. The ode to the nutmeg relays how flotillas of spice cargo from the Banda islands traversed the oceans of the Asia-Pacific to reach Western shores. In the tales of the bygone colonial era, despite the rise and fall of empires, the nutmeg thrived, and reigned supreme, with a handful of them being vastly sufficient to buy a house or a ship.

> Like a planet, a nutmeg too can never be seen in its entirety at one time. As with the moon or any spherical (or Quasi-spherical) object, a nutmeg has two hemispheres; when one is in the light, the other must be in darkness—for one to be seen by the human eye, the other must be hidden.[116]

Ghosh poetically puts forward the idea that the nutmeg's two hemispheres hold hidden meaning in today's world: one shell portraying its commercial merits as a spice and the other elusive crust remaining open to interpretation through parables passed on through the oral tradition.[117] Our present time bears no resemblance to colonial times. During the colonialist quest for spices, plants and botanical material could decide the fate of humans. The modern era is one in which human-made goods take precedence over natural products. Nations are however dependent on fossil fuels, another form of vegetal matter, though decomposed and dead. These fossil fuels have replaced spices in the material quest for wellbeing, but the voices of these spices still hold meaning in their stories of survival.

The time when the West invaded the East was one that resonated with colonial rivalries. European monarchs vied with each other to sign imperial ententes with the Indian Maharajas to seal the Spice Trade. In India, the Portuguese armada first arrived in Goa in 1496. The British merchant ships arrived in 1600, and Sir Thomas Roe, an ambassador of King James I, stayed in the Mughal Court of King Jehangir between 1615 and 1618. He penned accounts of the rich spices and the rare precious gems of India. After the British fleets embarked on the Spice Trade, the French *navires* typically followed the British a year later in 1601. Conflicts were often enacted across continents between the colonists. For instance, Anglo-Dutch rivalries fought in two fronts—the Banda massacre in Indonesia (1621) and the Pequot war (1636–1638) in Connecticut, US—were linked by haunting continuities. In both battle grounds, the Dutch Vereenigde Oostindische Compagnie (VOC) resorted to the dreaded Dutch-war tactic called *brandschattingen* when they mercilessly burnt villages and vegetation.[118]

Ghosh refers to Sir Frances Bacon, the Lord chancellor of England (1618–1621) who in his treatise *An Advertisement Touching An Holy War* refers to the colonised nations as "wayward countries" as "routs and shoals of people, as have utterly degenerated from the laws of nature."[119] The colonist voice endorses the colonialist conquest as a lawful, godly endeavour to wipe the uncivilized off the face of Gaia. The intent of extinguishing a tribe or nation is typical of the Oriental Quest of the West proclaiming to enlighten the East, of bringing Order to Chaos, thus clearly enunciating the European stance on why it was lawful for Christian Europeans to annihilate the savage East. This idea of supporting an extermination of savage people with the divine order, is typical of the Orientalist quest of undertaking a 'mission civilisatrice' and bringing the gifts of civilization to the so-called uncivilized East. Here, the European position of bringing Law and Order or free trade or material progress is considered as a Christian mission bearing the breath of God. The imperialistic stance of changing the very nature of free trade, taking complete control of the nutmeg trade due to its lucrative nature in the name of God, further reiterates the colonial intent to eventually appropriate the monopoly of its cultivation. The voiceless nutmeg and the people of its land succumbed to colonialism the curse of that time. This archaic reasoning of bringing Order to the degenerate East was also used to tame the Banda landscape when the Dutch decided to terraform the landscape by restricting nutmegs to the Banda islands and cloves to the neighbouring Ternate islands. Matter and nature were viewed as being ‘brute,’ ‘savage’ and ‘stupid’ from an anthropogenic viewpoint, in which human intellect was thought to supersede non-human existence.

Taste buds in Europe in the seventeenth century, however, changed. The pursuit for the exotic was replaced by one that favoured a bland diet. The nutmeg trade was thus in the turn of the century rendered non-lucrative. As the VOC launched on a campaign of extermination limiting cloves to Ambon islands, nutmegs to the Bandas, with their minions crawling on fours to chop down the spices, nature fought back, with the rich volcanic soil enabling the nutmegs to sprout back with fresh vigour making the extirpation process an impossible mission. Nature spoke by showing her capacity to shrug off forms imposed by the coloniser. Both spices, thus bore the names of ‘spices of curse’ as the Dutch proceeded with a campaign of extermination. Songs of the nutmegs are still sung in Maluka. In the Parable of the Nutmeg’s Curse, Ghosh relates the tale of how Martijn Sonck, a Dutch official stationed in Selamon, a village in the Banda archipelago, hears a lamp fall at nightfall. Imagining a surprise attack from the native Bandanese, Sonck, and his counsellors begin shooting into the dark of the night at the invisible enemy. One wonders if they killed friend or foe! Through this parable, Ghosh conveys the idea that an ambush on nature is a dual attack on humanity too. The VOC’s ambitious plans of terraforming included isolating and segregating individual spice species to different Indonesian islands—nutmegs on Banda islands and clove trees on Ambon islands. The French and the English did manage to smuggle seeds to other islands, and it survives today in Barbados, the ‘Nutmeg Island,’ and in Connecticut, the ‘Nutmeg State.’ As an inert resource, the nutmeg’s fate depends entirely on humans as it has no story-telling powers of its own. Ghosh’s parable of the Nutmeg’s travel is a didactic story that illustrates our engagement with nature and how life sustains through songs.

As in James Lovelock’s hypothesis of Gaia that speaks of the Earth as a living entity,[120] one may muse, like Ghosh: Is Gaia the battleground of eternal rivalries? Or is Gaia a trickster offering a golden apple to sow rivalries that ignite the Trojan war or planetary wars of our time? In a world of Big Carbon and Big Coal corporations, geological and carbon footprints on Gaia are measured through spatial distance and temporalities of convenience. Watermills have been abandoned in favour of displaceable pipelines; agri-businesses have erased forests to permit mass monoculture. Monstrous Gaia often expresses her discontent by displacing migrants, hurling hurricanes on whim, and spitting out pandemics at her vulnerable inhabitants. Her offspring like the cloves and nutmegs have managed to survive by being picky about where they sprout be it Mount Gamala or the Banda forests—“it is said that nutmegs must be able to smell the sea, whereas clove trees must be able to see it.”[121]

In the polyphonic space of a *The Nutmeg's Curse* voices and perspectives of those who are affected by Gaia's wrath are heard, like Khokon, a Bengali migrant who braves the Mediterranean Seas in pursuit of a better life; or even Shakespeare's Caliban, the brute in *The Tempest* (1611) whose master Prospero gave him the most important gift of words and the faculty of speech, albeit incomprehensible due his brute-like existence; and voices of British prisoners who died of overcrowding and asphyxiation in the Black Hole of Calcutta during the colonial wars. As for the nonhuman voices, Ghosh lets trees talk, communicate with each other, even reminding us that Buddha gained knowledge under the sacred Bodhi tree; and that stories may be heard even in migratory patterns of a flock of penguins who weave meaning out of experiences. Restoring nonhuman voices to their proper place, (can be done) through the medium of stories"[122]—be it a collection of objects in a cabinet that still resound with stories, or the falling of a lamp that kindles Ghosh's imagination of a colonialist ambush.

In Ghosh's works of fiction and nonfiction, the oceans have always silently witnessed and contributed to the "archives of unfair trade."[123] European colonisers have monopolized the colonial waterways to transport Opium, Teak, and Spices from the East to the West. Typical of Material Ecocriticism, Ghosh distrusts materialistic forces that plunder the planet's natural resources, and he takes part in the new emerging paradigm of making a Material Turn, thus considering possible ways to analyze language and reality, human and non-human life, mind and matter, without falling into dichotomous patterns of thinking.[124] Ghosh shows how the West's fascination for the East as seen in the Orientalist's initial quest for spices like nutmeg, cloves, pepper, coffee, cacao, sugar, and tea, lead eventually to the discovery of the addictive narcotic drug 'opium,' and eventually fueled and financed the opium wars.[125] It is interesting to refer to Carl Trocki's work *Opium, Empire and the Global Political Economy*, where he states that "the British Empire, the opium trade, and the rise of global capitalism all occurred together . . . gold and silver from the West" crossed the Atlantic or the Pacific, it ultimately found its way to Asia (east of Suez) to purchase the "riches of the East" and to allow the otherwise deprived inhabitants of the northwest Eurasian peninsula to share in the fabled Oriental splendors."[126] The postcolonial enterprise in countering what Edward Saïd describes as "the ineradicable distinction between Western superiority and Oriental inferiority,"[127] is evident in Ghosh's fiction and nonfiction. Ghosh writes back, and voices disapproval of the materialistic colonial intent of the past through Eco-parables. While terraforming the landscape, the Dutch VOC claimed to be abiding by the principles of fair trade, whereas the British declaration of war was waged in the name of freedom. Each coloniser justifies the means of subduing the voice of the colonised.

> The war when it comes, will not be for opium. It will be for the principle: for freedom—for the freedom of trade and for the freedom of the Chinese people. Free trade is first conferred on Man by God, and its principles apply as much to opium as to any other article of trade. More so perhaps, since in its absence many millions of natives would be denied the lasting advantages of British influence.[128]

As agents in the pursuit of a higher good, the colonists terraformed Gaia. The uncivilized captive East was subject to the colonist enterprise of bringing Order to Chaos.

By exhuming the materialistic colonial past and reconfiguring them as parables, Ghosh's parable conveys a vital message. Through parables of spices, he emphasizes the material inclinations of colonists, the terraforming of land and natural resources, and the alteration of the landscape from one bearing necessary crops to that of lucrative spices and narcotic drugs to balance the West's trade with the East. The parables throw light on the materialist past, emphasize the need to remember and record the long histories of injustice, voice the need to remove the obstacles in the way of building a just society, and protect Gaia. His ecocritical vision highlights the fact that "our best hope for universal emancipation lies in remaining unreconciled to the past and unconsoled by the present."[129] In today's world, the nutmeg and its sister spices no longer enjoy the status of coveted spices as oil and other fossilized botanical matter have replaced them. We continue to depend on nature in its various forms and will continue to do so, but we are also answerable to Gaia. It is interesting to consider Bahktin's view on answerability, "I have to answer with my own life for what I have experienced and understood in art, so that everything I have experienced and understood would not remain ineffectual in my life."[130] This duty to answer or answerability, is one where everyone has the obligation to act. Ghosh's literary enterprise through his discursive polyphonic parables shows this intent of responding, interacting with other voices and awaiting ethical responses of interpreters. These dialogic aspects challenge us readers, listeners, and interpreters to respond in ways that include ethical actions in our daily lives. Ghosh's polyphonic parables insist that "It is essential now, as the prospect of planetary catastrophe comes ever closer, that those nonhuman voices be restored to our stories. The fate of humans, and all our relatives, depends on it."[131]

MOBILIZING VOICES FOR GAIA

Gaia in all her generosity offers us her physical space but the task of sowing the seeds of the future is in our hands. Seed banks that collect seeds are worth more than any kind of monetary gain that a financial institution can offer to the planet. Sowing the seeds of hope and the need to protect Gaia lies in our capacity to mobilize voices for Gaia. Features of the Earth have figured in creation myths since time immemorial ranging from "canyons and lakes, mountains and arroyos, rocks and vacant fields—which together endow their lands with multiple forms of significance"[132] that mould and speak for human existence on Earth. These myths of the Nutmeg still bring to life not just the Banda language with its songs and stories of the Banda Mountain, but also "its blessing (or curse), the nutmeg."[133]

> we, pearls of wisdom
> the fruits of nutmeg have died.[134]

The song carries voices of the Bandanese with their stories that serve as pearls of wisdom and parables. The impoverished nutmeg of our times uses the epistolary form of a letter to voice its dying woes. The Bandanese weep, speak, lament, and moan of erstwhile times and is evident in the refrain of 'the nutmegs have died.' Voices of the past and present mingle and muse on whether nutmegs were a blessing or a curse. In the indigenous culture of the Bandanese, nature in the form of plants, animals, and elements have stories to relate as they have witnessed history from time immemorial. For the Dutch Vereenigde Oostindische Compagnie (VOC), trees, volcanoes, and landscapes of the Bandas held no significance other than monetary profit. Terraforming land into a vast nutmeg-producing factory was synonymous of the colonial quest of subjugating both people and nature, humans and non-human entities. Mass killing of humans and destruction of the forest fall into the categories of killing or '-cide,' namely 'genocide' and 'ecocide,' both dual acts of extermination to wipe out savage and brute forms of existence and make them malleable for colonial pursuit. Gaia deserves a voice in the face of apocalyptic violence. As Ghosh writes, "The planet will never come alive for you unless your songs and stories give life to all the beings, seen and unseen, that inhabit a living Earth—Gaia."[135]

NOTES

1. Amitav Ghosh, *The Great Derangement: Climate Change and the Unthinkable* (London: University of Chicago Press, 2016), 11.
2. Amitav Ghosh, *The Great Derangement*, 9.
3. Tate, "Art Terms," Tate, accessed June 29, 2023, https://www.tate.org.uk/art/art-terms/e.

4. Agnes Denes (1931–) is a concept-based artist who is internationally known for works created in a wide range of mediums. *Wheatfield—A Confrontation* is considered to be the first large scale site-specific piece portraying ecological concerns.

5. Katy Hessel, "A Field of Wheat on a $4.5bn Patch of New York: The Prophetic Eco Art of Agnes Denes," *Guardian*, July 18, 2022, https://www.theguardian.com/artanddesign/2022/jul/18/a-field-of-wheat-on-a-45bn-patch-of-new-york-the-prophetic-eco-art-of-agnes-denes.

6. Olafur Eliasson, "Ice Watch," Studio Olafur Eliasson, accessed July 24, 2023, https://olafureliasson.net/artwork/ice-watch-2014/.

7. José da Silva, "Olafur Eliasson Floods Museum and Removes Wall, Opening It 24-Hours-a-Day to 'Insects, Bats or Birds,'" *Art Newspaper—International art news and events*, September 28, 2021, https://www.theartnewspaper.com/2021/04/21/olafur-eliasson-floods-museum-and-removes-wall-opening-it-24-hours-a-day-to-insects-bats-or-birds-and-people.

8. Idem.

9. Sandra Sawatzky (1967–), a multidisciplinary artist based in Canada's energy rich province of Alberta, is a writer, filmmaker, artist/designer, and embroiderer. The stories depicted on her tapestry are based upon more than a year of meticulous research.

10. The Black Gold Tapestry, accessed June 29, 2023, https://www.theblackgoldtapestry.com/.

11. Andy Goldsworthy (1956–) is a British sculptor, land artist, and photographer known for his ephemeral works created outdoors from natural materials in nature.

12. Andy Goldsworthy, "Three River Works," Andy Goldsworthy—Official Website, May 3, 2023, https://andygoldsworthystudio.com/three-river-works/.

13. "Christo and Jeanne," Claude, accessed June 29, 2023, https://christojeanneclaude.net/artworks/arc-de-triomphe-wrapped/.

14. "Banksy: Trolley Hunters," Sothebys.com, November 18, 2021, https://www.sothebys.com/en/articles/banksy-trolley-hunters#:~:text=It%20highlights%20our%20inability%20to,in%20a%20Los%20Angeles%20warehouse.

15. Sebastien Laboureau, "Show Me the Monet, 2005," Banksy Explained, September 18, 2022, https://banksyexplained.com/show-me-the-monet-2005/.

16. "Girl with Balloon: From Graffiti to Art History Icon," Banksy Explained, July 13, 2021, https://banksyexplained.com/issue/girl-with-balloon-graffiti-legend/.

17. Amitav Ghosh, *The Great Derangement*, 9.

18. David Sillito, "Hashtag Is 'Children's Word of Year,'" BBC News, May 27, 2015, https://www.bbc.com/news/entertainment-arts-32902170.

19. Greta Thunberg, "'Our House Is on Fire': Greta Thunberg, 16, Urges Leaders to Act on Climate," *Guardian*, January 25, 2019, https://www.theguardian.com/environment/2019/jan/25/our-house-is-on-fire-greta-thunberg16-urges-leaders-to-act-on-climate.

20. The Annie E. Casey Foundation, "What the Statistics Say about Generation Z," The Annie E. Casey Foundation, November 14, 2020, https://www.aecf.org/blog/generation-z-statistics#:~:text=Meet%20Generation%20Z.,is%20adding%20members%20through%202025.

21. Kim Parker, "On the Cusp of Adulthood and Facing an Uncertain Future: What We Know about Gen Z so Far," Pew Research Center's Social & Demographic Trends Project, May 14, 2020, https://www.pewresearch.org/social-trends/2020/05/14/on-the-cusp-of-adulthood-and-facing-an-uncertain-future-what-we-know-about-gen-z-so-far-2/.

22. "Fridays for Future," Fridays for Future, February 27, 2023, https://fridaysforfuture.org/.

23. John Sutter and Lawrence Davidson, "Teen Tells Climate Negotiators They Aren't Mature Enough," CNN, December 17, 2018, https://edition.cnn.com/2018/12/16/world/greta-thunberg-cop24/index.html.

24. Maha El Dahan, "Davos 2023: Greta Thunberg Accuses Energy Firms of Throwing People 'under the Bus,'" *Reuters*, January 20, 2023, https://www.reuters.com/world/europe/davos-2023-greta-thunberg-says-energy-firms-throwing-people-under-bus-2023-01-19/.

25. 4ocean Team, "How Plastic Ingestion Impacts Dolphins and Porpoises," 4ocean, December 1, 2018, https://www.4ocean.com/blogs/cause-of-the-month/how-plastic-ingestion-impacts-dolphins-and-porpoises.

26. Vanessa Nakate, "Vanessa Nakate Bigger Picture: Climate Justice in Africa," *Time*, October 28, 2021, https://time.com/6109452/vanessa-nakate-climate-justice/.

27. World Bank Group, "Journey into the Congo Basin—the Lungs of Africa and Beating Heart of the World," World Bank, October 27, 2022, https://www.worldbank.org/en/news/feature/2022/10/24/journey-into-the-congo-basin-the-lungs-of-africa-and-beating-heart-of-the-world.

28. Tom van Ierland and Jessica M. Smith, "#NoDAPL and Online Activism: New Directions for Effectively Engaging with Critics," JPT, January 15, 2021, https://jpt.spe.org/nodapl-and-online-activism-new-directions-effectively-engaging-critics.

29. "World Environment Day 2023," UN Environment, accessed July 1, 2023, https://www.unep.org/news-and-stories/press-release/world-environment-day-2023-be-hosted-cote-divoire-focus-solutions#:~:text=The%20campaign%20for%20World%20Environment,the%20hashtag%20and%20slogan%20%23BeatPlasticPollution.&text=World%20Environment%20Day%20is%20the,and%20action%20for%20the%20environment.

30. Akshita Bhadauria, "How 'Child Climate Activist' Licypriya Kangujam Trends Twitter Hashtags As e-Aandolanjeevi," OpIndia, March 17, 2021, https://www.opindia.com/2021/03/licypriya-kangujam-twitter-hashtags-trends-random-causes/.

31. Cheryll Glotfelty, "Introduction: Literary Studies in an Age of Environmental Crisis," essay, in *The Ecocriticism Reader: Landmarks in Literary Ecology*, ed. Harold Fromm (Athens: University of Georgia Press, 1996), xv–xxxvii.

32. Iovino Serenella, *Material Ecocriticism* (Bloomington: Indiana University Press, 2014), 1–2.

33. Idem, 1–2.

34. Stephen Rust, Salma Monani, and Sean Cubbitt, *Ecomedia: Key Issues in Environment and Sustainability* (New York: Earthscan Routledge, 2016).

35. Bruno Latour, *Reassembling the Social: An Introduction to Actor-Network Theory* (Oxford: Oxford University Press, 2005).

36. *The Seeds of Vandana Shiva* (CORE), accessed June 30, 2023, https://core.live/foundation#impactviewers.

37. James Becket (1936–) is a filmmaker, developmental economist, human rights lawyer, author, and filmmaker who uses documentary film to address issues of social justice and environment issues.

38. Vandana Shiva and Kartikey Shiva, *Oneness vs. the 1%: Shattering Illusions, Seeding Freedom* (Vermont: Chelsea Green Publishing, 2020), 177.

39. *Vandana Shiva and Ors. v. Union of India and Ors* (Supreme Court of India, April 22, 1994).

40. *Priya and the Twirling Wind*, https://www.youtube.com/watch?v=cwaJya0jaBQ, 2022, accessed July 1, 2023.

41. Henry Jenkins, *Convergence Culture: Where Old and New Media Collide* (New York: New York University Press, 2008).

42. Chris Rapley (1947–) is a professor of climate science at University College London (UCL).

43. Simon Lewis is a professor of global change science at University College London (UCL).

44. Alexandria Villaseñor (2005) is an American child activist who co-founded the U.S. Youth Climate Strike movement, part of the youth led international Fridays for Future movement.

45. Ridhima Pandey (2008-) is a child activist from Uttarakhand in India who advocates action against climate change.

46. "Power of Priya," Power of Priya, accessed July 1, 2023, https://www.priyashakti.com/.

47. David B. Gowler, *The Parables After Jesus: Their Imaginative Receptions Across Two Millennia* (Grand Rapids: Baylor Academic, 2017), xi.

48. Idem, 1.

49. Edwin H. Palmer, *The Holy Bible, New International Version: Containing the Old Testament and the New Testament* (Grand Rapids: Zondervan, 1984), Matthew 13:31–33.

50. Idem, Matthew 13:1–9.

51. Idem, Matthew 13:11–17.

52. Ghosh, *The Great Derangement: Climate Change and the Unthinkable*.

53. Bakhtin, *Problems of Dostoevsky's Poetics* (Minneapolis: University of Minnesota Press, 1984), 110.

54. Susan VanZanten Gallagher, *Postcolonial Literature and the Biblical Call for Justice* (Jackson: University Press of Mississippi, 1994), 4–5.

55. Ghosh, *The Glass Palace*, 71.

56. Gowler, 3.

57. Ghosh, *The Glass Palace*, 71.

58. Ghosh, *The Hungry Tide* (New Delhi: Ravi Dayal, 2004).

59. Ghosh, 246.

60. Gowler, 5.

61. Ghosh, *The Hungry Tide*, 246.

62. Palmer, *The Holy Bible*, Mark 4:26–29.

63. Amitav Ghosh, *River of Smoke* (London: John Murray, 2011).

64. Gowler, 204.

65. Amitav Ghosh, *River of Smoke*, 39.

66. Pierre Poivre (1719–1786) was a French missionary-turned-entrepreneur whose enthusiasm for trade with Indochina sparked French colonial expansion. He was a horticulturist and botanist whose travels in Asia resulted in the propagation of plant species from the East in the West.

67. Philibert Commerson (1727–1773) was a French naturalist and explorer who established a botanical garden, enriched by his collecting trips around France. He was the royal botanist and physician who accepted a position as Bougainville's assistant in Papua New Guinea on his voyage around the world (1767–1768).

68. Ghosh, *River of Smoke*, 82–83.

69. Idem, 83.

70. Suhasini Vincent, "Narrating, Naming and Labelling the Environment in Amitav Ghosh's *The Hungry Tide*," essay, in *Ecocriticism and Environment—Rethinking Literature and Culture* (New Delhi: Primus, 2018), 173–85.

71. Amitav Ghosh, *Gun Island* (London: John Murray, 2020).

72. Idem, 7.

73. Bakhtin, *Problems of Dostoevsky's Poetics*, 197.

74. Joni Keefe, "Farms Finest: Green-Washing Tactics Abound," AspenTimes.com, August 24, 2016, https://www.aspentimes.com/news/farms-finest-green-washing-tactics-abound/.

75. Idem.

76. Idem.

77. Bayer, Bayer Closes Monsanto Acquisition, August 8, 2022, https://www.bayer.com/media/en-us/bayer-closes-monsanto-acquisition/.

78. Mark Schapiro, *Seeds of Resistance: The Fights to Save Our Food Supply.* (New York: Hot Books, 2018), 14.

79. *Bowman v. Monsanto Co*., (Unites States Supreme Court, May 13, 2013).

80. Neil Young and Daryl Hannah, "Let $289 Million Jury Award Stand in Monsanto Case," *San Francisco Chronicle*, October 14, 2018, https://www.sfchronicle.com/opinion/openforum/article/Let-289-million-jury-award-stand-in-Monsanto-case-13303640.php.

81. *Monsanto Technology LLC v. Nuziveedu Seeds Ltd* (Supreme Court of India, January 8, 2019).

82. *Monsanto Technology LLC v. Nuziveedu Seeds Ltd* (2019), section 1.

83. Idem, section 23.

84. Neel Kamal, "'Sc Hasn't Upheld Monsanto's Patents on Seeds': Chandigarh News—Times of India," *Times of India,* January 10, 2019, https://timesofindia.indiatimes.com/city/chandigarh/sc-hasnt-upheld-monsantos-patents-on-seeds/articleshow/67462493.cms.

85. *The Seeds of Vandana Shiva* (CORE), accessed June 30, 2023, https://core.live/foundation#impactviewers.

86. *Dewayne Johnson v. Monsanto Co.* (San Francisco District Court, January 28, 2016).

87. *Dewayne Johnson v. Monsanto Co.* (Superior Court of California, San Francisco County August 10, 2018).
88. *Dewayne Johnson v. Monsanto Co.* (Court of Appeal, State of California, July 20, 2020).
89. *Hardeman v. Monsanto Company* (US District Court, San Francisco, February 12, 2016).
90. *Pilliod et al. v. Monsanto* Co. (Alameda County Superior Court [Oakland] March 28, 2019).
91. *Pilliod et al. v. Monsanto Co.* (Supreme Court of the United States, June 27, 2022).
92. *S. Jagannath v. Union of India & Ors* (Supreme Court of India, December 11, 1996).
93. Idem, section 1.
94. Idem, section 1.
95. *Research Foundation for Science v. Union of India & Anr* (Supreme Court of India, July 6, 2012).
96. "Principle 7: UN Global Compact," Principle 7 | UN Global Compact, accessed July 3, 2023, https://unglobalcompact.org/what-is-gc/mission/principles/principle-7.
97. *Subhash Kumar v. State of Bihar and Ors* (Supreme Court of India, January 9, 1991).
98. Bharat Patel and Manisha Goswami, "In Vapi, Can Decades of Damage Be Finally Turned Around?," in *Making the Law Count: Ten Environmental Justice Stories by Community Paralegals in India* (New Delhi: Namati, 2018), 20–24.
99. Idem, 24.
100. *A.P. Pollution Control Board v. Prof.M.V. Nayudu (Retd.) & Other* (1999) (Supreme Court of India, January 27, 1999).
101. Idem, section 23.
102. Idem, section 31.
103. *Sukhdev Vihar Welfare Residents Association v. Union of India* (National Green Tribunal, New Delhi, February 2, 2017).
104.*104. Gaurav Bansal v. Union of India* (Supreme Court of India, July 23, 2015).
105. *Hindustan Zinc Ltd. v. Rajasthan Electricity Regulatory Commission* (Supreme Court of India, May 13, 2015).
106. *Court on its own motion v. State of Himachal Pradesh & Other*s (National Green Tribunal, New Delhi, September 20, 2018).
107. "The Energy Conservation (Amendment) Bill, 2022." PRS Legislative Research, July 3, 2023. https://prsindia.org/billtrack/the-energy-conservation-amendment-bill-2022.
108. Ty Johnson, "Google: Black-Owned Friday," Ty Johnson, November 15, 2022, https://tyjo.co/work/googlebof/.
109. *Ridhima Pandey v. Union of India* (National Green Tribunal, New Delhi January 15, 2019).
110. Idem, section 2.
111. Idem, section 3.

112. *Juliana v. United States* (United States District Court, Oregon, October 15, 2018).

113. *Ali v. Federation of Pakistan & Another* (Supreme Court of Pakistan, April 2, 2016).

114. Amitav Ghosh, *The Nutmeg's Curse: Parables for a Planet in Crisis* (Chicago: University of Chicago Press, 2021).

115. Idem, 9.

116. Idem, 11.

117. Idem, 10.

118. Idem, 10.

119. Idem, 26.

120. James Lovelock, *The Vanishing Face of Gaia* (London: Penguin, 2009).

121. Ghosh, *The Nutmeg's Curse: Parables for a Planet in Crisis*, 159.

122. Idem, 204.

123. For a detailed analysis refer to Suhasini Vincent, "Archives of Unfair Trade in Amitav Ghosh's Fiction," *Academia Letters*, August 17, 2021, https://doi.org/10.20935/al1185.

124. Refer to Suhasini Vincent, "An Eco-Critical Analysis of Climate Change and the Unthinkable in Amitav Ghosh's Fiction and Non-Fiction," *Humanities* 7, no. 2 (2018): 59, https://doi.org/10.3390/h7020059.

125. For a more detailed reading, refer to Suhasini Vincent, "Material Ecocriticism: Maritime Trade, Displacement and the Environment in Amitav Ghosh's Fictional Waterscape," in *Negotiating Waters: Seas, Oceans and Passageways in the Colonial and Postcolonial Anglophone World*, ed. Nancy Pedri and André Dodeman (Wilmington: Vernon Press, 2019), 149–65.

126. Carl A. Trocki, *Opium, Empire and the Global Political Economy* (London: Routledge, 1999), 7–8.

127. Edward Said, *Orientalism–Literary Theory: An Anthology* (Cornwall: Blackwell, 1998), 881.

128. Amitav Ghosh, *Sea of Poppies* (London: John Murray, 2008), 120.

129. Benita Parry, *Postcolonial Studies: A Materialist Critique* (New York: Routledge, 2005), 193.

130. Mikhail M. Bakhtin, *Art and Answerability Early Philosophical Essays*, ed. Michael Holquist and Vadim Liapunov (Austin: University of Texas Press, 1990), 1.

131. Amitav Ghosh, *The Nutmeg's Curse: Parables for a Planet in Crisis*, 257.

132. Idem, 35.

133. Idem, 35.

134. Idem, 36.

135. Idem, 84.

Chapter 8

Children of the Stars—The Symbiocene

I trace my fingers along the smooth nape
of your curves. I calligraph text on you
gently with my uneven nails, etching letters
permanently on your polished silk-skin—
jet-black granite, obsidian. I write on you,
in ink made from meteorite minerals—
embedded in our earth's core, in our hearts.
Syntax melds and multiplies, polyvocal.
Your linguistic matrix, a coded language—
only I decipher every syllable.
You and I are "children of the stars"—
conceived in the "cradle of humankind."[1]

Sudeep Sen, in his ekphrastic poem "Children of the Stars," engages in a literary representation of the Earth seen as an object of visual art. Like painters or sculptors who work creatively on an object and bring it to life by exhibiting artistic talent, Sen's poetic sleight of hand has chosen a silent object, the Vredefor Crater, situated in Johannesburg in South Africa. Geologists believe that this crater is the cradle of our civilization, formed when a giant asteroid hurtled towards the Earth about two billion years ago bringing with it the polyphonic awakening cries of around eight million life forms on our planet. Sen's poetic gaze on the ancient crater as seen in his photo captioned "Children of the Stars," in figure 8.1, infuses life into the inert rock form by endowing it with polyvocal abilities and a matrix of artificial intelligence in keeping with the present times. The smooth stone of the crater serves as the slate for the writer's verbal painting. The etching of calligraphy though uneven, results in the contact between man and stone. Granite, obsidian or glass-like solidified lava stone comes alive as the poet pens his thoughts with ink formed from ancient, meteorite ores, whose coloring compliment the

Figure 8.1. Children of the Stars. *Source*: Children of the Stars © Sudeep Sen.

jet-black stone. The amalgam of the different chemical elements results in a polyphony of voices where the Earth's voice is heard through its different elements, its creatures, its people who came into existence from its core. The connective linguistic matrix is one that demands symbiosis or an interaction of various elements necessary for the mutually beneficial existence of the 'children of the stars,' who were conceived at Vredefor, the cradle of humankind. The ekphrastic poem draws its strength from both the image and the written word.[2] Likewise in another haiku poem, "Storm," Sudeep Sen's polyphonic haiku set in the dialogic mode permits a symbiotic interaction of two different elements—Rain and Earth.

The soaked earth, ruddier—
the aroma, petrichor.
Under open-skies, I am
drenched. Aqua minerals
pacify my red rashes—
I bow to the rain gods.
Thunder-strike—firelights
the rugged bush terrain.
The soundscape—nature's
choral refrain, its guttural
enunciation—polyphonic.
Rain's language—heals.[3]

Rain, wet, life-giving rain, that douses heat, pierces the skin and penetrates the Earth is a frequent speaker in Sen's poetry. The flash storm's expression through thunder and lightning awakens both auditory and visual senses of the reader. The elements participate in the polyphonic contribution to the haiku's *kigo* or seasonal word of rainy weather. Further olfactory senses are awakened by metaphors of rain striking the parched Earth and emanating smells of petrichor or the smell of the first rain where aqua minerals combine with the soil to give new life to dormant Earth forms. Sen's ode to rain, ends with a poetic bow to acknowledge the rain gods that have healed the Earth. The alchemy of the elements of Earth and Rain in Sen's poem is reflective of the Earth emotion of Ghedeist or "the awareness of a spirit of force that holds all life together, a feeling of profound symbiotic interconnectedness in all life between the self and other beings (human and nonhuman) and their gathering together to live within shared Earth places and spaces."[4] This feeling of intense affinity and sense of mutual empathy for other beings speaks for an ushering in of the era of the Symbiocene, an era when humans are aware of their duty of care for the Earth and all her life forms needed to sustain the planet.

THE AGE OF THE GREEN ENTREPRENEUR

Symbiocene, the antidote to the Anthropocene, is yet another term coined by Glenn Albrecht to describe a time when human intelligence will replicate nature's ability to live together with other species and forge lifelong relationships to sustain each other.[5] Biologists refer to this relationship as Symbiosis, a term derived from the Greek words 'symbios' (living together with another) and 'bios' (life). Nature coexists in harmony through symbiotic relationships that permit the existence of coral reefs, forests, birds, and bees. Sea anemones live on a diet of plankton and small fish that get sucked into their tentacles. Clownfish that are immune to the anemone's venom thanks to the mucus that covers their body, can relax safely in the tentacles of the anemones, and are protected from potentially larger fish predators. As the clownfish have a vivid orange coloring, they attract small fish or food to the anemones. While the clownfish offers shelter, the anemones repay the favor by attracting food. Similarly, the aggressive, ever-hungry Nile crocodile is known for its unusual-friendly collaboration with the Egyptian plover or crocodile bird. After a heavy meal, the crocodile opens its huge jaws to let the waiting crocodile birds pick off tiny bits of remaining food that remain in the teeth. The crocodile thus avoids a visit to the dentist and the plover gets an easy meal. Symbiosis has a message for humans as it shows how animals survive through collaboration and cohabitation by sharing the same habitat and resources.

To move towards the Symbiocene, human intelligence will have to replicate nature by using the symbiotic and biodiverse reinforcing forms and processes found in living organisms in nature. In February 1984, Vaclav Havel, former president of the Czech Republic, wrote a speech entitled "Politics and Conscience" on being awarded an honorary doctorate from the University of Toulouse. As Havel did not attend the ceremony, his speech that was delivered by the English playwright Tom Stoppard. It gives an idea of the new science of Biomimicry for the Symbiocene.

> We must draw our standards from our natural world, heedless of ridicule, and reaffirm its denied validity. We must honor with the humility of the wise the limits of that natural world and the mystery which lies beyond them, admitting that there is something in the order of being which evidently exceeds all our competence.[6]

Among all the life organisms on the planet that has ever existed, man is the species that has developed the most with human intelligence simulating the flight of birds in aviation to circumnavigate the globe in a few hours faster than all other species on the planet. We have mined minerals, used different forms of energy to light up the dark hours of night, even lassoed the sun's energy, and have made strides in artificial intelligence to build self-reflective brains. With the planetary crisis of climate change, the call is now to turn to nature and innovate by drawing inspiration from nature and using our intelligence and known technologies for the planet's wellbeing. Biomimicry refers to "the conscious emulation of life's genius . . . doing it nature's way" and trying to "change the way we grow food, make materials, harness energy, heal ourselves, store information, and conduct business."[7] This word has its root from the Greek *bios* and *mimesis*, or imitation, and considers nature as a model from which human problems can be solved by imitating or taking inspiration from nature's design. As a new way of viewing and valuing nature, it introduces an era based not on what we can extract from the natural word, but on what we can learn from it.[8] A hand in glove harmony with nature necessitates what Janine M. Benyus calls a canon of nature's laws.

> Nature runs on sunlight.
> Nature uses only the energy it needs.
> Nature fits form to function.
> Nature recycles everything.
> Nature rewards cooperation.
> Nature banks on diversity.
> Nature demands local expertise.
> Nature curbs excesses from within.
> Nature taps the power of limits.[9]

In a biomimetic world of the Symbiocene, human beings have the potential to manufacture and produce like animals and plants do, as seen in the innovative use of the sun or solar-powered technology to transform CO_2 and plastic waste into sustainable fuels and cosmetics.[10] To solve the problem of noise exiting from train tunnels with a sonic boom, engineers of Japan's Shinkansen Bullet Train turned to biomimicry to find a quieter, faster, and more efficient solution. While the owl's serrated feathers inspired the pantograph which is the rig that connects the train to the electric wires above; the smooth body shape of the penguin inspired the pantograph's supporting shaft permitting lower wind resistance; and the kingfisher's unique pointed beak that enables it to dive efficiently to catch its prey was the new nose design of one of Japan's fastest trains, the Shinkansen Bullet Train. Janine Benyus suggests inviting biologists to the table of innovation and has shown how it is possible to compute like a cell, run a business like a redwood forest, build better air ventilation systems by studying prairie dog burrows to build, mimic shark skin to create bacteria-resistant plastic surfaces for hospitals, arrange wind turbines in the same drag-reducing pattern that schools of fish swim in, create a paint for a building like the self-cleaning leaves of a lotus, or copy the self-sufficiency skills of ants in software for autonomous cars. An entry to the Symbiocene will rely on a system like nature's capacity to recycle and reuse resources, which can be equated to a human circular economy where there will be no by-products or waste going into landfills. Ecosystems do not waste as everything is cyclically reused. A log is consumed by fungus that is eaten by small insects, which is food for animals, and these animals in turn are consumed by humans, who are then brought back to the soil. At the 2022, Techsauce Global Summit held in Bangkok in Thailand, climate activist Marc Buckley stated, "The world's first trillionaire will be a green entrepreneur operating in symbiosis with a regenerative platform system and dynamic business models."[11] In his speech, he said that humanity had achieved its pipe dream through a "Moonshot" and now it was time to think of an "Earthshot" by showing the Blue Marble photo of the *Apollo 17* astronauts to his audience. He predicts that the same technology used to go to the moon, can help humans to save the planet. It is now time for a new generation of rethinkers who instead of being guided by blinkers and tunnel vision will work with a greater vision of achieving the objectives of COP 27, that of averting climate disaster and keeping the planet at a safe 1°C. The six major transformation national priority goals or Sustainable Development goals (SDG) to be achieved before 2030 are education and gender equality; health, well-being, and demography; energy decarbonisation; sustainable food and land; digital revolution and Sustainable Development; and sustainable cities and communities.[12] In today's corporate goals, businesses just add one of the SDGs as add-ons, but what they really need to do is to look at the whole picture and engage collectively in rebooting the system.

Our Earth a remnant of the cosmic Big Bang, has its creatures who have crawled out of the primordial soup of gases that created the building blocks of life.[13] As "children of the stars,"[14] we are the Earth's stewards and need to work on Symbiosis or symbiotic relationships, and not be in competition as in the Darwinian notion of the survival of the fittest. The Symbiocene is the era for the biotechnologist-activist entrepreneur who will step away from exploitative capitalist models and will engage in circular economic models, shared platform structures and regenerative models of scale.

SUMBIOCRACY: THE RULE OF THE EARTH

Sumbiocracy, the form of government in the Symbiocene is one that will favor "the rule for the Earth, by the Earth, so we may all live together."[15] As seen in the cases in my study, the new legal phenomenon of Earth System law has resulted in Western and non-Western countries granting legal living status reserved conventionally to humans, to non-human entities of nature. The largest global research network on climate change, called the Earth System Governance Project, in its annual meeting in Toronto in 2022, voiced the need to encompass multiple world views in eco-governance and provide a multifaceted view of the rule of the Earth for the Earth.[16] In Earth System law, lawyers, writers, scientists, and activists collaborate in writing the judgements of the future. These judgments have a broader, political, and cultural significance in the wake of the new advent of the Rights of Nature laws.

In *Giudizio Universale (The Last Judgment)*, *A Sud v. Italy* (2021),[17] the petitioner-NGO, A Sud, filed a suit on behalf of 200 plaintiffs involved in a campaign called 'The Last Judgment' alleging that the Italian government had violated fundamental rights by not taking appropriate measures to meet the emission-reduction targets in the Paris Climate Agreement (2015). The plaintiffs sought an order stating that the Italian government must take steps to cut CO_2 emissions by 92 percent by 2030. The applicants argued that although a 29 percent reduction has been achieved since 1990, this level of reduction was insufficient to meet 1.5°C target of the Paris Agreement (2015). Drawing the name from the fresco of Italian renaissance painter, Michael Michelangelo, 'The Last Judgment,' the campaign makes an allegorical reference to judgment rendered by future generations upon the present and past generations, both complicit in the Great Acceleration towards climate change.

In *Democratic Youth Federation of India v. Union of India*,[18] the Supreme Court of India in a ruling on May 13, 2011, ruled on a Public Interest Petition filed by the Democratic Youth Federation of India (DYFI) by passing an ad-interim order banning the manufacture, sale, and use of the pesticide called Endosulfan throughout the country due to its adverse health effects. This decision was based on the Precautionary Principle and the right to life under Article 21 of the Indian Constitution. Continued activist petitions resulted in the Supreme Court issuing a new order on January 30, 2017, whereby the state governments were ordered to pay all victims of Endosulfan poisoning in Kasaragod district a compensation of Rs 5000,000, an equivalent of approximately US$ 6000 within three months of the order. In the various cases in this book, governments and private entities have been brought to task for tort-based claims, human rights issues, damage to the ecosystems, non-compliance with environmental regulation, and cases involving carbon and coal corruption, credits, and mismanagement. The Rights of Nature laws demonstrate "what the law could achieve in its attempts to dissolve hierarchies by deliberately embracing ecocentrism and care for the non-human world."[19] They consider the inseparable links that exist between "all human and non-human entities, components and processes making up the entire Earth system, from the local to the global sphere, (that) are vulnerable."[20]

Sixteen-year-old Greta Thunberg's admonishment to world leaders at the World Economic Forum at Davos on January 25, 2021, was an activist call for the Symbiocene, expressing through persuasive rhetoric, the need to work together as a planetary community, and respond together to meet the complex environmental challenges of our time that are increasingly linked with our health and well-being. She warned, "I don't want you to be hopeful. I want you to act as you would in a crisis. I want you to act as if our house is on fire."[21] Her wakeup call was one addressed to executive heads, legislators, and judges on the imperative need to protect the planet's biodiversity, its atmospheric common good, its ecosystems, landscapes, human and animal welfare. Our age of eco-activism has transformed how we perceive the role of the courts in natural resource disputes, and how it has changed the way lawyers and judges address environmental law's traditional principles, objectives, instruments, and institutions. Judges who belong to the legal branch of government usually exercise their knowledge and expertise without stepping on the toes of the executive and the legislative. Unlike the other two branches, they are not elected by constituencies and have no electors to woo. However, increasing climate change activism modifies these ancient premises of a separation of powers and has rattled judges' traditional ways of rendering justice. Justice Antonio Herman Benjamin states, "We should include courts in the climate change picture because we have no other option. No substitute exists for the court system. If judges are in charge of deciding all sorts of conflicts about life, death, love, human rights, and national security, it makes no sense to leave climate change outside the courtroom."[22] In the present ambience of climate change where intergenerational values reign supreme, judges can no longer claim that is a matter for the legislative to pass laws or the prerogative of the executive to execute them. They cannot function existing just within the traditional precincts of constitutionalism and the Rule of Law, as the judiciary has been on many occasions in the recent years forced to deliberate on issues extending well beyond the jurisdiction of local and national courts, thus exercising green climate jurisprudence. In the present global trend where voices are heard and swept across the planet through social media, judges find that their decision making will affect many who are spread across different countries, as their decisions will set a precedent that will be cited in other foreign jurisdictions. Judges who ruled traditionally on things that were real, that could be seen, heard, and touched are now ruling often on virtual possibilities of the unseen, the unheard, and the probable. Intangible categories of hyperobjects are under the microscope of the judicial eye, where judges must make pragmatic, legal, ethical, and institutional decisions. Judges can no longer step back, claiming a lack of jurisdiction or competence. As legal arbitrators in a new era of eco-activism, they are expected to deal with whole spectrum of environmental matters. Judicial enforcement has proved how it can bring forth fair and effective environmental adjudication to save the planet's rich biodiversity, biomes, ecosystems, species, and genetic diversity that are in desperate need of judicial justice and enforcement. Climate change has entered the courtroom and invaded the judicial sanctum of the erstwhile traditional judge, transforming the judge into one who is an activist-environmental judge setting precedent with environmental decisions that provoke new environmental legislation.[23] In the present spectrum, courts have shown that they are part of the constellation of actors engaged in protecting the planet. They arbitrate and resolve issues dealing with licenses and permits; they are engaged in environmental impact assessments; they consider the impact of climate change on a plethora of issues like protected areas, disaster management, rising sea levels, deforestation, water contamination, wetlands, toxic waste, dams for common good, seed patents, desertification, and Rights of Nature. They do retain the final, authoritative word. By ruling on decisions, they complement the working of the legislative and the executive in the formulation and execution of environmental policies. Judges do not pass laws, they only apply as permitted by the system of separation of powers, the laws approved by their parliaments. In other words, they implement laws and partake in judicial law implementation. The cases in this book have shown how Indian courtrooms have activist justices who have passed decisions reflecting their capacity to evolve with changing times and face the challenges of climate change. The new judicial technique of forming commissions in collaboration with the legislative has enabled judges to work closely with scientific experts to assess, measure and forecast the changing environment and take apt decisions to mitigate climate change. Judges have the unique capacity to hold governments accountable for meeting policy commitments, to force legislators to implement laws that have considered, researched, and analyzed credible scientific facts, to convince the various stakeholders to comply with legal obligations on climate change, to balance the after-effects and to protect citizen's rights to a good environment, thus closing the cracks through which people and ecosystems fall. They act thus as an interface through which justice can be rendered.

POSITIVE PSYCHOTERRATICA FOR THE SYMBIOCENE

Glenn Albrecht contemplates on how we will be viewed by future generations in the Symbiocene. He writes that the "Symbiocene heritage will tell the story of how we replaced 'Anthropocene heritage' with new creations that preserved their function but revolutionised their form and process."[24] The Symbiocene is one that will be conducive for humanity to feel positive Psychoterratica or Earth Emotions. In "Transmigration,"[25] a short story by Cécile Seiller, the reader absorbs and engages in a dialogic discovery of a kaleidoscopic perception of positive Psychoterratica or Earth Emotions. Seiller, a French academician with stints in Asian countries like India and Hongkong, as well as in the United States, gives a semiautobiographical account of her time as a postcolonial studies researcher in the foothills of the Himalayan Mountain ranges in the Indian state of Uttaranchal. The sojourn awakens Topophilia, the strong sense of love for a place.[26] The short story builds on how one's childhood memories of distant places, even foreign and unknown may create emotional and cognitive ties to a place. The story's diegesis takes place in the imaginary locale of Krishnapur, a name reminiscent of typically named Indian villages and towns of no precise fame.

> This place is a perfected substitute, where the inmates and I live free, unsupervised, unmedicated. We must be the freest and the most unsupervised beings on earth, high on something—but what, I cannot begin to say. It might have to do with the air. It is much thinner here, you can feel it, entering your nostrils, delivering its sharp, needle stabs. There is always this light wind in the morning, when mist and clouds recede and the mountains grow into full view above the pine trees. The landscape is so stunning I wish it remained secret.[27]

The idea of having accomplished the biophilic quest to find a place that is an alternative for the normal is evident in the oxymoron 'perfected substitute' and the accompanying contradictions of a 'free,' 'unsupervised,' 'unmedicated' life, to highlight the state of confined inmates being unchained, but left unattended and free from the influence of medicative grog doses. The curative, respiratory and olfactory therapy of inhaling the fresh mountain air triggers a fleet of other emotions as in the visual sense of perception that leads to an unveiling of the secret landscape of pine trees hidden from invasive trespassers. The feeling of Eutierra is evident in the way the first-person narrator's heart lifts on seeing the mountains materialize into full view after the swirling mist and clouds gradually vanish. The description of the breathtaking landscape as one that is 'stunning' releases positive feelings of Eutierra or "oneness with the Earth and its life forces, where the boundaries between the self and the rest of nature are obliterated."[28] The discovery of a landscape akin to one of her childhood memories is typical of Endemophilia, that is central to the love of a place that is rare and unique.[29] The uniqueness is evident in the experience of feeling small like a Lilliputian, beside majestic, towering mountains that bear crests and ridges, the natural frontiers separating India from its neighbors Nepal and Tibet. The lone human figure in the mountainous setting is one whose endemophilic love for the place revels in the immense peace and quiet of the rugged slopes. While absorbing the landscape, Seiller muses, "I bury myself in foreign, and the foreign becomes myself. I found a place to live. Everyone needs a place to live—or do they?"[30] In her quest to discover the new, she reveals her former vain attempts at attaining this rather illusory and elusive state of being. She contends that in a foreign setting, one's past is erased from view, as one sets out to figure out a new course of life. New configurations slowly take shape with life being "rewritten, reset" and adjusted to the new reconfiguration of a "blank slate as a reality." Experience forewarns Seiller of the usual patterns of Nostalgia that one encounters in a foreign country, with "familiar patterns of melancholy, despite foreign tongues, foreign weathers, foreign conditions."[31] In the land of the foreign, the Himalayan visit offsets the Earth Emotion of Biophilia, or the love of life, with the nostalgic longing for the known and the melancholy of the foreign, fading into the background.

> Every day I look at the horizon and see new things, new crests, new crevices, or so it seems, on the monumental canvas that is being exposed. I imagine the steepness of slopes, the texture of the snow up there above seven thousand meters, and I think I can spot lost souls, people looking for something up in the mist. I always imagine myself borne somewhere onto those heights. For nature does not exist in itself. The human mind either must recreate it or inhabit it, penetrate it, touch it from the inside, like the crazy alpinists we keep on meeting here, like Jason in his search for debunking the hidden. It is the first time nature does not make me crave cities.

The pursuit for the new as in the enumeration of 'new things, new crests, new crevices' in the unfathomable space of the unknown, speaks of emotions of

Biophilia or feelings that revel in life and growth in nature, considering it as an ethical good.[32] The wish to inhabit an unknown space shows her reverence for life that is in total alignment with nature that bestows humanity with its bounty. The biophilic experience sparks a love for a foreign space, infused with new, cultural identity. Seiller's account highlights the fact that there is no escaping this tryst with the unique biosphere of the Himalayas and its environment. It is an awareness of the perfect peace in nature that prompts her to embrace the quiet life in a remote mountainous part of the world and feel like a bird on free flight. She further contrasts her experience of life in a crowded city with the interlude in a foreign unknown village.

> Usually I feel better in big, packed cities, in buildings cramped with humans, in swarming buses. Over the years, crowded cities have saved me, they have kept me alive because they were huge forgiving organisms I could take for granted, and they were feeding me all right. But here the craving has not come yet.[33]

Through metaphors of packed cities, cramped buildings, swarming buses, and huge organisms, she highlights how modern cities abound in Topophobia that fills her with Topaversion, a feeling that is strongly averse to returning to a place that was once loved, appreciated, and enjoyed, but has been irrevocably changed for the worse.[34] In the polyphony of Earth emotions, it is interesting to highlight the fact that emotional forces that characterize the universe sits within the poles of what Albrecht refers to as *terraphthora* (Earth destroyer) and *terrascia* (Earth creator).[35] The dual presence of positive and negative Earth emotions and the interaction between terraphthoric and terranascient emotions is part of the dialogic nature of human existence where every human being has his or her own way of expressing the zeitgeist or the anxiety of the time. Seiller's story abounds with images of the ever-green *devdars* or conifers of the mountain slopes, white-sheets of pristine snow, pelting rain, and the discreet sun, thus revealing Ecodiversity. There is a synesthetic appreciation of the co-mingling of forest and winter colors, smells of the different seasons, and other sensory stimuli like the deep intake of breath to savor the clean mountain air. The biophilic love of life is one that awakens productive stimuli that makes Seiller feel "something new to the security of finding confirmation of the old . . . (and) enjoy life and all its manifestations rather than mere excitement.[36]

By penning a story from memories, Seiller engages in another Earth Emotion of Soliphilia, the process of converting the negative into a positive Earth Emotion, "the love of the totality of our place relationships and a willingness to accept the political responsibility for protecting and conserving them at all scales."[37] Seiller writes on how the mere mention of a place as in Borobudur, Siem Reap, Macao, Pathankot can awaken a panoply of positive

Earth Emotions. The places mentioned in Seiller's account are just not locales, but geographical spaces that contain ample "territories of meaning"[38] for each one of the protagonists. She uses the mode of the anecdote to relay reality while focusing on the unique. While writing of the circumstances and events that prompted her trajectory to the quaint, little Himalayan guesthouse, her polyphonic account of Earth Emotions is punctuated with further anecdotal accounts by the other protagonists in the dialogic space of the short story. Her account of the chance encounters with similar-minded guests of different nationalities are cosmopolitan meetings with the unknown, as the characters launch on philosophical discussions having their voices heard along with the author. Her verbal memory of the events is seen in how all characters in the polyphonic anecdote get to voice their views: the bellboy Mahendra has the capacity of dispelling the fear of poisonous, albeit dead scorpions; the garrulous landlord's warning of blood-sucking leeches instead of raising antennas of alarm, trigger waves of peace rendering the beasts non-venomous; sharp auditory sensitivity enables Seiller to catch the distinct dialectal differences in the well-modulated woodnotes of Dr. Kumar, the educated Indian, who switches the tone to a rough, gruff, hierarchy-conscious grunt when speaking to a lower menial; Alicja revels in the coolness of the Himalayan foothills; Jason, the bird watcher excels in his mimicry of bird calls. The biophilic space of the anecdotal short story thrives on the polyphonic engagement with the love of place. Truth of physical or ecological reality is no longer a goal but an instrument for pursuing the good life."[39] The anecdotal nature of the short story permits different voices to express different perspectives where the ideas are not presented in abstraction but are concretely embodied in the lives of the characters. Being a dialogic text and not a monologic one, there is no authorial finality. Seiller does not have the last word as the polyphonic space is one that is open-ended, permitting further reflection and debate with the dialogue not coming to an end.[40] There are many voices contributing towards the biophilic space of the story revealing how "verbal memory" as a free discursive act is a valued asset.[41] As in Bakhtin's notion of polyphonic dialogues, characters are transformed through dialogue, fusing their views with each other's discourse. Seiller reveals how the other's response can change everything in one's own consciousness as she ends her story stating, "I have not felt freer."[42] Being a nobody in a foreign place brings with it the twin assets of anonymity and freedom to choose a location that awakens the love for life. The literal re-incarnation of the protagonist into a bird is in keeping with the thematic line of a metaphorical rebirth and the migration to a better place filled with positive Earth Emotions.

EARTH POLYPHONY

In the Symbiocene, our heritage will be Our Whole Earth. So, it is time for *Nostos Erda* or the time of returning Home to Earth and stop consuming ecological capital, the base from which all nature's abundance flows.[43] *Nostos Erda* stems from a theme used in Ancient Greek literature of an epic hero's return home after weathering storms and trials at sea as in Odysseus's return home in Homer's *Odyssey*. Nostos means return and *Erda* means Earth. In Olafur Eliasson's poem that accompanied his *Time Magazine Cover* in the celebration of Earth Day 2022, he makes a plea to indulge in a creative endeavor of recreating the Blue Marble planet.[44] The cover image, entitled "Earthshot," was conceived by graphic artist Stéphanie Léonard. Different artistic approaches demonstrate the polyphony of techniques—water colors, shaded penciling and computer graphics. She shows how the Earth can be seen creatively from within. Aquarelle paints highlight the Earth's sun-lit surface and hallowed rim. Blue Marble Earth in her "Earthshot" figures with its swirling ocean currents, imaginary meridians, and geographical poles on a tilted axis. The green line that serpents around the globe and the dotted circles highlight the limits of the biosphere. Shaded grey pencils serve to highlight the contours of continents and the meridians, while blue lines hug the coastline. Constellations figure in pristine white. Her creative endeavor to create visuals that stand out despite the artistic mixing, speaks for polyphony in the art form where no technique is submerged by another, but stands out in the final assemblage of the cover image. Our Earth viewed from within needs the voices of her "Children of the stars" to survive.[45] Let me end with my acrostic voice for Our Whole Earth.

*E*arth seen anew resonates
*A*wakening Gaia's many soundscapes
*R*icochets of green woodlands
*T*errestrial songs of earthlings
*H*ums, twitters, and trills of birds
*P*olyvocal activists strike chords
*O*ceanic waves and vibrations
*L*iterary rhymes, assonances, and alliterations
*Y*earn to protect nature's small things
*P*olyphonic cries in world forums
*H*ope resonates in diverse voices
*O*ur Earth intones
Nostos Erda, return home to Earth, echoes
You and I, we are the Children of the Stars

NOTES

1. Sudeep Sen, "Storm," in *Red* (Gauteng, 2023), 29.
2. James A.W. Heffernan, *Museum of Words: The Poetics of Ekphrasis from Homer to Ashbery* (Chicago: The University of Chicago Press, 2008).
3. Sudeep Sen, "Storm," in *Red*, 76.
4. Glenn A Albrecht, *Earth Emotions: New Words for a New World* (Ithaca: Cornell University, 2019), 199. *Ghehd* in Old English has meanings of 'together' or 'to gather.' The neologism coined by Albrecht is formed with the *ghed*, or ghost, and an abbreviation of the German *Geist*, with its reference to the life forces of the spirit and mind.
5. Glenn A Albrecht, *Earth Emotions*.
6. Vaclav Havel, "Politics and Conscience," Library of Babel, February 13, 2017, https://tayiabr.wordpress.com/2017/02/13/politics-and-conscience-vaclav-ha)vel/.
7. Janine M. Benyus, *Biomimicry: Innovation Inspired by Nature* (HarperCollins), 1998, 2.
8. Idem, 1.
9. Idem, 1.
10. Erwin Reisner, "Solar-Powered Carbon Capture Breakthrough Could 'Cut Fossil Fuels Out,'" Euronews, June 23, 2023, https://www.euronews.com/green/2023/01/11/new-solar-powered-technology-can-transform-plastic-waste-into-sustainable-fuels-and-cosmet.
11. "Marc Buckley Taking 'Earthshots' and Inspiring Innovations for Purpose," Techsauce, accessed July 10, 2023, https://techsauce.co/en/sustainable-focus/marc-buckley-earthshots-innovation.
12. "Six National Priorities Towards Implementation of the 2030 Agenda," United Nations, accessed July 15, 2023, https://sdgs.un.org/partnerships/six-national-priorities-towards-implementation-2030-agenda.
13. The idea of the primordial soup was a theory proposed by British scientists Alexander Oparin and John Haldane, in the 1920s, as a possible explanation for the creation of life on our planet. They advanced the idea that energy added to the gases that made up Earth's early atmosphere, had resulted in the primary building blocks of life.
14. Sudeep Sen, "Children of the Stars," in *Red*, 19.
15. Glenn A. Albrecht, *Earth Emotions,* 106.
16. "2022 Toronto Conference on Earth System Governance," Earth System Governance, November 7, 2022, https://www.earthsystemgovernance.org/2022toronto/.
17. *A Sud et al. v. Italy* (Civil Court of Rome, June 5, 2021).
18. *Democratic Youth Federation of India v. Union of India* (Supreme Court of India, January 10, 2017).
19. Louis J. Kotzé, "Earth System Law for the Anthropocene." *Sustainability* 11, no. 23 (2019): 6796: 6 https://doi.org/10.3390/su11236796.
20. Louis J. Kotzé, "Earth System Law Vulnerability and Socio-Ecological Injustice in an Age of Human Rights." *Journal of Human Rights and the Environment* 10, no. 1 (2019): 64.

21. Greta Thunberg, "'Our House Is on Fire': Greta Thunberg, 16, Urges Leaders to Act on Climate," *Guardian*, January 25, 2019, https://www.theguardian.com/environment/2019/jan/25/our-house-is-on-fire-greta-thunberg16-urges-leaders-to-act-on-climate.

22. Antonio Herman Benjamin, *Climate Change, Coming Soon to a Court Near You* (Manila: Asian Development Bank, 2020).

23. Ryan Holifield, *Spaces of Environmental Justice* (Malden: Wiley-Blackwell, 2010).

24. Glenn A. Albrecht, "Public Heritage in the Symbiocene," *Oxford Handbooks Online*, 2018, https://doi.org/10.1093/oxfordhb/9780190676315.013.12.

25. Cécile Seiller, "Transmigration," *Another Chicago Magazine*, June 19, 2023, https://anotherchicagomagazine.net/2023/05/30/transmigration-by-cecile-seiller/.

26. Albrect, "*Earth Emotions*," 120.

27. Seiller, "Transmigration."

28. Albrect, "*Earth Emotions*," 127.

29. Idem, 124. *Endemophilia* is based on the English word *endemic*, or native, with the Greek roots of *endemia* referring to a 'dwelling,' *demos*, or 'people,' and *philia*, or love.

30. Seiller, "Transmigration."

31. Idem.

32. Albrect, "*Earth Emotions*," 127.

33. Seiller, "Transmigration."

34. Albrect, "*Earth Emotions,*" 79.

35. Idem.

36. Erich Fromm, *The Heart of Man: Its Genius for Good and Evil* (New York: American Mental Health Foundation Books., 2010), 43.

37. Albrect, "*Earth Emotions,*" 121.

38. Arild Holt-Jensen, *Geography, History & Concepts* (London: Sage Publications Limited, 1999), 224.

39. Sean Cubitt, *Anecdotal Evidence: Ecocritique from Hollywood to the Mass Image* (New York: Oxford University Press, 2020), 27.

40. Bakhtin, *Problems of Dostoevsky's Poetics*, 165.

41. Ong, 73.

42. Seiller, "Transmigration."

43. Benyus, 9.

44. Olafur Eliasson, "Read Olafur Eliasson's Poem to Accompany His New *Time* Cover," *Time*, October 27, 2022, https://time.com/6224840/olafur-eliasson-time-climate-poem/.

45. Sudeep Sen, "Storm," in *Red* (Gauteng, 2023), 29. A reference to life stemming from the cosmic soup.

Glossary of Climate Science

Anthropocene: a term coined by Paul Crutzen to describe the geologic time following the Holocene epoch, used to describe the most recent period in Earth's history when human activity started to have a significant impact on the planet's climate and ecosystems. It is still an unofficial term.

Bandwaggonocene: a term that expresses the bandwagon phenomenon in environmental discourse whereby certain terms, after becoming fashionable, weaken in meaning, and implies a sense of boredom with geological terms.

Biosphere: refers to all the parts of the Earth where life exists and extends from the deepest root systems of trees to the ocean trenches, to lush rain forests and high mountaintops.

Black carbon emissions: the black soot emitted from gas and diesel engines, coal-fired power plants, and other sources that burn fossil fuel.

Capitalocene: a term that locates climate change within the history of capitalism and colonialism and suggests the role of the neoliberal state and multilateral governance institution system in managing human-environment relations within a global capitalist framework.

Carbon footprint: the total amount of greenhouse gases that are generated by our actions. It stems from the older idea of ecological footprint.

Carbon majors: entities, companies, and countries on Earth that possess fossil fuel reserves that will, if produced and emitted, intensify anthropogenic climate change.

Carbon negative: the intentional removal of carbon dioxide from the atmosphere, whereby a company removes more carbon than it produces.

Carbon net zero: the situation when the amount of carbon we add to the atmosphere is no more than the amount removed. There is a balance between the carbon emitted into the atmosphere, and the carbon removed from it.

Carbon neutral: having the right balance between emitting carbon and absorbing carbon from the atmosphere in carbon sinks.

Carbon pledge: a commitment to reach net-zero carbon emissions by 2040, ten years ahead of the Paris Agreement (2015).

Carbon sink: organic matter like plants, ocean, soil, and fossil fuels that absorb more carbon from the atmosphere than they release.

Carbon free: using clean energy sources like wind and solar power to produce electricity, and not use fossil fuels, thus resulting in no emissions of carbon.

Climate positive: when the activity goes beyond achieving net-zero carbon emissions to create an environmental benefit by removing additional carbon dioxide from the atmosphere.

Cryosphere: refers to the frozen parts of the planet including ice on land, ice caps, glaciers, permafrost, and sea ice. This sphere reflects incoming solar radiation back into space and helps maintain Earth's climate.

Desertification: the process by which vegetation in drylands like arid and semi-arid lands, such as grasslands or shrublands, decreases due to climate variations or anthropogenic activity, and eventually disappears giving way to deserts.

Ecological footprint: a concept invented in the early 1990s by William Rees and Mathis Wackernagel and refers to the total area of land, water and resources needed to sustain an activity or a population.

Ecosphere: another word for the biosphere that refers to that part of the Earth's environment in which living organisms are found on land, air, and water.

Ghedeist: a term coined by Glenn Albrecht from the German *geist* with its meanings of spirit and mind to refer to the spirit or force which holds things together, creating a feeling of symbiotic interconnectedness in life between human and non-human beings and their gathering together to live within the shared Earth places and spaces.

Greenhouse gases: a term coined by the Swedish physicist and chemist Svante Arrhenius in 1896 to describe gases in the Earth's atmosphere that trap heat like water vapour (H_2O), carbon dioxide (CO_2), nitrous oxide(N_2O), methane (CH_4), and ozone (O_3).

Green washing: when a company makes an environmental, green claim about the organization's policy of having a positive effect on the environment, but such a misleading spin is merely intended to promote a false sense of environmental practice or concern.

Holocene: the geologic time that began 11,700 years ago after the last major ice age. It is officially the current epoch and considered as a warm and stable epoch for life forms on Earth.

Homogenocene: a term used to describe the present ecological era where one recognizes and acknowledges the homogenization of species that is a part of the anthropocene, and all its anthropogenic activities.

Hydrosphere: refers to the sum of Earth's water, found in the ocean, the ground, on the surface, and in the air.

Hyperobject: a term coined by Timothy Morton to describe objects that are so massively distributed in time and space as to transcend spatiotemporal specificity, such as global warming, styrofoam, and radioactive plutonium.

Lithosphere: the the solid, outer part of Earth that includes the brittle upper portion of the mantle and the crust.

Myxocene: a term coined by the oceanographer Daniel Pauly to represent changes to the ocean state.

Pedosphere: refers to the soil mantle of the Earth that covers much of the Earth's land surface and the bottom of stable waterbodies. It serves as the Earth's biogeomembrane, which is analogous to the biomembranes of living organisms.

Planthroposcene: an aspirational episteme or scene in which people work with plants and their allies to make a livable world for all.

Plantationcene: a proposed alternate name for the present epoch of the Anthropocene, that addresses multiple forms of plantations, past and present, and lays emphasis on colonialism, capitalism, and enduring racial hierarchies at the center of the discourse and considers how past and future modes of resistance might emerge.

Terra Firma: dry land or solid ground that is distinct from the sea or air.

Thanatocene: an epoch that traces the natural history of destruction where the blame lies with the large-scale war efforts implemented by the industrial and military powers.

Stratosphere: refers to the atmospheric layer composed of stratified temperature layers, with the warmer layers of air remaining high in the sky and the cooler layers of air in the low sky moving close to the planetary surface of the Earth.

Symbiocene: a term for an epoch of deeper symbiosis between humankind and the natural world where the focus will be on discovering mutually reinforcing life-reproducing forms and processes found in living systems.

Zero-carbon: a state when no carbon emissions are being produced from a product or service as in the case of a wind farm generating electricity, or a battery deploying electricity.

Glossary of Ecocriticism

Animal Turn: a term invented by American anthropologist Sarah Franklin in 2003 to refer to a renewed interest in animal entities, especially in their dichotomy and relationship with humans, and animal studies.

Biophilia: a term conceived by Harvard naturalist, Edward O. Wilson to refer to a human tendency to interact or be closely associated with other forms of life in nature.

Biomimicry: a term coined by Jenine Benyus to study nature's biological models and then imitated by engineers who draw inspiration from these designs and processes to solve human problems.

Ecocriticism: a term coined by William Rueckert in 1978 and refers to a field of study that applies ecology and ecological concepts to explore how the natural world is portrayed in literature, typically in relation to modern environmental concerns, like human-nature relationships, actor networks, feminist perspectives, and Earth-centred system of values.

Eco-centric approach: derived from *ecocentrism* that adopts as world view whereby there is serious concern attributed to environmental issues and non-human life on Earth and lays stress on protecting the inherent intrinsic value of nature.

Ecodiversity: refers to the diverse array of ecosystems (grasslands, tundra, deserts, rainforests, and terrestrial and marine spaces) including diverse niches or habitat diversity existing in in a geographical location and their overall effects on humans and the environment.

Eco-feminism: a movement that proposes the idea of a connection between the exploitation and degradation of the natural world and the subordination and oppression of women.

Endemophilia: a word derived from the French *endémique* and the Greek *philia* to express a particular local and distinctive love that people feel for a place.

Eutierra: a word from the *eu*, or "good," and *tierra*, or Earth, to express a positive feeling of oneness with the Earth and its life forces.

Deep Ecology: a movement begun in 1972 by the philosopher Arne Naess that insisted on nature having inherent value like all living beings and opposed the practice of shallow ecology that viewed nature as a mere resource to be exploited.

Material Ecocriticism: a new material paradigm proposed by Karen Barad and Donna Haraway for the study of the way material forms, organic and inorganic forms of matter, bodies, things and nature, intra-act with each other and with human beings to produce configurations of meanings and discourses that can be interpreted as stories.

Material Turn: a term conceived by Serenella Iovino and Serpil Oppermann to engage in the quest for new conceptual models to theorize the connections between matter and agency on the one hand, and the intertwining of bodies, natures, and meanings on the other hand.

Mermosity: a term coined by Glenn Albrecht to refer to the anticipated state of being worried about the likely passing of the familiar and its adverse effect on one's sense of place.

Meteoranxiety: a term coined by Glenn Albrecht to refer to the anxiety one feels concerning the vicissitudes of the weather.

Novums: a term coined by Darko Suvin to refer to science fiction that specializes in constructions of 'new' other-worlds, that are extraterrestrial, futuristic, and scientifically plausible.

Psychoterratic: a term coined by Glenn Albrecht from the Greek '*psykhe*,' which means soul, mind, spirit, or invisible animating entity. It refers to Earth emotions that people feel in relation to the Earth.

Solastalgia: a term coined by Glenn Albrecht to refer to the feelings of nostalgia, solace, and desolation caused by environmentally induced stress. The word is a combination of the Latin word *solacium*, meaning 'comfort,' or the English language derivative 'solace,' and the root word *-algia* from the Greek word *algos*, meaning 'pain,' and 'nostalgia,' as in homesickness.

Soliphilia: a concept that has its origins from the French *solidaire*, the Latin *solidus*, and the Greek *philia*, to refer to the love of the totality of our place relationships, and a willingness to accept the political responsibility for protecting and conserving them at all scales.

Sumbiocracy: a term invented by Glenn Albrecht to refer to a form of government where humans govern keeping in mind all the reciprocal relationships of the Earth, and where there is a rule of the Earth for the Earth. The term is from the Greek *sumbioun* meaning 'to live together.'

Symbiosis: refers to the close, prolonged association or mutually beneficial relationship between two or more different biological species.

Terraforming: a term coined by Jack Williamson for the process of modifying a planet, moon or other body to a more habitable atmosphere, temperature, or ecology.

Terranascia: a term formed by Glenn Albrecht to refer to Earth creators or Terranascient humans who strive to protect nature and live symbiotically with the rest of life in the Symbiocene. It is formed from *terra*, the Latin word for Earth, and the Greek word *nātūra*, meaning 'to be born.'

Terraphthora: a term created by Glenn Albrecht to refer to Earth destroyers or *Terraphthorans* in the Anthropocene. It is formed from *terra*, the Latin word for Earth, and the Greek word *phthorá*, meaning 'destruction.'

Topaversion: a term used by Glenn Albrecht to refer to a feeling one experiences when one is strongly averse to returning to a place that was once loved, as it has faced environmental degradation.

Topophilia: from the Greek *topos*, meaning place, and *philia*, or love, referring to a strong sense of place, which is often associated with the sense of cultural identity among certain people and a love of certain aspects of such a place.

Glossary of Indian Words

Aagariyas: a subcaste of the Gond tribe, believed to be ancient miners, who are now pygmy-sized farmers due to the lack of sustenance.
Abhaya: Hindi word meaning 'fearlessness.'
Adivasis: an original name for the scheduled tribes or various ethnic groups considered to be the original inhabitants of the Indian sub-continent.
Agni: the *vedic* fire God in Hindu mythology who is regarded as the friend and protector of humanity.
Asur: Hindi word meaning 'demon' or an 'evil person.'
Baigas: forest dwelling tribe in central India known for their colorful attire, dances, and tattoos.
Bajra: *pennisetum glaucum* or pearl millet.
Bengali: language spoken in the Indian states of Jharkhand, West Bengal, and in Bangladesh.
Bhils: tribal indigenous people known to be excellent archers who live in the forests of Chhattisgarh, Gujarat, Karnataka, Madhya Pradesh, Maharashtra, Andhra Pradesh, and Rajasthan.
Bhilalas: tribal folk of huntsmen who live in the forests of Malwa and Nimar of the Central Provinces and in Central India.
Bhumkal: Hindi word meaning 'earthquake,' referring to the Adivasi rebellion in 1910 against the British Raj in the princely state of Bastar.
Bhutaa: Hindi word for 'maize,' *Zea mays*.
Black bhat: *glygcine max* or black soya bean.
Brahma: a *Hindu* god, referred to as 'the Creator' in the Trimurti, the trinity of supreme divinity that includes Vishnu and Shiva.
Brahmin: a person belonging to the priestly caste in India.
Brinjal: *solanum melongena*, also known as eggplant or aubergine.
Champa: *magnolia champaka*, or plumeria, a tropical flowering plant.
Chappals: a pair of sandals.

Char sau bees: the number 420 from section 420 IPC of the Indian Penal Code that is the basis for charging a person with the offence of cheating. The maximum punishment is a term of seven years and a fine.

Chipko: *Hindi* word meaning 'to hug' or 'to cling to.'

Dada Log: a tribal term for Maoists.

Dalit: a member of the scheduled caste or scheduled tribe in India.

Devdars: *Pinus deodora*, or green cedar.

Dhak: *butea monosperma*, known as the flame of the Forest or palash or dhak or bastard teak.

Gandharaja: *gardenia jasminoides*, or gardenia, are fragrant summer flowers.

Ghandian: of or relating to the principles of Mahatma Gandhi.

Gomal: lands reserved for cattle pasturage.

Gonds: tribes from Gondwana forest regions in central India who cultivate land on the hill slopes.

Gram Sabha: the general legislative assembly in a village in India, where those who have attained the age of eighteen years, can participate directly, and seek answers from their elected representatives.

Halbas: tribal community found in Chhattisgarh, Maharashtra, Madhya Pradesh, and Orissa in India who are farmers.

Hindi: the official language of India as per Article 343 (1) of the Constitution of India and that is spoken by approximately 585 million people in the world.

Hindu: a follower of Hinduism and does not refer to the people of India.

Holi: the two-day festival of colors in India that celebrates the eternal love between Radha and Lord Krishna.

Jallikattu: the traditional bull-taming sport played during Pongal, the harvest festival to tame, in which people embrace the bull and retrieve the coins in its horns.

Jehana: Hindi word meaning 'destiny' or 'artistic creativity.'

Jhangora: *echinochloa frumentacea*, or Indian barnyard millet.

Jowar: *sorghum bicolor*, or new quinoa is a gluten-free and protein-rich millet.

Keria: tribal ethnic group from east-central India who depend on the forest roots, tubers, and fruits for their sustenance.

Leng: means 'voice' in *Gondi*, or the language of the *Gonds*.

Lodhas: tribal folk from West Bengal and Odisha who live a life of seclusion in the forests.

Maroa: means 'food grain' in the *Aagariya* dialect.

Molksha: Hindi word meaning liberation from the cycle of birth, death, and rebirth.

Moong dal: *phaseolus aureus*, or green gram.

Mundas: tribal folk who live of the produce of the forests in south and east Chhotanagpur plateau region of Jharkhand, Odisha, and West Bengal.

Murias: a tribal community of the Bastar district of Chhattisgarh whose livelihood from the forests has been affected by the war between the *Naxalite* unrest.

Nagesias: tribal folk from Odisha, West Bengal, and Jharkhand who are traditional farmers and a food-gathering people of the forests.

Narmada Bachao Andolan: Save the River Narmada Movement.

Navarangi: suggests that these lentils have nine colors of grains. It is a specialty pulse of Uttarkhand which is rich in protein.

Naxalite: a member of an extreme Maoist group in India. The name originates from the armed peasant revolt in 1967 in the Naxalbari block of Siliguri subdivision in Darjeeling district, West Bengal.

Okra: *Abelmoschus esculentus*, known as lady's fingers, is a tropical vegetable of the mallow family. It has edible green seed pods.

Oraons: tribal folk who live in the forested uplands of east-central India. They have now migrated to work in the tea plantations of Assam.

Padayatra: a Hindi word meaning a journey undertaken on foot for religious, political, social, or charitable purposes.

Parhaiyas: tribal folk whose name means 'burners of the forest' or 'forest dwellers' as they depend on the forests for sustenance. They live in the Sonbhadra District of the Uttar Pradesh in North India.

Pasupathi: the name given to Lord Shiva in Hindu mythology, meaning the Lord of all Animals and Human Beings.

Pavras: the name for the tribal folk, the *Bhils* in the Satpura mountain ranges in Gujarat, Madhya Pradesh, and Maharashtra in India.

Prakriti: Hindi word meaning 'nature' referring to all the animals, plants, and other things in the world that are not made by people, and all the events and processes that are not caused by people.

Ragi: *eleusine coracana*, or finger millet.

Sansis: nomadic tribal people of people of Rajasthan, Punjab, Haryana, who were known for their illegal but non-violent activities during the British Era.

Sanskrit: the standardized dialect of old Indo-Aryan, originating as Vedic Sanskrit as early as 1700–1200 BCE. It is of the oldest Indo-European languages. It believed to have been the general language of the greater Indian Subcontinent in ancient times, thus providing the root to Indian languages and dialects.

Santals: tribal group found in the states of Odisha, Bihar, and Assam who work in coal mines or as agricultural laborers.

Saras: Hindi word meaning 'stork.'

Satyagraha: the policy of non-violent resistance adopted by Mahatma Gandhi to fight for Indian independence.

Shiva: a Hindu god, referred to as 'the Destroyer' in the Trimurti, the trinity of supreme divinity that includes Vishnu and Shiva.

Sunderbans: Bengali word meaning 'beautiful forests' for the mangrove forests of India.

Tadvi: an agriculturist tribe who live in the states of Maharashtra, Gujarat, Madhya Pradesh, and Rajasthan in India.

Tahsildar: a land revenue officer at the district level in India supervises the work given to the *Patwari* or administrative officer and makes sure that the land records are maintained properly, and that land revenue is collected on time.

Til: *sesamum indicum*, or sesame seeds.

Upanishads: a genre of texts found in the *Vedas* which speculates about the ontological connection between humanity and the cosmos.

Urad dal: *vigna mungo*, or black gram.

Vassawa: an indigenous tribe of farmers who rent the land they work on and are part of the Bhil ethnic community who live in the states of Gujarat, Maharashtra, and Rajasthan.

Vedas: ancient Indian religious texts of Hinduism consisting of four books: *Rig Veda* (knowledge of the Verses), *Yajur Veda* (knowledge of the Sacrifice), the *Sama Veda* (knowledge of the Chants), and *Athara Veda* (knowledge of the Fire Priest).

Vishnu: a Hindu god, referred to as 'the Preserver' in the Trimurti, the trinity of supreme divinity that includes Brahma and Shiva.

Yatra: a Sanskrit word meaning 'journey,' 'expedition' or 'travel.'

Yatri: a traveler who sets out on a journey.

Glossary of Legal English Terms

Absolute liability: rule that makes the individual completely liable for actions caused due to escape of a dangerous object in the non-natural use of land, without any exception.

Affidavit: a written court statement sworn before a person having authority to administer an oath or a court testimony.

Aggrieved person: a person sufficiently harmed by a legal judgment, decree, or order to have standing to contest a particular judicial or administrative decision.

Amicus curiae: from the Latin, 'friend of the court,' when the person has a strong interest in the case and submits the brief intending to influence the court's decision.

Cassation appeal: an extraordinary appeal against judicial decisions limited to questions of law, whereby the Supreme Court or the High Courts of Justice review the application of the law that has been previously carried out by the lower courts.

Certiorari: from the Latin 'to be certified' or 'to be informed'; a writ issued by a higher court to a lower court ordering it to transfer a pending case or to quash their order in a case. It may be issued on the grounds of an excess of jurisdiction or lack of jurisdiction or error of law.

Compensatory damages: damages awarded by a court equivalent to the loss a party suffered.

Concur (v.): to agree.

Concurring opinion: an opinion filed by a judge who agrees with the majority or plurality opinion on the case but is written to express a particular judge's reasoning on different reasons or on a different view of the case.

Continuing mandamus: when the matter is not disposed of even after the court has given directions, instead the court maintains a supervisory role through continuous reports in reasonable intervals, to ensure compliance and enforcement of its directions within a stipulated period, without delay.

Counter affidavit: an affidavit filed by the respondent in reply to a petition.

Curative petition: the last chance available to the petitioner to invoke the protection for the compensation of injustice in the court after the review petition is dismissed or has been exhausted.

Declaratory judgment: a party may seek a court's authoritative opinion regarding the exact nature of the legal matter and whether the parties would be entitled to relief without requiring the parties to do anything.

Dissent (v.): to disagree.

Dissenting opinion: an opinion filed by a judge who disagrees with the majority decision of a case.

**Forum*: court of justice which has jurisdiction to hold a trial of a particular lawsuit.[1]

Forum non conveniens: a common law legal doctrine that refers to a court's discretionary power to decline to exercise its jurisdiction or authority, when it deems that there is another court, or forum that may more conveniently hear a case.

Habeas Corpus: from the Latin 'you may have the body'; a writ issued by a court or judge to produce a person who has been detained before a court and to release him if such detention is found illegal.

In limine: from the Latin, 'at the threshold'; a pretrial motion made at the start of the trial requesting the court to find certain evidence be found inadmissible.

**Injunction*: a court order which requires one party to the case to do or to refrain from doing something for the benefit of the other party; it is an equitable remedy.

Inter Alia: from the Latin, 'among other things' to specify one example out of many possibilities.

Judicial activism: the practice of using the courts' authority to examine state actions, thus resulting in the proactive role of the Judiciary in protecting the rights of citizens.

Judicial restraint: a theory of judicial interpretation whereby judges limit the exercise of their own power.

Judicial review: the federal courts' power to review the constitutionality of the federal executive or legislative acts.

**Jurisprudence*: the concept of jurisprudence in European legal English is synonymous with case law; in the context of EU law, both terms are used interchangeably; however, in the context of English law, the word jurisprudence refers to the science of law (doctrine); in the latter case, it is not to be confused with the French jurisprudence which is translated by case law in English. Only when they deal with an EU issue, English court cases use the term *jurisprudence* to mean case law.

**Lift/pierce the corporate veil*: a fact for the courts to set aside the corporate personality of a company to impose liability on its members when the company was set up for fraudulent purposes, as a sham entity or to evade liability.

Limited jurisdiction: when a court's jurisdiction or authority is limited to hear and decide on a particular subject matter.

Locus standi: from the Latin *locus*, which means "place," and *standi* means "the right to bring an action to a court of law," or "to appear in a court."

Loco parentis: from the Latin 'in the place of a parent' and refers to a common law doctrine that denotes the legal responsibility of some person or organization to perform some of the functions or responsibilities of a parent.

Mandamus: from the Latin 'we command'; a writ is used by the court to order the public official who has failed to perform his duty or refused to do his duty, to resume his work. Besides public officials, it can be issued against any public body, a corporation, an inferior court, a tribunal, or government for the same purpose.

Majority opinion: a judicial opinion that is given by more than half the judges deciding a case.

Mandate: the official authority to carry out a particular task or policy.

Minority opinion: an opinion by one or more judges in a legal case who disagree with the decision reached by the majority.

Memorandum of Law: A comprehensive and organized written document that summarizes and analyzes relevant laws to support a conclusion on a particular legal issue.

Moot: US federal courts only have authority to resolve actual disputes between real parties, a federal court cannot hear a case once the issue at hand has been resolved by other means. This matter is then said to be "moot."

Non sui juris: from the Latin 'not of one's own right' that signifies that the person is not able to make decisions or enter into legal agreements on his own without the help of a guardian or other legal representative.

**Onus*: the burden of proof

**Obiter Dicta*: from the Latin 'by the way'; comments made by the court, which are different from the ratio decidendi, but logically lead to a legal ruling being rendered; *obiter dicta* only have a persuasive effect.

Parens patriae: from the Latin for 'parent of the country or homeland,' a doctrine under which a state or court has a paternal and protective role over its citizens or others subject to its jurisdiction.

**Patent*: exclusive legal right enjoyed by an inventor or company to manufacture, sell, and use his or its invention for a certain number of years thanks to the permission granted by a government.

Per se: from the Latin for 'by itself,' in other words, inherently.

Precautionary principle: a principle that states that in the absence of scientific evidence, precautionary measures must be taken to anticipate and prevent the causes of environmental degradation as it is the social responsibility of the State to protect the public from any plausible risk.

Precedent: the rule of law established in earlier court decisions that is considered as an authority for deciding subsequent cases and must be followed by other courts according to the doctrine of *stare decisis*.

Prohibition: a writ issued by a higher court to a lower court to forbid the latter from exceeding its jurisdiction or usurping a jurisdiction that it does not possess.

Polluter Pays Principle: a principle that imposes liability on a person who pollutes the environment to compensate for the damage caused and return the environment to its original state regardless of the intent.

Public Interest Litigation: a lawsuit filed in a court of law by a socially conscious member or a public-spirited NGO to espouse a public cause by seeking judicial for redressal of public injury.

Public Trust Doctrine: a legal principle establishing that certain natural and cultural resources are reserved for public use. It entrusts the Government with the task of protecting the resources for the enjoyment of the public rather than to permit their use for private ownership or commercial purposes.

Punitive damages: awarded in addition to actual damages and are typically awarded at the court's discretion when the defendant's behavior is found to be especially harmful.

Sine qua non: from the Latin for 'without which not' to describe a necessary or indispensable requirement.

Sub judice: from the Latin for 'under a judge,' referring to a particular case or matter being under trial or being considered by a judge or court.

**Trademark*: mark indicating that the goods and services in connection with which it is used are certified by the proprietor of the mark in respect of origin, material, mode of manufacture, quality, or other characteristics.

Quo Warranto: from the Latin 'by what authority or warrant'; the court's enquiry into the legality of a claim of a person to a public office to prevent illegal usurpation of a public office by a person.

**Ratio decidendi*: from the Latin 'meaning of decision'; legal ruling which is essential in a court decision.

Rule of Law: a principle of governance in which all persons, institutions, and entities, public and private, including the State itself, are accountable to laws that are publicly promulgated, equally enforced, and independently adjudicated, and which are consistent with international human rights norms and standards.

Standing: the litigant's capacity to either bring a claim before a court, or to appeal or petition the court.

**Stare Decisis*: from the Latin 'let the decision stand'; courts' policy to comply with decisions made in earlier cases, so long as they raised similar issues of fact and mostly, law.

Strict Liability: the rule that a person can be held liable even there is no negligence on his part.

Sustainable development: an approach to economic planning that attempts to foster economic growth of the present without compromising the ability of future generations to equitably meet developmental and environmental needs.

Writ: a formal, legal document drafted by a court that orders a person or entity to perform or to cease performing a specific action or deed.

Writ jurisdiction: a court order ordering a person or authority to conduct or abstain from executing a certain activity

NOTE

1. All legal terms preceded with an asterisk are from *Glossaire de droit anglais: Méthode, traduction et approche comparative* (2019).

Bibliography

"10 Animals That Are Now Extinct." OneKindPlanet, September 22, 2017. https://onekindplanet.org/top-10/top-10-worlds-extinct-animals/.

"10 of the World's Most Endangered Animals." WWF. Accessed April 15, 2023. https://www.wwf.org.uk/learn/wildlife/endangered-animals.

101 Dalmatians. Walt Disney Pictures, 1996.

"15 Amazing Hybrid Animals That Actually Exist." YouTube, 2020. https://www.youtube.com/watch?v=twGnn8niQYE.

"2022 Toronto Conference on Earth System Governance." Earth System Governance, November 7, 2022. https://www.earthsystemgovernance.org/2022toronto/.

"50 Years of Environmental Conservation." WWF. Accessed September 10, 2023. https://wwf.panda.org/discover/knowledge_hub/history/.

"A Dry Lake Hamun Means More Dust Storms." NASA. Accessed June 8, 2023. https://earthobservatory.nasa.gov/images/150941/a-dry-lake-hamun-means-more-dust-storms.

A. Periyakaruppan v. The Principal Secretary & Anr (Madras High Court, April 19, 2022).

A.P. Pollution Control Board v. Prof.M.V. Nayudu (Retd.) & Other (1999) (Supreme Court of India, January 27, 1999).

A Life on Our Planet. Netflix, 2020. https://www.netflix.com/title/80216393.

A Sud et al. v. Italy (Civil Court of Rome, June 5, 2021).

Acción de habeas corpus Decision AHC4806 (Colombia Supreme Court of Justice, July 26, 2017).

Acción de hábeas corpus presentada por la Asociación de Funcionarios y Abogados por los Derechos de los Animales (AFADA) (Tercer Juzgado de Garantías Poder Judicial Mendoza, November 3, 2016).

Ahlawat, Himanshu, and Sujith Koonan. "Environmental Rule of Law in India: A Transformative Principle or Old Wine in a New Bottle?" *Journal of Indian Law and Society* 13, no. 1 (2022): 133–45.

Ahmed, Umaima R. "Freedom in Sight for Kaavan, 'the World's Loneliest Elephant.'" Global Voices, December 1, 2020. https://globalvoices.org/2020/10/31/freedom-in-sight-for-Kaavan-the-worlds-loneliest-elephant/.

Albrecht, Glenn A. "Solastalgia: A New Concept in Human Health and Identity." *PAN (Philosophy, Activism, Nature)* 3 (2005): 44–59.

Albrecht, Glenn A. *Earth Emotions: New Words for a New World* Ithaca: Cornell University, 2019.

Albrecht, Glenn A. "Public Heritage in the Symbiocene." *Oxford Handbooks Online*, 2018. https://doi.org/10.1093/oxfordhb/9780190676315.013.12.

Alejandro de la Garza, "Matt Damon Wants You to Care about Water." *Time*, March 29, 2022. https://time.com/6160927/matt-damon-water/.

Ali v. Federation of Pakistan & Another (Supreme Court of Pakistan, April 2, 2016).

Alaknanda Hydro Power Company Ltd v. Anuj Joshi and Ors (Supreme Court of India, August 13, 2013).

Allers, Roger and Rob Minkoff. *The Lion King*. United States: Buena Vista Pictures, 1994.

"American Airlines." Cool Effect, September 1, 2021. https://www.cooleffect.org/american-airlines.

Amit Maru v. Ministry of Environment and Forest (National Green Tribunal, Pune, October 1, 2014).

Anderson, Benedict. *Imagined Communities: Reflections on the Origin and Spread of Nationalism*. London: Verso, 1991.

"Animal Protection Index." World Animal Protection | Animal Protection Index. Accessed April 16, 2023. https://api.worldanimalprotection.org/.

Animal Welfare Board of India v. A. Nagaraja & Ors (Supreme Court of India, May 7, 2014).

Anirudh Kumar v. Municipal Corporation of Delhi & Ors (Supreme Court of India, March 20, 2015).

"Article 21: Protection of Life and Personal Liberty." Constitution of India, March 31, 2023. https://www.constitutionofindia.net/articles/article-21-protection-of-life-and-personal-liberty/.

Asghar Leghari v. Federation of Pakistan (Lahore High Court, Pakistan, April 4, 2015).

"Asia for Animals Coalition: Network." Asia for Animals. Accessed April 15, 2023. https://www.asiaforanimals.com/.

Asociación de Funcionarios y Abogados por los Derechos de los Animales y otros contra GCBA (Juzgado No. 4 on Contentious Administrative and Tax Matters, October 21, 2015).

Augé, Marc. *Les Nouvelles Peurs*. Paris: Payot, 2013.

Ayferam, Gashaw. The Nile dispute: Beyond water security—Carnegie endowment, January 19, 2023. https://carnegieendowment.org/sada/88842.

Aysegül Kibaroglu, "An Analysis of Turkey's Water Diplomacy and Its Evolving Position Vis-à-Vis International Water Law." *Water International* 40, no. 1 (2014): 153–67. https://doi.org/10.1080/02508060.2014.978971.

Bailey, Sarah Pulliam. "The Dakota Access Pipeline Isn't Just about the Environment. It's about Religion." *Washington Post*. WP Company, October 27, 2021. https://www.washingtonpost.com/news/acts-of-faith/wp/2016/12/05/the-dakota-access-pipeline-isnt-just-about-the-environment-its-about-religion/.

Bakhtin, Mikhail Mikhailovich. *The Dialogic Imagination*. Austin: University of Texas Press, 1981.

Bakhtin, Mikhail Mikhailovich. *Problems of Dostoevsky's Poetics*. Minneapolis: University of Minnesota Press, 1984.

Bakhtin, Mikhail M. *Art and Answerability: Early Philosophical Essays*, edited by Michael Holquist and Vadim Liapunov. Austin: University of Texas Press, 1990.

Balachandra Bhikaji Nalwade v. Union of India (Delhi High Court, September 18, 2009).

Banka, Neha. "In West Bengal, Marine Strandings of Endangered Horseshoe Crabs Are Increasing." *Indian Express*, August 16, 2022. https://indianexpress.com/article/cities/kolkata/west-bengal-marine-strandings-endangered-horseshoe-crabs-increasing-8091777/.

"Banksy: Trolley Hunters." Sothebys.com, November 18, 2021. https://www.sothebys.com/en/articles/banksy-trolley-hunters#:~:text=It%20highlights%20our%20inability%20to,in%20a%20Los%20Angeles%20warehouse.

Bano v. Union Carbide Corporation (Southern District Court of New York, November 15, 2001).

Barnes, Sara. "Giant 'Faucet' Spewing Single-Use Plastic Urges Us to Reconsider Our Plastic Use." My Modern Met, October 5, 2021. https://mymodernmet.com/benjamin-von-wong-giant-plastic-tap/.

Bayer. Bayer Closes Monsanto Acquisition, August 8, 2022. https://www.bayer.com/media/en-us/bayer-closes-monsanto-acquisition/.

Beattie, Ainslie. "Pacific Climate Warriors." Transition Network, September 7, 2018. https://transitionnetwork.org/news/pacific-climate-warriors/.

Benjamin, Antonio Herman. *Climate Change, Coming Soon to a Court Near You*. Manila: Asian Development Bank, 2020.

Benyus, Janine M. *Biomimicry: Innovation Inspired by Nature*. HarperCollins, 1998.

Bhabha, Homi K. "The Location of Culture." In *Literary Theory: An Anthology*, edited by Julie Rivkin and Michael Ryan, 936–44, Oxford: Blackwell, 1998.

Bhadauria, Akshita. "How 'child Climate Activist' Licypriya Kangujam Trends Twitter Hashtags as e-Aandolanjeevi." OpIndia, March 17, 2021. https://www.opindia.com/2021/03/licypriya-kangujam-twitter-hashtags-trends-random-causes/.

Billy Rose's Jumbo. Metro-Goldwyn-Mayer, 1962.

Black Hills Institute of Geological Research (BHI) v. Fort Peck Paleontology et al. (US District Court for the District of Montana, November 22, 2010).

Bladow, Kyle, Jennifer Ladino. "Introduction. In *Affective Ecocriticism: Emotion, Embodiment, Environment*, edited by Kyle Bladow, 1–24, University of Nebraska Press, 2018.

Braddick, Ian. "'Anthropocene Monument'—Professor Lise Autogena Exhibiting at Symposium-Performance and Exhibition in Toulouse." The CCRI Impact Blog, July 26, 2018. https://blogs.shu.ac.uk/c3riimpact/lise-autogena-anthopocene-monument-france/.

"Brundtland Report of the World Commission on Environment and Development:" United Nations. Accessed July 14, 2023. https://digitallibrary.un.org/record/139811?ln=fr.

Bout, Marie. "5 Reasons We Need Wildlife in Order to Survive." Greenpeace International, March 8, 2021. https://www.greenpeace.org/international/story/46591/5-reasons-wildlife-human-survive-climate-change/.

Boguslaw, Daniel. "The CIA Just Invested in Woolly Mammoth Resurrection Technology." *The Intercept*, September 28, 2022. https://theintercept.com/2022/09/28/cia-extinction-woolly-mammoth-dna/.

Booth, Wayne C. "Introduction." In Problems of Dostoevsky's Poetics, xiii–xxvii. Minneapolis: University of Minnesota Press, 1984.

Bout, Marie. "5 Reasons We Need Wildlife in Order to Survive." Greenpeace Aotearoa, March 8, 2021. https://www.greenpeace.org/aotearoa/story/5-reasons-we-need-wildlife-in-order-to-survive/.

Brasch, Sam. "10 Farm Animal Hybrids You Didn't Know Existed." *Modern Farmer*, October 2, 2018. https://modernfarmer.com/2014/01/10-farm-animal-hybrids-didnt-know-existed/.

Brunon-Ernst, Anne, Armelle Sabatier, Suhasini Vincent, and Justin Beplate. *Glossaire de droit anglais: Méthode, traduction et approche comparative*, edited by Géraldine Gadbin-George. Paris: Dalloz, 2019.

Buell, Lawrence. "The Emergence of Environmental Criticism." In *The Future of Environmental Criticism*, 1–28, Malden: Blackwell, 2005.

Bulga Milbrodale Progress Association Inc. v. Minister for Planning and Infrastructure and Warkworth Mining Limited (Land and Environmental Court of New South Wales, April 15, 2013).

Callaghan, Paul. "Visiting the Algae All-Stars in Spain." *Brave Blue World*, June 25, 2019. https://www.braveblue.world/blog/2019/5/20/visiting-the-algae-all-stars-in-spain-6xnse.

Calzavara, Mark. "Breaking: Nestle Sells Water Business to Wall St for $4.3 Billion." Council of Canadians, July 26, 2022. https://canadians.org/analysis/breaking-nestle-sells-water-business-wall-st-43-billion/.

Campbell, Nancy. *The Library of Ice. Readings from a Cold Climate*. Bompiani: Scribner, 2018.

"Canoes vs. Coal Ships—Blockading Newcastle Harbour—Stories & Images." Stories & images, December 18, 2020. https://storiesandimages.net/cases/climate-movement/pacific-warriors/blockade/.

Carson, Rachel L. *Silent Spring*. Boston: Mifflin, 1962.

Center for Environmental Law WWF-1 v. Union of India (1999), (Supreme Court of India, April 15, 2013).

Center for Social Justice Studies et al. v. Presidency of the Republic et al. Judgment T-622/16 (Constitutional Court of Colombia, November 10, 2016).

Chevron Corporation and Texaco Petroleum Corporation v. Republic of Ecuador, PCA Case No. 2009-23, Second Partial Award on Track II (30 Aug. 2018).

Chadha, Pavneet Singh. "Why Did Goa See a Spate of Forest Fires in March?" *Indian Express*, May 8, 2023. https://indianexpress.com/article/explained/explained-climate/goa-forest-fires-in-march-2023-explained-8596719/.

Charlie Faulkner, "Water Crisis Heightens the Risk of Famine in Afghanistan." The Third Pole, August 17, 2021. https://www.thethirdpole.net/en/food/bone-dry-afghanistan-stares-at-future-famines/.

Chakrabarty, Dipesh. "The Climate of History: Four Theses." *Critical Enquiry* 35 (2009): 197–210.

Chakrabarty, Dipesh. "Anthropocene Time." *History and Theory* 57, no. 1 (2018): 5–32. https://doi.org/10.1111/hith.12044.

Chapter 3—Global Warming of 1.5°c—IPCC. Accessed July 5, 2023. https://www.ipcc.ch/sr15/chapter/chapter-3/.

"Christo and Jeanne." Claude. Accessed June 29, 2023. https://christojeanneclaude.net/artworks/arc-de-triomphe-wrapped/.

Cinelli, Antonella. "Italy's Water Crisis Exacerbated by Leaky Pipes, Data Shows." Reuters, March 21, 2023. https://www.reuters.com/business/environment/italys-water-crisis-exacerbated-by-leaky-pipes-data-shows-2023-03-21/.

"Climate Change 2022: Mitigation of Climate Change—Sixth Annual Assessment Report." IPCC. Accessed June 25, 2023. https://www.ipcc.ch/report/ar6/wg3/.

Cohen, Michael. "Will Cape Town Run out of Water?" Bloomberg.com, December 8, 2017. https://www.bloomberg.com/news/features/2017-12-08/will-cape-town-run-out-of-water.

Colorado River Ecosystem v. State of Colorado (Colorado Federal District Court, December 4, 2017).

"Constitution of India." Constitution of India | Legislative Department | India. Accessed April 23, 2023. https://legislative.gov.in/constitution-of-india/.

Construction of Park at Noida Near Okhla Bird Sanctuary v. State (The Supreme Court of India, December 3, 2010).

Connolly, Kate. "Climate Activists 'Prepared to Risk Lives' to Stop German Coalmine." *Guardian*, January 10, 2023. https://www.theguardian.com/world/2023/jan/10/climate-activists-prepared-risk-lives-stop-german-coalmine-lutzerath.

Cooperrider, Kensy. "How We Make Sense of Time." *Scientific American*, November 1, 2016. https://www.scientificamerican.com/article/how-we-make-sense-of-time/.

"COP27 Ends with Announcement of Historic Loss and Damage Fund." UNEP. Accessed June 24, 2023. https://www.unep.org/news-and-stories/story/cop27-ends-announcement-historic-loss-and-damage-fund.

Corgan, Billy. "Doomsday Clock." Smashing Pumpkins—Doomsday Clock Lyrics | Lyrics.com. https://www.lyrics.com/lyric/26597212/Smashing+Pumpkins/Doomsday+Clock.

Court on its own motion v. State of Himachal Pradesh & Others (National Green Tribunal, New Delhi, September 20, 2018).

Cozzi, Laura, Olivia Chen, and Hyeji Kim. "The World's Top 1% of Emitters Produce Over 1000 Times More CO2 than the Bottom 1%." IEA, February 22, 2023. https://www.iea.org/commentaries/the-world-s-top-1-of-emitters-produce-over-1000-times-more-co2-than-the-bottom-1.

Crichton, Michael. *Jurassic Park*. New York: Random House, 1990.

Crutzen, Paul J. "Geology of Mankind." *Nature* 415, no. 6867 (2002): 1–23. https://doi.org/10.1038/415023a.

Cubitt, Sean. *Anecdotal Evidence: Ecocritique from Hollywood to the Mass Image*. New York: Oxford University Press, 2020.

"Customer Carbon Offsetting: Ryanair's Corporate Website." Customer Carbon Offsetting | Ryanair's Corporate Website. Accessed June 24, 2023. https://corporate.ryanair.com/sustainability/customer-carbon-offsetting/.

D. G. Khan Cement Company v. Government of Punjab (The Supreme Court of Pakistan, April 15, 2021).

Dahan, Maha El. "Davos 2023: Greta Thunberg Accuses Energy Firms of Throwing People 'under the Bus." Reuters, January 20, 2023. https://www.reuters.com/world/europe/davos-2023-greta-thunberg-says-energy-firms-throwing-people-under-bus-2023-01-19/.

Danone. "Danone: A Solid Set of Full-Year 2021 Results; a Strong Finish to the Year." GlobeNewswire Newsroom, February 23, 2022. https://www.globenewswire.com/news-release/2022/02/23/2389984/0/en/DANONE-A-solid-set-of-Full-Year-2021-results-A-strong-finish-to-the-year.html.

Decision -/CP.27 Sharm el-Sheikh implementation plan—UNFCCC. Accessed July 5, 2023. https://unfccc.int/sites/default/files/resource/cop27_auv_2_cover%20decision.pdf.

Deep Impact. Paramount Pictures, 1998. https://www.netflix.com/title/11819345.

"Defending Mother Earth in Bolivia." Cultural Survival. Accessed June 16, 2023. https://www.culturalsurvival.org/news/defending-mother-earth-bolivia.

Democratic Youth Federation of India v. Union of India (Supreme Court of India, January 10, 2017).

Dewayne Johnson v. Monsanto Company (San Francisco District Court, January 28, 2016).

Dewayne Johnson v. Monsanto Company (Superior Court of California, San Francisco County, August 10, 2018).

Dewayne Johnson v. Monsanto Company (Court of Appeal, State of California, July 20, 2020).

Devi, Mahasweta. "Little Ones." In *Bitter Soil*, trans. Ipsita Chanda, 1–20, Calcutta: Seagull Books, 1998.

Devi, Mahasweta. "Pterodactyl, Puran Sahay and Pirtha." In *Imaginary Maps*, 95–196, New York: Routledge, 1995.

Devi, Mahasweta. *The Book of the Hunter*, trans. Sagaree Sengupta and Mandira Sengupta. Calcutta: Seagull Books, 2002.

Derrida, Jacques. "The Animal That Therefore I Am (More to Follow)," *Critical Enquiry* 28, no. 2 (2002): 369–83.

Di Pippo, Simonetta. United Nations OOSA Director Simonetta Di Pippo on Space Sustainability. Oxford University Space and Astronomy Society. YouTube, 2021. https://www.youtube.com/watch?v=cEJa2bp6nhU.

Directive 2008/50/EC of the European Parliament and of the Council of 21 May 2008, on ambient air quality and cleaner air for Europe. Queen's Printer of Acts of Parliament. Accessed April 17, 2023. https://www.legislation.gov.uk/eudr/2008/50/contents.

Docplexus. "Ban On Diclofenac Sodium Injection: DCGI Order." Docplexus. Accessed April 16, 2023. https://www.docplexus.com/posts/ban-on-diclofenac-sodium-injection-dcgi-order.

Donnellon-May, Genevieve. "China's Super Hydropower Dam and Fears of Sino-Indian Water Wars." *Diplomat*, December 12, 2022. https://thediplomat.com/2022/12/chinas-super-hydropower-dam-and-fears-of-sino-indian-water-wars/.

Dovey, Jon. "Documentary Ecosystems: Collaboration and Exploitation." In *New Documentary Ecologies: Emerging Platforms, Practices and Discourses*, edited by Kate Nash, Craig Hight, and Catherine Summerhayes, 11–32. Palgrave Macmillan, 2014.

Dominey-Howes, Dale. "Hazards and Disasters in the Anthropocene: Some Critical Reflections for the Future." *Geoscience Letters* 5, no. 1 (2018): 1–15.

Donnellon-May, Genevieve. "China's Super Hydropower Dam and Fears of Sino-Indian Water Wars." *Diplomat*, December 12, 2022. https://thediplomat.com/2022/12/chinas-super-hydropower-dam-and-fears-of-sino-indian-water-wars/.

Don't Look UP. Netflix Official Site, 2021. https://www.netflix.com/title/81252357.

Doxiades, Konstantinos Apostolou, and J. G. Papaioannou. *Ecumenopolis: The Inevitable City of the Future*. New York: Norton, 1974.

Drake, David, Bret Shaw, and Mary Magnuson. "Coyotes Are Here to Stay in North American Cities–Here's How to Appreciate Them from a Distance." *Conversation*, September 13, 2022. https://theconversation.com/coyotes-are-here-to-stay-in-north-american-cities-heres-how-to-appreciate-them-from-a-distance-186893.

Drewes Farms P'ship v. City of Toledo (United States District Court, N.D. Ohio, Western Division, February 27, 2020).

Dutta, Sagnik. "Mines of Scam." *Frontline*, September 19, 2014.

"Earth's Freshwater." Education. Accessed June 12, 2023. https://education.nationalgeographic.org/resource/earths-fresh-water/#:~:text=Only%20about%20three%20percent%20of,buried%20deep%20in%20the%20ground.

"Eau La La!" Perrier History | Perrier UK. Accessed June 9, 2023. https://www.perrier.com/uk/since-1863/history/eau-la-la.

Eckerman, Ingrid. *The Bhopal Saga: Causes and consequences of the world's largest industrial disaster*. Hyderabad: Universities Press, 2005.

Ecuador's Constitution of 2008—constituteproject.org. Accessed June 16, 2023. https://www.constituteproject.org/constitution/Ecuador_2008.pdf.

Edwards, Linda H. "Once Upon a Time in Law: Myth, Metaphor, and Authority." *Tennessee Law Review* 77: 883–916.

Egan, Dan. "The Wizard of Phosphorus: One Man's Quest to Turn Sewage into Eco-Gold." Big Think, March 8, 2023. https://bigthink.com/life/capture-phosphorus-sewage-wastewater/#:~:text="Phosphate%20is%20a%20biological%20accelerant,process%2C%20and%20apply%20chemical%20fertilizer.

Egerton, F. N. "Changing Concepts of the Balance of Nature." *Quarterly Review of Biology* 48 (1973): 322–50.

"Egypt Addresses UN Security Council over Ethiopia's Continued Filling of Gerd." *Egypt Independent*, August 4, 2022. https://egyptindependent.com/egypt-addresses-un-security-council-over-ethiopias-continued-filling-of-gerd/.

Eliasson, Olafur. "Ice Watch." Studio Olafur Eliasson. Accessed July 24, 2023. https://olafureliasson.net/artwork/ice-watch-2014/.

En ejercicio de sus atribuciones constitucionales y legales, expide la siguiente caso no. 1149-19-jp/20 (el pleno de la corte constitucional del ecuador 10 November 2021).

"Endangered Species." Education. Accessed April 15, 2023. https://education.nationalgeographic.org/resource/endangered-species/.

"Ende Gelände." Ende Gelände. Accessed June 28, 2023. https://www.ende-gelaende.org/en/news/ende-gelaende-ends-a-successful-week-of-action-major-gas-consumers-and-liquefied-natural-gas-terminal-construction-site-blocked-port-of-hamburg-paralyzed-for-nine-hours/.

"Every Satellite Orbiting Earth and Who Owns Them." Dewesoft. Accessed March 24, 2023. https://dewesoft.com/daq/every-satellite-orbiting-earth-and-who-owns-them.

"Evian—Danone Eaux." Danone, March 20, 2023. https://www.danone.com/fr/brands/waters/evian.html. Egypt Independent. "Egypt Addresses UN Security Council over Ethiopia's Continued Filling of Faulkner, Charlie." "Water Crisis Heightens the Risk of Famine in Afghanistan." The Third Pole, August 17, 2021. https://www.thethirdpole.net/en/food/bone-dry-afghanistan-stares-at-future-famines/.

"Federal Judge Strikes Down 'Lake Erie Bill of Rights.'" Animal Legal Defense Fund, March 29, 2021. https://aldf.org/article/federal-judge-strikes-down-lake-erie-bill-of-rights/.

"Fighting the Deadly Exotic Pet Trade to Keep Wild Animals Where They Belong–in the Wild." World Animal Protection, March 25, 2020. https://www.worldanimalprotection.org/our-work/animals-wild/exotic-pets.

Fischer, Hannah. "Investigating Animal Bites & Attacks." BOAH. Accessed April 15, 2023. https://www.in.gov/boah/files/9.-Presentation-Animal-Bite-Investigations.pdf.

Fisher, Richard. "The Environmental Case for Buying a Coal Mine." BBC Future, March 18, 2022. https://www.bbc.com/future/article/20220118-the-environmental-case-for-buying-a-coal-mine.

Fitterman, Su T. "The Dakota Access Pipeline (DAPL)—Environmental & Energy Law Program." Harvard Law School, February 28, 2023. https://eelp.law.harvard.edu/2017/10/dakota-access-pipeline/.

Flannery, Tim F. *The Weather Makers: The History and Future Impact of Climate Change*. Melbourne: Text Publishing, 2008.

Friends of the Earth, Incorporated v. Laidlaw Environmental Services (Supreme Court of the USA, January 2, 2000).

Friends of the Earth v. The Governor in Council and Others (Federal Court of Vancouver, October 20, 2008).

"Fridays for Future." Fridays for Future, February 27, 2023. https://fridaysforfuture.org/.

Fromm, Erich. *The Heart of Man: Its Genius for Good and Evil*. New York: American Mental Health Foundation Books., 2010.

Fürstenau, Marcel. "Opinion: German Coalition Government Exceeds Its Reputation ." dw.com, December 12, 2022. https://www.dw.com/en/opinion-the-german-coalition-government-exceeds-its-reputation/a-64021360.

Gallagher, Susan VanZanten. *Postcolonial Literature and the Biblical Call for Justice*. Jackson: University Press of Mississippi, 1994.

Garrard, Greg. *Ecocriticism*. London: Routledge, 2004.

Garza, Alejandro de la. "Matt Damon Wants You to Care about Water." *Time*, March 29, 2022. https://time.com/6160927/matt-damon-water/.

Gashaw Ayferam, "The Nile Dispute: Beyond water security," Carnegie Endowment, January 19, 2023. https://carnegieendowment.org/sada/88842.

Gaurav Bansal v. Union of India (Supreme Court of India, July 23, 2015).

Ghosh, Amitav. *The Glass Palace.* London: HarperCollins, 2000.

Ghosh, Amitav. *Sea of Poppies*. London: John Murray, 2008.

Ghosh, Amitav. *River of Smoke*. London: John Murray, 2011.

Ghosh, Amitav. *The Great Derangement: Climate Change and the Unthinkable*. London: University of Chicago Press, 2016.

Ghosh, Amitav. *Gun Island*. London: John Murray, 2020.

Ghosh, Amitav. *The Nutmeg's Curse: Parables for a Planet in Crisis*. Chicago: University of Chicago Press, 2021.

Gies, Erica. "Why Peru Is Reviving a Pre-Incan Technology for Water." BBC Future, May 11, 2022. https://www.bbc.com/future/article/20210510-perus-urgent-search-for-slow-water.

Gill, Gitanjali Nain. *Environmental Justice in India: The National Green Tribunal*. London: Routledge, Taylor & Francis Group, 2018.

"Girl with Balloon: From Graffiti to Art History Icon." Banksy Explained, July 13, 2021. https://banksyexplained.com/issue/girl-with-balloon-graffiti-legend/.

Gleick, Peter H. "Water, War & Peace in the Middle East." *Environment: Science and Policy for Sustainable Development* 36, no. 3 (1994): 6–42. "Global Risks Report 2023." World Economic Forum. Accessed May 17, 2023. https://www.weforum.org/reports/global-risks-report-2023, 57–58.

Glotfelty, Cheryll, and Harold Fromm. "Introduction: Literary Studies in an Age of Environmental Crisis." In *The Ecocriticism Reader: Landmarks in Literary Ecology*, edited by Cheryll Glotfelty, xv–xxxvii, Athens: University of Georgia Press, 1996.

Graham Huggan. "Greening Postcolonialism: Ecocritical Perspectives." *Modern Fiction Studies* 50, no. 3 (2004): 701–33.

"Greta Thunberg: *Time*'s Person of the Year 2019." *Time*, December 4, 2019. https://time.com/person-of-the-year-2019-greta-thunberg/.

Goldsworthy, Andy. "Three River Works." Andy Goldsworthy—Official Website, May 3, 2023. https://andygoldsworthystudio.com/three-river-works/.

"'Good Food, Good Life': Célébration des 150 ans de Nestlé." Nestlé. Accessed June 9, 2023. https://www.nestle.ch/fr/media/newsandfeatures/150-ans-de-nestl%C3%A9.

Gould, Stephen Jay. *Time's Arrow: Time's Cycle. Myth and Metaphor in the Discovery of Geological Time*. Cambridge, MA: Harvard University Press, 1987.

Gowler, David B. *The Parables After Jesus: Their Imaginative Receptions Across Two Millennia*. Grand Rapids: Baylor Academic, 2017.

Green, Joy. "Quebec's Magpie River Granted Legal Personhood." The Futures Centre, March 24, 2021. https://www.thefuturescentre.org/signal/quebecs-magpie-river-granted-legal-personhood/.

Green Fares: Fly More Sustainably | Lufthansa. Accessed June 24, 2023. https://www.lufthansa.com/us/en/green-fare.

Greenberg, Chris. "Carbon Offsets Are a Scam." Greenpeace International, May 10, 2023. https://www.greenpeace.org/international/story/50689/carbon-offsets-net-zero-greenwashing-scam/.

Greenpeace India. "Mahan Forests Inviolate—No Go for Mining Says MoEF." Greenpeace India. Accessed June 22, 2023. https://www.greenpeace.org/india/en/press/2353/mahan-forests-inviolate-no-go-for-mining-says-moef/.

Greenwashing "The Climate Disaster." Greens/EFA, January 9, 2023. https://www.greens-efa.eu/opinions/greenwashing-the-climate-disaster/.

Griffin, Paul. "Carbon Majors Report 2017." CDP, July 2017. https://www.cdp.net/en/articles/media/new-report-shows-just-100-companies-are-source-of-over-70-of-emissions.

Grush, Loren. "Virgin Galactic Says First Customers Headed to Space Soon." *Bloomberg News*, February 28, 2023. https://www.bloomberg.com/news/articles/2023-02-28/virgin-galactic-says-first-customers-head-to-space-within-months?leadSource=uverify%20wall.

"HM Courts & Tribunals Service." GOV.UK. Accessed April 17, 2023. https://www.gov.uk/government/organisations/hm-courts-and-tribunals-service.

Hannah, Neil Young and Daryl. "Let $289 Million Jury Award Stand in Monsanto Case." *San Francisco Chronicle*, October 14, 2018. https://www.sfchronicle.com/opinion/openforum/article/Let-289-million-jury-award-stand-in-Monsanto-case-13303640.php.

Hanuman Laxman Aroskar v. Union of India (The Supreme Court of India, January 16, 2020).

Hardeman v. Monsanto Company (US District Court of Francisco, February 12, 2016).

Hardeman v. Monsanto Company (United States Court of Appeal, Ninth Circuit, May 14, 2021).

Havel, Vaclav. "Politics and Conscience." *Library of Babel*, February 13, 2017. https://tayiabr.wordpress.com/2017/02/13/politics-and-conscience-vaclav-havel/.

Heffernan, James A.W. *Museum of Words: The Poetics of Ekphrasis from Homer to Ashbery*. Chicago: The University of Chicago Press, 2008.

Henderson, John, and Thomas Bewick. *Aesop's Human Zoo: Roman Stories about Our Bodies*. Chicago: University of Chicago, 2004.

Hennessy, Hannah. "Americas | Andes Drought Leaves Lima Thirsty." BBC News, May 9, 2004. http://news.bbc.co.uk/2/hi/americas/3697647.stm.

"Hérault: Un Chat Savannah Confondu Avec Un Léopard Mobilise Les Gendarmes." France 3 Occitanie. Accessed April 15, 2023. https://france3-regions.francetvinfo

.fr/occitanie/herault/montpellier/herault-chat-savannah-confondu-leopard-mobilise-gendarmes-1434175.html.

Hessel, Katy. "A Field of Wheat on a $4.5bn Patch of New York: The Prophetic Eco Art of Agnes Denes." *Guardian*, July 18, 2022. https://www.theguardian.com/artanddesign/2022/jul/18/a-field-of-wheat-on-a-45bn-patch-of-new-york-the-prophetic-eco-art-of-agnes-denes.

Hindustan Zinc Ltd. v. Rajasthan Electricity Regulatory Commission (Supreme Court of India, May 13, 2015).

Holifield, Ryan. *Spaces of environmental justice*. Malden: Wiley-Blackwell, 2010.

Holt-Jensen, Arild. *Geography, History & Concepts*. London: Sage Publications Limited, 1999.

Hofste, Rutger Willem, Paul Reig, and Leah Schleifer. "17 Countries, Home to One-Quarter of the World's Population, Face Extremely High-Water Stress." World Resources Institute, August 6, 2019. https://www.wri.org/insights/17-countries-home-one-quarter-worlds-population-face-extremely-high-water-stress.

How Animals Are Rapidly Evolving Because of Climate Change | WIRED. YouTube. WIRED, 2021. https://www.youtube.com/watch?v=uMxsflmpaYM.

"How Much Does It Cost?" ESA. Accessed March 24, 2023. https://www.esa.int/Science_Exploration/Human_and_Robotic_Exploration/International_Space_Station/How_much_does_it_cost.

Huggan, Graham, and Tiffin, Helen. *Postcolonial Ecocriticism: Literature, Animals, Environment*. New York: Routledge, 2010.

Human Rights and Peace for Bangladesh (HPRB) and others v. Secretary of the Ministry of Shipping and others (High Court of Bangladesh, January 30, 2019).

Ierland, Tom van, and Jessica M. Smith. "#NoDAPL and Online Activism: New Directions for Effectively Engaging with Critics." JPT, January 15, 2021. https://jpt.spe.org/nodapl-and-online-activism-new-directions-effectively-engaging-critics.

"India, China Sign Two MoUs on Sharing of Brahmaputra River Data, Rice Supply." The Wire, June 9, 2018. https://thewire.in/uncategorised/india-china-sign-two-mous-on-sharing-of-brahmaputra-river-data-rice-supply.

"India: Court Decision Requires Dow Chemical to Respond to Bhopal Gas Tragedy." Amnesty International, August 17, 2021. https://www.amnesty.org/en/latest/news/2013/07/india-court-decision-requires-dowchemical-respond-bhopal-gas-tragedy/.

"India Ranks Better in Animal Protection Index 2020, but Still Needs Improvements." *Business Standard*, March 12, 2020. https://www.business-standard.com/article/news-ani/india-ranks-better-in-animal-protection-index-2020-but-still-needs-improvements-120031200558_1.html.

Indian Council for Enviro-Legal Action v. Union of India and Ors (Supreme Court of India, February 13, 1996).

International Campaign for Justice in Bhopal. Accessed June 27, 2023. https://www.bhopal.net/what-happened/contamination/court-cases-environmental-liability/.

Iovino, Serenella, and Serpil Oppermann. *Material Ecocriticism*. Bloomington: Indiana University Press, 2014.

Islamabad Wildlife Management Board v. Metropolitan Corporation Islamabad & others (Islamabad High Court, May 21, 2020).

Islamic Republic of Pakistan v. Republic of India—Press Release (The Hague, May 17, 2023).

"Italy Drought: Rome Forced to Cut Water Pressure at Night." BBC News, August 29, 2017. https://www.bbc.com/news/world-europe-41081066.

Jackson, Michael. *Earth Song*. YouTube, 2015. https://www.youtube.com/watch?v =gbAd62jzrNI.

Jackson, Michael. "Michael Jackson—Earth Song." Genius. Accessed June 29, 2023. https://genius.com/Michael-jackson-earth-song-lyrics.

Jan Chetna v. Ministry of Environment & Forests (The National Green Tribunal, New Delhi, May 11, 2012).

"January 2023 Global Climate Report." January 2023 Global Climate Report | National Centers for Environmental Information (NCEI). Accessed July 5, 2023. https:// www.ncei.noaa.gov/access/monitoring/monthly-report/global/202301.

Jeff Bezos Speaks at Amazon India Event. YouTube, 2020. https://www.youtube.com /watch?v=jzfXlg-wyUU.

Jenkins, Henry. *Convergence Culture: Where Old and New Media Collide*. New York: New York University Press, 2008.

Johnson, Ty. "Google: Black-Owned Friday." Ty Johnson, November 15, 2022. https: //tyjo.co/work/googlebof/.

Jonsson H. Herbert. *Haikai Poetics: Buson, Kito and the Interpretation of Renku Poetry*. Stockholm: Stockholm University Press, 2006.

Juliana v. United States (United States District Court, Oregon, October 15, 2018).

Jurassic Park—Life Finds a Way. Universal Pictures, 1993.

Kamal, Neel. "'Sc Hasn't Upheld Monsanto's Patents on Seeds': Chandigarh News—*Times* of India." *Times of India*, January 10, 2019. https://timesofindia.indiatimes .com/city/chandigarh/sc-hasnt-upheld-monsantos-patents-on-seeds/articleshow /67462493.cms.

Karnail Singh & Ors v. State of Haryana (Punjab-Haryana High Court, May 31, 2019).

Karnataka Industrial Areas Development Board v. Sri C. Kenchappa & Ors (The Supreme Court of India, May 12, 2006).

Kashyap, Aruna, Becker, Jo, and Ganguly, Meenakshi. "'Being Neutral Is Our Biggest Crime': Government, Vigilante, and Naxalite Abuses in Chhattisgarh State." New York: Human Rights Watch, 2008.

Keefe, Joni. "Farms Finest: Green-Washing Tactics Abound." AspenTimes.com, August 24, 2016. https://www.aspentimes.com/news/farms-finest-green-washing -tactics-abound/.

Kelsen, Hans. *Introduction to the Problems of Legal Theory: A Translation of the First Edition of the Reine Rechtslehre or Pure Theory of Law*. Oxford University Press: New York, 1992.

Khan, Ilyas M. "Kaavan, the World's Loneliest Elephant, Is Finally Going Free." BBC News. BBC, November 28, 2020. https://www.bbc.com/news/world-asia -55060433.

Kipling, Rudyard. *The Jungle Books*. Oxford: Oxford World's Classics, 1996.

Kipling, Rudyard. "Beyond the Pale." In *Plain Tales from the Hills*, 127–32, Oxford: Oxford University Press, 1996.

Kobilinsky, Dana. "Climate Warming Changes Bird Migration Timing and Body Size." The Wildlife Society, January 8, 2023. https://wildlife.org/climate-warming-changes-bird-migration-timing-and-body-size/.

Koigi, Beth. "Majik Water." Beth Koigi: Majik water | TED Talk. Accessed June 9, 2023. https://www.ted.com/talks/beth_koigi_majik_water.

Kowitt, Beth. "Can Monsanto Save the Planet?" Fortune, June 7, 2021. https://fortune.com/longform/monsanto-fortune-500-gmo-foods/#:~:text=Monsanto%20sells%20not%20only%20its,million%20acres%20around%20the%20globe.

Kumar, Ruchi. "Iran and Afghanistan Face off over Sharing Helmand Waters." The National, May 28, 2023. https://www.thenationalnews.com/mena/2023/05/28/iran-and-afghanistan-face-off-over-sharing-helmand-waters/.

Kumar, Ananth. "How Perungudi Dump Yard Has Made Life Difficult for Residents in Chennai's IT Corridor." Citizen Matters, Chennai, June 8, 2023. https://chennai.citizenmatters.in/perungudi-dumpyard-mashland-pallikaranai-fire-pollution-biomining-75904.

"La Société Protectrice des Animaux." SPA. Accessed April 15, 2023. https://www.la-spa.fr/.

Lalit Miglani v. State of Uttarakhand & Others (High Court of Nainital, Uttarakhand, March 30, 2017).

Lanari, Nora, and John Overton. "Dam Stories: Using Narrative Analysis to Understand the Debate over Water Security and the Waimea Community Dam." New Zealand Geographer 78, no. 1 (2022): 51–62. https://doi.org/10.1111/nzg.12329.

Land and Environment Court of New South Wales. Accessed April 17, 2023. https://www.lec.nsw.gov.au/.

Laboureau, Sebastien. "Show Me the Monet, 2005." Banksy Explained, September 18, 2022. https://banksyexplained.com/show-me-the-monet-2005/.

Latour, Bruno. *Facing Gaia: Eight Lectures on the New Climatic Regime*. Cambridge: Polity, 2017.

Latour, Bruno. *Reassembling the Social: An Introduction to Actor-Network Theory*. Oxford: Oxford University Press, 2005.

Le Monde with AP and AFP. "Greta Thunberg Detained at German Coal Mine Protest." *Le Monde*, January 17, 2023. https://www.lemonde.fr/en/germany/article/2023/01/17/greta-thunberg-detained-at-german-coal-mine-protest_6011960_146.html.

"Learn about the Amazon Rainforest." WWF. Accessed April 15, 2023. https://www.wwf.org.uk/where-we-work/amazon.

Liebman, Alex. "Trickle-down Hegemony? China's 'Peaceful Rise' and Dam Building on the Mekong." *Contemporary Southeast Asia* 27, no. 2 (2005): 281–304. https://doi.org/10.1355/cs27-2f.

Life Insurance Corporation of India v. Escorts Ltd. & Ors (Supreme Court of India, December 19, 1985).

Litigation and Entitlement Kendra & Ors v. State of U. P. & Ors (Supreme Court of India, March 12, 1985).

Lovelock, James. *Gaia: A New Look at Life on Earth*. Oxford: Oxford University Press, 1979.

Lovelock, James. *The Vanishing Face of Gaia*. London: Penguin, 2009.

Ludka, Alexandra. “Hitchcock’s ‘The Birds’: Mystery Solved.” ABC News. ABC News Network, December 28, 2011. https://abcnews.go.com/blogs/entertainment/2011/12/hitchcocks-the-birds-mystery-solved.

Lui, Ana. “33 Is the Magic Number—to Being 33 Forever.” Ana Lui Photography I Ibiza & Mallorca Editorial Commercial Travel Photographer, August 3, 2016. https://www.analuiphotography.com/blog/33-is-the-magic-number#:~:text=Number%2033%20is%20a%20Master,number%20that%20symbolizes%20%27guidance%27.

M.C. Mehta v. Union of India & Ors (The Supreme Court of India, July 8, 1996).

“Major Fire in Perungudi Dumpyard.” *Hindu*, April 27, 2022. https://www.thehindu.com/news/cities/chennai/major-fire-in-perungudi-dumpyard/article65361006.ece.

Manes, Christopher. “Nature and Silence.” In *The Ecocriticism Reader: Landmarks in Literary Ecology*, edited by Cheryll Glotfelty and Harold Fromm, 15–29. Athens: University of Georgia Press, 1996.

Manohar Lal Sharma v. The Principal Secretary & Ors (Supreme Court of India, August 25, 2014).

“Map of Private Exotic Pet Ownership Laws.” Animal Law Legal Center. Accessed April 16, 2023. https://www.animallaw.info/content/map-private-exotic-pet-ownership-laws.

“Marc Buckley Taking ‘Earthshots’ and Inspiring Innovations for Purpose.” Techsauce. Accessed July 10, 2023. https://techsauce.co/en/sustainable-focus/marc-buckley-earthshots-innovation.

“Martyl Langsdorf. Designer of the Doomsday Clock.” Bulletin of the Atomic Scientists, Accessed March 23, 2023. https://thebulletin.org/virtual-tour/martyl-langsdorf-designer-of-the-doomsday-clock/.

Massachusetts v. Environmental Protection Agency (Supreme Court of the USA, April 2, 2007).

“May Prehistory Thunder Forward: The Resurrection of the Woolly Mammoth.” Colossal, October 10, 2022. https://colossal.com/mammoth/.

Mecklin, John. “Current Time—2023.” Bulletin of the Atomic Scientists, January 24, 2023. https://thebulletin.org/doomsday-clock/current-time/.

Meet the Water Sommelier. CBS Sunday Morning. YouTube, 2021. https://www.youtube.com/watch?v=7YKbeh3cKpY.

Meredith, Sam. “Boris Johnson Warns It’s ‘One Minute to Midnight’ to Prevent Climate Catastrophe.” CNBC. CNBC, November 1, 2021. https://www.cnbc.com/2021/11/01/cop26-boris-johnson-says-one-minute-to-midnight-amid-climate-crisis.html.

Millar, Will. “Doomsday Clock: What Is It, How Close Is It to Midnight, and What Time Have Scientists Set It to in 2023?” January 24, 2023. Accessed March 2023. https://www.londonworld.com/read-this/doomsday-clock-what-is-it

-how-close-is-it-to-midnight-and-what-time-are-scientists-due-to-set-it-in-2023-3999447.

Mohammed Salim v. State of Uttarakhand & others (High Court of Uttarakhand, Nainital, March 20, 2017).

Mohanta, Nibedita. "How Many Satellites Are Orbiting around Earth in 2022?" Geospatial World, January 6, 2023. https://www.geospatialworld.net/prime/how-many-satellites-orbiting-earth/.

Monsanto Technology LLC v. Nuziveedu Seeds Ltd (Delhi High Court, March 28, 2017).

Monsanto Technology LLC v. Nuziveedu Seeds Ltd (Supreme Court of India, January 8, 2019).

Morton, Timothy. "This Is Not My Beautiful Biosphere." In *A Cultural History of Climate Change*, edited by Tom Bristow and Thomas Ford, 229–38, New York: Routledge, 2016.

Mukherjee, Pablo. "'Tomorrow There Will Be More of Us': Toxic Postcoloniality in Animal's People." In *Postcolonial Ecologies: Literatures of the Environment*, edited by George B. Handley and Elizabeth M DeLoughrey. New York: Oxford University Press, 2011.

"Online Rally: Respect Wangan and Jagalingou." Stop Adani. Accessed July 13, 2023. https://www.stopadani.com/respect_wangan_and_jagalingou_online.

N.R Nair & others v. Union of India (Kerala High Court, June 6, 2000).

Nain, Gitanjali Gill. *Environmental Justice in India: The National Green Tribunal*. Earthscan from Routledge, New York, 2017.

Nakate, Vanessa. "Vanessa Nakate Bigger Picture: Climate Justice in Africa." *Time*, October 28, 2021. https://time.com/6109452/vanessa-nakate-climate-justice/.

Nanda, Meera. *Prophets Facing Backward: Postmodern Critiques of Science and Hindu Nationalism in India*. New Brunswick: Rutgers University Press, 2003.

Nandi, Jayashree. "115% Rise in Forest Fires This Month." *Hindustan Times*, March 13, 2023. https://www.hindustantimes.com/india-news/115-rise-in-forest-fires-this-month-101678733527908.html.

Namjoshi, Suniti. *The Blue Donkey Fables*. London: Women's Press, 1988.

Namjoshi, Suniti. *Dangerous Pursuits*. New Delhi: Penguin Zubaan, 2022.

Narayan Dutt Bhatt v. Union of India and Others (Uttaranchal High Court, July 4, 2018).

Narmada Bachao Andolan v. Union of India & Ors (Supreme Court of India, March 15, 2005).

Naruto v. David Slater (United States Court of Appeals for the Ninth Circuit, July 12, 2017).

Nasrat Sayed and Said Hashmat Sadat. "Climate Change Compounds Longstanding Displacement in Afghanistan." migrationpolicy.org, June 29, 2022. https://www.migrationpolicy.org/article/climate-change-displacement-afghanistan.

National Green Tribunal. Accessed April 17, 2023. https://www.greentribunal.gov.in/.

Nelson, Prince Rogers. "1999." Prince—1999 Lyrics | Lyrics.com. Accessed March 21, 2023. https://www.lyrics.com/lyric/8706616/1999.

"Nestlé Reports Full-Year Results for 2022." Nestlé Global. Accessed June 9, 2023. https://www.nestle.com/media/pressreleases/allpressreleases/full-year-results-2022.

"New Legislation for Carbon Reduction in India." Infineum Insight, March 20, 2023. https://www.infineuminsight.com/en-gb/articles/new-legislation-for-carbon-reduction-in-india/#:~:text=After%20being%20approved%20by%20both,aims%20to%20reduce%20carbon%20emissions.

"New Water Treatment Plant Tests Stanford Technology for Cleaning Wastewater While Creating Energy." Stanford News Service, May 11, 2018. https://news.stanford.edu/press-releases/2018/05/11/new-plant-tests-treat-wastewater/.

New Zealand Māori Council v. Attorney-General (New Zealand Supreme Court, August 29, 2013).

Nolan, Connor, Jonathan T. Overpeck, Judy R. Allen, Patricia M. Anderson, Julio L. Betancourt, Heather A. Binney, Simon Brewer, et al. "Past and Future Global Transformation of Terrestrial Ecosystems under Climate Change." *Science* 361, no. 6405 (2018): 920–23.

Nonhuman Rights Project, Inc. v. Breheny (Court of Appeals of New York, June 14, 2022).

Nuziveedu Seeds Ltd v. Monsanto Technology LLC (Delhi High Court, April 11, 2018).

Ocampo-Peñuela, Natalia, John Garcia-Ulloa, Itto Kornecki, Christopher D. Philipson, and Jaboury Ghazoul. "Impacts of Four Decades of Forest Loss on Vertebrate Functional Habitat on Borneo." Frontiers, April 9, 2020. https://www.frontiersin.org/articles/10.3389/ffgc.2020.00053/full.

Olivier, Mark. "Banksy's Painted Elephant Is Illegal, Say Officials." *Guardian*. Guardian News and Media, September 18, 2006. https://www.theguardian.com/uk/2006/sep/18/arts.artsnews.

Olsen, Jan M. "Norway's Government Apologizes to Sami Reindeer Herders." AP NEWS. Associated Press, March 2, 2023. https://apnews.com/article/norway-protest-wind-farm-sami-reindeer-904e83b5be17d8c4c8febf131227ef4b.

"On Quit India Day, Modi-Shivraj Asked to Quit Narmada Valley." TwoCircles.net, August 9, 2015. http://twocircles.net/2015aug09/1439131493.html.

"One Planet. One Health." Danone, November 4, 2019. https://www.danone.com/fr/stories/one-planet-one-health.html.

"One Water Spotlight: Stickney Water Reclamation Plant." One Water Spotlight: Stickney Water Reclamation Plant | US Water Alliance. Accessed June 9, 2023. https://uswateralliance.org/resources/one-water-spotlight-stickney-water-reclamation-plant.

Ong, Walter J. *Orality and literacy: The Technologizing of the Word*. London and New York: Routledge, 2002.

Oppermann, Serpil. "Ecocriticism: Natural World in the Literary Viewfinder." *Journal of Faculty Letters*, Hateceppe University of Ankara Turkey, 1999, 1–16.

Oppermann, Serpil. "Material Ecocriticism and the Creativity of Storied Matter." *Frame* 26, no. 2 (November 2013): 55–69.

Orr, David. *Ecological Literacy: Education and the Transition to a Postmodern World*. Albany: State University of New York Press, 1992.

Palanichamy, Raj Bhagat. "How Does a Flood-Prone City Run out of Water? Inside Chennai's 'Day Zero' Crisis." World Resources Institute, June 25, 2019. https://www.wri.org/insights/how-does-flood-prone-city-run-out-water-inside-chennais-day-zero-crisis.

Palmer, Edwin H. *The Holy Bible, New International Version: Containing the Old Testament and the New Testament*. Grand Rapids: Zondervan, 1984.

Patkar, Medha. "Narmada: Petition for President, CJ, PM, Saying 2 Lakh People May Face Submergence—Counterview—30.8.19." Narmada Bachao Andolan, August 31, 2019. https://narmadaandolan.org/narmada-petition-for-president-cj-pm-saying-2-lakh-people-may-face-submergence-counterview-30-8-19/.

Patel, Bharat, and Manisha Goswami. "In Vapi, Can Decades of Damage Be Finally Turned Around?" In *Making the Law Count: Ten Environmental Justice Stories by Community Paralegals in India*, 20–24. New Delhi: Namati, 2018.

"People for the Ethical Treatment of Animals (PETA)." PETA. Accessed April 24, 2023. https://www.peta.org/.

People's Charioteer Organization v. Union of India (Supreme Court of India, March 29, 2023).

Pierini, Jean-Bernard. "Carbon Offsetting—Greenfield, Patrick. "Revealed: More than 90% of Rainforest Carbon Offsets by Biggest Certifier Are Worthless, Analysis Shows." *Guardian*, January 18, 2023. https://www.theguardian.com/environment/2023/jan/18/revealed-forest-carbon-offsets-biggest-provider-worthless-verra-aoe.

Pilliod et al. v. Monsanto Company (Alameda County Superior Court (Oakland) March 28, 2019).

Pilliod v. Monsanto Company (Court of Appeal, First District, Division 2, California August 9, 2021).

Pilliod et al. v. Monsanto Company (Supreme Court of the United States, June 27, 2022).

Pine, D. W. "Behind Time's Optical Illusion Climate Change Cover." *Time*, October 27, 2022. https://time.com/6224632/olafur-eliasson-time-magazine-cover/.

"Planet: BA Sustainability, Carbon Reduction & Net Zero." Planet | BA Sustainability, Carbon Reduction & Net Zero. Accessed June 25, 2023. https://www.britishairways.com/en-gb/information/about-ba/ba-better-world/planet.

"Power Stocks Fall up to 7 P.C. on SC Order on Coal Allocation." *Hindu*, November 16, 2021. https://www.thehindu.com/business/markets/power-stocks-fall-up-to-7-pc-on-sc-order-on-coal-allocation/article6353862.ece?utm_source=RSS_Feed&utm_medium=RSS&utm_campaign=RSS_Syndication.

"Power of Priya." Power of Priya. Accessed July 1, 2023. https://www.priyashakti.com/.

"Principle 7: UN Global Compact." Principle 7 | UN Global Compact. Accessed July 3, 2023. https://unglobalcompact.org/what-is-gc/mission/principles/principle-7.

"Principle 10." UNEP. Accessed April 16, 2023. https://www.unep.org/civil-society-engagement/partnerships/principle-10.

Priya and the Twirling Wind. https://www.youtube.com/watch?v=cwaJya0jaBQ, n.d. Accessed July 1, 2023.

"Progress on Household Drinking Water, Sanitation and Hygiene, 2000–2020: Five Years into the Sdgs." UNICEF DATA, June 16, 2022. https://data.unicef.org/resources/progress-on-household-drinking-water-sanitation-and-hygiene-2000-2020/.

Punamchand v. Union of India & Ors (National Green Tribunal, Pune April 16, 2014).

"Q'inti the Hummingbird—A Quechen Story." The Flight of the Hummingbird. Accessed June 22, 2023. https://www.hummingbird.vancouveropera.ca/story.

R (on the application of ClientEarth) v. The Secretary of State for the Environment, Food and Rural Affairs (CJEU November 19, 2014).

R (on the application of ClientEarth) v. Secretary of State for the Environment, Food and Rural Affairs (UKSC April 29, 2015).

Rajagopal, Krishnadas. "There Will Be at Least One Constitution Bench in Supreme Court throughout the Year: CJI-Designate U.U. Lalit." *Hindu*, August 26, 2022. https://www.thehindu.com/news/national/there-will-be-at-least-one-constitution-bench-in-supreme-court-throughout-the-year-cji-designate-uu-lalit/article65814413.ece.

Rajiv Dutta v. Union of India (National Green Tribunal, New Delhi May 2, 2019).

Ramnath, Kalyani. "The Runaway Judgment: Law-as-Literature, Courtcraft and Constitutional Vision." *Journal of Indian Law and Society* 3 (2011).

Rathod, Vijay. "Saving Sangam from Mining." *In Making the Law Count: Ten Environmental Justice Stories by Community Paralegals in India*, 8–10. New Delhi: Namati, 2018.

Reisner, Erwin. "Solar-Powered Carbon Capture Breakthrough Could 'Cut Fossil Fuels Out.'" Euronews, June 23, 2023. https://www.euronews.com/green/2023/01/11/new-solar-powered-technology-can-transform-plastic-waste-into-sustainable-fuels-and-cosmet.

"Report High Level Committee to Review Various Acts Administered by Ministry of Environment, Forest & Climate Change, Government of India November 2014." Accessed April 17, 2023. https://www.naredco.in/notification/pdfs/Final_Report_of_HLC.pdf.

Research Foundation for Science v. Union of India & Anr (Supreme Court of India, July 6, 2012).

"Rhône. Villeurbanne: Un Félin Attaque Des Lapins Et Échappe Aux Recherches." Rhône. Villeurbanne: un félin attaque des lapins et échappe aux recherches. Le Progrès, January 4, 2016. https://www.leprogres.fr/rhone/2016/01/03/villeurbanne-un-felin-attaque-des-lapins-et-echappe-aux-recherches.

Richard Frederick Wheeler y Eleanor Geer Huddle c/ Gobierno Provincial de Loja, juicio 11121-2011-0010 (March 30, 2011).

Ridhima Pandey v. Union of India (National Green Tribunal, New Delhi, January 15, 2019).

Roy, Arundhati. "Walking with the Comrades." In *Broken Republic: Three Essays*, 37–146. New Delhi: Hamish Hamilton, 2011.

Roy, Arundhati. "Mr Chidambaram's War." In *Broken Republic: Three Essays*, 1–36. New Delhi, 2011.
Roy, Arundhati. "There's No Escape from the Corporations That Run India | Arundhati Roy." *Guardian*, March 19, 2012. https://www.theguardian.com/commentisfree/2012/mar/19/corporations-india-arundhati-roy.
Roy, Arundhati. *Capitalism: A Ghost Story*. London: Verso Books, 2015.
Roy, Arundhati. "On Citizen's Rights to Express Dissent." In *My Seditious Heart: Collected Non-Fiction*, 150–59. Gurgaon: Hamish Hamilton, 2019.
Rueckert, William. "Literature and Ecology: An Experiment in Ecocriticism." In *The Ecocriticism Reader: Landmarks in Literary Ecology*, edited by Cheryll Glotfelty and Harold Fromm, 105–23. Athens: University of Georgia Press, 1996.
Rushdie, Salman. *Grimus*. London: Gollancz, 1975.
Rust, Stephen, Salma Monani, and Sean Cubbitt. *Ecomedia: Key Issues in Environment and Sustainability*. New York: Earthscan Routledge, 2016.
Ryding, Sara, and Matthew Symonds. "Animals Are Changing Their Body Shapes to Cope with Climate Change." World Economic Forum, September 13, 2021. https://www.weforum.org/agenda/2021/09/climate-change-animals-global-warming-shape.
Rylands v. Fletcher (House of Lords, July 17, 1868).
S. Jagannath v. Union of India & Ors (Supreme Court of India, December 11, 1996).
Sahu v. Union Carbide Corporation (Southern District Court of New York, September 22, 2009).
Said, Edward. *Culture and Imperialism*. London: Chatto and Windus, 1996.
Said, Edward. *Orientalism—Literary Theory: An Anthology*. Cornwall: Blackwell, 1998.
Samvaad, Dhanush. "Ministry of Tribal Affairs, Government of India." Ministry of Tribal Affairs—Government of India. Accessed June 16, 2023. https://tribal.nic.in/FRA.aspx.
Sandy, Matt. "Why Is the Amazon Rain Forest Disappearing?" *Time*. Accessed June 19, 2023. https://time.com/amazon-rainforest-disappearing/.
Sayed, Nasrat, and Said Hashmat Sadat. "Climate Change Compounds Longstanding Displacement in Afghanistan." migrationpolicy.org, June 29, 2022. https://www.migrationpolicy.org/article/climate-change-displacement-afghanistan.
Schapiro, Mark. *Seeds of Resistance: The Fights to Save our Food Supply*. New York: Hot Books, 2018.
Schlosberg, David. *Defining Environmental Justice: Theories, Movements, and Nature*. Oxford: Oxford University Press, 2007.
Scott-Geddes, Arthur. "Un Space Chief Calls for Mass Action to Save Earth and Cosmos." *The National*, July 4, 2021. https://www.thenationalnews.com/uae/environment/un-space-chief-for-mass-action-to-save-earth-and-cosmos-1.1085174.
Seiller, Cécile. "Transmigration." *Another Chicago Magazine*, June 19, 2023. https://anotherchicagomagazine.net/2023/05/30/transmigration-by-cecile-seiller/.
Sen, Sudeep. *Anthropocene: Climate Change, Contagion, Consolation*. Sutton: Pippa Rann Books & Media, 2021.
Sen, Sudeep. *Red*. Gauteng: Nirox Foundation, 2023.

Serenella, Iovino. *Material Ecocriticism*. Bloomington: Indiana University Press, 2014.
Sethi, Nitin. "Dow Re-Labelled, Sold UCC Products to Evade Law: India News—Times of India." *Times of India*, January 29, 2012. https://timesofindia.indiatimes.com/india/dow-re-labelled-sold-ucc-products-to-evade-law/articleshow/11669179.cms?utm_source=contentofinterest&utm_medium=text&utm_campaign=cppst.
Shanahan, Ed. "Happy the Elephant Isn't Legally a Person, Top New York Court Rules." *New York Times*, June 14, 2022. https://www.nytimes.com/2022/06/14/nyregion/happy-elephant-animal-rights.html.
Shepherd, Nick. "Making Sense of 'Day Zero': Slow Catastrophes, Anthropocene Futures, and the Story of Cape Town's Water Crisis." *Water* 11, no. 9 (2019): 1–19. https://doi.org/10.3390/w11091744.
Shiva, Vandana. *Staying Alive: Women, Ecology, and Development*. Berkeley: North Atlantic Books, 2016.
Shiva, Vandana, and Kartikey Shiva. *Oneness vs. the 1%: Shattering Illusions, Seeding Freedom*. Vermont: Chelsea Green Publishing, 2020.
Sierra Club v. Morton, 405 U.S. 727 (U.S. Supreme Court, April 19, 1972).
Sillito, David. "Hashtag Is 'Children's Word of Year.'" BBC News, May 27, 2015. https://www.bbc.com/news/entertainment-arts-32902170.
Silva, José da. "Olafur Eliasson Floods Museum and Removes Wall, Opening It 24-Hours-a-Day to 'Insects, Bats or Birds.'" *The Art Newspaper—International art news and events*, September 28, 2021. https://www.theartnewspaper.com/2021/04/21/olafur-eliasson-floods-museum-and-removes-wall-opening-it-24-hours-a-day-to-insects-bats-or-birds-and-people.
"Six National Priorities Towards Implementation Of The 2030 Agenda." United Nations. Accessed July 15, 2023. https://sdgs.un.org/partnerships/six-national-priorities-towards-implementation-2030-agenda.
Shores of Silence | The Slaughter of Whales Sharks in India. YouTube, 2017. https://www.youtube.com/watch?v=TVMW_6_dVhE. Stromberg, Joseph, and Sarah Zielinski.
Slater, David J. *Wildlife Personalities*. New York: Blurb, Wildlife Personalities Ltd, 2014.
Shut Shit Down—An Activist's Guide to Ende Gelände. Accessed June 28, 2023. https://www.ende-gelaende.org/wp-content/uploads/2021/02/Basics-Ende-Gelaende-online-version.pdf.
Singh, Vandana. *The Woman Who Thought She Was a Planet*. Penguin Random House India Private Limited, 2008.
Sinha, Indra. *Animal's People*. London: Simon & Schuster, 2007.
Slovic, Scott. "Ecocriticism: Containing Multitudes, Practising Doctrine." In *The Green Studies Reader: From Romanticism to Ecocriticism*, edited by Laurence Coupe, 160–62. London: Routledge, 2000.
Smith, Adrian, Dickinson, Bruce. "2 Minutes to Midnight." Iron Maiden—2 Minutes to Midnight Lyrics | Lyrics.com. Accessed March 23, 2023. https://www.lyrics.com/lyric/4937868/Iron+Maiden/2+Minutes+to+Midnight.

Smith, Brad. "Microsoft Will Be Carbon Negative by 2030." *The Official Microsoft Blog*, July 23, 2020. https://blogs.microsoft.com/blog/2020/01/16/microsoft-will-be-carbon-negative-by-2030/.

Smith, Jonathan. "This Biotech Uses Bacterial Proteins to Purify Water Faster." Labiotech.eu, June 24, 2022. https://www.labiotech.eu/startup-scout/water-purification-aquaporin-osmosis/.

Society for Protection of Environment and Biodiversity v. Union of India (National Green Tribunal, December 8, 2017).

Solastalgia—Stiller/Tremblay. Solastalgia, 2019. https://www.solastalgia.ca.

"Solastalgia." Kalmar Art Museum. Accessed June 24, 2023. https://www.kalmarkonstmuseum.se/en/exhibition/solastalgia/.

"Steelcase Announces Carbon Neutrality and Goal to Be Carbon Negative by 2030." Steelcase, October 14, 2020. https://www.steelcase.com/press-releases/steelcase-announces-carbon-neutrality-goal-carbon-negative-2030/.

Som, Reba. "Ektuku Chhoya Lage." In *Rabindranath Tagore: The Singer and His Song*. New Delhi: Penguin, 2017.

State of Andhra Pradesh v. State of Karnataka (Supreme Court of India, September 28, 2022).

State of Uttaranchal v. Balwant Singh Chaufal & Ors (Supreme Court of India, January 18, 2010).

Stevens, Wallace. *Collected Poems of Wallace Stevens*. New York: Alfred K. Knopf, 1971.

Stipe, Michael. "It's the End of the World Lyrics by R.E.M. from Blast from the Past Soundtrack." It's The End of the World Lyrics—STLyrics.com. Accessed March 23, 2023. https://www.stlyrics.com/lyrics/blastfromthepast/itstheendoftheworld.htm.

Subhash C. Pandey v. Union of India (The Green Tribunal, August 20, 2014).

Subhash Kumar v. State of Bihar and Ors (Supreme Court of India, January 9, 1991).

Sukhdev Vihar Welfare Residents Association v. Union of India (National Green Tribunal, New Delhi, February 2, 2017).

"Summary for Policymakers." Global Warming of 1.5 °C. Accessed April 15, 2023. https://www.ipcc.ch/sr15/chapter/spm/.

"Sundargarh: Why Tribals of Kharia Community Protesting against Odisha Govt?" Ground Report, October 22, 2022. https://groundreport.in/sundargarh-why-tribals-of-kharia-community-protesting-against-odisha-govt/.

Sutter, John, and Lawrence Davidson. "Teen Tells Climate Negotiators They Aren't Mature Enough." CNN, December 17, 2018. https://edition.cnn.com/2018/12/16/world/greta-thunberg-cop24/index.html.

Suvin, Darko. *Metamorphoses of Science Fiction: On the Poetics and History of a Literary Genre*. New Haven: Yale University Press, 1079.

Tamil Nadu Pollution Control Board v. Sterlite Industries (I) Ltd. (Supreme Court of India February 18, 2019), section 124.

Tate. "Art Terms." Tate. Accessed June 29, 2023. https://www.tate.org.uk/art/art-terms/e.

Team, 4ocean. "How Plastic Ingestion Impacts Dolphins and Porpoises." 4ocean, December 1, 2018. https://www.4ocean.com/blogs/cause-of-the-month/how-plastic-ingestion-impacts-dolphins-and-porpoises.

Tejpal, Cara. "'Not Just Films': Exploring Conservation with Riverbank Studios." Sanctuary Nature Foundation, April 14, 2021. https://sanctuarynaturefoundation.org/article/%22not-just-films%22%3A-exploring-conservation-with-riverbank-studios.

"Ten Threatened and Endangered Species Used in Traditional Medicine." Smithsonian.com. Smithsonian Institution, October 18, 2011. https://www.smithsonianmag.com/science-nature/ten-threatened-and-endangered-species-used-in-traditional-medicine-112814487/.

The Goa Foundation Anr v. Union of India Ors (National Green Tribunal, New Delhi, July 18, 2013).

The Hidden Lives of Pets. Netflix, 2022. https://www.netflix.com/title/81318943.

"Tensions over Nearly Finished Gerd Rooted in National Identity, Experts Say." Africa Defense Forum, April 18, 2023. https://adf-magazine.com/2023/04/tensions-over-nearly-finished-gerd-rooted-in-national-identity-experts-say/.

"The Animal Turn." NC State University Libraries. Accessed April 24, 2023. https://www.lib.ncsu.edu/animal-turn.

The Annie E. Casey Foundation. "What the Statistics Say about Generation Z." The Annie E. Casey Foundation, November 14, 2020. https://www.aecf.org/blog/generation-z-statistics#:~:text=Meet%20Generation%20Z.,is%20adding%20members%20through%202025.

The Black Gold Tapestry. Accessed June 29, 2023. https://www.theblackgoldtapestry.com/.

"#RiseUpMovement." website. Accessed July 1, 2023. https://www.riseupmov.org/.

"The Climate Pledge." The Climate Pledge—Amazon, November 17, 2021. https://www.aboutamazon.eu/planet/the-climate-pledge.

"The Constitutional Scheme of Animal Rights in India." Animal Law Legal Center, January 1, 1970. https://www.animallaw.info/article/constitutional-scheme-animal-rights-india#:~:text=Article%2048A%20lays%20down%20the,and%20wildlife%20of%20the%20country.

"The European Union Legislation on Animal Welfare: State of Play, Enforcement and Future Activities." La Fondation Droit Animal, Ethique et Sciences, February 16, 2021. https://www.fondation-droit-animal.org/proceedings-aw/the-european-union-legislation-on-animal-welfare/.

"The Impact of Climate Change on Our Planet's Animals." IFAW. Accessed April 15, 2023. https://www.ifaw.org/uk/journal/impact-climate-change-animals.

The Last Migration. YouTube. YouTube, 2013. https://www.youtube.com/watch?v=WHVwd91pzKg.

"The Origins & History of the RSPCA." RSPCA. Accessed April 15, 2023. https://www.rspca.org.uk/whatwedo/whoweare/history. Vincendon, Salomé. "Renards, Sangliers, Ours . . . Que Viennent Faire Les Animaux Sauvages En Ville?" BFMTV. Accessed April 15, 2023. https://www.bfmtv.com/animaux/renard-sangliers-ours-que-viennent-faire-les-animaux-sauvages-en-ville_AN-202208210013.html.

The Seeds of Vandana Shiva. CORE, 2022. core.live/movies/the-seeds-of-vandana-shiva-movie.

"The Water Box: Jaden Smith's ambitious plan to provide clean water in Flint—and the rest of America." Accessed June 9, 2023. https://www.fastcompany.com/90400006/the-water-box-jaden-smiths-ambitious-plan-to-provide-clean-water-in-flint-and-the-rest-of-america.

The Yes Men. United Artists—MGM, 2003.

"The Yes Men Are Revolting," 2015. https://i-d.vice.com/en/article/bjnqk5/the-yes-men-turn-their-media-spoofing-stunts-to-tackling-climate-change.

The Yes Men Fix the World. YouTube, 2010. https://www.youtube.com/watch?v=JszDiLiY7EY.

Thunberg, Greta. "'Our House Is on Fire': Greta Thunberg, 16, Urges Leaders to Act on Climate." *Guardian*, January 25, 2019. https://www.theguardian.com/environment/2019/jan/25/our-house-is-on-fire-greta-thunberg16-urges-leaders-to-act-on-climate.

"Thoraipakkam Residents Raise a Stink Over Biomining at Perungudi Dump Yard." *Hindu*, November 30, 2022. https://www.thehindu.com/news/cities/chennai/thoraipakkam-residents-raise-a-stink-over-biomining-at-perungudi-dump-yard/article66206156.ece.

Tigris-Euphrates Alluvial Salt Marsh." One Earth. Accessed May 18, 2023. https://www.oneearth.org/ecoregions/tigris-euphrates-alluvial-salt-marsh/.

Tilikum v. Sea World Parks Sea World Parks & Entertainment, Inc (United States District Court of California, February 8, 2012).

"*Time* Magazine Cover: Endangered Earth, Planet of the Year." *Time*, January 2, 1989. https://content.time.com/time/covers/0,16641,19890102,00.html.

"*Time* Magazine Cover: Heroes of the Environment—Oct. 5, 2009." *Time*, October 5, 2009. https://content.time.com/time/covers/asia/0,16641,20091005,00.html.

Tolkien, John Ronald Reuel. *The Lord of the Rings*. London: Houghton Mifflin Company, 2004.

"Top 20 Countries with the most Number of Dams." Numerical.co.in. Accessed June 11, 2023. https://numerical.co.in/numerons/collection/60e1d4b6ef7874158890333f.

Trocki, Carl A. *Opium, Empire and the Global Political Economy*. London: Routledge, 1999.

Twain, Mark. *The Stolen White Elephant*. London: Chatto & Windus, 1918.

"Un Manchot Géant Se Dresse Devant La Gare de Reims." Actus—Champagne FM, January 11, 2022. https://www.champagnefm.com/un-manchot-gant-se-dresse-devant-la-gare-de-reims#:~:text=Il%20s%27agit%20d%27une,aux%20dangers%20du%20réchauffement%20climatique.

"UN Environment Document Repository Home." UNEP. Accessed April 17, 2023. https://wedocs.unep.org/bitstream/handle/20.500.11822/29567/ELGP1StockD.pdf.

"UN Framework Convention on Climate Change." Unfccc.int. Accessed April 17, 2023. https://unfccc.int/.

"Update 3-Vattenfall Eyes Sale of German Lignite Assets after Posting Huge Loss." Reuters, October 30, 2014. https://www.reuters.com/article/vattenfall-results-idUKL5N0SP1XE20141030.

U.S. v. Larson (United States Court of Appeals, Eighth Circuit April 10, 1997).

*Union of India v. Union Carbide Corporatio*n (Supreme Court of India, March 14, 2023).

Urgenda Foundation v. The Netherlands (Supreme Court of the Netherlands, December 20, 2019).

Vandana Shiva and Ors. v. Union of India and Ors (Supreme Court of India, April 22, 1994).

Vanishing Giants. YouTube, 2009. https://www.youtube.com/watch?v=8bG103hHkUU.

Vellore Citizens' Welfare Forum v. Union of India (Supreme Court of India, August 28, 2006).

"Velsicol Chemical vs. Rachel Carson—the Lawsuit That Didn't Happen." Millard Fillmore's Bathtub, December 5, 2015. https://timpanogos.blog/2010/08/23/velsicol-chemical-vs-rachel-carson-the-lawsuit-that-didnt-happen/.

Vimal Bhai & Others v. Ministry of Environment & Forests (National Green Tribunal, New Delhi, December 14, 2011).

Virender Gaur and Ors. v. State of Haryana and Ors (Supreme Court of India, November 24, 1994).

Vincent, Suhasini. "Narrating, Naming and Labelling the Environment in Amitav Ghosh's The Hungry Tide." In *Ecocriticism and Environment—Rethinking Literature and Culture*, 173–85. New Delhi: Primus, 2018.

Vincent, Suhasini. "An Eco-Critical Analysis of Climate Change and the Unthinkable in Amitav Ghosh's Fiction and Non-Fiction." *Humanities* 7, no. 2 (2018): 59. https://doi.org/10.3390/h7020059.

Vincent, Suhasini. "Material Ecocriticism: Maritime Trade, Displacement and the Environment in Amitav Ghosh's Fictional Waterscape." In *Negotiating Waters: Seas, Oceans and Passageways in the Colonial and Postcolonial Anglophone World*, edited by Nancy Pedri and André Dodeman, 149–65. Wilmington: Vernon Press, 2019.

Vincent, Suhasini. "Archives of Unfair Trade in Amitav Ghosh's Fiction." *Academia Letters*, August 17, 2021. https://doi.org/10.20935/al1185.

Wash on the brink—UNICEF. Accessed May 17, 2023. https://www.unicef.org/media/118356/file/%20UNICEF%20Afghanistan%20WASH%20on%20the%20Brink%202022.pdf.

Watch the Yes Men Impersonate Shell, Make "Last Iceberg" Snow Cones. YouTube, 2015. https://www.youtube.com/watch?v=nkqO-qOHFT8.

"Water Made by Nature." *Aquaporin*, November 9, 2022. https://aquaporin.com/.

"Water, Peace & Security Partnership." World Resources Institute, August 29, 2022. https://www.wri.org/initiatives/water-peace-security-partnership.

Watson, Lara Herrington. "James Elser Hopes Phosphate Recycling Can Solve Two Environmental Problems." American Association for the Advancement of Science (AAAS). Accessed June 9, 2023. https://www.aaas.org/james-elser-hopes-phosphate-recycling-can-solve-two-environmental-problems.

"Welcome to the Anthropocene." *Economist*, May 26, 2011. https://www.economist.com/leaders/2011/05/26/welcome-to-the-anthropocene.

"What Is Coal Scam?" *Indian Express*, May 22, 2017. https://indianexpress.com/article/what-is/manmohan-singh-cbi-coalgate-coal-block-allocation-cag-report-what-is-coal-scam-4668265/.

"What Is Taj Heritage Corridor?" *Hans India*. March 30, 2015. https://www.thehansindia.com/posts/index/Education-and-Careers/2015-03-30/What-is-Taj-Heritage-Corridor/140716?infinitescroll=1.

"When the Big Dams Came Up." *Hindu*, March 19, 2015. https://www.thehindu.com/news/national/when-the-big-dams-came-up/article7012590.ece.

"Where Did Earth's Water Come From?" Earth & Planets. Accessed June 3, 2023. https://epl.carnegiescience.edu/news/where-did-earths-water-come.

Wildlife First and Ors v. Ministry of Forest (Supreme Court of India, February 13, 2019).

Wilfred J. v. Ministry of Environment & Forests (National Green Tribunal, New Delhi, July 17, 2014).

Willoquet-Maricondi, Paula. *Framing the World: Explorations in Ecocriticism and Film*. Charlottesville: University of Virginia Press, 2010.

Winterson, Jeanette. *The Stone Gods*. London: Hamish Hamilton, 2007.

"Working Group on the 'Anthropocene.'" Sub commission on quaternary stratigraphy. Accessed March 23, 2023. http://quaternary.stratigraphy.org/working-groups/anthropocene/.

World Bank Group. "Journey into the Congo Basin—the Lungs of Africa and Beating Heart of the World." World Bank, October 27, 2022. https://www.worldbank.org/en/news/feature/2022/10/24/journey-into-the-congo-basin-the-lungs-of-africa-and-beating-heart-of-the-world.

"World Environment Day 2023." UN Environment. Accessed July 1, 2023. https://www.unep.org/news-and-stories/press-release/world-environment-day-2023-be-hosted-cote-divoire-focus-solutions#:~:text=The%20campaign%20for%20World%20Environment,the%20hashtag%20and%20slogan%20%23BeatPlasticPollution.&text=World%20Environment%20Day%20is%20the,and%20action%20for%20the%20environment.

"World Water Day." United Nations. Accessed June 8, 2023. https://www.un.org/en/observances/water-day.

Worland, Justin. "The Selfish Case for Climate Justice." *Time*, November 7, 2022.

Wright, Lawrence. "The Elephant in the Courtroom." *New Yorker*, February 28, 2022. https://www.newyorker.com/magazine/2022/03/07/the-elephant-in-the-courtroom.

Index

About the Author

Suhasini Vincent is an associate professor (Maître de conférences) at Paris Pantheon Assas University, where she teaches legal English. She was born in New Delhi, grew up in Chennai in South India, and now lives in Reims, in France's Grand Est region. She defended her doctoral thesis on Experimental Writing within the Postcolonial Framework on Indian Writing through a joint-supervision programme between the University of Paris 3—Sorbonne Nouvelle and the University of Madras in 2006. In 2009, she was awarded the second-place prize for the best defended thesis on topics relating to the Commonwealth, organised under the aegis of the SEPC (Société d'études des Pays du Commonwealth). Her research focusses on the legal scope of environmental laws in postcolonial countries and explores ecocritical activism in the essays and literary works of diasporic and non-diasporic Indian writers. Her research on hybridity and experimental writing contemplates on how the protean novel serves as a canvas for polyphonic expression permitting various genres to be included in its pages. Voice constitutes the horizon of all the texts in her research, serving as the backbone to relate to textuality and serving as a metonymy for different kinds of discourse—migration, feminism, ecocriticism, and postcolonialism. Her analysis of a polyphony of voices aims to explore both production and reception: production as in the position or locus from which a text is written, the representation of the world by the author to a reader or a certain stratum of readership; reception as in the act of perception by the reader in his deciphering of meaning and context. Her research shows how the hybrid space of postcolonial novels with self-conscious and self-questioning narrators, validates the ideas and pronouncements of authors with various experimental modes ranging from magical realism, fable, myth, magical realism, songs, travelogue, anecdote, oral folklore, parable, and poetry. During her research track, she has published articles on Indian writers in peer-evaluated international journals and presented papers in conferences in France and abroad. Her current research project is on the new horizons of ecocriticism.

www.ingramcontent.com/pod-product-compliance
Ingram Content Group UK Ltd.
Pitfield, Milton Keynes, MK11 3LW, UK
UKHW041450071026
15587UKWH00010B/726

9 781666 951561